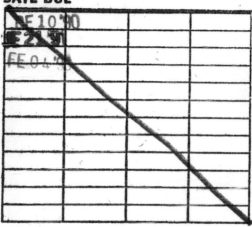

TEACHING

THE

LEARNING DISABLED

Deborah Deutsch Smith

University of New Mexico

PRENTICE-HALL, INC., Englewood Cliffs, New Jersey 07632

Library of Congress Cataloging in Publication Data

Smith, Deborah Deutsch
    Teaching the learning disabled

    Includes bibliographies and index.
    1. Learning disabilities.   I. Title.
LC4704.S62   371.9   80-21036
ISBN   0-13-893511-4

Editorial supervision and interior design: Serena Hoffman
Cover design: RD Graphics
Photography: Allen Madans
Manufacturing buyer: Edmund W. Leone

PRINTED IN THE UNITED STATES OF AMERICA

10   9   8   7   6   5   4   3   2   1

PRENTICE-HALL INTERNATIONAL, INC., *London*
PRENTICE-HALL OF AUSTRALIA PTY. LIMITED, *Sydney*
PRENTICE-HALL OF CANADA, LTD., *Toronto*
PRENTICE-HALL OF INDIA PRIVATE LIMITED, *New Delhi*
PRENTICE-HALL OF JAPAN, INC. *Tokyo*
PRENTICE-HALL OF SOUTHEAST ASIA PTE. LTD., *Singapore*
WHITEHALL BOOKS LIMITED, *Wellington, New Zealand*

CONTENTS

EVALUATION OF INSTRUCTION 34

INTERVENTION STRATEGIES: PART 1
INCREASING STUDENTS' PERFORMANCES

ORAL LANGUAGE 184

READING 217

WRITTEN COMMUNICATION 260

11   MATHEMATICS   283

12   LIFE-CENTERED CAREER EDUCATION   307

**COMMUNICATING WITH OTHERS:
PARENTS AND PROFESSIONALS** **327**

DEDICATION

It is difficult to dedicate a book, for you offend many by their omission and embarrass those you mention. This book cannot be dedicated to one person, but must be dedicated to the many who have shaped my personal and professional life.

First, I wish to dedicate this book to my family. My sincere thanks go to my parents, who gave unrelentingly through so many degrees and so much education. To my immediate family, I hope this product makes them proud and compensates for the time and patience I denied them.

I also want to dedicate this book to my professional family. I am very proud of my professional lineage and of the academic roots from which I come. To my academic father, my doctoral advisor and mentor, Dr. Tom Lovitt, I hope that he feels that I have given fair credit when credit is due. His influence on my professional opinions about learning disabled youngsters and their education has been profound. Although we do not always agree, his influence can be found throughout the contents of this text. I wish to thank Dr. Lovitt's academic father, Dr. James O. Smith—my husband, colleague, and coauthor—for his encouragement, support, and guidance. Dr. Smith's doctoral advisor, Dr. Lloyd Dunn, by the exacting standards he demonstrated in our professional and collaborative relationships, taught me to strive for quality in all the work I present to the field. And last, but certainly not least, to my academic great-great-grandfather, Dr. Samuel Kirk—the father of the field of learning disabilities—my thanks for his warmth and friendship. My place in this genealogy of special education gives me a great obligation and a unique and humble perspective for my own work.

I also wish to acknowledge and dedicate this book to the women models who molded and influenced my professional life. In particular, I am most grateful to Sybil Richardson and Ruth Monroe for demonstrating to me that it is possible for women to make contributions to a scholarly field. I hope this effort will serve as a model to other women, and will spur them to achievements far beyond mine. This will only benefit the field and the lives of very special children.

Deborah Deutsch Smith

PREFACE

The sincere hope of this author is for this text to serve as a resource both to those preparing to work with and to those facing the day-to-day challenge of students the educational system has come to call learning disabled. An attempt was made to bridge some of the philosophic differences that have divided and troubled this field within special education. Such debates are best held in academic arenas. Teachers must concern themselves with what works best with those students placed in their charge. The teaching methods and procedures suggested in this book have been verified through research and practice. My optimism rests on the thought that learning disabled youngsters' school experiences may be enriched by the contents of this text.

I would like to take this opportunity to thank those who contributed to and enhanced this book. My deepest appreciation goes to June Maker and Vicki Risko. Dr. Maker's development of the chapter about problem-solving skills makes this book more comprehensive and thorough than the texts on procedures that preceded it. Dr. Risko's efforts and contributions to the language and reading chapters make this text unique by building a bridge between the various pedagogic philosophies that have separated and divided this field. This book, clearly, is better because of their efforts, for their depth of knowledge in those areas strengthened the material presented immeasurably. My sincere gratitude is extended to these two fine scholars and practitioners.

The next individual I must thank and acknowledge is very special to me. My appreciation and professional debt to him only deepens across the years. Dr. Tom Lovitt shaped my thoughts about learning disabled students and their teachers, and helped me to formulate most of the positions that were presented in this text. Through my earliest research efforts, which were guided, supervised, and sponsored by Dr. Lovitt, the seeds for this book were born. Dr. Lovitt's reviews of the first three chapters were so helpful that the writing of the remaining chapters was much improved by his earlier input. I hope he is pleased by the product of his labor.

I want to express my deepest thanks to those individuals who gave of themselves and their skills to help me develop this book. I would like to thank Nancy Roi and Marilyn Smith, graduate students at the University of New Mexico, for their help and input. Sandra Bourgeault's editorial and technical assistance on many chapters should make the reader's task much simpler. It is impossible to show my true appreciation for two loyal and diligent research assistants who saw me through this incredible adventure with poise, patience, and a standard for excellence that even surpasses mine: Anne (Bambi) Udall and Kevin Rodgers. Without them, this book would still not be completed.

I wish to thank the University of New Mexico, the College of Education, and the Department of Special Education (and particularly my chairperson, Gary Adamson) for facilitating this venture and lending support and encouragement throughout the project.

Many students at the University of New Mexico gave unselfishly of their feedback and patience while helping me to field-test this book. To all those students enrolled in my courses who either read a part or all of the text, the book is greatly improved because of your help. Thank you.

A number of youngsters and their teachers also helped make this book a better product. I thank them and their teachers—Marci Moore, Nancy Hyatt, Kyle Higgins, and Bonnie Everett—for allowing me to intrude on their school time. I also want to thank the fine and creative photographer, Allen Madans, who visited classes with me to obtain photographs for this book. Further appreciation is expressed to Vicki Risko and James F. Smith for supplemental photographs provided.

Finally, but certainly not least, I wish to thank my secretaries: Elaine Blaire, Judy Baca, and Anne Sethre.

The text you are about to read is the product of the combined efforts of many people. We all wish you good reading.

1 INTRODUCTION

The education of youngsters we now call learning disabled has been a concern of parents and teachers for a long time. However, specific attention to these students' educational requirements began only several decades ago. Because it is one of the newest areas within special education, many rapid and dramatic changes in philosophy and practice have occurred as this field has emerged. The history and evolution of the field of learning disabilities is well documented,[1] and the purpose of this text is not to recount that development, but rather to present a technology for instruction, offering validated instructional procedures and techniques.

One of the author's main intents was to develop a text bridging the various gaps that professionals in the field of learning disabilities have created. While professionals debate and researchers investigate the efficacy of various instructional procedures, practitioners must teach. This text is meant to provide the practitioner with information reflecting the most current research findings, the views of many professionals, and the validated practices of many who work with learning disabled persons. Some of the procedures suggested will be effective with some learning disabled youngsters, but no one strategy has yet been identified that produces uniform results with all learners; therefore, many different procedures are suggested in the following chapters. Possibly someday a system that efficiently matches students with instructional procedures and materials will be developed. Unfortunately, that lies in the future. At present, learning disabilities teachers must be armed with an assortment of techniques and be prepared to try a variety of them with their individual students.

[1]Interested readers should refer to Cruickshank (1977), Kirk (1977), and Weiderholt (1974).

Much discussion has centered on who is learning disabled—which students learning disabilities experts should serve.[2] Although little consensus exists on this issue, there is agreement on some general principles. First, learning disabled students are different from their normal classmates. Second, they require specialized educational services to make satisfactory progress in school. Third, there are discrepancies between the academic and social skills of these students and their potential, and these delays cannot be explained by the existence of other primary handicapping conditions (mental retardation, deafness, visual impairment). Again, the confusion and debate over a definition of learning disabilities is not within the scope of this text. Many experts, teacher trainers, and researchers have adopted as their full-time mission the resolution of these issues. In fact, the federal government has charged five national research institutes with this mandate, and the field awaits their findings.[3] Meanwhile, learning disabled students must be served and their educational needs met as best as possible. Today's students cannot wait for these theoretical and philosophical issues to be resolved; today's practitioners must meet the challenges that these students present.

There are many reasons for the considerable public attention the field of learning disabilities has received, mostly stemming from its many, baffling aspects. Continuing hope for remediation characterizes the field, stimulated by examples of those unique individuals who purportedly had severe learning disabilities in their youth yet made significant contributions to society as adults. Individuals such as Thomas Edison, George Patton, Woodrow Wilson, Albert Einstein, and many other distinguished men are said to have had a learning disability (Thompson, 1971). Even one of the world's most famous writers of children's literature, Hans Christian Andersen, had a severe reading disability (Arden, 1979).

These reports have influenced the field in several important ways. First, they have given parents and teachers the hope that learning disabilities can be "cured" or compensated for, and therein lies the hope that these students will have prosperous and successful futures. Unfortunately, these reports have helped to make some parents and teachers victims of passing fads and dubious educational practices. When traditional educational procedures are unsuccessful and special education techniques do not produce satisfactory results, many parents of learning disabled youngsters begin the frustrating and usually unproductive search for a cure for their child's disability. In most cases, considerable expenditures in time and money are made, to no avail. Teachers of learning disabled students have a moral and ethical obligation to those students and their families to become knowledge-

[2]Interested readers should refer to the following sources for more detail: Hallahan (1975), Hallahan and Kauffman (1977), Myers and Hammill (1976), and Reger (1979).

[3]A summary of the scope of work for each of the learning disabilities research institutes can be found in the Winter 1978 issue of *Learning Disability Quarterly* in an article edited by Deshler (1978a). More specific information can be obtained by writing to each of the institutes' directors: Dale Bryant, Columbia University; Tanis Bryan and Maurice Eash, University of Illinois—Chicago Circle; Edward Meyen and Donald Deshler, University of Kansas; James Ysseldyke, Mark Shinn, and Martha Thurlow, University of Minnesota; and Daniel Hallahan, University of Virginia.

able resources, so that they can help them obtain the best proven remedial services available.

SERVICE DELIVERY OPTIONS

Learning disabled students and their teachers can find themselves in a variety of educational settings, each having different demands, expectations, and limits. There are a number of special education service delivery options available among the various levels of school.

Cascade of
Services

Although variation exists from state to state, each usually offers its handicapped students different educational schemes. In most states six options are available: consultation to regular educators, itinerant special education, resource room assistance, partially self-contained classrooms, self-contained classrooms, and self-contained schools (usually private). The state of New Mexico has adopted and implemented a statewide plan that includes most of the options previously identified, and is typical of those used by most states. A diagram of this plan is found in Figure 1.1. The implementation of this system allows students to move from one type of service to another as the need arises.

One commonly used option was designed for students having few difficulties in school. The learning disabilities expert is a consultant who provides support assistance to regular educators, suggesting various techniques and procedures that might be beneficial and providing special instructional materials. The purpose of this service option is to support regular educators' efforts to maintain learning disabled students in regular programs. In some instances, these specialists do not work directly with students, while in others, they come to regular education classrooms to tutor the learning disabled students. Usually these teachers (or consultants) are itinerant, serving many teachers at many schools.

One innovative and successful itinerant consulting program is the Prevention Intervention Project (PIP) (Cantrell & Cantrell, 1976), which used teachers as consultants to regular educators who were specially trained in behavioral principles, basic evaluation techniques, program relevant assessments, contingency management, group process, and ecological management of exceptional students. The purpose of this project was to resolve youngsters' school problems before referral for formal services became necessary. The project's success was demonstrated through reduced referral rates from those regular educators who received support assistance from the itinerant consulting special educators. Unfortunately, such preventative special programs are rare, and learning disabilities experts often are confronted with problems that have been long in developing.

Currently, the most common service delivery option used is the resource room or learning center. The learning disabilities teacher has a classroom where students come for specialized assistance. The majority of the student's day is spent in the regular program. In Iowa, students spend anywhere from one to six hours per week in the resource room (Brown,

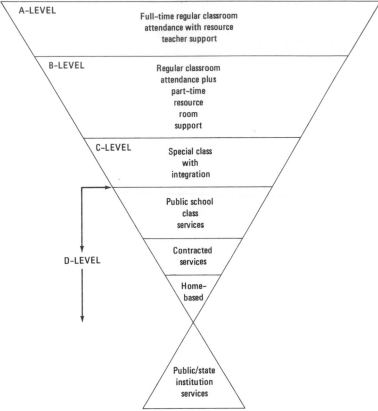

LEAST RESTRICTIVE EDUCATIONAL SETTING

A-LEVEL — Full-time regular classroom attendance with resource teacher support

B-LEVEL — Regular classroom attendance plus part-time resource room support

C-LEVEL — Special class with integration

Public school class services

D-LEVEL — Contracted services

Home-based

Public/state institution services

Figure 1.1   A plan for the delivery of special education services for the state of New Mexico. (State Department of Education, Special Education Division, State of New Mexico; see Note 1.)

Kiraly, & McKinnon, Note 2). Resource room teachers usually tutor handicapped students in content areas, attempt to remediate ability deficits, and provide assistance in other problem areas (social behavior, survival skills).

Traditional special education service delivery options still are used for many learning disabled students. The self-contained classroom (for either part or most of the school day) is necessary for some students at some time during their school careers. This setting affords the learning disabilities teacher the opportunity to concentrate remedial efforts for substantial periods of time. Although these options are criticized by the proponents of the mainstreaming movement, the self-contained situation is the most appropriate placement for some learning disabled students. Those who are far behind their classmates in academic subject areas cannot participate fully in the instructional situation. To remain in the regular education program could be devastating for some youngsters, leading to serious emotional problems and resulting in little or no academic growth. Martin (1974) stresses that out of human concern, handicapped youngsters must be included within regular education programs; they must be within the sight and mind of the general public. He also cautions that handicapped students must have the fullest measure of our educational resources. Unfortunately, for a few, this requires separation from the mainstream for some period of time.

Level of School   Historically, learning disabilities programs were provided only through grade six; only recently have these programs been incorporated into middle and high schools. Services at the elementary level, therefore, are more coordinated and established. Usually these teachers aim at the remediation of basic academic and social skills and conceptual deficits. Elementary services tend to use all six service delivery options.

Middle or junior high school programs are not as well developed and some concern exists about what their content should be, whom they should serve, and what materials should be used. Middle school special educators have several advantages over elementary level teachers, but they must also cope with several obstacles to efficient instruction. Middle school teachers have great resources available that elementary teachers do not. Unlike the elementary school, the middle school has a variety of content experts and also has counselors on staff. These resources can be utilized to enrich middle school programs for learning disabled students. A disadvantage of the middle school situation is the large number of school personnel whose efforts must be coordinated, requiring considerable effort on the part of the learning disabilities teachers. Paroz, Siegenthaler, and Tatum (1977) feel that special education middle school personnel must attend to transitions in life, seek to maintain attendance in regular classes, work with a number of other teachers, individualize instruction, and develop significant relationships between themselves and each student.

Educational programs for learning disabled students attending high schools are very new, and are not always available because of a shortage of trained personnel. Secondary programs are new for several reasons. Many felt that since learning disabilities were remediable, if specialized assistance were given during the elementary years such services would not be necessary during the later school years. Unfortunately, this has not proven to be the case. As Deshler (1978b) points out, in many cases learning disabilities are resistant to remediation and currently available intervention strategies lack the power necessary to reduce or eliminate the consequences of the learning disability. According to Deshler, there are different types of secondary programs. The first could be referred to as remedial. The second attempts to teach students to compensate for their disabilities by giving them strategies for acquiring information through nontraditional means. The third option centers around alternative education for life adjustment with emphasis on survival skills.

The problems facing the secondary learning disabilities specialists can at times seem insurmountable. Academic difficulties are not the only problems confronting the learning disabled adolescent. Other psychosocial deficits frequently become apparent (Kronick, 1978). In addition, the home situation often begins to deteriorate as the hope for the disappearance of the disability begins to fade. Also, secondary learning disabilities teachers serve a range of students. In an attempt to delimit the numbers and types of students these teachers serve, Goodman and Price (1978) propose that students whose basic skills fall below sixth grade achievement levels be placed in specialized programs. Those students whose skills are above this level would be assigned to regular education programs because these authors believe that they possess minimal requisite skills. Possibly there is a need for different kinds of learning disabilities programs at the high school level, each monitored by different specialists. At present, there is little agreement about what the complexion of secondary learning disabilities programs should be. There is agreement, however, that there is a need for specialized educational services for these youngsters at the high school level.

TEACHER COMPETENCIES

The concern about what competencies teachers should possess is not new (Olson, 1935). However, mounting evidence, collected over the past fifteen years, clearly demonstrates that teachers do control the performances of their students. Even unplanned actions of teachers influence occurrences within and outside of the classroom. Thomas, Becker, and Armstrong (1968) make this point well:

> *Teachers are sometimes unaware of the effects of their actions in the behavior of their students. Many teachers assume that if a child performs disruptive acts in the classroom then the child must have a problem at home, or at the very least, must not have reached sufficient maturity to function adequately in the school situation. However, an increasing body of evidence indicates that many of the behaviors which teachers find disruptive are actually within their control. A teacher can modify and control the behavior of her students by controlling her own responses.* (p. 35)

Such evidence has left many professionals concerned about what skills teachers need to ensure social and academic growth in their students.

The growing question of what minimal skills teachers of learning disabled students should possess comes from many different sources: researchers, institutions of higher education, school administrators, and professional organizations. Some research efforts have been directed toward the identification of those skills which help successful teachers. For example, Melton (1978) finds that the use of behavioral objectives (particularly when they are stated to the learner) enhances student performance. Drabman (1976) believes that the ability to use systematic praise and ignoring techniques should be part of every teacher's instructional repertoire. He also indicates that teachers should monitor the influence of instructional techniques by gathering evaluation data on their students' classroom performances. Fine, Nesbitt, and Tyler (1974) believe that if behavior change programs are to be successful, teachers must have specific training and be

It is important for teachers of learning disabled children to develop a meaningful relationship with their students. Here, this teacher also is sharing the evaluation data from her reading assignment.

able to define target behaviors, record behavior change, systematically apply instructional procedures, determine the feasibility of educational programs designed for specific students, and develop meaningful teacher-student interactions. In one teacher survey, resource personnel were polled in an attempt to determine what facilitates the amelioration of student problems. The following were indicated as most important: music, health education, social studies, hygiene, cooperation with rehabilitation agencies, directing students in leisure time, and domestic arts.

Another research study investigated specific variables that contribute to teacher success, as defined by substantial changes in student performance. Although not conducted with teachers of learning disabled youngsters, these findings are important to all classroom situations. Fredericks, Anderson, Baldwin, Grove, Moore, and Baird (Note 3) found that the most significant indicator of teacher success was the total amount of time the children spent each day in instruction: more instruction yielded more learning. The second competency indicator was the percentage of instructional units that were task analyzed. One other finding of their research is important and has implications for a broad set of skills that teachers need: All of the teachers in the group showing substantial child-change gains maintained systems of daily data gathering within the classroom situation.

Many institutions of higher education have long been concerned about what skills teachers should possess, for this has direct bearing on the training program provided to prospective teachers. College and university personnel must adjust course content and field-based experiences to guarantee that their trainees become effective agents of child-change. These programs use the information available from research efforts and professional judgment to continually modify training activities. The 1970s saw a move toward competency-based teacher education programs. These programs sought to develop meaningful didactic and field-based experiences, and required their trainees to demonstrate specific skills. One notable example of such a program was developed and implemented at the University of Vermont (Robie, Pierce, & Burdett, 1979). This training program, referred to as The Responsive Teacher Program, was task analyzed and is highly structured. All of the trainees are expected to demonstrate a set of minimum skills in each of the following areas: basic skills, measurement systems, individualized instruction, and learning theory.

On another front, local school district administrators have expressed a need for guidelines to help them select qualified teachers from an ever growing pool of applicants. Many of these administrators are not special educators and require assistance to determine who can best serve the needs of their learning disabled students. To meet this need, some school districts have developed lists of competencies they expect of their instructional personnel. For instance, Riverside County in California developed a minimum competency list to assist their administrative staff in the selection and evaluation of learning disabilities personnel (Riverside County, Note 4). In that competency statement, five general skill areas were deemed requisite: assessment, instruction, evaluation, interpersonal relationships, and general knowledge.

Because efforts to develop and implement teacher competencies were scattered and because little consistency existed, the professional organization for learning disabilities personnel, the Council for Exceptional Children's Division for Children with Learning Disabilities (DCLD), set out to develop a policy statement. The competency committee, chaired by Phyllis Newcomer, was assigned the task of creating a comprehensive competency statement. Because of the diverse skills needed by learning disabilities personnel who work in a variety of service delivery options from kindergarten to high school, the committee included all aspects of assessment, instruction, management, and consultation for content as well as affective areas. The intent was for this set of minimum competencies to become the guidelines used by institutions of higher education to develop new or modify existing training programs, by school districts to develop criteria for employment, by state departments of instruction to establish certification standards, and by the professional organization to monitor ongoing professional practices. Because of the importance of this committee's work, several years were spent developing competency lists and testing them with a wide range of professionals. The final competency list became available in 1978 (Newcomer, 1978) and is included in Figure 1.2. Since its publication, a research study was conducted to determine whether practitioners agreed with the DCLD statement. Through this study, Freeman and Becker (1979) found that the DCLD statement does reflect the opinions of practicing professionals. Because of its import and acceptance, it is worthwhile for every educator concerned with the education of learning disabled students to study the DCLD competency statement.

Oral Language

I. General Knowledge

The teacher:
1. understands the association learning, linguistically oriented, and cognitive theories of language.

II. Assessment

1. can administer and interpret standardized language tests in the areas of phonology, semantics, morphology, and syntax.

III. Instruction

1. can select and use appropriate commercial developmental materials and programs.

Reading

I. General Knowledge
   A. Developmental Reading
   B. Specialized Reading
      1. Corrective Reading

      2. Remedial Reading

II. Assessment
   A. Screening

   B. Evaluation

   C. Diagnosis

   D. Formative/Summative

III. Instruction
   A. Corrective Reading

   B. Remedial Reading

The teacher:
1. understands basic theories related to the field of reading.

1. understands that corrective reading instruction is a system for planning and delivering classroom instruction to students who experience minor deficiencies in the elements of developmental reading.
1. understands that remedial reading instruction is a system for delivering intensive individualized instruction to students who have major reading problems in word recognition, comprehension, and fluency.

1. has knowledge of the appropriate instruments and techniques for general screening for reading.
1. has knowledge of the appropriate instruments and techniques for specific assessment of the students' level of reading achievement and the areas that warrant specific attention.
1. can select and administer formal and informal diagnostic instruments for specific skills related to reading.
1. can develop and use tests to monitor students' ongoing and final level of mastery.

1. can plan and implement instruction for minor problems associated with gaps or deficiencies in the developmental reading process.
1. can plan and implement intensive individualized instruction in the skill areas associated with remedial reading.

Written Expression

I. General Knowledge

The teacher:
1. recognizes written expression as a method of conveying ideas or meanings.

II. Assessment

1. can administer and interpret standardized achievement tests of written expression.

III. Instruction

1. can plan and implement an instructional program incorporating the basic components for writing.
   1.1 purpose of composition
   1.2 arrangement of ideas

Figure 1.2 DCLD Competency statement. (Newcomer, P. L. Competencies for professionals in learning disabilities. *Learning Disability Quarterly*, 1978, *1*, pp. 73–76. Reprinted by permission.)

1.3 compare and contrast skills
1.4 organization of ideas
1.5 types of prose, e.g., narrative, descriptive, expository, argumentation
1.6 poetry

Spelling

I. General Knowledge

II. Assessment

III. Instruction

The teacher:
1. understands the nature and rules of English orthography.
1. can administer and interpret the spelling sections of standardized achievement tests.
1. can teach spelling skills using a planned sequence of activities.

Mathematics

I. General Knowledge
  A. Number Theory
  B. Addition and Subtraction

  C. Multiplication and Division

  D. Fractions, Decimals, and Percentage

  E. Geometry
  F. Measurement

  G. Money
  H. Verbal Problem Solving

II. Assessment

III. Instruction

The teacher:
1. understands all the concepts involved in numeration and counting.
1. understands the computation process involved in adding and subtracting whole numbers.
1. understands the computational process involved in solving multiplication and division problems.
1. understands all the operations involved in adding, subtracting, multiplying, and dividing fractions, decimal numbers, and numbers expressed as percentages.
1. understands simple common plane geometric figures, e.g., circle, square.
1. understands all concepts involved in measurement of: time, linear planes, weight, liquids, and temperature.
1. understands the U.S. monetary system.
1. understands the variables that contribute to difficulty in verbal problem solving, e.g., reading level, level of syntactic complexity, distractors, etc.
1. can administer and interpret the mathematics portion of standardized group achievement tests.
1. can teach a specific mathematical skill by developing and following a planned sequence of activities.

Cognition

I. General Knowledge
  A. Nature of Thought
  B. Piagetian Theories

  C. Association Theory

  D. Information Processing Theories

  E. Gestalt Theories

  F. Theories of Intelligence

The teacher:
1. understands various theories regarding thought and process of thinking.
1. understands the implications of a stage theory such as Piaget's and can compare it with age theories.
1. understands the implications of association theory and can analyze learning situations into stimulus and response components.
1. understands the implications of information processing theory as a model of human intelligence.
1. understands theories which view learning wholistically and can analyze:
    1.1 discovery learning
    1.2 perceptual arousal
    1.3 creative or original responses
1. understands Q-factor theory, "g," and special abilities.

II. Assessment	1. can administer and interpret standardized tests of intelligence.
A. Formal	1. can devise tasks which reveal children's skills at problem solving, inferential thinking and concept development.
B. Informal	
III. Instruction	1. can incorporate information regarding cognitive development into general instructional programming.

Behavioral Management

I. General Knowledge	The teacher:
	1. understands general theoretical positions related to:
	1.1 theories of learning
	1.2 theories of personality and psychopathology
	1.3 child development (normal and atypical)
II. Assessment	1. can define target behaviors.
III. Instruction	1. can use remedial instructional procedures to modify behavior.

Counseling and Consulting

I. Consulting with Teachers and Administrators	The teacher:
	1. must have knowledge about working with exceptional children in school settings involving handicapped and nonhandicapped students.
II. Counseling and Consulting with Parents	1. can establish and maintain rapport with parents.
III. Counseling and Consulting with Children	1. must establish and maintain rapport with children.

Career/Vocational Education

I. General Knowledge	The teacher:
A. Knowledge of Individual Characteristics	1. is aware that each individual has unique patterns of abilities and limitations which affect career/vocational decisions.
B. Knowledge of Career and Occupational Opportunities	1. has comprehensive knowledge of a wide variety of occupational families.
II. Assessment	1. can administer and interpret standardized vocational/career interest and aptitude tests.
III. Instruction	1. will provide information pertaining to a wide variety of career opportunities.

Educational Operations

I. Assessment	The teacher:
	1. is able to establish rapport during assessment.
II. Materials	1. can determine student needs to be met by curricula.
III. A/V	1. can identify and select media appropriate for stated instructional objectives.
IV. Environment	1. can identify variables which influence learning in the school and classroom environment.
V. Instruction	1. can plan and implement a sequential remedial program for a student.

Historical-Theoretical Perspectives

I. History of Learning Disabilities	The teacher:
	1. can identify early contributors to the field of learning disabilities.
II. Program Models	1. can explain various program models used to deliver services to learning disabled children.
III. Professional Organizations	1. is aware of various professional organizations in learning disabilities.

SUMMARY

The intent of this text is to inform teachers of learning disabled students about various verified instructional strategies and procedures that should enhance the school performances of their students. The material included in the following chapters should become a resource as the planning, implementation, and evaluation stages of learning disabled students' instructional programs are actualized. In this chapter, discussions were included on the overall purpose of this text, service delivery options, and the numerous competencies, skills, and knowledge that learning disabilities practitioners must possess. It is hoped that the reader has already come to understand that the responsibilities of learning disabilities personnel are great and the obligations are serious, but the work is exciting, challenging, and hopeful. The aim of this text is to facilitate the improvement of learning disabled students' social and academic growth by providing their teachers with a vast array of procedures and techniques that have proved to be beneficial for other youngsters.

REFERENCE NOTES

1. New Mexico State Department of Education. *A plan for the delivery of special education services in New Mexico. Part three: Regulations* (2nd ed.). Santa Fe, N.M.: State Department of Education, Special Education Division, 1976.

2. BROWN, L. F., KIRALY, J., & McKINNON, A. *State-wide survey of special education resource room programs* (Research report). Iowa City, Ia.: University of Iowa, 1978.

3. FREDERICKS, H. D. N., ANDERSON, R., BALDWIN, V., GROVE, D., MOORE, M., & BAIRD, J. H. *The identification of competencies of teachers of the severely handicapped* (Project supported through Grant #OEG-0-74-2775, U.S. Bureau of Education for the Handicapped). Corvallis, Ore.: Oregon State University, undated.

4. Riverside County, Office of Superintendent of Schools. *Competency handbook for the learning handicapped specialist credential* (Handbook used in teacher training project for personnel working with exceptional children). Riverside County, Calif.: Office of Riverside County Superintendent of Schools, 1977.

REFERENCES

ARDEN, H. The magic world of Hans Christian Andersen. *National Geographic*, 1979, *156*, 825–849.

CANTRELL, R. P., & CANTRELL, M. L. Preventive mainstreaming: Impact of a supportive services program on pupils. *Exceptional Children*, 1976, *42*, 381–386.

CRUICKSHANK, W. M. Myths and realities in learning disabilities. *Journal of Learning Disabilities*, 1977, *10*, 51–58.

DESHLER, D. D. New research institutes for the study of learning disabilities. *Learning Disability Quarterly*, 1978, *1*, 68–78. (a)

DESHLER, D. D. Issues related to the education of learning disabled adolescents. *Learning Disability Quarterly*, 1978, *1*, 2–10. (b)

DRABMAN, R. S. Behavior modification in the classroom. In W. E. Craighead, A. E. Kazdin, & M. J. Mahoney (Eds.), *Behavior modification: Principles, issues, and applications*. Boston: Houghton Mifflin Co., 1976.

FINE, M. J., NESBITT, J. A., & TYLER, M. M. Analysis of a failing attempt at behavior modification. *Journal of Learning Disabilities*, 1974, *7*, 70–75.

FREEMAN, M. A., & BECKER, R. L. Competencies for professionals in LD: An analysis of teacher perceptions. *Learning Disability Quarterly*, 1979, *2*, 7–78.

GOODMAN, L., & PRICE, M. BEH final regulations for learning disabilities: Implications for the secondary school. *Learning Disability Quarterly*, 1978, *1*, 73–79.

HALLAHAN, D. P. Comparative research studies on the psychological characteristics of learning disabled children. In W. M. Cruickshank & D. P. Hallahan (Eds.), *Perceptual and learning disabilities*, Vol. 1: *Psychoeducational practices.* Syracuse, N.Y.: Syracuse University Press, 1975.

HALLAHAN, D. P., & KAUFFMAN, J. M. Labels, categories, behaviors: ED, LD, and EMR reconsidered. *The Journal of Special Education*, 1977, *11*, 139–149.

KIRK, S. A. Specific learning disabilities. *Journal of Clinical Child Psychology*, 1977, *6*, 23–26.

KRONICK, D. An examination of psychosocial aspects of learning disabled adolescents. *Learning Disability Quarterly*, 1978, *1*, 86–93.

MARTIN, E. W. Some thoughts on mainstreaming. *Exceptional Children*, 1974, *41*, 150–153.

MELTON, R. F. Resolution of conflicting claims concerning the effect of behavioral objectives on student learning. *Review of Educational Research*, 1978, *48*, 291–302.

MYERS, P. I., & HAMMILL, D. D. *Methods for learning disorders* (2nd ed.). New York: John Wiley & Sons, 1976.

NEWCOMER, P. L. Competencies for professionals in learning disabilities. *Learning Disability Quarterly*, 1978, *1*, 69–77.

OLSON, W. C. The diagnosis and treatment of behavior disorders of children. In the Thirty-Fourth Yearbook of the National Society for the Study of Education (Eds.), *Educational diagnosis.* Bloomington, Ill.: Public Schools Publishing Co., 1935.

PAROZ, J., SIEGENTHALER, L. S., & TATUM, V. H. A model for a middle-school resource room. *Journal of Learning Disabilities*, 1977, *10*, 1–9.

REGER, R. Learning disabilities: Futile attempts at a simplisitic definition. *Journal of Learning Disabilities*, 1979, *12*, 529–532.

ROBIE, D. E., PIERCE, M. M., & BURDETT, C. Vermont's responsive teacher program: Competency based teacher training. *Exceptional Children*, 1979, *45*, 365–367.

THOMAS, D. R., BECKER, W. C., & ARMSTRONG, M. Production and elimination of disruptive classroom behavior by systematically varying teacher's behavior. *Journal of Applied Behavior Analysis*, 1968, *1*, 35–45.

THOMPSON, L. J. Language disabilities in men of eminence. *Journal of Learning Disabilities*, 1971, *4*, 34–45.

WIEDERHOLT, J. L. Historical perspectives on the education of the learning disabled. In L. Mann & D. A. Sabatino (Eds.), *The second review of special education.* Philadelphia: The JSE Press, 1974.

2 THE INDIVIDUALIZED
EDUCATIONAL PROGRAM PROCESS

In 1975 Congress enacted Public Law 94-142, The Education for All Handicapped Children Act, entitling all exceptional youngsters to an appropriate education through the public school system. The implications of this law are far reaching and have direct impact on classroom activities, changing drastically the roles and responsibilities of parents and school personnel (administrators, diagnosticians, counselors, and teachers).

P. L. 94-142 requires that all handicapped children and youth be provided with appropriate educational services from ages three to twenty-one (effective September 1980). Documented evidence must be submitted indicating that efforts were made to locate every handicapped school-aged person in each state. The law states that every handicapped student is entitled to participate in activities enjoyed by nonhandicapped youngsters (transportation, counseling, recreation, physical education, employment, special interest groups, athletics, and clubs). Also, the law requires that prior to placement in special education, the youngster must receive a full, nondiscriminatory, individual evaluation (tests administered in the child's native language by properly trained personnel).

For each student identified as handicapped, an *individual educational program* (IEP) must be developed, implemented, and evaluated. The components of the IEP are specified in the law (and outlined in detail in a later section of this chapter). The IEP necessitates the writing of a detailed set of goals and objectives for each student, as well as a meeting with teacher, parent, and other school officials. Also, a check and balance system is guaranteed by the option of due process hearings that may be initiated by either parents or school officials. If properly implemented, the individualized educational program process should result in improved educational programs for all handicapped students.

To be able to fulfill the requirements of P. L. 94-142 and implement the IEP process, teachers must not only be knowledgeable about the process, but also must possess some prerequisite knowledge and skills. Therefore, the first section of this chapter is devoted to this prerequisite information; the second section of this chapter is allocated to a technical description of the individualized educational program process from the initial referral to the evaluation of the special education services rendered. Content information—the goals and objectives for individual students—is provided in chapters 6–13 of this text.

PREREQUISITE KNOWLEDGE

As indicated above, before the individualized educational program process can be implemented for any student, the teacher must possess certain skills and knowledge. For example, before writing an IEP (which contains long-term and short-term goals and objectives), teachers must be able to write objective statements. To sequence these goals and objectives, teachers must conduct task analyses. In addition, teachers must know how to determine students' current functioning levels; therefore, knowledge of assessment procedures and devices is necessary. These, then, are some of the prerequisite skills teachers must possess before they approach the task of initiating the IEP process.

Behavioral Goals and Objectives

For almost twenty years, teachers have specified the desired products of their instruction in terms of child-change information. Recently, evidence has indicated that instruction is more efficient and coordination of services is facilitated when goals and objectives have been specified (Carr, 1979). The statement of the desired outcomes of instruction is presented in the form of behavioral goals and objectives (Mager, 1962, 1975; Popham & Baker, 1970). Behavioral goals usually are global in nature and are composed of specific objectives. The crucial elements of any behavioral statements are precise wording and outcomes described in such a way that reliable measurement and evaluation are guaranteed. Therefore, the behavior must be defined precisely and in observable terms, with criteria for mastery noted. An example of a poor behavioral goal is: Johnny and his classmates will like each other better. Although worthy, this statement is not precise, is not suitable for reliable measurement, and does not include a provision for mastery. Without more specificity, independent observers will not be able to measure or collect data on the behavior of interest. Table 2.1 provides a list of behavioral goals and objectives that are stated appropriately and include mastery or criteria statements.

Task Analysis

For efficient instruction to occur, behavioral goals and objectives must be sequenced; their order of presentation determined. Lists of goals and objectives can be helpful to teachers as they decide what will comprise students'

Table 2.1 **Overall goal: to understand and use time**
Immediate goal: to tell time using a standard clockface with Arabic numerals

Abbreviated Objective	Behavioral Statement	Criterion
Hand discrimination	2.01 The student is able to point to and name both the hour and minute hand	2.01 with 100% accuracy within 15 seconds
Hour hand	2.02 The student is able to identify all hour hand placements 2.02.01 The student is able to identify the hour for exact hour hand placements 2.02.02 The student is able to identify the hour for any hour hand placement	2.02 with 100% (.01– accuracy .02) within 10 seconds
Minute hand	2.03 The student is able to identify all minute placements 2.03.01 The student is able to identify the minute for minute hand placements on any interval of five 2.03.02 The student is able to identify the minute for exact minute hand placements 2.03.03 The student is able to identify fractions of hours using the minute hand (e.g., quarter after)	2.03 with 100% (.01– accuracy .03) within 10 seconds
Combination of hour and minute hand	2.04 The student is able to identify the correct time using both the hour and minute hand 2.04.01 The student is able to identify the time for the ''o'clock'' times 2.04.02 The student can identify the time for all intervals of five 2.04.03 The student is able to identify the exact time 2.04.04 The student can identify the time for fractions of the hour	2.04 with 100% (.01– accuracy .04) within 10 seconds

instructional programs. Without a sequence, however, no indication is available regarding *when* an objective becomes the target of instruction. The purpose of a task analysis is to determine the priority of goals and objectives and provide a plan for the sequence of instruction.

Teachers do not have to conduct task analyses for every skill they teach. In fact, valuable teacher time should not be spent conducting unnecessary task analyses. For students who profit from the standard mathematics sequences used as outlines for elementary basal texts, the sequence of instruction already is determined through the combined efforts of researchers and professionals from that discipline. In some cases, the mathematics textbook does not include an area that particular learning disabled students need to master. For example, the use and understanding of time is a very important area, often neglected or inadequately programmed in mathematics texts. In such instances, teachers should search for already available instructional materials. Only if appropriate instructional programs are not available should teachers create their own sequences and materials. The time and expertise involved in the development of good instructional materials often is far beyond what an already very busy teacher can justify expending.

Teacher-made task analyses are necessary at other times also. Sometimes, instructional programs are available for every goal and objective necessary for a particular student. For example, a program was found for each mathematics area identified for instruction for an entire academic year (computation, time telling, change making, and problem solving). After considerable searching, the teacher located twenty specific instructional programs. Because they were from a variety of sources, the order in which they should be taught had to be determined by conducting a task analysis.

There are various ways to structure the task analysis process. Some processes specify the strategies and procedures as well as the sequence to use when instruction is initiated (see Gold, Note 1). Some systems are complicated and complex, but yield comprehensive information about the task being analyzed (Resnick, Wang, & Kaplan, 1973; Resnick, 1976). Others (Smith, Smith, & Edgar, 1976; Smith & Snell, 1978) propose the adoption of a simple system that merely provides an outline or blueprint of the instructional sequence. When such a system is used, only a skeletal outline of the proposed ordering of objectives is presented. This, however, is all that is necessary when sequencing instructional units.

The lattice system.   The lattice system was originated by Myron Woolman (Note 2) and has been useful to many teachers as they attempt to organize and sequence educational activities (Bricker, 1972; Budde, 1972; Budde & Menolascino, 1971; Smith et al., 1976; Smith & Smith, Note 3). A procedural lattice diagramming the technical steps followed to construct a lattice is shown in Figure 2.1.

The lattice system requires the graphic display of the instructional sequence. To use the lattice system for task analysis, the teacher requires some knowledge of the rules for this system plus competence in the subject matter. The teacher first identifies the skill to be developed as precisely and specifically as possible. The words used need not be as complete or thorough as those used in behavioral objective statements, but the implied intent must be recognizable to the users. The entry behaviors (those prerequisite skills expected of the student before the instructional program is initiated) must be specified. The actual skill to be taught is then broken down into small teaching units or component parts. This is accomplished by having the person conducting the task analysis execute the steps identified over and over until the sequence is crystalized.

Once the cell components (the precise behaviors the task or skill is composed of) are identified, the lattice is constructed. The terminal behavior (the achievement of the goal) is stated concisely and placed in a box or cell in the far right-hand corner. The major subgoals leading to the completion of the terminal behavior are placed in the ridgeline. The ridgeline is the stair-step section of the lattice that reads left to right and leads the reader to attainment of the terminal behavior or goal. The en-route objectives are those behaviors that make up each subgoal and are placed below their appropriate ridgeline box.

Some rules or conventions are followed as lattices are constructed so that communication is consistent among lattice readers. The lines connecting

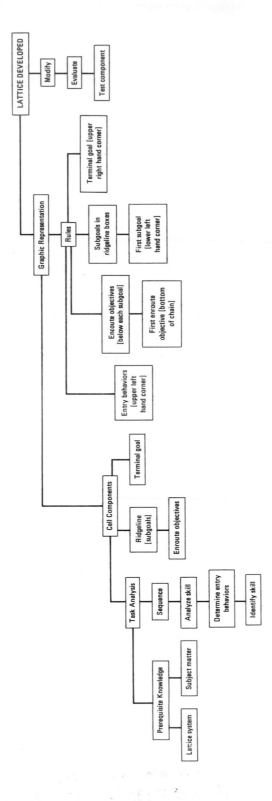

Figure 2.1 Procedural lattice for lattice development. (D. D. Smith, J. O. Smith, and E. Edgar. A prototypic model for developing instructional materials for the severely handicapped. In N. G. Haring and L. J. Brown [Eds.], *Teaching the severely handicapped*. New York: Grune & Stratton, 1976, p. 159. Reprinted by permission.)

the ridgeline boxes form right angles (with the angle at the top) and are arranged in such a way that the ridgeline's first box (the first subgoal to be taught) is the lowest and the terminal behavior is the highest. Whenever possible, the en-route objective boxes are connected to each other and the appropriate subgoal box with straight lines. When two en-route objectives are not necessarily sequential, they may be placed next to each other, and each connects directly with the subgoal box.

It is important to remember that lattices are only blueprints for instruction. They do not necessarily indicate what instructional techniques or aids will be used. They do, however, outline the instructional sequence planned and can be useful as a year's set of goals and objectives is arranged for particular students (see Figure 2.2 for an example).

Knowledge of Assessment Procedures and Instruments

As mentioned earlier, P. L. 94-142 requires that careful assessment of each student recommended for special education services be conducted. Currently, most diagnostic information relies heavily on the use of standardized tests. Although there has been much debate regarding the appropriateness and usefulness of standardized assessment instruments, the major issues are not resolved. At least for awhile, debates will continue to rage, and the status quo is ensured. Regardless of the philosophical position an individual educator holds regarding the merits of traditional assessment instruments and procedures, full knowledge about the process is imperative.[1] If teachers are to be active, participating members in the IEP process, they must be cognizant of commonly used evaluation methods and their purposes and appropriate uses.

The assessment debate. Standardized diagnostic tests have been criticized in recent years (Eaton & Lovitt, 1972; Lovitt, 1967; Van Etten & Van Etten, 1976). Many tests are discriminatory and their results are biased toward youngsters from affluent backgrounds and against those from multicultural or bilingual families.

Standardized test scores represent typical (or expected) growth patterns of students from different geographical regions. For example, when a student's pre- and post-performance on a standardized achievement test is evaluated, a comparison can be made between that individual's past and present performances. The scores are evaluated against an often ambiguous national norm or average. If, according to a test's scoring system, a student gained only eight months over a period of a year, some would say that the student was behind and did not progress according to expectations on the material tested. Certainly the student did not progress as much as the nation's average student. If, however, an entire school district's average growth rate for that period of time was only eight months, then, our sample student's growth rate was equal to the growth rate of the peer group.

---

[1]Because space does not allow for a comprehensive overview of diagnostic procedures, their specific uses, or the many instruments that can be used, only general information as it relates to the IEP process is presented in this chapter. Interested readers should refer to texts that solely address the diagnosis of handicapped persons (Mauser, 1976; Salvia & Ysseldyke, 1978) and various related chapters in introductory learning disabilities texts (Lerner, 1976; Mercer, 1979).

ALPHABETIZING

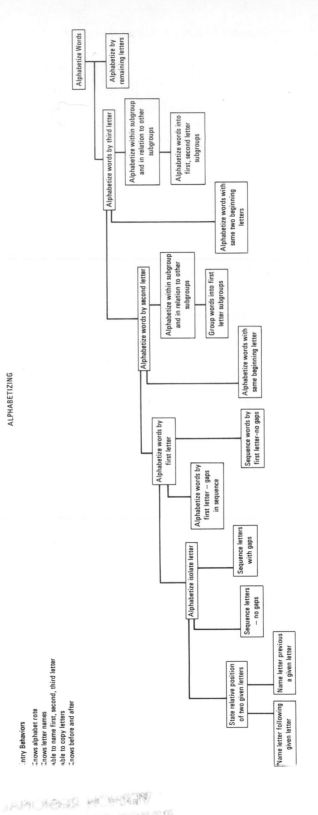

Figure 2.2   The lattice system applied to a sample skill—alphabetizing. (National Institute of Education Grant OEG-0-70-3916 [607] under the direction of Norris Haring.)

Caution must be taken when evaluating student progress against the national norm. In one school district, a learning disabilities "epidemic" raged. Close examination of all students' scores determined that the district's average was two years behind the national norm. Therefore, all those children two years "behind" actually were "average," and only those children four years below the national average should have been considered for assistance from the learning disabilities specialists because of severe academic deficiencies.

The debate about assessments of school-aged children has raged for years. At the center of the debate are some important issues: What is the purpose of the diagnosis? Who should do the diagnosis? Who should interpret the results of the diagnosis? Does testing violate a child's right to privacy? What is a nondiscriminatory test? Quick and easy answers to these questions are not available. Interpretations of the meanings of these questions and their implications vary from school district to school district and state department of education to state department of education. One gauge or perspective, however, can be offered for the testing issue: standardized tests can only be justified if they are useful to the school system, the teacher, the parent, *and* the child.

Purposes of assessment. Generally, there are seven diagnostic categories, each having a different purpose. Intelligence tests, such as the *Stanford-*

Standardized and criterion-referenced tests can give regular and special education teachers information to help them plan for individual students.

Binet (Terman & Merrill, 1960) and the *Wechsler Intelligence Scale for Children, Revised* (Wechsler, 1974), are supposed to provide an indication of an individual's potential abilities. Tests of personality, such as the *Minnesota Multiphasic Personality Inventory* (Hathaway & McKinley, 1967), are supposed to indicate levels of social and personal adjustment. Tests of acuity provide an indication of deficits in a sensory channel (hearing, sight). Tests of learning style are used to determine strengths and weaknesses. An example of this type of test is *The Illinois Test of Psycholinguistic Abilities* (Kirk, McCarthy, & Kirk, 1968). Achievement tests, such as the *Wide Range Achievement Test* (Jastak & Jastak, 1978), the *Metropolitan Achievement Test* (Durost, Bixler, Hildreth, Lund, & Wrightstone, 1959), and the *Peabody Individual Achievement Test* (Dunn & Markwardt, 1970), provide the evaluator with an estimate of a student's grade level achievement in academic subject areas. Criterion-referenced tests, examples of which include the *Mann-Suiter Diagnostic Inventories* (Mann & Suiter, 1974) and the *Brigance Diagnostic Inventory of Essential Skills* (Brigance, 1979), although usually not standardized, indicate whether an individual has mastered a skill or curriculum area. They tell a teacher what skills a student does and does not possess. Because of their structure, they not only help evaluate student skill levels, but also indicate to the teacher which skills should be taught next. Direct and daily measurements (procedures delineated in the next chapter) also are used for assessing or evaluating student progress. These assessments are taken from the materials used in the classroom (for example, oral reading samples from the assigned basal readers) for a number of school days.

Before any student is submitted to the testing (assessment) situation, the purposes of the testing must be determined. Where a child fits in the cascade of educational services (Deno, 1970) should be decided accurately and efficiently. Standardized tests of intelligence, learning style, and achievement can facilitate this decision-making process.

The IEP process requires each student to have a set of annual goals and objectives that are monitored periodically to determine whether progress is being made toward the attainment of the stated goals and objectives. Various tests and assessment procedures can facilitate program evaluation. Criterion-referenced tests, achievement tests and direct and daily measurements are useful in determining year-to-year gains and losses, the necessity for continuation of special services, etc.

Teachers also need assessment information to plan and to make decisions about classroom organization and instruction based upon each student's skills. Specifically, they need to know when an objective is met, when to re-instruct on particular topics, when to terminate daily instruction, when one intervention tactic is no longer effective, and when a specific kind of tactic is needed. This kind of information only results from sensitive and reliable measurements. For example, an ongoing, continuous measurement system can be developed for daily or frequent classroom and student evaluations. The applied behavior analysis evaluation procedures (described in detail in the next chapter) can be useful evaluation tools.

DEVELOPING THE INDIVIDUAL EDUCATION PROGRAM[2]

Since the enactment of P. L. 94-142, there has been much discussion about the purposes and implications of the IEP. Several excellent books (Lerner, Dawson, & Horvath, 1980; Shrag, 1977; Torres, 1977; Turnbull, Strickland, & Brantley, 1978) and articles (Turnbull, Strickland, & Hammer, 1978a, 1978b) provide thorough discussion about the IEP. Although there may be some disagreement about minor issues (of how much detail the IEP must include and how the evaluation should be accomplished), a specific sequence must be followed during the IEP process. The flow chart in Figure 2.3 illustrates the steps and the intended sequence required by the law.

Referral

Children are referred for special education services in various ways. Not every student referred actually qualifies for assistance from specially trained personnel. Some parents know that their child will need special education before the child starts school (for example, the parents of severely handicapped students). Preschoolers whose language development is delayed are usually identified before kindergarten as potential students for the speech clinician or language developmentalist. However, most students who receive educational services for learning disabilities are referred initially by the regular classroom teacher. Sometimes the referral occurs very early in a student's academic career; other times, referral does not occur until middle elementary grades.

The referring teacher notifies the principal and the special services committee about a student who is having difficulties in school. This special services committee, sometimes referred to as the appraisal and review committee or the child study team, should be composed of relevant school personnel. Permanent committee members should be the school's special education resource room teacher(s), principal, counselor, and school psychologist. Rotating members are the child's classroom teacher, the child's parents, and the social service agency representatives who deal with the child and the family (Turnbull, Strickland, & Brantley, 1978). If, after consultation, the committee decides that a formal evaluation of a referred student is warranted, a written notification and request for permission is sent to the child's parents.

The primary referring agent, usually the regular classroom teacher, should indicate to the special services committee the reasons for the referral and some data or justification. Information from general screening instruments, from classroom academic performance in relation to classmates, and from observations about social behavior problems should accompany a written request for referral. After reviewing the referral request and considering other information from additional school personnel (supplemental service teachers such as the physical education teacher, the music teacher, or the art

---

[2]It is important to note that considerable variation in the interpretation of the mandate of P.L. 94-142 exists from state to state and from school district to school district. This section attempts to indicate the minimum procedures to follow to comply with the federal mandate.

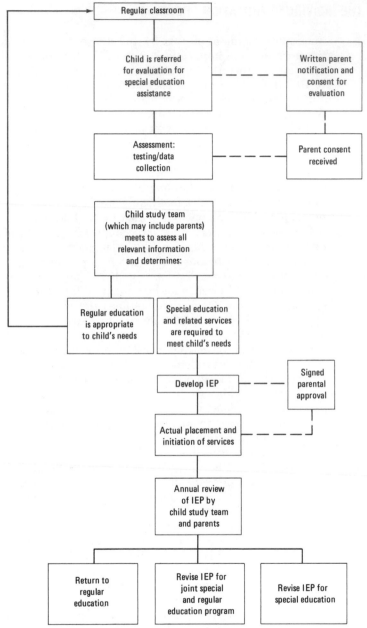

Figure 2.3   Flow chart for the individualized education program process.

The special services committee is discussing the placement and program for a youngster. Present are the child's parents, the special education teacher, the regular education teacher, the principal, and the counselor/diagnostician.

teacher), the special service committee may decide that a formal evaluation or assessment is necessary.

Assessment

To receive special education services, the student must qualify by meeting the criteria specified in the definition of that category of special education. For the category of learning disabilities, a student must: (1) be of average or above average intelligence; (2) be behind academically (often specified as two or more years behind); and (3) be without physical impairments, retardation, or severe behavioral disorder. Many states also include a fourth category specifying that a student must be weak in any one or a combination of psychological processes such as memory, auditory processing, visual processing, or conceptualization.

To determine whether a student can qualify for special education and receive specialized help from the learning disabilities teacher, certain kinds of formal assessment instruments must be used. Specifically, a test of intelligence (to determine whether the student falls within the normal range), a test of academic achievement (to determine whether the student is two years behind his or her peer group), and screening tests of acuity (to be certain that school difficulties are not a function of poor, uncorrected vision or hearing) should be part of the assessment battery. In addition, many special services committees strongly recommend that other assessments be included, such as direct and daily measurements, tests of learning style, and behavioral checklists. Once all of the assessment information is collected, the special services committee must evaluate its completeness. If further data are needed, they may request additional testing or referral to other diagnostic specialists (for example, the medical profession).

Consideration for special services. After a complete formal assessment, many students return to the regular education program and do not receive specialized services because they do not meet the qualifications. For students identified as learning disabled, however, placement decisions must be made. A variety of service delivery options are available in most school districts: itinerant teachers, resource rooms, partially self-contained and self-contained classrooms. The special services team decides what kind of service delivery option is most suitable for each student, and what additional special services are required for the implementation of a complete and appropriate educational program. For example, many learning disabled students require specialized assistance from language developmentalists or recreational therapists. The appropriateness of these services to the student's educational needs must be considered. If warranted, they must be guaranteed.

The student's parents must be informed of the evaluation results and the ensuing decisions and recommendations about their child's educational program. Parents are to be included in the IEP meeting (at which their child's individual education program for the academic year is developed). They must be notified of the date, place, and time of the meeting. If they cannot attend, parent conferences, telephone calls, and home meetings may be used instead. In most cases, parents and schools are in agreement and share their concerns and program recommendations. Parents do have the right to challenge the committee's evaluation or program recommendations. In instances where agreement cannot be reached between the two parties, a due process hearing may be called; decisions are then made by an impartial hearing officer.

Writing the IEP. Once the special services committee decides that a child should be placed in special education, the IEP must be written. P. L. 94-142 requires that this be completed within thirty days of the special education decision. The IEP is a management and administrative tool. Although it provides guidelines for the content of a student's educational program, it need not be an instructional plan.

Parents should be encouraged to participate actively in the development of the goals and objectives included in their child's IEP. They must be at least aware of its content and indicate their approval by signing the IEP. The intent is that parents' involvement in their child's educational program will continue after the approval of the IEP. Unfortunately, some parents' interest and concern stop at this point. Once they have signed the IEP, their legal commitment is completed. If, however, a more complete educational program is to be implemented, parents and teachers should work together throughout the academic year. Some authorities (Goldstein, Strickland,

The parents must sign their child's Individualized Education Plan.

Turnbull, & Curry, 1980) suggest that for this to occur, many parents will need special training.

A number of requirements for the IEP and its content are specified in the law. Table 2.2 indicates the items that must be included in each IEP. A portion of one student's IEP, shown in Figure 2.4, delineates only one goal area, mathematics. For most learning disabled students, a substantial number of goals and their ensuing objectives are necessary.

As specified by P. L. 94-142, the IEP is developed by a team of people consisting of the student's teacher(s), a representative from special education administration, the student's parent(s) or guardian(s), a diagnostician (preferably one who assisted in the identification process), and (if appropriate) the student. Although some school districts do not insist that the student's teacher(s) for the coming academic year be present, it is advantageous for their input and involvement to come at the beginning, when the development of a student's yearly program is being planned. The teacher is the one who must implement the IEP, select educational programs and materials, write daily lesson plans, and evaluate student progress toward the goals and objectives stated in the IEP. Since the teacher is the one person best able to monitor the delivery of related services, his or her involvement is critical in the early developmental stages. Competent learning disabilities specialists can facilitate the development of IEPs and should insist on participation. Also, if the student attends regular education classes part time, that teacher

Figure 2.4. Sample individualized educational program plan form with individualized program goals in one subject area.

Sandra Bourgeault
(Student's Name)

6/15/71
(Birthdate)

Ms. Hyatt
(Teacher)

September 2
(Date of Last Assessment)

September 15
(Date)

9
(Age)

Valley Vista
(School)

STRENGTHS:

Sandra relates well with her peers and does not display any social behavior problems.

She follows instructions and seems to benefit greatly from individualized instruction.

WEAKNESSES:

She has an articulation problem that interferes with her oral language, which results in her hesitancy to speak before the group.

She is several grade levels behind in reading and does not demonstrate sufficient word attack skills.

She is behind her classmates in computational arithmetic and has not mastered many basic facts.

Prioritized Annual Goals:

1. Articulation deficits will be remediated.
2. Computational arithmetic skills (addition, subtraction, and multiplication facts and processes like carrying and borrowing) will be mastered.
3. Decoding skills in reading will be mastered.

Description of Student's Current Program:
Special Education Resource Room, Regular Education 4th grade, and Speech Therapy.

Committee Members Present:

Mr. Petre
(Diagnostician)

Mr. & Mrs. Bourgeault
(Parent or Guardian/Advocate)

Mr. Porec—Speech

Ms. Pepe (Reg. Ed.)
(Teacher)

Mr. Martinez
(School Representative)

Ms. Hyatt (Sp. Ed.)

Computational Arithmetic
(Area)

Sandra Bourgeault
(Student's Name)

September 15
(Date)

ANNUAL GOAL: To demonstrate mastery of computational facts from three computational areas (addition, subtraction, and multiplication) and to demonstrate mastery of process problems for two computational areas (addition and subtraction).

REVIEW DATES: 11/15 2/15 4/15

Short-term Objectives	Methods, Materials, and Procedures	Person Responsible	Start Date	Target Date	Date Objective Met	Comments and Revisions
1. Sandra will demonstrate mastery of all addition facts by meeting the criterion of correct rate (CR) score of 25 and an error rate (ER) score of 0.	Teacher-made worksheets, flash cards, error drill, free-time reinforcement.	Ms. Hyatt	9/15	10/15		
2. Sandra will demonstrate mastery of all subtraction facts by meeting the criterion of CR at 25 and ER at 0.	Teacher-made worksheets, language master, error drill, free-time reinforcement.	Ms. Hyatt	10/15	12/15		
3. Sandra will demonstrate mastery of all multiplication facts by meeting the criterion of CR at 20 and ER at 0.	Teacher-made worksheets, crib sheet, certificate from regular education teacher.	Ms. Hyatt and Ms. Pepe	1/15	3/15		
4. Sandra will demonstrate her ability to compute addition problems that require carrying by achieving three consecutive scores of 95% of better.	Teacher-made worksheets, teacher demonstrations, certificate of success.	Ms. Hyatt	10/1	11/5		
5. Sandra will demonstrate her ability to calculate subtraction problems that do not require borrowing by achieving three consecutive scores of 95% or better.	Teacher-made worksheets, demonstrations, response cost for errors (minutes from recess).	Ms. Hyatt	11/5	11/25		
6. Sandra will demonstrate her ability to calculate subtraction problems that require borrowing without zeros in the minuend by achieving three consecutive scores of at least 95%.	Teacher-made worksheets, demonstrations, reinforcement of special privilege.	Ms. Hyatt	11/26	12/20		
7. Sandra will demonstrate her ability to compute subtraction problems that require borrowing with zeros in the minuend by obtaining three consecutive correct percentage scores of at least 95%.	Teacher-made worksheets, demonstrations, peer tutoring, certificate of success from regular education teacher.	Ms. Hyatt and Ms. Pepe	1/15	2/25		

Table 2.2   **Information that must be included in the IEP**

Area	Specifications
I. Present functioning levels	1. A statement of the child's present levels of educational performance should be provided for at least each of the following areas: a) academic achievement b) social adaptation c) prevocational and vocational skills d) psychomotor skills e) self-help skills
II. Annual goals	1. Annual goal statements should be included for each of the areas listed above. 2. These should describe the educational performance levels expected at the end of the school year. 3. They should be individually tailored for each student in line with information provided for present functioning levels.
III. Short-term behavioral objectives	1. Short-term behavioral objectives should be developed for each of the annual goals. 2. These should be measurable intermediate steps leading to the attainment of the stated goals. 3. Appropriate criteria and evaluation procedures must be delineated to indicate whether the short-term objectives have been achieved.
IV. Special and related services	1. A description of the kind of education services required should be included. 2. A justification for the type of special education class placement is required (resource room, partially self-contained, etc.). 3. A listing of specialized related services must be included (language therapy, physical education, etc.). 4. Projected dates for the initiation and anticipated duration of service should be provided.
V. Regular education	1. A description of the extent to which the student will participate in regular education programs must be included. 2. Care must be taken to ensure that the student receives an appropriate education in the least restrictive setting possible.
VI. Responsibility	1. Individuals responsible for implementing and monitoring the student's IEP must be designated.
VII. Evaluation	1. Methods and procedures to be used to review each IEP must be specified. 2. A schedule for review must be indicated. 3. Reviews must take place at least annually.
VIII. Parent involvement	1. The parents of the student should be encouraged to help develop the IEP goals and objectives. 2. They must be aware of the content of the IEP. 3. They must demonstrate approval of the IEP by signing it.

should be included to maintain consistency within the total program for the child.

Implementation.   Implementation of the IEP begins the first day the student comes to class. Related services specified in the IEP should be initiated according to the schedule indicated. Continual monitoring of goals and objectives is advisable, even necessary, if efficient progress is to be made. Each day throughout the school year, the attainment of the IEP goals and objectives should be of utmost concern to all those concerned with the educational performance and progress of the student. The responsibility is onerous, but the result can be rewarding.

Evaluation. Although the law does not mandate continual evaluation of student performance (evaluation and review are only necessary annually), without frequent information about the influence of the program planned, there is a higher probability that the student will fall short of the stated goals. The law does mandate that each student's goals and objectives be monitored and that criteria for mastery be indicated.

At the time of the required annual review, decisions about placement, related services, and development of new goals and objectives are made. For some learning disabled students, return to regular education is appropriate, while for others, continuation of special education and related services is required to maintain growth.

SUMMARY

Over the past thirty years, special education has changed the face of regular education. To many, the changes brought about by special education were made slowly; to others the changes were achieved too quickly. Possibly no other single piece of legislation effected as many changes as quickly across the whole of the United States as P. L. 94-142. The IEP process mandated by this law has far-reaching implications for all of education, some of which are only beginning to be felt.

One important implication of the IEP process is the increased visibility and participation of the handicapped in schools. More teachers, both regular and special, now work with handicapped learners. Since most handicapped students spend at least part of each school day with their normal counterparts, both the teachers and students who fully participate in regular education programs must adjust to and accommodate for individual differences.

The implications of the IEP process have even more impact for special educators. The IEP process requires more curriculum planning, more specification for each student's goals and objectives, and more accountability through the evaluation and monitoring of progress. Although few would question the merit of developing individualized goals and objectives for every student, Buckley and Walker (1978) do offer one caution. They warn that specified goals and objectives can become self-fulfilling prophecies which, if set too low, could hinder students from achieving their maximum potential.

In addition, this process has forced many special educators to form a partnership with the parents of their students, an unheard of venture in the recent past. These new relationships have direct bearing on the type and quality of the instructional program for each youngster.

Also, the IEP process has made the entire educational system more aware of the multiple educational needs of handicapped learners. No longer are these students viewed as the sole domain of the special education teacher. They are now pupils of professionals from a myriad of disciplines within the school system. This has forced the special education teacher into assuming new, complex roles (advocate, multidisciplinary team leader, evaluation coordinator).

Clearly, many changes have been made over the past few years. Most were mandated by federal law and implemented by local school districts. The IEP process has been a jolt to many, but it has initiated the realization of appropriate educational services as the guaranteed right of all handicapped students.

REFERENCE NOTES

1. GOLD, M. W. *Task analysis: A statement and an example using acquisition and production of a complex assembly task by the retarded blind* (National Institute of Child Health and Human Development Program, Project Grant No. HD05951). Urbana, Ill.: University of Illinois, Institute for Child Behavior and Development, undated.

2. WOOLMAN, M. *The concept of the program lattice* (working paper). Washington, D.C.: Institute of Educational Research, Inc., 1962.

3. SMITH, J. O., & SMITH, D. D. Research and application of instructional material development. In N. G. Haring (Ed.), *Annual report: A program project for the investigation and application of procedures of analysis and modification of behavior of handicapped children* (National Institute of Education, Grant OEG-0-70-3916, 607). Washington, D.C.: National Institute of Education, 1974.

REFERENCES

BRICKER, W. A. A systematic approach to language training. In R. L. Schiefelbusch (Ed.), *Language of the mentally retarded*. Baltimore: University Park Press, 1972.

BRIGANCE, A. H. *The Brigance diagnostic inventory of essential skills*. Woburn, Mass.: Curriculum Associates, Inc., 1979.

BUCKLEY, N. K., & WALKER, H. M. *Modifying classroom behavior: A manual for classroom teachers* (rev. ed.). Champaign, Illinois: Research Press Company, 1978.

BUDDE, J. F. The lattice systems approach: Systems technology for human development. *Educational Technology*, 1972, *12*, 75–79.

BUDDE, J. F., & MENOLASCINO, F. J. Systems technology and retardation: Applications to vocational habilitation. *Mental Retardation*, 1971, *9*, 11–16.

CARR, R. A. Goal attainment scaling as a useful tool for evaluating progress in special education. *Exceptional Children*, 1979, *46*, 88–95.

DENO, E. Special education as developmental capital. *Exceptional Children*, 1970, *37*, 229–237.

DUNN, L. M., & MARKWARDT, F. C., JR. *Peabody individual achievement test*. Circle Pines, Minn.: American Guidance Service, 1970.

DUROST, W. N., BIXLER, H. H., HILDRETH, G. H., LUND, K. W., & WRIGHTSTONE, J. W. *Metropolitan achievement tests*. New York: Harcourt, Brace & World, 1959.

EATON, M. D., & LOVITT, T. C. Achievement tests vs. direct and daily measurement. In G. Semb (Ed.), *Behavior analysis and education—1972*. Lawrence, Kan.: University of Kansas, 1972.

GOLDSTEIN, S., STRICKLAND, B., TURNBULL, A. P., & CURRY, L. An observational analysis of the IEP conference. *Exceptional Children*, 1980, *46*, 278–286.

HATHAWAY, S. R., & McKINLEY, J. C. *Minnesota multiphasic personality inventory*. New York: The Psychological Corporation, 1967.

JASTAK, J. F., & JASTAK, S. R. *The wide range achievement test* (rev. ed.). Los Angeles: Western Psychological Services, 1978.

KIRK, S. A., McCARTHY, J. J., & KIRK, W. D. *Illinois test of psycholinguistic abilities* (rev. ed.). Urbana, Ill.: University of Illinois Press, 1968.

LERNER, J. W. *Children with learning disabilities* (2nd ed.). Boston: Houghton Mifflin Co., 1976.

LERNER, J., DAWSON, D., & HORVATH, L. *Cases in learning and behavior problems: A guide to individualized education programs.* Boston: Houghton Mifflin Co., 1980.

LOVITT, T. C. Assessment of children with learning disabilities. *Exceptional Children*, 1967, *34*, 233–239.

MAGER, R. F. *Preparing instructional objectives.* Palo Alto, Calif.: Fearon Publishers, 1962.

MAGER, R. F. *Preparing instructional objectives* (2nd ed.). Belmont, Calif.: Fearon Publishers, 1975.

MANN, P. H., & SUITER, P. *Teacher's handbook of diagnostic inventories: Spelling-reading-handwriting-arithmetic.* Boston: Allyn & Bacon, 1974.

MAUSER, A. J. *Assessing the learning disabled: Selected instruments.* San Rafael, Calif.: Academic Therapy Publications, 1976.

MERCER, C. D. *Children and adolescents with learning disabilities.* Columbus, Ohio: Charles E. Merrill Publishing Co., 1979.

POPHAM, W. J., & BAKER, E. L. *Planning an instructional sequence.* Englewood Cliffs, N.J.: Prentice-Hall, 1970.

RESNICK, L. B. Task analysis in instructional design: Some cases from mathematics. In D. Klohr (Ed.), *Cognition and instruction.* Hillsdale, N.J.: John Wiley & Sons, 1976.

RESNICK, L. B., WANG, M. C., & KAPLAN, J. Task analysis in curriculum design: A hierarchically sequenced introductory mathematics curriculum. *Journal of Applied Behavior Analysis*, 1973, *6*, 679–710.

SALVIA, J., & YSSELDYKE, J. E. *Assessment in special and remedial education.* Boston: Houghton Mifflin Co., 1978.

SHRAG, J. A. *Individualized educational programming (IEP): A child study team process.* Austin, Tex.: Learning Concepts, 1977.

SMITH, D. D., SMITH, J. O., & EDGAR, E. A prototypic model for developing instructional materials for the severely handicapped. In N. G. Haring & L. J. Brown (Eds.), *Teaching the severely handicapped* (Vol. 1). New York: Grune & Stratton, 1976.

SMITH, D. D., & SNELL, M. E. Classroom management and instructional planning. In M. E. Snell (Ed.), *Systematic instruction of the moderately and severely handicapped.* Columbus, Ohio: Charles E. Merrill Publishing Co., 1978.

TERMAN, L., & MERRILL, M. *Stanford-Binet intelligence scale* (revised I.Q. tables by S. R. Pinneau). New York: Houghton Mifflin Co., 1960.

TORRES, S. (Ed.) *A primer on individualized education programs for handicapped children.* Reston, Va.: The Foundation for Exceptional Children, 1977.

TURNBULL, A. P., STRICKLAND, B. B., & BRANTLEY, J. C. *Developing and implementing individualized education programs.* Columbus, Ohio: Charles E. Merrill Publishing Co., 1978.

TURNBULL, A. P., STRICKLAND, B., & HAMMER, S. E. The individualized education program—Part 1: Procedural guidelines. *Journal of Learning Disabilities*, 1978, 11, 40–46.

TURNBULL, A. P., STRICKLAND, B., & HAMMER, S. E. The individualized education program—Part 2: Translating law into practice. *Journal of Learning Disabilities*, 1978, *11*, 67–72.

VAN ETTEN, C., & VAN ETTEN, G. The measurement of pupil progress and selecting instructional materials. *Journal of Learning Disabilities*, 1976, 9, 469–480.

WECHSLER, D. *Wechsler intelligence scale for children—Revised.* New York: The Psychological Corporation, 1974.

3 EVALUATION OF INSTRUCTION

Youngsters are sent to school to gain knowledge and enhance their abilities. They are expected to learn how to perform academic tasks, interact with others in socially appropriate ways, and develop skills to make them productive members of society. Achievement of these overall goals is the awesome responsibility of teachers. Whether they are appropriate goals for schools to assume is not for debate here. It seems, however, that society has charged the schools and the educational system with the obligation of meeting these somewhat ambiguous yet certainly ambitious goals for each and every individual. The taxpayers' concern with allocation and dispersement of revenue for education, the courts' and state legislatures' demands for the establishment of minimum competency levels, and the implementation of P.L. 94-142 requiring accountability in education—all emphasize society's concern about education and the educational process (Van Etten & Van Etten, 1976).

Monitoring the learning of students is not an impossible task. In fact, evaluation of student performance has been typical school routine for many years. Traditionally, students' progress is measured at the beginning and at the end of each school year and before each grade report. This noncontinuous system, however, does not provide teachers with enough information to assist them in scheduling appropriate instructional activities. Neither does it provide immediate feedback about the effectiveness of teaching procedures. For those students who make adequate progress in school, traditional evaluation procedures may be sufficient. For the learning disabled student, more precise evaluation methods are necessary.

Recommendations about frequent, direct evaluation of student performance in the classroom are neither new nor novel. Olson (1935) stressed the importance of measuring children's behavior in the classroom to ensure greater precision in the discovery of relationships between the environment and student behavior. He advocated systematic measurement and precise record keeping for use with children possessing undesirable behavioral deviations. Certainly the collection of information about target students and their behavioral repertoires should be an integral part of the instructional process.

Although it is possible to measure almost every classroom and student occurrence, it is unreasonable to expect this of teachers who must work within current teacher-student ratios and financial constraints. There are times, however, when social behavior or academic learning is problematic for every student and specific instruction is required. In these instances, teachers must be certain that the instructional activities planned and implemented are effective. Many authorities (Cooper & Johnson, 1979; Jenkins, Mayhall, Peschka, & Townsend, 1974; Kazdin, 1973; Lovitt, 1975; Van Etten & Van Etten, 1976) have stressed eloquently the merits of directly evaluating student performance in conjunction with the application of instructional procedures. All concur that evaluation must become part of every teacher's classroom routine.

Standard measurement procedures should be employed so that evaluation becomes the collection of facts, not just the interpretation of subjective feelings about the learning situation. White and Liberty (1976) make this point well:

> Without guidelines, observations of children and the world in which they move are often shaded by what we think we should see, or perhaps, by unusual and dramatic sidelights to the performance of the child which have nothing to do with learning, per se. Decisions based upon such information are subject to grave errors. Programs in which a child grows are altered. Programs which doom a child to eventual failure are continued. And so it goes. (p. 32)

Evaluation procedures need to be sensitive to the learning situation so that immediate feedback about the influence of instructional procedures can be obtained. The learning disabled student cannot afford to lose instructional time because of prolonged use of ineffective techniques. This kind of teacher accountability is warranted whether mandated by society or not.

Standard and sensitive evaluation procedures need not be expensive in teacher time or effort. They should be easily incorporated into teaching situations, and a variety of persons (pupils, aides, and volunteers) should be able to implement them. This chapter provides an overview of evaluation procedures that have been in use in classrooms for over a decade. Guidelines for choosing data collection systems are included, as are methods for analyzing and evaluating the product (data) of the evaluation process.

DATA COLLECTION

The purpose of collecting information on student performance is to evaluate the teacher's and student's progress toward achieving goals and objectives. To justify the time spent measuring, the data collected must be meaningful.

Therefore, the information gathered should relate directly to the target behavior. If oral reading is the current behavior of concern, words read orally by the student in his or her assigned reader should be the behavior measured.

Direct measurement of the specified behavior alone, however, does not guarantee meaningful data. Student performance must be evaluated across time. This means that direct data should be gathered daily or at least frequently. For teachers who do not see the student daily, measurement of the target behavior should occur each time the student receives instruction.

The data gathered must be of equivalent or comparable scale, in order that one day's performance can be judged against other days' performances to assess whether progress has been made. To have equivalent data, several factors must be constant. First, the behavior measured must remain the same across time. If rate of oral reading is the target behavior, the child should read orally from comparable passages each day—not oral reading on Monday, silent reading on Tuesday, oral reading comprehension on Wednesday, and so on. These other reading targets might also need to be assessed frequently, but they are separate targets, not interchangeable ones. The measurement system chosen must also remain constant. If reading rate is the appropriate measurement system, it must be used consistently. The interspersing of one system with another renders all the data meaningless.

To determine whether the scheduled instruction was responsible for changes in student performance, it is important to keep other situational variables as constant as possible. For example, if a child is asked to read

Data gathered on a child's performance must be meaningful so reliable communication can occur. This will lead to accurate decisions about changes in students' educational programs.

orally in the morning one day, after lunch the next day, and before recess the following day, the changes in that student's oral reading might not be due to the materials presented or the instruction given. Likewise, if the location of the student's reading desk is changed daily, variations in performance might be more attributable to those moves than to actual change in reading ability. Naturally, everything cannot be held constant. The health of the student or the events that happened the previous evening or during the morning on the way to school can affect the way a student performs at school. Frequent measures of performance, however, place those variables in perspective, and an accurate picture of the student's abilities in target areas becomes apparent.

It is important to choose a measurement system that adequately reflects the target behavior, is sensitive to changes in performance, and can be implemented with relative ease. A number of different measurement systems are available. They render different kinds of information and are applicable to specific situations. The remainder of this chapter discusses the advantages and disadvantages of each measurement system.

Anecdotal Logs   Historically, teachers kept information about their students through anecdotal logs. Most often such records were kept in diary format through an abbreviated narrative; naughty or otherwise unacceptable social behavior was noted at the end of the school day (see Figure 3.1 for an example).

Although attempts were made to keep daily records of student behavior, the value of the information was questionable. Noted at the end of the day, the recollections of a tired teacher over a six-hour period had to be trusted. The accuracy and detail of these records were suspect at best, for they relied on the teacher's memory and subjective feelings. Although the reliability of the measurement is in doubt, a busy teacher can use this system

Figure 3.1   Anecdotal records for recording behavioral information.

initially. The teacher should note occurrences of certain behaviors to determine whether their frequency is sufficient to warrant the scheduling of a complex data collection system.

Antecedent
Behavior
Consequence
(ABC) Analysis

A more sophisticated form of anecdotal record keeping is available for monitoring social behavior as it naturally occurs. The ABC Analysis method lends some structure and organization to the collection of observational information. Instead of relying on recollection at the end of a school day or an academic period, the teacher is required to keep a record of classroom or playground events *as they occur*. The notations are organized on a time basis. Events that antecede the target behavior are noted in the first column of a prepared form (see Figure 3.2). The behavior of concern for a target student is marked in the middle column, and events occurring subsequent to the behavior under consideration are indicated in the last column.

This system is helpful when teachers are attempting to specify exactly what problem behavior should be considered for remediation. For example, often a teacher indicates that a student is "aggressive," but is not certain

---

Student's Name: *Steve S.*

Period: *Reading*

Teacher's Name: *Ms. Tidall*

Observation Time: *10:10 - 10:25*

Antecedent	Behavior	Consequence
John whispers to Steve	S. Clowns	Class laughs
Class still laughing	S. tells joke	Class laughs
Teacher tells S. to stop	S. laughs	Class quiets down
Teacher tells S. to sit in hall	S. leaves class	

Figure 3.2 ABC Analysis reporting form.

about the forms the student's aggression takes, the frequency of such acts, the victims of the aggression, or what events tend to stimulate these episodes.

After watching an aggressive student on the playground for several days and keeping a record of his behavior using this format, one teacher was able to define the behavior more precisely. Bill's aggression, for example, was composed of distinct components: not following the rules of the game, hitting and kicking others, and swearing. By counting the number of times each of these categories of behavior occurred, the teacher had a rough estimate of the frequency of occurrences and which was the most prevalent.

The ABC Analysis method of note-taking also yields additional useful information. Other children who are directly or indirectly involved in the target student's acts of aggression can be identified. For example, Bill only exhibited aggressive behavior when Tom and Susie were present, and Pete most frequently was the victim. Information about other students who might be contributing to the situation is helpful to the teacher in taking steps to reduce aggressive occurrences in the future. Also, certain environmental situations tend to be present when the aggressive acts occur. In Bill's case, the probability of trouble increased when he was playing baseball. The variables contributing to problematic behavioral episodes are almost infinite in number, but being cognizant of their presence and their interactive capabilities certainly facilitates the selection of an appropriate intervention strategy.

Both forms of anecdotal notes, the traditional log and the ABC Analysis, are useful initially to pinpoint and define social behaviors.[1] However, both methods are too cumbersome to implement for a long period of time because they require the teacher to make records of behavior in longhand and do not allow for quick review of behavioral changes noted for days, weeks, or months of student performance. Once the target behavior is identified, the teacher should select one of the following measurement systems to evaluate changes in student performance.

Frequency

The simplest system of data collection is frequency. Frequency data indicate the number of times a behavior occurred and are gathered by merely recording each time the behavior is observed. Teachers can collect such data by making hatch marks on an index card taped to a convenient place; data can be collected by aides, volunteers, peers, or by the target student. Many situations lend themselves well to the frequency system. For example, the number of disruptive acts, talk-outs, out-of-seats, correct math problems, correct spelling words, and instances of tardiness can all be measured by the collection of frequency data.

Frequency data should not be used in all situations. Systematic measurement devices are needed to translate behavioral occurrences so that one day's performance can be compared with another's, and so that how often the

---

[1]When academic tasks are being considered for remediation, anecdotal notes do not provide the desired information. In these instances, criterion-referenced tests, task analyses, and various skill sequences are more useful.

behavior occurs across time can be determined. By merely counting the frequency of the behavior, however, commonality of the data is not guaranteed. Let's suppose that Liz talked back to the music teacher a lot. The teacher decided to count how many times this happened. According to the teacher's data, Liz talked back five times on Monday, Tuesday, and Wednesday, four times on Thursday, and three times on Friday. Can the teacher accurately say that Liz's performance was improving? That is impossible to determine from the data provided, for there is no indication whether session time was held constant. If music period lasted for fifty minutes on Monday, forty minutes on Tuesday and Wednesday, twenty minutes on Thursday, and only ten minutes on Friday, Liz's behavior did not improve across the week. In fact, she was even worse on Friday than Monday! This example demonstrates that if frequency data are to be kept, session time must be held constant.

A corollary is also true. If the number of correct responses is the target of interest, the number of opportunities to respond must be held constant (rather than session time). If frequency data are used in this situation, the only way to determine whether spelling accuracy increases is to keep the number of spelling words dictated the same each time.

Duration Sometimes the important question is not "How many times does a certain behavior occur?" but rather "How long does the behavior last?" To illustrate this point, two students' tantrums were compared. Both students had two tantrums during the entire school day. One student's tantrums lasted a total of two minutes. In this case, the teacher decided that for the present no direct action was warranted, but the student's tantrums would be monitored periodically to be certain that neither the frequency nor the duration warranted remediation. The second student presented another problem. He also had an average of only two tantrums each day, but the average time spent having tantrums over a week was forty-five minutes daily. Although this student did not have a high frequency of tantrums, the duration was high and indicated a need for remediation. In some cases, both the frequency *and* duration of a social behavior are of concern. When this occurs, both aspects of the target behavior can be measured concurrently.

Duration data are not difficult to obtain if the teacher has a stopwatch at his or her disposal. Each time a tantrum begins, the teacher or a classmate of the target child starts the watch. When a tantrum ceases, the watch is stopped. Without erasing the time accumulated, when another tantrum begins the stopwatch is started and the process repeated until the observation period is completed. The amount of time the student spent having tantrums and the day's data are revealed by merely reading the stopwatch.

As with frequency data, a major precaution must be considered when duration data are kept. For the same reasons that either number of opportunities or session time must be held constant in the frequency situation, session time must remain the same for all data collection sessions. If data are kept for the whole day or even for the morning, the time is of sufficient length so that the teacher need not be concerned that each daily recording session is equivalent to the minute. When duration data cannot be collected over an entire school day, morning, or afternoon, a precise observation time (for example, thirty minutes) should be established.

Percent

When neither frequency nor duration data can be collected appropriately because situational variables cannot be controlled, it is necessary to translate the data into a ratio so comparisons can be made from one day's data to another. If the number of spelling words included on each test is the same, frequency data (counting number of correctly spelled words) are appropriate. If, however, the number of words presented varies per test, the raw data must be converted to an equivalent form. A comparable situation exists for duration data. When observation time cannot be held constant, the raw data must be translated into another form to ensure that the data have meaning and can serve to evaluate and reflect changes in student performance accurately across time. Percent scores (percent correct, percent of occurence) can serve this purpose.

Percent correct. This measurement system gives an indication of quality or accuracy of performance. Percent correct does not give information about the quantity or amount of work completed, but is a very appropriate measurement system to select when the accuracy of student performance is of concern.

Percent correct scores are calculated by using the following formula:

$$\frac{\text{number of correct responses}}{\text{number of correct and incorrect responses}} \times 100 = \text{percent correct}$$

For example, the percent correct score for one day's spelling test is determined by dividing the number of correctly spelled words by the total number of words on the test, multiplied by 100 (to remove the decimal point). Kyle spelled 4 words correctly on a 15 word test. The percent correct score was calculated by dividing 4 by 15 and then multiplying the quotient by 100 and putting a percentage sign after the product. In this case, the correct percentage score was 27 percent.

The number of opportunities to respond affects the score a student can obtain, as does the student's performance. If there are only five questions on one social studies quiz and thirty questions on the next quiz, a student who misses only one question on each test receives vastly different percentage scores (80 percent and 97 percent). To remedy this situation, some teachers make certain that all quizzes are of sufficient length so that scores are not biased as in the above example.

Percent of occurrence. When session time cannot be or is not held constant while duration data are collected, the raw data must be transformed into a ratio so the data can be compared with each other. Therefore, in these instances two different kinds of information must be gathered for each session: the length of observation time and the total amount of time the student engaged in the target activity. The desired percentage score is obtained by using the following formula:

$$\frac{\text{number of minutes engaged in target behavior}}{\text{session time}} \times 100 = \text{percent of occurrence}$$

It should be remembered that although session time may vary from day to day when this type of percentage score is used, it is advisable to keep the observation times comparable and not allow great fluctuations.

Rate

Speed of performance is important for almost everything adults do, particularly in job situations. Unfortunately, it is an area that special education teachers often neglect because they are so concerned with instilling student accuracy. In many academic situations, however, indication of accuracy is not sufficient to evaluate a student's true academic progress. It is possible to get every item attempted on a test correct, but fail academically because assignments are not completed on time. Students who are learning to become better silent readers, for example, must be able to read passages accurately and also quickly enough to keep up with classmates. In these instances, both *accuracy* and *speed* (quality and quantity) of student performance are of vital importance.

Rate is a measurement system that gives an indication of speed of performance. In oral reading the teacher can hear each word read. In silent reading the teacher is not able to determine how accurately the student read each word in the passage; a test of comprehension has to serve this purpose. By calculating reading rate, however, it is possible to assess students' proficiency or speed of reading. This is accomplished by dividing the number of words read during a silent reading session by the time it took to complete the passage.

There are two ways to determine the amount of time it took a student to complete a passage. One is to have the students write on a page the time they began and concluded the passage, then subtract the start time from the stop time. Another is to provide them with stopwatches and have them start the watch when they begin reading and stop the watch when they complete the passage. The time indicated on the stopwatch face is the amount of time it took to complete the passage. The number of words read is obtained by either counting the words in the section or using a text with precounted passages.

Correct rate and error rate.   In the example provided above, it is impossible to gain information about the quality and quantity of performance by using one measurement system. Percent of comprehension questions answered correctly and rate of silent reading had to be the measures used. For many academic areas, however, it is possible to gain an indication of speed of performance and accuracy through the use of one measurement system. Correct and error rates, when used together, provide the teacher with an indication of quality and quantity of student performance. Oral reading, calculation of math facts, assembly line tasks, and other job skills lend themselves well to the application of the correct and error rate measurement system.

Unlike percent correct, in which only one score per evaluation session is sufficient, two scores per session are required for correct and error rate. With percent, the correct percentage score is inversely related to the incorrect percentage score. A perfect score is always 100 percent and never more than that; it is impossible to obtain a correct percentage score of 150 percent. Therefore, if the correct percentage score is 90 percent, the error percentage score is 10 percent. If the correct percentage score is 60 percent, the error percentage score is 40 percent. Correct and error rate scores are not so related. Error rate scores for an entire school week can be zero and the correct rates can be different each day (Monday's correct rate was 30, error rate was 0; Tuesday's correct rate was 45, error rate 0; Wednesday's correct rate 46, error rate 0; Thursday's correct rate 42, error rate 0; Friday's correct rate 55, error rate 0). Although it might be impossible for a correct rate to go above a certain level, that is a function of the target area and not the measurement system itself. For example, it is possible to read silently at a rate of 300 words per minute; to read orally at a correct rate of 175; and calculate math facts at 75 per minute. One might even surpass these scores, while one cannot surpass 100 percent.

Correct and error rates are calculated by using these two formulas:

$$\frac{\text{number of correct responses}}{\text{session time (minutes)}} = \text{correct rate}$$

$$\frac{\text{number of incorrect responses}}{\text{session time (minutes)}} = \text{error rate}$$

Since the correct and error rate measurement system is employed commonly in oral reading, that situation is used for illustration. Jenni was a poor reader and her teacher decided that until substantial changes in her reading skills were noted, Jenni's reading progress would be monitored daily. Each day Jenni read orally to her teacher from her assigned basal text for five minutes. As Jenni read, the teacher marked those words read incorrectly in her copy of the text. At the conclusion of the session, the teacher counted the number of errors made and the number of correctly read words. On one day, Jenni read a total of 205 words correctly and made fifteen errors. These raw data were calculated into correct and error rate scores by dividing by five minutes (session time). Therefore, the correct rate for this day was 41 ($205 \div 5 = 41$ correct words per minute) and the error rate was 3 ($15 \div 5 = 3$ incorrect words per minute).

Both scores were necessary to evaluate Jenni's progress because they are not dependent on each other (the knowledge of one score does not yield the information necessary to determine the other). It is possible for her correct rate scores to increase, decrease, or stay the same while her error rate scores stayed the same, decreased, or increased. Figure 3.3 shows possible variations in correct and error rate score patterns.

The independence of correct rate and error rate scores is important to consider in evaluating student performance. Figure 3.3 illustrates this point.

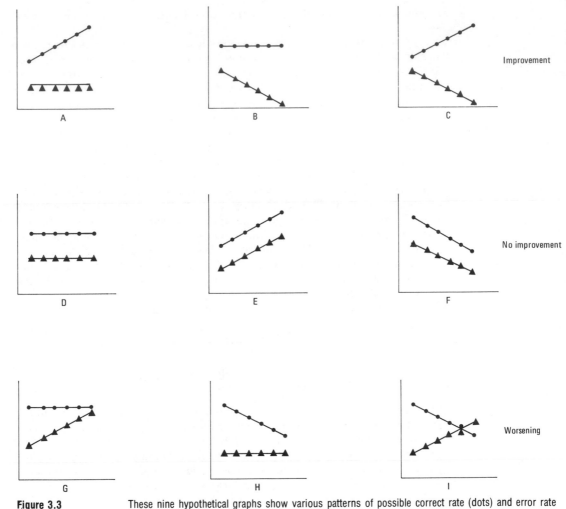

Figure 3.3

These nine hypothetical graphs show various patterns of possible correct rate (dots) and error rate (triangles). Correct rate scores and error rate scores are not reciprocal; one set of scores may decrease, while the other set may also decrease, stay at the same level, or increase. In the top row all three graphs indicate improvement, although the data patterns differ. In the second row all three graphs indicate no improvement. In the bottom row performance is worsening.

Correct rate scores are indicated by the use of dots, while error rate scores are indicated by triangles. The top row of graphs (A, B, and C) displays data that indicate student improvement. In Case A, the student's error rate scores are remaining the same. In Case B, the reverse is true; the student is making fewer errors while not showing any change in correct performance. Case C is what every teacher wishes for: overall improvement in both measures of performance. In the middle row of graphs (D, E, and F), the students are not improving at all. In Case D, both sets of scores are remaining static. In Case E, both correct and error rate scores are accelerating at approximately the same pace; the student is merely doing his or her work faster. In the last graph, Case F, the student is slowing down across time, but proportionally. The quality of performance has not improved as overall production has vastly decreased. The bottom row of examples (Cases G, II, and I) are all those instances teachers hope not to see. In Case G, correct rate scores are remaining static as the error rate scores are accelerating; and in Case H, the student's error rates are remaining the same but correct rates are rapidly decelerating. The last example is every teacher's nightmare. The student started out on the first day of measurement performing the task relatively well, but across time performance deteriorated so that by the final day the student's error rate score exceeded the correct rate score.

The importance of examining both scores should become apparent as one looks only at the correct rates for Case E. The correct rate scores were increasing and one might feel that the student's performance was improving. When the error rate scores are evaluated, however, the contrary is found to be true. If one were to study the error rate pattern that appears in Case F, one might feel that the student's performance was improving, for the error rate scores are decreasing. When the correct rate scores also are considered, however, one can see that the student is not getting any better at all. From these examples one can see that although correct and error rate information are gathered simultaneously, they are not dependent measures: both are needed to evaluate accurately student performance when quality and quantity (proficiency) of student performance is of concern.

Observational Recording

This category of data collection systems was designed to evaluate social behavior through observation of the actions and interactions of students. Only a brief discussion follows because these procedures require the use of outside personnel and are too complex for teachers to implement along with their other responsibilities (Salzberg, Wheeler, Devar, & Hopkins, 1971). Those readers requiring more details about observational measurement systems are referred to Hersen and Barlow (1976), Kazdin (1973), Martin and Pear (1978), and Sulzer-Azaroff and Mayer (1977). Although classroom teachers are not likely to select one of these complex systems, they should be aware of their existence and characteristics, for situations might arise warranting their use.

Basically, there are two versions of observational recording systems: continuous and sampling. In the continuous system, data are kept for a period of time and everything occurring in that period is recorded through the use of observational codes. This system provides a complete "transcript" of the behavioral incident that transpired during the prescribed time. The difficulties involved with collecting and analyzing the voluminous amount of data generated using this system are enormous. Computerized data collection systems are available in which a data collector can enter information about the target environment into a tape recorder, which allows for computerized analysis later.

Observational data, taken in the classroom, can reveal social interaction patterns in need of remediation.

Time sampling procedures have been used and refined over a long period of time. Olson and Cunningham (1934), in their review of time sampling techniques, indicate the prevalence of the use of this observational measurement system during the 1920s and 1930s. The sampling method does not require the recording of all the incidents, but rather records the events during slices of time. In these cases, fixed time samples might be used. For example, an hour can be divided into twelve five-minute intervals. At the end of every five minutes, the teacher could count the number of children out of their seats. The number of children out of their seats each of the twelve times that the teacher counted is averaged to arrive at the day's data.

Since the teacher is not able to concurrently collect the data and teach, outside personnel are necessary to insure that the data are collected accurately and reliably. One suggestion is to seek help from a neighboring college's psychology or special education department, after gaining permission from the administration.

Summary of Data Collection Systems Table 3.1 summarizes those data collection systems teachers are most likely to employ. They range in sophistication from frequency to rate and can be applied appropriately in social and academic situations.

Table 3.1   **Summary of data collection systems**

Measurement System	Definition	Formula	Limitations
Frequency	Number of occurrences; how often the behavior occurs	Count or tally	Session time or number of opportunities must be held constant.
Duration	Total amount of time the individual engaged in an activity; how long the behavior lasts	Cumulative time; time of each episode added together	Session time must be held constant.
Percent correct	The proportion or ratio between correct and incorrect responses	$\dfrac{\text{no. of correct}}{\text{no. of correct + incorrect}} \times 100$	Data are biased by the number of opportunities—only an indication of accuracy with no indication of quantity or speed of performance.
Percent of occurrence	The ratio between the amount of time the student engaged in the target activity and session time	$\dfrac{\text{no. of minutes engaged in the target activity}}{\text{session time}} \times 100$	Data are biased if some sessions are very short in length.
Rate	How fast an activity is performed, transposed into a per minute score	$\dfrac{\text{no. of responses}}{\text{time}}$	Sheer rate provides no indication of quality of performance, only quantity.
Correct rate and error rate	Indicates how many correct and error responses were made per minute	$\dfrac{\text{no. of correct responses}}{\text{session time}}$ $\dfrac{\text{no. of error responses}}{\text{session time}}$	Correct rate and error rate cannot be used alone; both scores must be kept per session.

DATA ANALYSIS

One important component of the evaluation process is the analysis of data collected on student performance. While the data are being gathered, the teacher must be able to judge the effectiveness of those procedures scheduled in light of student progress. Many different ways to analyze data are now available to the teacher and researcher. Some of these methods are simple to execute; others are not. Since the purpose of this chapter is to help *teachers* and other school personnel evaluate the success or failure of the events planned at school, those design and analysis procedures that fall into the exclusive domain of researchers are not discussed.[2]

For school personnel to evaluate instruction, steps must be taken beyond the mere collection of data. The data collection and the intervention application must be submitted to some structure, which involves selecting

[2]Those teachers who wish to conduct classroom research are referred to the following sources: Kerlinger (1964); Hersen and Barlow (1976); Craighead, Kazdin, and Mahoney (1976); Baer (1975); and Campbell and Stanley (1963).

an appropriate evaluation design and submitting the teaching process to that format. This allows for precise teacher judgment based on student performance and systematically observed changes.

Evaluation Designs

One important key to the evaluation of instruction is the structure to which the learning situation is submitted. First, the teacher must be fully aware of those events that might be functioning in the school situation. Although a vast number of events can contribute to student performance, a determination must be made of those variables which, when manipulated, will achieve the desired aim: enhanced student performance. To facilitate the teacher's efforts in identifying those events contributing to undesirable situations and those encouraging student progress, a number of evaluation designs are simple to employ and provide the teacher with the needed information.

It is important to note that all of the designs discussed require certain information from the teacher. The target student(s) must be identified and the target behavior(s) selected. This can be accomplished through the structured observation methods described in the ABC Analysis section, by using checklists, criterion-referenced tests, or collecting some preliminary data. This prebaseline or predesign implementation period, which need only last a few days, can save the teacher a substantial amount of time and facilitate the selection of the most advantageous evaluation design.

Reversal or ABAB.   Although a number of variations of this design have been developed and refined over the years, the basic format remains as it was outlined by Baer, Wolf, and Risley (1968). Usually, there are four basic elements or phases of this design: *baseline, intervention, return-to-baseline,* and *return-to-intervention.*

The purpose of the baseline phase is to assess the target behavior over time. By measuring or collecting data on the target behavior during the usual classroom routine for a period of time, the teacher learns about the nature of the target, its components, and functioning level. This usually takes anywhere from three to five data days. The data gathered during the baseline phase can help the teacher select the intervention strategy having the highest probability of producing the desired changes in the target behavior.

The second phase of the reversal design is the intervention condition. Each day during this phase, the teacher teaches in about the same way. If instruction is selected as the intervention strategy, it is provided every day that the conditions prescribed are in effect. Changes in the intervention strategy should not be made haphazardly. For example, on day three, feedback should not be added; on day four, reinforcement should not be scheduled. The first intervention should be given a chance to operate. If, after four or five data days, the amount of change in the target behavior is not sufficient, a new phase is implemented that adds to the first intervention or substitutes a different strategy.

If the first intervention strategy produced the desired changes in student performance, a return-to-baseline condition (removal of the intervention) usually is scheduled to be certain that the desired changes were influenced by the intervention and not some yet unidentified environmental factor. When this design is selected, it is assumed that the target behavior will reverse or return to the performance levels of the initial baseline period.

Typically, social behaviors (talking out, out of seat, aggression, and disruption) fluctuate in this manner. Once verification (that the intervention was the cause of the changes in the target behavior) is obtained by a return of the scores to the approximate levels of the first baseline phase, the intervention procedures are reapplied. A graph of data submitted to an ABAB design is shown in Figure 3.4.

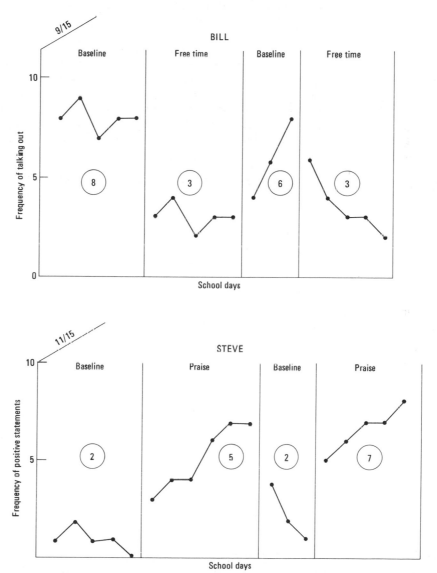

Figure 3.4   These two graphs show expected patterns for data gathered by the reversal design. In each graph the dots represent daily frequency scores. Each phase is labeled. The score of central tendency (median) for each condition is circled.

However, an adaptation of the reversal design was described for non-research situations (Smith & Snell, 1978). In the situation related above, the performance levels are expected to return to the initial levels when the intervention is withdrawn. When learned behavior is the target (acquisition of sight words, spelling words, or math facts), the hope is that when the intervention is withdrawn, the learned behavior will not return to the poor performance levels of the baseline period, but rather remain at mastery levels of performance. In these situations, application of the reversal design is not appropriate. A variation, however, is helpful to teachers and students as they monitor progress in the acquisition of specific skills. In this modified version of the reversal design, the initial baseline and intervention phases are similar to those described above. In the baseline condition, an assessment of student performance is made; in the second condition an intervention is scheduled. If criterion for mastery is achieved in the second condition, the intervention is discontinued to determine whether the student can perform the task without the help offered during intervention. If the student can again demonstrate mastery of the learned behavior, performance is monitored on a weekly posttest basis to insure that learning is maintained over time. An example of this version of the reversal design is found in Figure 3.5. In this instance, the procedures are reversed (no instruction, instruction, no instruction), but the data do not reverse (low, high, high).

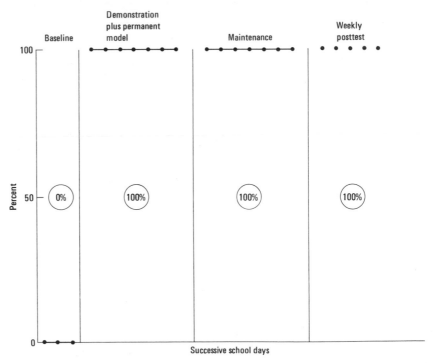

Figure 3.5 This graph illustrates the desired pattern for the data collected when a modified reversal design is used. The dots represent each day's percent correct score. Each phase is labeled to indicate what procedures were in effect, and the median score for each phase is circled.

Changing the criterion.   Another variation of the modified reversal design just discussed is the changing criterion design. As with the second reversal design presented, the expectation is for the data gathered during the return-to-baseline condition not to reverse to the original, undesirable state. Usually this design is composed of three conditions: baseline, intervention, and return-to-baseline or maintenance. Within the intervention condition, a number of minor changes are scheduled. The criterion for acceptable performance becomes more stringent as the target behavior improves.

To use oral reading as an example, Kevin's initial performance level was far below that of his classmates. A changing criterion design was selected for him. During the baseline condition, he obtained an average correct rate score of 20 words per minute. His classmates all read around 80 correct words per minute. In the initial period of the intervention condition, the teacher set a correct rate aim of 30. On any day Kevin did not achieve this aim, he received no reinforcement; he only received a reward when he obtained a correct rate score above 29. After he demonstrated achievement of this objective for three days, the aim score was increased to a correct rate of 40. The procedures were repeated until this objective was met and then the aim score was reset again and again until the final objective was achieved. Another example of this design is provided in Figure 3.6.

Task analysis.   This design is selected most appropriately when either a behavioral checklist, criterion-referenced test, or teacher-made instructional sequence is followed. This graphing system allows for the monitoring of the

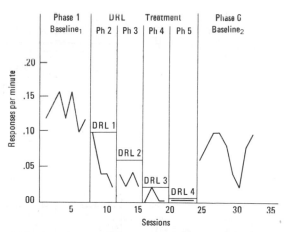

Figure 3.6

An example of the changing-criterion design: the rate of subject changes for a class of high school senior girls during baseline 1, treatment, and baseline 2 phases. "Free" Fridays could be earned by the group if they made fewer than the specified number of responses for each of the first four days of the week. The limit for the first treatment week was five or fewer responses during the 50-minute sessions (DRL 1). DRL 2 required three or fewer responses. DRL 3 required one or fewer responses and DRL 4 required zero responses. (S. M. Dietz & A. C. Repp. Decreasing classroom misbehavior through the use of DRL schedules of reinforcement. *Journal of Applied Behavior Analysis*, 1973, *6*, 457–463. Copyright 1973 by the Society for the Experimental Analysis of Behavior, Inc. Reprinted by permission.)

mastery of each component of a complex task or skill. In the example shown in Figure 3.7, the skill of subtraction was first submitted to a task analysis. The components of subtraction were identified, sequenced, and placed along the vertical axis of the graph. Weekly checks were made on the student to determine whether mastery (90 percent) was achieved for each class of problems. Those classes in which mastery was achieved were given a plus, those not meeting the aim score were given a minus, and those not yet tested were left blank. The overview of skill attainment illustrated by this kind of graphic display can be useful to both teacher and student as evaluation of progress made toward the mastery of an entire skill is monitored.

Multiple baseline. As the name of this design implies, more than one measurement of performance is kept at a time. Measurements on several

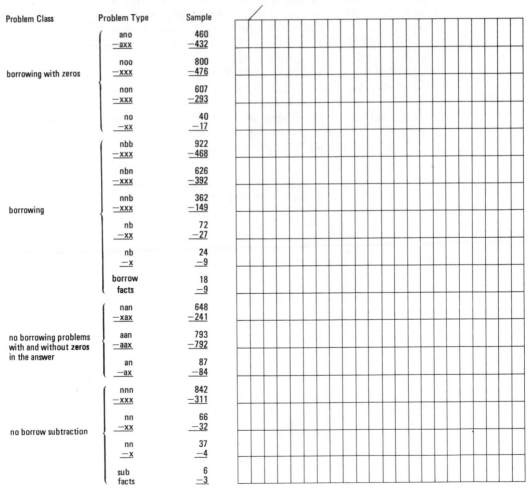

Problem Class	Problem Type	Sample
	ano −axx	460 −432
borrowing with zeros	noo −xxx	800 −476
	non −xxx	607 −293
	no −xx	40 −17
	nbb −xxx	922 −468
	nbn −xxx	626 −392
borrowing	nnb −xxx	362 −149
	nb −xx	72 −27
	nb −x	24 −9
	borrow facts	18 −9
	nan −xax	648 −241
no borrowing problems with and without zeros in the answer	aan −aax	793 −792
	an −ax	87 −84
	nnn −xxx	842 −311
no borrow subtraction	nn −xx	66 −32
	nn −x	37 −4
	sub facts	6 −3

Figure 3.7 An example of a task analysis design.

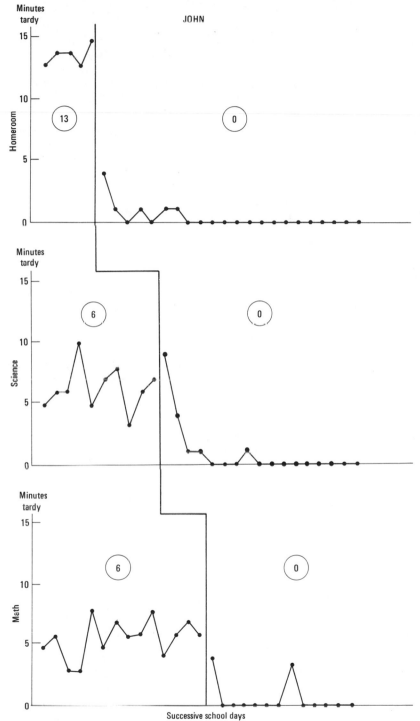

Figure 3.8   An example of a multiple baseline design.

targets are begun at the same time, but intervention is scheduled first for one target, then another, and so on. The general format for this design is shown in Figure 3.8. There are several variations of the multiple baseline design, across individuals, settings, or target behaviors.

One commonly used variation of this design follows a student across settings. For example, some high school students were frequently tardy in reporting to their various classes. The teachers discussed this problem and found that John was tardy to homeroom, science, and math class too often. The teachers decided that action must be taken. All of the teachers involved measured the amount of time that John was late to each class every day (see Figure 3.8). From the data, it was determined that John was late to homeroom most often. Together, the teachers decided that homeroom tardiness would be targeted first. For every minute that John was late to homeroom, he missed a minute from gym (an activity of great importance for John). Once his tardiness decreased for homeroom, the procedure was scheduled for science. Finally, it was applied to math.

Multiple baseline designs frequently are used in across-setting situations. The following are clusters of settings that might be used for multiple baseline applications in school situations: recess, hallway, and lunchroom; resource room, regular classroom, and home; before morning recess, after morning recess, and after lunch. For many students, it is most advantageous to target intervention first in one setting, then in another, and finally in all situations where the behavior or skill is of concern. This seems to be more acceptable to students and more manageable for teachers than attempting to handle remediation efforts in all situations initially.

The multiple baseline design also is useful when monitoring several behaviors or skills at the same time, as when a student is learning to compute subtraction problems requiring borrowing. The teacher presents the student each day with three sheets of borrowing problems, each containing problems of different types. After a baseline period on all three pages, intervention (demonstration and instruction) is scheduled for one of the three. Once some improvement is noted on the targeted page, instruction is given for the second class of problems. Finally, instruction is provided for all three pages until mastery is achieved for any or all of the pages.

In the last variation of the multiple baseline design, the performance of several students who present a common problem is monitored concurrently. Remediation efforts are aimed first at only one of the students. Progressively, each student receives direct intervention until all are being helped simultaneously. This version of the multiple baseline design is least desirable in classroom settings, for it is usually more convenient to group youngsters with common problems and schedule their interventions concurrently.

The evaluation designs presented here are arranged to give structure to the teaching situation so that student and teacher performance may be subjected to some objective scrutiny. Each has distinctive features that allow for differences in the teaching situation. The teacher must match these designs with the salient features of the instructional situation.

Data Calculations Once data are gathered, it is necessary to perform several calculations to render the data more meaningful. When the effectiveness of an intervention strategy is being evaluated, comparative scores can be useful. It is important to be able to compare a student's performance in one condition to the next, so that a judgment about whether or not a procedure should be discontinued can be made. The following discussions center on those calculations that give the data referents.

Central tendency. There are three different ways to calculate central tendency for the data within a condition: mean, median, and mode. The mode is the score occurring most often and one that serves no purpose for the evaluation of student performance. The mean and median are, however, useful measures. The mean is the average score (total of all scores within a condition divided by the number of scores). The median is the middle score by rank order; with practice, it is very simple to determine. First, count the number of scores in the condition. Divide that by two to determine which place is in the middle. Using rank order (not temporal sequence), count until that place is reached. The score in the middle place is the median. See Figure 3.9 for examples.

Another way to determine the median score follows the same general theme, but instead of a raw data sheet (and the actual scores), the graphed data are used. In this second method, the teacher again counts the number of scores in a phase, but then uses the horizontal lines on the graph to help determine the rank order of the scores. See Figure 3.9 for an example.

A score representing central tendency, *either* a mean *or* median, should be calculated for each set of scores for every condition. If correct and error rate scores are the measures used, then two scores of central tendency are calculated for each condition.

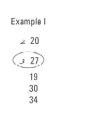

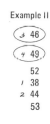

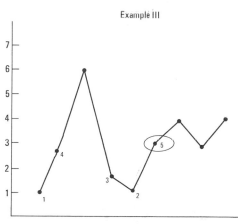

Figure 3.9 Calculating medians. In Example I there are five scores; the third (27) score is the median. In Example II there are six scores; the median (47.5) is half way between scores 3 and 4. In Example III there are nine scores; the fifth score (3) is the median.

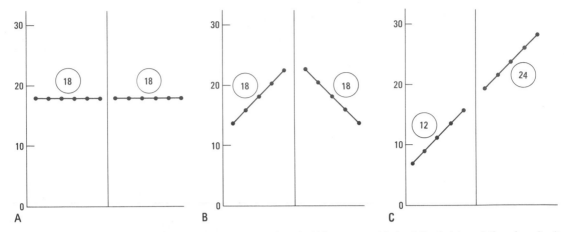

Figure 3.10   Possible combinations of data trends and middle scores and their relation to interpretation of results. It is important to note the central tendency (mean or median) for each condition, but the trend of the data should also be considered. In Graph A, no improvement across conditions was noted. In Graph B, the central tendency scores for both conditions are the same, but the trends of the data are different; in this case, the student's performance worsened. In Graph C, the student's performance improved across conditions; the trend indicates that the improvement continued during the second condition. The intervention scheduled during the second condition cannot be credited for the improvement indicated by the changes in central tendency scores.

Trend.   Although no details are given here about precise ways of calculating trend lines,[3] it is important to include consideration of the trend or direction of the data as part of the evaluation process. Data can follow three basic trends: increasing, decreasing, or flat. One reason that it is not sufficient to use only the mean or median is illustrated in Figure 3.10. In Part A, the median scores for each condition are the same—18; the profile shown is that which most people envision when the medians or means are the same for two conditions. The two conditions shown in Part B also have the same median scores, but the trends and interpretation of the data are different. In Part C an entirely different point is made. If one considers only the central tendency scores for each condition, it is possible to conclude that the student improved greatly from one condition to the next. When the *trend* is considered, however, it becomes apparent that there is no improvement at all, only a maintenance of the trend initiated in the first condition. Both the scores of central tendency and the trend or direction of the data must be considered before declaring a tactic successful, because of the changes noted from one condition to the next.

Aim scores.   There are two general types of aim scores possible for individual students: long term and short term. The long-term goal for a student might be to read fast enough to keep up with classmates in the in-class reading assignments in social studies, since the student's present functioning level is far below that level. Therefore, several goals (and aim scores) are

[3]Interested readers are referred to Hersen & Barlow (1976) and White & Haring (1976).

established for this student: one that is attainable in the near future and one that is the ultimate aim. In fact, as student performance improves, a number of short-term aims might be established in the course of reaching the final goal.

Sometimes aim scores are referred to as levels of mastery. In percent situations, teachers often demand three days above 90 percent before moving the student to a new task. Some even require three consecutive days at 100 percent correct. Why these particular criteria are used, no one knows. Keeping some pupils from learning new skills because they cannot obtain three consecutive 100 percent scores does not seem pragmatic. The teacher should judge what the aim score should be for an individual and what information should be learned. It is important, however, for the teacher to make such a determination before or at the time instruction is initiated.

Aim scores also are used in rate situations. Many refer to these aim scores as *desired rates*. In general, students should be able to function with their classmates. One way to determine aim scores is to test the skills of sample students from the regular classroom to which the student is returning or is a member. If members of the regular class calculate math facts at a rate of forty, the target student should be able to do about the same. Otherwise, the student cannot succeed in this situation.

Criteria for change of phase.   There should be two different criteria for concluding a condition: failure of a tactic or attainment of the aim score. It is vital to instructional planning to know when a tactic is insufficiently effective or totally ineffective. Sometimes an intervention does not work for a particular student; after four days of very little or no change in the data, another intervention should be scheduled. In some cases, an intervention is effective for awhile, but then ceases to be. In such instances, it is important to know when substantial change is not occurring so that another intervention can be added to the first or scheduled alone. Although no precise rules exist, some guidelines are available (White & Liberty, 1976; White & Haring, 1976). After a condition is at least five days long and the last two days' scores fall below the scores obtained on the two previous days, a new intervention should be selected. Of course, other guidelines can be developed. The important point is that guidelines be established so that ineffective procedures are not followed too long.

Needless to say, when criterion for mastery or the aim score is reached and maintained for several days, new procedures should be implemented. If the aim score is reached during an intervention condition, it is advisable to discontinue the intervention procedures to determine whether the student can remain at the desired levels of performance without the help of the intervention procedure. If the preestablished aim score level is maintained, it is time to move on to the next step in the instructional sequence.

DATA DISPLAY

Data gathered on student performance are easier to evaluate if transformed into a visual display as they are collected. When data are presented graphically, analysis becomes obvious and evaluation almost automatic. In fact, performance has been shown to improve when graphs are shown to students (Brandstetter & Merz, 1978).

Data should be graphed when collected and not after long intervals. Many times the need to change intervention strategies becomes apparent only when the data are displayed visually. Time lost because data were not analyzed cannot be justified.

Raw Data Form   As data are being collected, scores describing student performance (math worksheets, spelling tests, pages of creative writing) can soon be overwhelming; it is advisable to transpose the data to one sheet of paper for easy reference. The same is true for other products of student performance that do not leave a permanent record (oral reading, social behavior, and oral language). In these cases, it is even more important that data be stored in a convenient place in an orderly fashion. A sample data sheet is shown in, Figure 3.11. Other versions can be developed to suit individuals and specific learning situations better.

Student's name _____   Subject area _____

Teacher's name _____   Specific target _____

Date D/M/Y	D A Y	Number		Percent Correct	Time	Rate	
		Correct	Error			Correct	Error
/ /	M						
	T						
	W						
	T						
	F						
/ /	M						
	T						
	W						
	T						
	F						
/ /	M						
	T						
	W						
	T						
	F						
/ /	M						
	T						
	W						
	T						
	F						

Figure 3.11   Sample raw data sheet.

Student performance data are displayed most conveniently in a graph, drawn on standard arithmetic graph paper available in most bookstores.[4] Standard procedures to follow when setting up a graph, such as labeling the axis and noting preestablished criteria, are discussed in the following sections.

The vertical axis. The scores are shown on the *ordinate*, or vertical axis (a line that goes up and down). The axis must be labeled with the name of the measurement system used (frequency, duration, percent correct, rate per minute), and hatch marks should be noted so quick reference can be made as a specific score is plotted (for example, 25, 50, 75, and 100 for percent; 5, 10, 15, and 20 for frequency).

If rate is the measure chosen, a special arrangement of the vertical axis is often required. If a student's correct and error rate scores are close together, there is no need for any change in the vertical axis. Most often, the correct rate scores cluster in one area of the graph and the error rate scores in another. Using the typical arrangement of a graph, changes in correct rate scores are clearly visible.

Error rate scores can present a different problem, however. A number of plots are possible between a score of one and zero (.2, .1, .5). Without some adjustment of the vertical axis, changes in error rate performance go unnoticed. For this reason, many teachers break the vertical axis into two parts: one for the correct rate scores, and one for the error rate scores. The correct rate axis must be deep enough to allow for change in performance, both positive and negative. Therefore, it is advisable to get an estimate of a student's correct rate performance before the graph is made. Allowance must be made so that some decrease and a substantial amount of change in the desired direction can be noted.

The arrangement of the vertical axis for error rate scores is determined by looking at student performance and the scores possible. First, if a student is making about ten errors per minute initially, room must be left for scores of ten and slightly above that level. Also, a place to enter a zero score and room for those scores that can fall below one and above zero (.5, .2) must be provided. A sample rate graph is shown in Figure 3.12.

The horizontal axis. Session days are represented on the *abscissa* (a line that goes across the page). This axis is labeled in accordance with the frequency of data collection. If the teacher is in a resource room and sees the student only three times a week, the abscissa is labeled "Session Days." If data are collected daily, the horizontal axis is labeled "School Days." Some teachers like to see the days of each week cluster together. To accomplish this, the horizontal axis is labeled "Successive Calendar Days," and day lines are held for Saturday and Sunday although they are never used.

---

[4]The use of semilogarithmic graph paper for the display of rate data is not discussed in this chapter. Research findings indicate that arithmetic displays are more understandable to youngsters and greater changes in performance are noted when linear rather then semilogarithmic graphs are shown to pupils (Brandstetter & Merz, 1978). Those desiring information about this system are referred to White and Haring (1976).

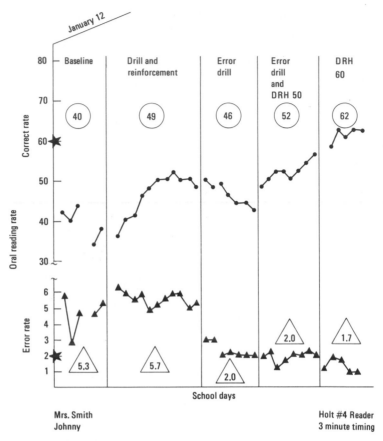

Figure 3.12

An example of an oral reading rate graph where the vertical axis is broken and different scale units are used for the correct rate (dots) and the error rate (triangles) scores. The aim scores for each are indicated by stars on the vertical axis. Each condition is labeled to indicate the procedures in effect. Also, central tendency scores for each condition are noted. Because daily correct rate and error rates were calculated, two central tendency scores appear for each condition. The correct rate central tendencies are circled; error rates are shown inside large triangles.

Once the abscissa is labeled, the days are represented by vertical lines that cross the horizontal axis. If "School Days" is the label chosen, the lines representing Monday, Tuesday, Wednesday, etc. always represent those days. If a student was absent on Monday, that day line is left open and Tuesday's data are plotted on the next line, the line designated for Tuesday.

Other labels. It is necessary to have the following information clearly visible on every graph so that one student's chart is not confused with another's, or math is not thought to be reading. The teacher's name should be on the graph. If more than one person teaches the student, their names should appear somewhere on the chart also. The homeroom teacher's name always should be noted to facilitate compilation of a student's graphs for any given year. Besides the names of the teacher(s) and the student, information about the target behavior sufficient to distinguish one graph from another is necessary. In some cases a brief notation like "oral reading from the Holt #4 reader" is enough; in other situations more information about the target behavior and materials used is needed.

The date for the first data plot should be indicated on the graph. Often it is desirable to indicate the day line that stands for the first data day of each month.

Along the vertical axis additional data notations can appear. It is helpful to both student and teacher to mark the short-term aim score on the graph by placing stars on the vertical axis at the levels of the aim scores. The notations and aim scores for both correct and error rates appear on the sample graph shown in Figure 3.12.

Entering Data on Graph

As mentioned earlier, it is important that data be plotted immediately upon collection and calculation, so that continual evaluation of student performance can occur.

Plotting conventions. Data plots are placed on a graph in such a way that the scores fall directly *on* day lines (vertical lines) and at the appropriate gradients as indicated on the vertical axis. The score of 12 percent is placed on the day line for the day on which it was collected at the correct level for 12 percent—between the 10 percent and 15 percent designated places.

Plots are connected within a phase or condition. When a student is absent, that day line is left blank and the plots preceding and subsequent to the absence are *not* connected. No-chance days (hearing screening test, fire drill, field trip, teacher lost the data) are noted on the graph by a blank day line, but the data before and after a no-chance day *are* connected.

If Saturday and Sunday day lines are included in a graph, they are left blank, because no data are collected on these days. In this situation, Friday and Monday plots are *not* connected, so a week's set of data cluster together visually. If the graph is labeled "School Days," there are no day lines to represent Saturday and Sunday, and the Friday and Monday data plots *are* connected.

If correct rate and error rate are used as the measures of performance, two plots appear on each day line: one for correct rate and one for error rate. To distinguish these two sets of data, a dot is used to indicate correct rate and a filled-in triangle is used for the error rate score. When connecting the plots, the rules provided above hold; but correct rate plots are connected to the other correct rates, and the error rates are connected to error rates. An example is provided in Figure 3.12.

A change in condition is indicated by a solid vertical line drawn between the two day lines that represent the last plot for one condition and the first plot for a new condition. This line is referred to as a *phase change line* and serves to separate the data from two different conditions. To facilitate the visual separation of the data from two phases, plots are *not* connected

Checklist for constructing evaluation graphs

Done

1. Set Up Graph.
    _____   a. Draw abscissa line (horizontal axis).
    _____   b. Draw ordinate line (vertical axis).
    _____   c. Label abscissa.
    _____   d. Label ordinate.
    _____   e. Note target (spelling, etc.; indicate material used).
    _____   f. Note teacher's name.
    _____   g. Note student's name.
    _____   h. Date graph.
    _____   i. Note aim score(s).

2. Calculate data.
    _____   a. Set up raw data sheet.
    _____   b. Calculate scores.

3. Plot data.
    _____   a. Place plot(s) on appropriate day line.
    _____   b. Connect plots for successive data days.
    _____   c. Do not connect plots if student was absent.
    _____   d. Connect plots for no-chance days.
    _____   e. Note phase changes with a solid vertical line.
    _____   f. Label phase.

4. Analyze data.
    _____   a. Calculate either mean or median scores by condition.
    _____   b. Enter scores of central tendency on graph for each phase.

across phase change lines. Also, each phase is labeled so the teacher quickly can recall the procedures used in each different phase.

Central tendency.   Scores to indicate central tendency, either the mean or median, must be calculated for each condition and each set of scores. After the calculations are completed at the conclusion of each phase, the score is entered on the graph centered within the phase, but not in such a way that it covers the data. Usually it is written in the center of a phase and a large circle drawn around it. If correct rate and error rate scores are used, there are two central tendency scores per phase. The correct rate central tendency score is placed in a large, open circle; the error rate central tendency score is placed in a large, open triangle.

Checklist   To ensure that all of the steps necessary to construct a meaningful evaluation graph are completed, a checklist is provided in Table 3.2. This checklist also serves as a summary of this section (Data Display) of the chapter.

SUMMARY

This chapter has served as an overview of the steps teachers follow to evaluate the influence of the intervention strategies they select for individual students. These evaluation procedures test such influences by judging the amount of progress made or not made in a given situation. Teachers follow a general sequence of steps, although clearly not linear, as they establish the structure necessary to evaluate instruction. A general delineation of those steps follows.

Prebaseline

During this initial stage of the evaluation process, answers to some fundamental questions are sought. What are the behaviors of concern and in need of remediation? Which and what level of materials should be utilized? Which measurement system should be selected? Which evaluation design might be most appropriate?

Answers to these critical questions are found through systematic observation and testing. An ABC Analysis might be used when social behavior is under consideration. A criterion-referenced test or task analyzed skill-sequence checklist might answer initial material and placement questions for academic situations. Trying out several curriculum materials with the student also might be beneficial. Once the target behavior is identified and the level of the student's performance determined, the selection of the measurement and evaluation design is facilitated.

Before formal data collection procedures are implemented, a number of other details must be handled. First, a consistent time and place for data collection must be established. Formats for data collection and analysis must be designed. A raw data sheet must be developed. A graph should be set up to reflect the needs of the data system used.

Baseline

During this and all of the conditions that follow, data are collected and plotted regularly and frequently. Systematic and frequent assessment of the student's performance is conducted to obtain knowledge about the characteristics of the target behavior. The initial performance levels of the student are judged against a long-range aim score, and a short-term aim is established. The final decision about the intervention strategy to try first is made after observing systematically the student's performance. Criteria for change of phase are set. Once the teacher feels confident that an understanding of the student and his or her performance characteristics has been achieved, a central tendency score is calculated and the baseline phase terminated.

Intervention Conditions

During instructional conditions, the student is learning to perform a target assignment at more desirable levels of performance or is learning not to exhibit undesirable behavior. A specific intervention procedure is applied systematically and consistently each day of instruction. Again, evaluation data are collected, plotted, and analyzed to insure that desired changes in student performance continually occur. If a tactic loses its effectiveness, and meets the criteria for change of phase, another tactic is added to the first, or a new strategy is scheduled. The changes in procedures are submitted to the same evaluation system.

If a reversal design was selected, return-to-baseline conditions are established. After several days the effective procedures are reinstituted and, it is hoped, desired changes in student performance reoccur.

Once the desired change is achieved, the aim score or mastery criterion reached, and a score of central tendency calculated, the intervention procedures are discontinued.

Maintenance

The last phase of the implementation of daily or frequent data collection is designed to insure maintenance or retention of the desired level of performance without the intervention strategy. Can the student perform the task on his or her own? This is the ultimate test of the teaching procedures implemented. Once the student again demonstrates mastery or achievement of the aim score, frequent testing of the target behavior can be stopped.

Posttest

After the target skill is learned and maintained, it is important to be certain that it remains at the desired levels. Therefore, weekly posttests are recommended for awhile followed by monthly posttests for the remainder of the school year. It is important to monitor student performance, for the monitoring process in and of itself can facilitate retention.

REFERENCES

BAER, D. M. In the beginning, there was the response. In E. Ramp & G. Semb (Eds.), *Behavior analysis: Areas of research and application.* Englewood Cliffs, N.J.: Prentice-Hall, 1975.

BAER, D. M., WOLF, M. M. & RISLEY, T. R. Some current dimensions of applied behavior analysis. *Journal of Applied Behavior Analysis*, 1968, *1*, 91–97.

BRANDSTETTER, G., & MERZ, C. Charting scores in precision teaching for skill acquisition. *Exceptional Children*, 1978, *45*, 42–48.

CAMPBELL, D. T., & STANLEY, J. C. *Experimental and quasi-experimental designs for research.* Chicago: Rand McNally & Co., 1963.

COOPER, J. O., & JOHNSON, J. Guideline for direct and continuous measurement of academic behavior, *The Directive Teacher*, 1979, *1*, 10–11; 21.

CRAIGHEAD, W. E., KAZDIN, A. E., & MAHONEY, M. J. *Behavior modification: Principles, issues, and applications.* Boston: Houghton Mifflin Co., 1976.

DIETZ, S. M., & REPP, A. C. Decreasing classroom misbehavior through the use of DRL schedules of reinforcement. *Journal of Applied Behavior Analysis*, 1973, *6*, 457–463.

HERSEN, M., & BARLOW, D. H. *Single-case experimental designs: Strategies for studying behavior change.* Elmsford, N.Y.: Pergamon Press, 1976.

JENKINS, J. R., MAYHALL, W. F., PESCHKA, C. M., & TOWNSEND, V. Using direct and daily measures to increase learning. *Journal of Learning Disabilities,* 1974, *7*, 605–608.

KAZDIN, A. E. Role of instructions and reinforcement in behavior changes in token reinforcement programs. *Journal of Educational Psychology*, 1973, *64*, 63–71.

KERLINGER, F. N. *Foundations of behavioral research: Educational and psychological inquiry.* New York: Holt, Rinehart & Winston, 1964.

LOVITT, T. C. Applied behavior analysis and learning disabilities. Part II: Specific research recommendations and suggestions for practitioners. *Journal of Learning Disabilities*, 1975, *8*, 504–518.

MARTIN, G., & PEAR, J. *Behavior modification: What it is and how to do it.* Englewood Cliffs, N.J.: Prentice-Hall, 1978.

OLSON, W. C. The diagnosis and treatment of behavior disorders of children. In the Thirty-Fourth Yearbook of the National Society for the Study of Education (Eds.), *Educational diagnosis.* Bloomington, Ill.: Public Schools Publishing Co., 1935.

OLSON, W. C. & CUNNINGHAM, E. M. Time-sampling techniques. *Child Development,* 1934, *5,* 41–58.

SALZBERG, B. H., WHEELER, A. J., DEVAR, L. T., & HOPKINS, B. L. The effect of intermittent feedback and intermittent contingent access to play on printing of kindergarten children. *Journal of Applied Behavior Analysis,* 1971, *4,* 163–171.

SMITH, D. D., & SNELL, M. E. Classroom management and instructional planning. In M. E. Snell (Ed.), *Systematic instruction of the moderately and severely handicapped.* Columbus, Ohio: Charles E. Merrill Publishing Co., 1978.

SULZER-AZAROFF, B., & MAYER, G. R. *Applying behavior-analysis procedures with children and youth.* New York: Holt, Rinehart & Winston, 1977.

VANETTEN, C., & VANETTEN, G. The measurement of pupil progress and selecting instructional materials. *Journal of Learning Disabilities,* 1976, *9,* 469–480.

WHITE, O. R., & HARING, N. G. *Exceptional teaching for exceptional children.* Columbus, Ohio: Charles E. Merrill Publishing Co., 1976.

WHITE, O. R., & LIBERTY, K. A. Behavioral assessment and precise educational measurement. In N. G. Haring & R. L. Schiefelbusch (Eds.), *Teaching special children.* New York: McGraw-Hill, 1976.

4 INTERVENTION STRATEGIES : PART 1 INCREASING STUDENTS' PERFORMANCES

This chapter and the next provide summaries of general intervention strategies. The combined material presented in Chapters 4 and 5 should be viewed as a detailed glossary of terms used in later chapters of this text. Providing definitions and examples of generic intervention strategies in these two chapters, rather than throughout the text, avoids redundancy. The intent is for these chapters to serve as a foundation by presenting information about general principles of learning and procedures that are beneficial across academic and social situations. Intervention strategies pertaining to specific skill areas, such as reading and handwriting, are presented in later chapters.

There are many ways to organize information about general remedial interventions. One is to divide tactics on a time basis. For example, some strategies usually are *antecedent* to the target behavior, and others are *subsequent* to the target behavior; feedback, for example, comes after the student performs. Time-based organization can become confusing because many interventions (drill, instructions) can be scheduled either before or after student performance.

Another way of classifying intervention strategies is based on the aim or purpose of the procedure. Although it is a simplistic view of educational situations, it is possible to organize procedures by whether the attempt is to increase or decrease the frequency of the behavior's occurrence. Often, teachers of learning disabled students have a list of behaviors they hope to decrease or eliminate from a student's repertoire (aggression, disruption), and another list of behaviors whose aim is to increase performance levels (cooperation, reading, arithmetic). Certain educational procedures are more appropriate in the first situation, and others are more effective in the second.

Some, however, may be used in both situations. This chapter discusses tactics that facilitate students' increased performance levels. Chapter 5 discusses tactics that decrease performance.

When the aim is to increase performance, a further classification is required. It is apparent from both research and practice that the effectiveness of many interventions depends on the entry level of the student. Certain tactics are most effective when a youngster is first learning how to perform a task; other tactics seem to be influential only when a student knows how to perform a task but needs to become more skilled in its execution. For example, the tactics teachers use to teach sight words or math facts are different from those used to teach fluency in reading or budgeting skills. Descriptions of the various stages of learning people pass through to achieve ultimate mastery of skills are provided first. Later, specific tactics are correlated with the stages of learning.

STAGES OF LEARNING

A number of researchers (Affleck, Lowenbraun, & Archer, 1980; Buckley & Walker, 1978; Haring, Lovitt, Eaton, & Hansen, 1978; Smith, 1973, Haring [Note 1]; White & Liberty [Note 2]) have found that the influence of specific intervention strategies depends on the entry level of the student. Some procedures facilitate more automatic performances; others encourage maintenance of satisfactory levels.

During the 1960s, much to the surprise of some researchers, it was discovered that rewards are not *always* effective. Ayllon and Azrin (1964) and Hopkins (1968), for example, found reinforcement to be unsuccessful initially. Instructions had to be implemented to get the target behavior to a level at which rewards were effective. In research designed specifically to study this phenomenon, Smith and Lovitt (1976) found that when students had to learn how to solve computational arithmetic problems, reinforcement was ineffective. When they had to compute arithmetic problems more quickly, however, reinforcement contingencies were influential.

For better communication, some researchers feel that it is important to describe the entry level of the learner in terms of the stage of learning. Some contend that much of the equivocal results found in research might be explained if the entry level of the subjects were reexamined. Five stages of learning have been identified so far; further delineation probably will be made through future research, but at least there tends to be agreement at present about these gross and general descriptions of students' entry levels.

The five stages of learning are: *acquisition, proficiency, maintenance, generalization*, and *adaption*. A simplified linear diagram of these stages and students' learning levels is displayed in Figure 4.1. These stages are applicable while students are learning skills and increasing performance levels.

During the *acquisition* stage the learner could enter the learning process at zero percent, indicating no knowledge of how to perform the task accurately. After a period of instruction, some learners indicate that they can perform the task or skill accurately (90 percent–100 percent); they have

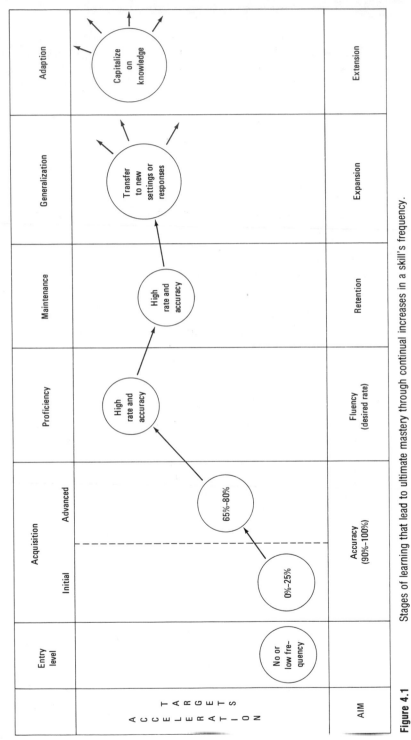

Figure 4.1 Stages of learning that lead to ultimate mastery through continual increases in a skill's frequency.

passed through the acquisition stage of learning. Others, however, need further direct instruction, at the advanced acquisition phase, to achieve sufficiently high levels of accuracy.

During the acquisition stage, the aim is for the individual to learn how to perform the skill accurately. This, however, is not where the educational process should stop. The individual must also be able to perform the skill quickly enough to execute it at a rather automatic level. During the *proficiency* stage of learning, the aim is for the learner to perform the task with both quality (accuracy) and sufficient quantity (speed). The tactics used differ from those used in the acquisition stage; they direct the learner to increase speed of performance.

There are some very important reasons why proficient levels of performance are necessary targets. For example, if a student can correctly form the letters of the alphabet but does so too slowly, he or she will not be able to complete assignments that require writing as a basic tool (written composition, spelling tests) on time. Thus, the student who writes slowly might not be able to keep up with the teacher's dictation of spelling words on weekly tests. Low spelling scores might be the result of slow writing, not poor spelling ability. This situation exists across most academic and vocationally related tasks.

Once proficient levels of performance are achieved, the learner enters into the *maintenance* stage of learning. The hope is for the learned behavior to remain at the high levels of the two previous stages. Retention of learning is important to all teachers and their students. For some learning disabled students this is the most frustrating stage of learning; often learned skills are not retained once direct instruction is withdrawn. For this reason, many teachers set aims in the proficiency situation slightly higher than necessary, so some loss in speed can be accepted. For individuals who tend not to retain desired speed of performance, teachers must plan for maintenance by periodically evaluating retention and implementing direct intervention on an infrequent basis.

After maintenance comes a period of *generalization*, in which the learned behavior should occur in all situations that are appropriate, regardless of setting. For many learning disabled students, skills learned in the classroom do not appear automatically in other settings without direct instruction. For example, a youngster who has demonstrated mastery of specific language and grammatical skills might speak appropriately in the classroom, but not on the playground or at home. For this student, direct instruction is necessary in various settings to guarantee generalization. Other students seem to generalize without direct intervention from the teacher, and only periodic *probes* (spot checks) need be conducted to ensure that setting generalization did occur. Unfortunately, this is not the case for all learners.

Another type of generalization that is also important to teachers of learning disabled students is response generalization. When some students are taught in mathematics to borrow, for example, they do so in all situations requiring that process $(23 - 7=)$ $(422 - 79=)$. Others do not generalize across response classes, and direct instruction must be provided for each different instance. For these students generalization must be programmed. Possibly the skill of generalizing should be taught.

The last stage has not received much attention from either researchers or teachers. The *adaption* stage of learning requires the individual to capitalize on previous learning and extend knowledge and skills already acquired. In new situations, the learner must be able to problem solve in order to determine what the appropriate response actually is. Although it is important to teach learning disabled students to extend their knowledge and skills so they can be more flexible in life situations, this stage of learning and the skills related to it are most often neglected. Possibly adaption abilities could be enhanced by using a discovery approach for some learning situations (Strike, 1975).

It is important for teachers to be conscious of these various stages of learning. The tactics that are most efficient and effective in one stage might not be suitable in another. Also, the measurement systems chosen for the purpose of evaluating instruction differ depending on the stage of learning (see Chapter 3 for review). In acquisition, percentage is a useful measurement system. In proficiency, rate (correct and error rate) tends to be more appropriate. In the more advanced stages, periodic rate probes (spot checks) are most useful. The next section of this chapter discusses interventions that correlate with these stages of learning.

Tactics that Aim to Increase Performance

Although some tactics are effective in more than one stage of learning, many tactics tend to be influential only in a specific stage. Because of these differential effects, teachers have a higher probability of producing the desired changes in student performance with certain interventions. Because of the relationship between student entry levels and the selection of the most effective interventions, the discussion of intervention procedures will be presented by stages of learning.

ACQUISITION STAGE

During this first stage of learning, the aim is to instill the target skill in the student's repertoire. In the initial phase of acquisition (correct percentage scores of zero percent), a number of useful intervention strategies are available to help students perform skills, although at rudimentary levels. These are referred to as *priming* tactics. As the name implies, they serve to prime or bring the skill into the repertoire of the youngster so further instruction can be beneficial. Several general procedures are available that incorporate specific priming tactics into the instructional process. These are referred to as *programming* procedures and provide structure and sequence to the instructional situation.

Sometimes another phase of the acquisition stage of learning becomes a concern of teachers. Often, students learn a skill but do not achieve mastery levels of performance. For example, when being taught the processes of computational arithmetic, many students learn to compute the problems, but their percent correct scores are not sufficient to move on to the next class of arithmetic problems. Some students obtain correct scores of 75 percent, but seem to need additional instruction to meet a mastery criterion of 90 percent or better. A number of tactics are available for improving accuracy once the student is capable of performing the task. These *refinement* tactics are scheduled appropriately in the later phases of acquisition and facilitate improved accuracy.

Priming Tactics   Many students come to some instructional situations without the elements of the target skill in their repertoires; they cannot perform the task at all. This situation occurs among all age and achievement levels, for whenever one learns a new skill one begins the instructional task at the initial acquisition level. In some cases only a minimal amount of time has to be spent at this level because skills learned in the past facilitate the acquisition of the new behavior. In other cases, however, a considerable amount of time and energy has to be spent merely getting the target skill within the individual's repertoire, so that further instruction can be beneficial. This situation occurs for children as well as adults.

Teachers should understand the difficulties and frustrations involved in this initial acquisition period. Many adults do not even attempt new skills because of the frustration this stage of learning presents. Some try but give up and say, "I'm too old to learn how to do that." Most adults do not remember how they learned to read, write, or calculate, but an example may illustrate the pains of acquiring new skills. Consider Elaine, who has never played any sport using a racket and ball but who wants to learn to play tennis. Thus, she enters the learning of tennis at the initial acquisition stage. Elaine's coach must spend substantial amounts of time and energy using priming tactics to help her learn to swing the racket and hit the ball with some accuracy; Elaine must spend a remarkable amount of time and energy in learning. Many learning disabled students acquiring basic academic skills experience the same frustrations as Elaine faced in trying to learn how to play tennis. Teachers must recognize the discomfort associated with the acquisition stage.

Many priming tactics require a one-to-one teaching situation and are very expensive in teacher time. Therefore, they should only be used with those students who truly need such direct instruction. Possibly the use of aides or parent helpers could relieve the scheduling and time problems.

Physical guidance.   This tactic is used when motor skills are involved. Physical guidance, sometimes referred to as molding or manual guidance, requires the teacher actually to participate in the execution of the skill. When teachers take preschool children's hands to help them cut paper, the tactic of physical guidance is being used. Dressing skills, handwriting, assembly tasks, and many vocational skills can be acquired initially through the use of physical guidance. A speech clinician helping a student to pronounce a deficient articulation sound often physically guides the correct formation of the student's lips. This direct contact with students should be used only in the early phases of acquiring a skill and should be *faded* (gradually eliminated) as soon as possible.

Shaping.   This procedure involves the careful reinforcement of successive approximations of the target response. The student is rewarded first for attempting to perform the new skill. Gradually, rewards are offered only as closer and closer approximations of the skill are performed by the student. Finally, only accurate responses are rewarded.

Let us return to our example of Elaine learning how to play tennis. She is learning how to swing the racket. At first, her coach praises her for any swing in the right direction. Soon, she is praised only when the racket is positioned correctly and the swing is straight. After awhile, praise is only given when the swing is correct and Elaine follows through with the racket. Gradually, her coach shapes an accurate or correct swing, and eventually she is praised only for completely accurate (although not yet proficient) swings of the racket.

Shaping can be useful in building new skills. Certainly handwriting is a prime target for the application of shaping procedures. At first, an approximation of the correct formation of a letter is rewarded; later only better and better attempts at letter formation are rewarded. Clearly, the use of shaping, rather than allowing students to learn through trial and error, allows less chance of learning incorrect responses.

Modeling.   Bandura (1965, 1969), through his pioneer research, stresses that modeling procedures are most efficacious in transmitting new response patterns to individuals. Modeling simply involves the active participation of at least two individuals: one demonstrates the desired behavior to one or more observers. The observers then are required to imitate or copy all parts of the target skill. The ability of the observer to imitate is crucial to the process. Because that skill comes early in normal human development, teachers of learning disabled students normally do not have to teach it.[1] Most children come to school already possessing a developed repertoire of imitative skills, for it is primarily through the modeling-imitation paradigm that infants, toddlers, and preschool children learn a wide variety of language, social, and academic skills before they come to school.

Although most often researched in the acquisition situation, modeling is effective across a wide variety of social and academic situations (Kauffman, LaFleur, Hallahan, & Chanes, 1975; Cullinan, Kauffman, & LaFleur, 1975). Clearly, however, modeling is a powerful tactic when academic subjects need to be learned. Smith and Lovitt (1975) provide a clear example of the power of modeling when students have to acquire an ability to compute various process problems in computational arithmetic (borrowing and carrying). In all cases, demonstrating how to solve a problem from the target class each day during the intervention condition caused mastery of the computational process within a matter of several school days. When used with a group of students, modeling sometimes is equivocal, resulting in learning for some class members but not others. One reason for this may be the varying entry levels of the students. When modeling is used for an entire class, the

---

[1]Those interested in developing imitative repertoires in deficient students should refer to procedures texts in the area of the moderately handicapped (see Snell, 1978).

likelihood is that the students are not at the same place in their learning. One student might already know how to perform the task being presented by the teacher, while others might not have mastered the preceding components of the skill or previous skills in an overall sequence. When this situation occurs, not all of the class can benefit from the teacher's instructional demonstration. If modeling is to be used, the teacher should be clearly aware of the students' differing entry levels and group students accordingly to ensure more efficient learning.

Match-to-sample. This acquisition tactic is included in many commercially available workbooks, and has been used in many specially designed materials for learning disabled youngsters. The student is provided with the correct answer and is required to select from a number of choices the item matching the one provided initially. For example, in a letter identification worksheet, the student is shown a series of letters in the first column and must circle its match in the next column. Figure 4.2 shows an example of a match-to-sample worksheet.

Another form of match-to-sample instruction was used by Beck (Note 3), in which students learned to compute basic arithmetic facts $(4 + 5 =) (7 + 8 =)$. Across the top of the students' worksheets in random order were facts with the answers provided. During a specified time period, the students were required to solve all of the facts on their worksheets. If they needed to, they could refer to the sample problems at the top of their sheets. Gradually, these were eliminated and the students were required to solve the problems on their own.

Telling. The use of verbal directions or instructions to help students acquire new skills has been part of the educational routine since time immemorial. Unfortunately, many learning disabled youngsters seem not to profit from instructions or directions and many researchers (Kandin, 1973, O'Leary, Becker, Evans, & Saudargas, 1969) have come to doubt their general effectiveness. Telling students how to perform the target skill can be efficient in the acquisition situation, but it must be handled with more care and concern than usually is the case. Lovitt and Smith (1972), for example, found instructions to be useful in helping a youngster expand his language abilities. It is important to note, however, that the instructions provided were consistent and specific to the goals the instructor had for the student (varied sentence beginnings, expanded length of sentences, and more elaboration). Other researchers (Ayllon & Azrin, 1964; Hopkins, 1968) concur; instructions can be useful in the acquisition situation. These researchers, however, contend that reinforcement procedures should be added to maintain the positive changes of the initial instructional period.

Lovitt and Smith found that teachers have a propensity for using instructions. From the data gathered, they estimated that many teachers use over 200 instructional statements per day. Most of these, however, are not specific to either student or situation. When instructions are provided systematically, they can serve to efficiently direct the student to perform the desired skill without the necessity of scheduling time-consuming, elaborate, or expensive educational procedures.

Look at the first picture in each row and mark the other picture in the row that looks just like it.

Figure 4.2   An illustration of a match-to-sample worksheet to teach discrimination skills. (T. G. Thurstone and D. L. Lillie, *Beginning to learn perceptual skills: A multileveled program for developing visual perception.* Chicago: Science Research Associates, Inc., 1972. Reprinted by permission of the publisher.)

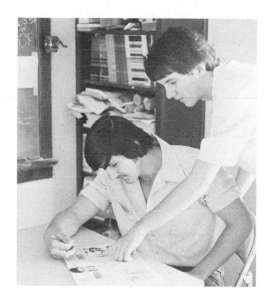

Sometimes, merely clarifying the instructions—making certain that the student understands what he is supposed to do—is sufficient to cause notable improvement in performance.

Cueing and prompting. These procedures are used during the early acquisition phase, but do not necessarily stimulate first occurrences of the target behavior. Both cueing and prompting help students make a correct response, and can be added to the priming tactics discussed earlier.

There are three kinds of cues: movement, position, and redundancy. When movement cues are provided, the teacher points to, touches, or taps the correct response. Position cues require that the correct choice is placed closest to the student. Redundancy cues pair the correct choice on one of several dimensions (color, shape, size, or position). For example, the correct choice is physically larger than the other items. The purpose of using cues is for the student to make as few errors as possible during instruction.

Prompts often are used in reading, but can be used in other academic areas. When prompts are used in reading, the teacher first forms his or her lips as though to say the correct initial sound, then actually says the first sound of the unknown word, then sounds out the word in its phonetic units. At any time the student has figured out the correct response, he or she is encouraged to provide it. Prompts provide the student with "hints" in the hope that the student will emit the correct response before the teacher must provide the answer.

Time delay. This is a relatively new procedure and one that is still in the developmental stages. During the first few trials the student is told the answer ("4 plus 5 is 9"). During the ensuing trials, the teacher waits (for gradually increasing time periods) before telling the student the answer. At first the delay may be only two or three seconds; later the teacher may wait up to twenty seconds for the student to provide the answer. Time delay has considerable potential because of several important advantages. It is easy for

75

the teacher to administer, places the student in control of the instructional situation, and is automatically discontinued when the student no longer needs the tactic. It has been used to facilitate learning disabled students' acquisition of spelling, recognition of sight words, and multiplication facts (Gast, Wilhoite, & Evans, Note 4).

Programming Procedures

A number of the tactics described in this first section can be incorporated into some general programming procedures to help the student acquire specific skills. In a sense, these programming procedures are ways to sequence or organize instruction so that learning will occur more efficiently. Many of these procedures can become laborious for both student and teacher and should be used only when necessary (when the student seems unable to acquire the skill through less arduous ways).

Chaining.   Chaining dictates the sequence in which units of a skill are taught. To use this procedure, the target skill must have been submitted to a task analysis and the component parts of the skill clearly identified. The components are taught in one of two general sequences: in order of their occurrence or in reverse order. In *forward chaining*, the first component of the skill taught is the first component of the skill executed. In *backwards chaining*, the last step in the sequence is taught first. Once that is mastered, the next to last step is taught and the student is required to perform both subskills. Chaining does not dictate what procedures to use; rather, it indicates the instructional sequence.

Errorless learning.   Errorless learning is a concept as well as a programming procedure. The rationale behind errorless learning is based on the student making no (or few) errors during the instructional period. The theory is to reduce the opportunity for error and to program for correct responses throughout the instructional sequence.

Errorless learning is very time consuming for both student and teacher because isolated, minute increments of each skill are presented in an orderly fashion. For many learning disabled students, only the concept of errorless learning needs to be kept in mind: reduce the opportunity for errors. Very few learning disabled ever require a complete application of errorless learning procedures for specific learning situations. When they do, teachers should refer to other texts (Skinner, 1968) for specific instructions on how to implement these procedures.

Refinement Tactics

As stated earlier, many times the tactic selected to influence the initial acquisition of a target skill is not sufficient to cause complete mastery of the skill. Often, students who start the instructional process at zero percent do not reach the criteria for mastery or their aim score (such as, three consecutive days of 90 percent or better) in a reasonable length of time. When this occurs, teachers must either discontinue the first intervention and schedule a new tactic, or add a new tactic to the first. The interventions described in this section are designed to help students achieve their aim scores once the target behavior is in their repertoires.

Feedback.   Kulhavy (1977) defines feedback as including any of the numerous processes that serve to inform students about the accuracy of their responses. Several researchers (Anderson & Faust, 1974; Kulhavy, 1977) suggest that the tactics forming the category of feedback fall along a continuum (ranging from a simple yes or no, right or wrong, to more thorough and complex forms reminiscent of instructional tactics).

Some studies (Buss, Braden, Orgel, & Buss, 1956; Buss & Buss, 1956; Buss, Weiner, & Buss, 1954) compared knowledge of correct answers to knowledge of errors and to knowledge of both correct and incorrect answers. There seems to be some consistency across these studies; knowledge about which answers are correct and incorrect is far superior to only identifying correct answers. It seems, then, that students should have their errors pointed out to them if feedback is to be effective. Many learning disabilities teachers feel that their students have been subjected to sufficient failure and need not be made aware of their errors. In these situations, students usually are praised for correct answers and errors are ignored. In a different type of study, McGee (1970) found that errors should not be ignored, observing that many mildly handicapped students are oversheltered and that teachers create artificial success experiences that do not match the student's relationship with the real world. When the students in McGee's study were subjected to moderate amounts of error (and knowledge of that error), 75 percent of them improved their performances.

Other studies about the influence of feedback challenge another commonly held belief. For years, teachers were taught that feedback should be given on all student assignments and that it should be immediate. Many an afternoon has been spent correcting that day's student work. Fortunately, that necessity does not tend to be supported through research. A number of studies have compared immediate with delayed feedback. Researchers (Kulhavy & Anderson, 1972, Surber & Anderson, 1975) have found that feedback delayed more than one day actually increases retention and improves scores on follow-up tests. They found that immediately after difficult tests, students tend not to pay attention to the feedback provided. Several days later, however, the students pay attention, study their errors more before the next test, and profit from the knowledge of results.- - -

Directions.   As mentioned earlier, specific instructions carefully applied can be useful in increasing students' academic performance. Simply telling youngsters to be more careful as they do their assignments can cause increases in their percent correct scores. Smith and Lovitt (1975) found that some of their students made careless errors in their arithmetic assignments, and, therefore, did not reach percentage scores that indicated mastery. These students' scores averaged about 75 percent. Telling the students to be more careful as they computed the problem was sufficient, and the students obtained scores indicating mastery (in these cases, three consecutive days at 100 percent).

For students who have acquired the basic processes involved but whose accuracy is still of concern, further explanation or redirection might be helpful. Sometimes only minor instructional statements relating to the way the student is completing the assignment facilitate final acquisition of the task. Once this is accomplished, proficiency can become the target.

Error drill.   Along the same lines, error drill can cause necessary increases in accuracy. For students who are unsure of the correct answer and get the correct solution one day and not the next, error drill specifically on those items not definitely mastered can be sufficient to increase accuracy. Error drill can be effectively applied to the acquisition of sight words, arithmetic facts, spelling, handwriting, and many other academic areas.

Reward for accuracy.   Sometimes students need an extra incentive to encourage them to put out the extra effort required to achieve mastery level percentage scores. The various incentive systems, described under the reinforcement heading in the next section, can be applied to increase accuracy. Students could receive extra bonuses or privileges for perfect papers. Special certificates of commendation, perfect papers placed on a bulletin board, notes home to parents, extra recess or leisure time, and other special activities could be scheduled for final mastery of academic tasks.

Response cost.   A full description of response cost tactics appears in the next chapter. For some students, directions, error drill, or rewards do not achieve the aim of increased accuracy. For students whose frequency of errors is too high, withdrawing the opportunity for privileges contingent upon errors is one way to stimulate increased correct percentage scores. Lovitt and Smith (1974) found that withdrawing minutes from recess served

To attain mastery of this sight word reading task, this youngster needed an extra incentive. Here, poker chips were used as immediate indications for correct answers. They were redeemable later for extra privileges.

to drastically reduce a young girl's errors in arithmetic. One caution about this technique should be noted, however. The teacher must be certain that the student can perform the desired task before response cost is applied. It is not fair to punish a student for something he or she is not capable of doing. When the teacher is certain that the reason for unsatisfactory percentage scores is not unknown answers but rather an unwillingness to provide the correct answer, response cost might well be a beneficial tactic to select.

PROFICIENCY STAGE

A number of interventions are effective in one stage of learning, but not in others. The most notable of these is reinforcement, which is most effective when the target skill is performed frequently enough to be reinforced. Once students have acquired a skill, it is important for them to become proficient at it; rate of performance is the important issue. The tactics discussed in this section increase rate of performance, and, therefore, increase proficiency.

Instructional Tactics

Several instructional tactics facilitate proficiency. Modeling, telling, and drill improve the quality and quantity of students' academic performances. It might be best to try these instructional tactics before scheduling complicated reinforcement procedures, because they are more natural to normal classroom situations. For some youngsters, however, they are not sufficient to cause substantial increases in rates of performance: reinforcement procedures are then necessary.

Modeling.   Modeling was discussed in some detail in the acquisition section of this chapter, and is most commonly and appropriately applied there. However, modeling has proven to be instrumental in building proficiency in some students' academic performances. Smith (1978, 1979), for example, used a modeling tactic to increase students' oral reading proficiency. The students had to increase their correct rates of oral reading. During the intervention conditions, the teacher read the first passage from the students' basal text at the desired rate (approximately 100 words per minute). The students then continued reading from the text for the allotted time. Modeling substantially and positively influenced the students' oral reading performances. Although there are few examples of the use of modeling in proficiency building situations, modeling is natural to the instructional situation; it is easy to schedule and might be a worthwhile tactic to try.

Telling.   Another simple tactic natural to instructional situations frequently is underused. Sometimes students do not know what is expected of them. Are they supposed to fill the math period with the seatwork given to them at the beginning of the period? Are they supposed to concentrate on accuracy? If students are privy to the teacher's aims, improved performance in line with the desired outcome might occur without the scheduling of elaborate techniques.

Lovitt (1978) reports several instances in which students' proficiency performance levels were achieved through the use of instructions. These students were told to work faster, to compute as many problems as they could, or to read faster. Simply clarifying the goals of the instructional situation for the students produced the desired results. Often, teachers forget to tell their students what is expected of them in academic situations. This might be a good first tactic to apply when fluency or proficiency must be enhanced.

Drill.   A tactic used in schools for many, many years is the use of drill and practice. Music teachers help students become more proficient at playing musical instruments by insisting on drill and practice. Handwriting is taught almost exclusively through the use of these tactics. Haring et al. (1978) suggests that drill in various forms can increase proficiency in a number of academic areas. Drill on errors seems to enhance oral reading, handwriting, and computational arithmetic. These researchers feel that drill has particular merit in the proficiency stage and suggest its specific application when fluency is the target. It should be noted, however, that many older students find drill uninteresting and refuse to practice tasks over and over when drill is scheduled alone. Teachers might have to add incentives to the drill procedures so that these students will practice sufficiently.

Positive
Reinforcement

The deliberate use of reinforcement procedures was introduced into classroom situations over fifteen years ago (Birnbrauer, Bijou, Wolf, & Kidder, 1965; Staats, Staats, Schultz, & Wolf, 1962; Zimmerman & Zimmerman, 1962). Although reinforcement has gained in popularity and use since then and the number of variations are now almost infinite, it is not a new discovery. It is documented (Lane, 1976) that Itard, in 1802, incorporated reinforcement procedures in his remediation program to normalize a retarded boy, Victor. Although Itard relied heavily on shaping procedures, he used contingent rewards (milk) and specific praise to reinforce Victor's development of specific skills.

Reinforcement can be defined as the application of an event that increases the likelihood that the behavior it follows will occur again. Reinforcement is applied after a behavior occurs and is functionally related to an increase in frequency of that behavior. An event is a reinforcer only if it causes an increase in the target behavior. What might be a reinforcer for one student might not be for another. Except in the case of primary reinforcers (food, sleep, water), it cannot be assumed that any tactic is a reinforcer. Data must be kept to determine this.

Most reinforcers used in school situations are termed secondary reinforcers, for their value must be learned. Events such as free time, for example, are not naturally reinforcing; the teacher must arrange for students to learn their reinforcing value. Ayllon, Layman, & Burke (1972) arranged for their students to experience a short priming period. The students first received noncontingently the rewards they worked for later, to help them learn the reinforcing value of the events. This idea has merit. Students will not work for library time if they do not know what library time is or that it can be fun and rewarding. Many of the events that are highly motivating in school can be used as positive reinforcers, but students must first be aware of their reinforcing value. A priming period, as suggested by Ayllon et al., might be helpful.

Tangible reinforcement.   When this form of reinforcement is used, the student receives as the reward something concrete—something that can be held. One common form of tangible reinforcement is the token. Elaborate systems have been created around the token, its dispensement, its value, etc. Therefore, an entire section of the next chapter is devoted to the discussion of token economies.

Tangible reinforcement also comes in the form of items given contingently (toy models, trinkets, and other objects). The accumulation of points earned daily for improved performance eventually leads to the purchase of a specific object. Toy models were used as reinforcers to increase performance during arithmetic period (Smith & Lovitt, 1976; Walker & Buckley, 1968) and goldfish for improved reading (Roberts, 1977).

This system can be useful to teachers working with youngsters who need a concrete object as a display of their achievement. Schultz and Sherman (1976) state that tangible reinforcers become effective around the ages of five or six. Probably they are most appropriate for elementary-age students. Teachers of older students also find them valuable when a youngster still requires a concrete representation of school achievement. As with the case of primary reinforcers, teachers should not use tangible rewards indefinitely, but help students learn the reinforcing value of other types of rewards. However, for youngsters who find school work frustrating and not intrinsically motivating, this level of reinforcement might well be a good place to start.

Adult attention.   Teacher attention is an integral part of the instructional process, but, unfortunately, it frequently is not used to its true potential. Although a natural part of the classroom situation, it is not used consistently, systematically, or appropriately. Its application should cause increases in the target behavior, but used carelessly it might not produce the desired results. Solomon and Wahler (1973) found that even highly trained teachers attend to disruption more than to appropriate classroom behavior; this can lead to even higher levels of disruption. Heller and White (1975) found that many junior high school teachers expressed more disapproving statements to their lower ability classes than to their higher ability classes. Most disapproving statements were aimed at managing disruption.

Careful application of teacher, or adult, attention has yielded remarkable results. In a classic study, Allen, Hart, Buell, Harris, and Wolf (1964) demonstrated the power of adult attention for a nursery school student's social interaction with her peers. Contingent use of adult attention also has increased students' rates of following instructions (Schutte & Hopkins, 1970), attention to academic task (Hall, Lund, & Jackson, 1968), and studying by junior high school students (Broden, Hall, Dunlap, & Clark, 1970). Teacher attention seems to be most powerful with lower elementary-age students, for young students are most interested in gaining attention from adults while older students are most interested in gaining the attention of their peers. Despite this age-related factor, teacher attention is powerful and should be used consciously.

Praise.   One form of teacher attention, studied for a number of years, is praise. Gilchrist (1916) found that in English classes the praised group of learners' achievement far surpassed that of another group admonished for poor work. According to Kennedy and Willcutt (1964) in their review of praise and blame as incentives in the classroom, the influence of praise was studied carefully as early as 1897 by Binet and Vaschide. Throughout the years this tactic seems to be stable, consistently influencing positive changes in student performance.

White (1975) studied the natural rates of approving and disapproving statements used by teachers in all grade levels (first through twelfth grade). A total of 105 teachers was studied. The results of her research are fascinating. Evidently, first and second grade teachers have high praise or approval rates; the rates stabilize at about eighth grade (one per five to ten minutes). Therefore, in a forty-minute class period, as few as four approving statements might be made. Disapproving rates also are higher in the primary grades, and lower disapproval rates occur in the higher elementary grades. In the middle schools, students more often hear disapproving statements than approving ones. By high school, students hear little of either kind. In all grades, students hear more disapproving statements for misbehavior and more positive statements for academics. According to White, children almost never hear, "I'm glad you're on time," or "You are all acting so nicely."

White's study was replicated (using different rating scales) by Thomas, Presland, Grant, and Glynn (1978), who report similar findings. Of the ten seventh grade teachers they studied, seven had higher disapproval than approval statement rates. The findings of these research projects are disturbing. If classrooms are to be positive learning environments, students should be praised and receive teacher attention for appropriate social behavior as well as for improved academic performance. Praise and attention should be specific so students understand why they are receiving reinforcement. A statement like, "I like the way Susie is sitting at her desk ready to work" is certainly superior to "Susie is good." Before scheduling elaborate reinforcement programs, teachers should examine their own rates of attention to determine whether they could be altered to produce positive changes in their students' performances.

Premack Principle.   The Premack Principle, sometimes referred to as Gramma's Rule (Snell & Smith, 1978), deals with the time arrangement of activities. Those activities the student likes to engage in follow those activities the student does not like. "Finish your vegetables, then you may have dessert," and "Complete your arithmetic assignment, then you may work on your art project" are examples of the application of the Premack Principle. Premack (1959), through a series of laboratory studies, formulated this hypothesis: high strength activities can serve as reinforcers for low strength activities.

The first deliberate application of this principle in a classroom situation was probably conducted by Homme, deBaca, Devine, Steinhorst, and Rickert (1963). The three-year-old nursery school students who participated in this study spent an inordinate amount of time running and screaming. This distracted from the "academic" routine. During the intervention condition, children were allowed to run and scream for a period of time contingent upon how long they sat in their chairs, paid attention to the teacher, and engaged in organized activities. In other words, an organized schedule was imposed on the situation. The children were still allowed to engage in their favorite activities, but this was contingent upon behavior the teaching staff considered most desirable.

In some cases, rescheduling the academic routine can effect positive changes in student performance. Some students while away time when given an assignment they do not like. If that assignment were scheduled first, and activity enjoyable to the students followed, they would have an incentive to complete the tedious activity so they could move on to one they liked. For example, if Ruth hates arithmetic and loves reading, arithmetic seatwork would be given to her first. The longer she spends on the arithmetic assignment (both completing it and correcting errors made), the less time left for reading. Before resorting to more complicated or elaborate intervention procedures, teachers might consider trying an application of the Premack Principle by rescheduling academic assignments according to student preferences.

The most common application of the Premack Principle in classroom situations is *free time*. When contingent free time is used, students earn minutes to spend in activities of their choice contingent upon appropriate behavior or desirable academic performance. Usually there are a number of free-time activities from which the student can choose (working on an art project, leisure reading, working puzzles, or playing quietly with a friend). It is advisable, however, to allow students to work on free-time activities only during time they have earned. If a student can engage in these activities at any time (earned or not), the incentive for earning minutes of free time, and thereby improving performance, diminishes.

Contingent free time has been effective in reducing time spent out of seat (Osborne, 1969), reducing general disruption of elementary and junior high school students (Broden, et al., 1970; Cowen, Jones, & Bellack, 1979), improving handwriting performance (Hopkins, Schutte, & Garton, 1971), improving spelling (Evans & Oswalt, 1968; Lovitt, Guppy, & Blattner, 1969), and improving arithmetic performance (Brooks & Snow, 1972). A wide variety of target behaviors can be selected for modification through the use of free time made contingent upon improvement. The incorporation of free time into the school situation has several advantages. First, the activities used during free time can be natural to the school setting, not requiring the use of expensive or outside materials; monetary or tangible rewards need not be used. Second, students learn to manage leisure time for themselves. This is an important aspect for many learning disabled students whose school routine is so established that they do not learn how to manage independent activities and leisure time in constructive ways. For some students, free time can prove to be a valuable learning experience in itself.

Special events.   Throughout the course of a school year, many events and activities are scheduled for the students. These range from special assemblies, rehearsals of drama and music clubs, and educational field trips to parties centering on holidays. Usually these events and related activities are scheduled noncontingently; participation seems to be an inalienable right of students. Thus, an opportunity to utilize a potentially high strength set of reinforcers goes untapped, since for many students, participation in special events is the most exciting part of the school year.

The incorporation of special activities into the classroom routine for the purpose of being used contingent upon improved school performance can add an element of fun to learning and also serve as extra motivation. One caution, however, must be noted. Arrangements must be made for students who do not earn the privilege of participating in special activities. Another teacher, aide, or other supervisory personnel must be available to monitor those students who are not included.

Schedules of reinforcement.   All reinforcement tactics (tangible reinforcement, adult attention, praise) may be used according to various schedules or patterns of application. Each instance of an application of a reinforcement procedure is often called a unit of reinforcement. These units, then, may be delivered according to the following schedules. Some of these schedules are more appropriately applied in one stage of learning than another (those most appropriate in the maintenance situation are discussed in that section).

The *continuous reinforcement* (CRF) schedule is most appropriate in the acquisition stage of learning: discussion is provided here for clarity and convenience. The student receives a unit of reinforcement for each occur-

As a reward for good classroom behavior, these boys asked their teacher to read them a story.

rence of the target behavior. Each time Johnny begins his assignment on time, the teacher praises him. As the teacher corrects Mary's arithmetic seatwork, for each correct answer he or she places a star next to the problem and praises Mary.

Although continuous reinforcement is very useful at first, the frequency of reinforcement should be reduced as soon as possible. There are several important reasons for *leaning* (reducing) the schedule of reinforcement from continuous to intermittent. First, the application of a CRF schedule of reinforcement is very expensive in teacher time, requiring a considerable amount of one-to-one attention. Second, CRF schedules are subject to extinction: if reinforcement is given each time the target behavior occurs, when the reinforcement is withdrawn, the desirable behavior tends to disappear and the frequency drops to zero. The last reason for only using CRF schedules initially is a phenomenon referred to as *satiation*. When one reinforcing event is used again and again, its power is often lost. The student who is praised over and over again soon becomes bored with praise and the tactic no longer serves its original purpose. CRF schedules tend to overuse specific tactics and soon meet with the phenomenon of satiation. Therefore, although CRF schedules of reinforcement often are initially very effective in building a positive set of behaviors for a youngster, it is advisable to move to a less frequent delivery system as soon as possible.

The *fixed interval* (FI) reinforcement schedule allows for reinforcement for every selected period of appropriate behavior. FI schedules usually are applied to improve social behavior, on task behavior, study time, or "attending." A kitchen timer can be used to indicate when the fixed time period has passed and reinforcement should either be received or not. For example, Sue needed to increase the amount of time she spent in her seat calculating problems in her arithmetic workbook. The teacher selected an FI schedule of 5:1. For each five-minute time period over the twenty-minute arithmetic study time planned for each day, Sue could earn one point. Each point was exchangeable for an extra minute of recess time. A total of four extra minutes of recess could be earned each day. A kitchen timer was set for five minutes. If she was in her seat working on her assignment during the five-minute segment, she received one point. If she was out of her seat during that segment, she did not receive a point. The timer was then reset and another five-minute segment was initiated.

When *fixed ratio* (FR) schedules of reinforcement are used, the individual receives a unit of reinforcement after so many occurrences of the target behavior. This is probably the most common schedule of reinforcement used in academic situations, for it allows the teacher to count the number of correct responses made by a student, apply the ratio, and deliver the specified amount of reinforcement. For example, if John has an FR 10:1 schedule arranged for his arithmetic seatwork assignments, for every ten problems he computes correctly, he receives one unit of reinforcement (minute of free time, point toward a tangible reinforcer). One difficulty with FR schedules is that reinforcement is earned even for unsatisfactory performances. Although not many units of reinforcement are earned, minimum performance levels allow the student reinforcement. If John only computes ten problems accurately (even if fifty was the aim), he earns one minute of free time.

To avoid this situation, a slightly more sophisticated tactic may be added to the FR schedule. When *differentially reinforcing higher rates of responding* (DRH) schedules are applied, reinforcement is earned only when the student's scores surpass a specified level—the central tendency score of the previous condition or current functioning level. Because of the confusing name of this schedule of reinforcement, children often refer to it as a "Go/No-Go Contingency." As its name clearly implies, reinforcement is received for really good work or it is not received at all.

A comparable schedule of reinforcement used to decrease rather than increase students' performances is called *differentially reinforcing lower rates of responding* (DRL) and is often paired with a DRH schedule. When correct and error rate scores are used as the daily measures, teachers often place reinforcement contingencies on improved correct rate scores *and* decreased error rate scores. A DRL schedule sets a maximum number of occurrences of a behavior each day, if reinforcement is to be received. In one case, Henry's error rate scores in oral reading were too high (mean of ten per minute). The teacher decided to implement a DRL schedule for Henry's error rate. She decided that the daily desired error rate would be five, and the achievement of that score was worth five minutes of extra recess. On any day his error rate rose above ten he would receive no reinforcement. Once Henry's error rate scores decreased, the teacher could then implement an even stricter DRL schedule to influence an even greater drop in errors made during oral reading. She might even consider placing Go/No-Go contingencies (DRH and DRL) on both correct and error rates for this student. The clear advantage of these differential schedules of reinforcement is that they do not allow for students to perform at unsatisfactory levels and still receive units of reinforcement.

Multiple ratio schedules of reinforcement are slightly more difficult to establish initially, but they are the most sophisticated form of reinforcement delivery systems used in classrooms and academic situations. The logic behind their implementation is that greater levels of improvement should be worth more units of reinforcement. In the schedules of reinforcement described above, the same ratio is applied regardless of how much improvement is made by the student. The Go/No-Go contingency feature accounts for unsatisfactory performance, but the ratio is applied consistently at all levels. The multiple ratio schedule allows little reinforcement when small amounts of improvement are achieved and substantial reinforcement for greater amounts of improvement. Details for determining multiple ratios are provided in the section on how to establish a point system (found later in this chapter).

Using reinforcement successfully.   A number of reinforcing events or activities easily can be included in classroom situations aimed at stimulating students' behavioral and academic improvement. Reinforcers, by definition, increase the likelihood of a target behavior increasing in frequency. The number of interventions serving this purpose is vast, and the selection of specific reinforcers should be done with the student in mind. The age of the student is an important variable. For preschoolers, primary reinforcers (food) might be appropriate at first. Young elementary-age students often find concrete items of great reinforcing value. Specific praise and contingent teacher attention also serve as powerful reinforcers for this age group. Older youngsters, however, find other things within the school environment more interesting. Upper elementary and middle school students enjoy such privileges as displaying good work on the bulletin board, selecting games during gym time, gaining free or leisure time, determining where they sit in the class, extra library time, special films, and other comparable activities. High school students often find earning a free period, writing or participating in a class play or skit, earning extra minutes for lunch time, being able to go off campus for lunch, or attending a rehearsal of a local theater group exciting enough to spend the extra energy required to improve academic or behavioral performance.

Also, the student's interests must be considered. Allowing a student to display a graph of his or her performance when that would only prove to be an embarrassment in front of classmates is an illustration of an inappropriate selection of a reinforcer. Allowing a student to earn more library time when that student dislikes everything related to reading again would not be the most advantageous reinforcer. For some students, sending home a note regarding good work at school is reinforcing. For others it is not. Teachers must know their students' interests. Teachers can discuss with their students which activities are of reinforcing value and which are not. Simply asking students to list their favorite activities in school is a start. Careful observation also often reveals those activities students self-select. These can then be made contingent upon improved school performance.

Lovitt (1978) provides some interesting and useful observations about the use of reinforcement in classroom situations.

> *A word of caution, teachers should be careful when they arrange reinforcers, particularly those that are expensive or habit forming. Ordinarily, once a reinforcer is used to change a behavior, it should be removed as soon as the behavior is changed. Like a medicine or any other therapy, a reinforcer can, if used unwisely, effect a cure that is worse than the problem.* (p. 4)

How to Set Up a Point System

The schedules of reinforcement are used to determine how many units of reinforcement a student earns for the improved performance. Once the teacher has decided what type of schedule (FR, multiple ratio) will be used, he or she must determine the actual ratio to be utilized. In this section examples are provided for the fixed ratio, DRH, and multiple ratio situations, which can be used for tangible reinforcement, special privileges, or free time.

Fixed ratio point systems are fairly easy to arrange and manage. Figure 4.3 provides a formula to follow to arrive at the desired ratio, and two examples of its implementation. First, the mean or median score from the

Fixed Ratio Reinforcement System

Steps to follow
1. Determine current functioning level
2. Determine short-term aim score
3. Decide reward you want to give for achieving aim score
4. Calculate ratio of reinforcement (aim score ÷ reward)

Example 1:   Previous mean rate = 25
Desired rate = 2 × 25 = 50
Reward for achieving aim = 5
Ratio = 50 ÷ 5 = 10:1

RATE	CALCULATE	REWARD
20	20 ÷ 10 =	2
30	30 ÷ 10 =	3
40	40 ÷ 10 =	4

Example 2:   Previous mean rate = 35
Desired rate = 2 × 35 = 70
Reward for achieving aim = 10
Ratio = 70 ÷ 10 = 7:1

RATE	CALCULATE	REWARD
25	25 ÷ 7 =	3
35	35 ÷ 7 =	5
45	45 ÷ 7 =	6
55	55 ÷ 7 =	8
65	65 ÷ 7 =	9
75	75 ÷ 7 =	10

Figure 4.3   A list of steps to follow and two examples of the implementation of fixed ratio schedules.

previous condition (or baseline) must be determined. This current level of functioning is the basis for determining the amount of improvement attainable. The short-term aim score then must be set in accordance with the student's current functioning level. In the examples provided, the aim score or desired rate was calculated by requiring a doubling of the current functioning level (central tendency score from the previous condition). The teacher then arbitrarily decided that any day the aim score was reached was worth a specific number of reinforcement units. In Example 1, the teacher decided that reaching the aim score was worth five units of reinforcement; in Example 2, it was worth ten. By dividing the aim score by the amount of reinforcement decided upon in Step 3, the fixed ratio of reinforcement was determined. That ratio becomes a constant for that intervention condition and is used each day to determine the number of units of reinforcement the student earned for that day's performance.

The DRH or Go/No-Go Contingency system merely adds to the fixed ratio situation. Reinforcement is only given to the student if the daily score surpasses a certain level. When fixed ratio schedules are applied, reinforcement (although not much) is given to the student even when performance levels are not desirable (see Figure 4.3). This does not happen when a DRH schedule is applied. The fixed ratio is calculated and implemented as described above, but now reinforcement is earned only when the student's score surpasses a specified level: the central tendency score of the previous condition or current functioning level. Steps to follow and two examples of a DRH reinforcement schedule are provided in Figure 4.4.

The multiple ratio procedures are the same as those used in arriving at the fixed ratio. The last step is different, however. Once the maximum *ratio* is determined, it is placed by the aim score. Ratios that yield fewer units of reinforcement are then placed by lower and lower possible daily scores (this is not accomplished through the use of formulas, but is an arbitrary decision of the teacher). See the example provided in Figure 4.5. It is advisable when using multiple ratio schedules to work out daily bands of reinforcement units that correlate with possible scores the student might make before the multiple ratio intervention is implemented. These bands, placed on an index card, indicate to both student and teacher how many units of reinforcement a

DRH or Go/No-Go Contingency

Steps to follow
1. Determine current functioning level
2. Determine short-term aim score
3. Decide reward you want to give for achieving aim score
4. Calculate ratio of reinforcement (aim score ÷ reward)

Example 1:   Previous rate = 25
Desired rate = $2 \times 25 = 50$
Reward for achieving aim = 5
Ratio = $50 \div 5 = 10{:}1$
Below 25 no reward

RATE	CALCULATE	REWARD
20	below 25	0
30	$30 \div 10 =$	3
40	$40 \div 10 =$	4

Example 2:   Previous mean rate = 35
Desired rate = $2 \times 35 = 70$
Reward for achieving aim = 10
Ratio = $70 \div 10 = 7{:}1$
Below 35, no reward

RATE	CALCULATE	REWARD
25	below 35	0
35	$35 \div 7 =$	5
45	$45 \div 7 =$	6
55	$55 \div 7 =$	8
65	$65 \div 7 =$	9
75	$75 \div 7 =$	10

Figure 4.4   A list of steps to follow and two examples of DRH schedules of reinforcement.

Multiple Ratio with a Go/No-Go Contingency

Steps to follow
1. Determine current functioning level
2. Determine short-term aim score
3. Decide reward you want to give for achieving aim score
4. Calculate ratio of reinforcement (aim score ÷ reward)
5. Adjust ratios so fewer points are earned for lower scores

Example 1: Previous mean rate = 25
Desired rate = 2 × 25 = 50
Reward for achieving aim = 5
Maximum ratio = 50 ÷ 5 = 10:1
Below 25 no reward

RATE	CALCULATE	REWARD
20	below 25	0
30	30 ÷ 15 =	2
40	40 ÷ 13 =	3
50	50 ÷ 10 =	5

Example 2: Previous mean rate = 35
Desired rate = 2 × 35 = 70
Reward for achieving aim = 10
Maximum ratio = 70 ÷ 10 = 7:1
Below 35 no reward

RATE	CALCULATE	REWARD
25	below 35	0
35	35 ÷ 11 =	3
45	45 ÷ 10 =	5
55	55 ÷ 9 =	6
65	65 ÷ 8 =	8
75	75 ÷ 7 =	11

Figure 4.5   Steps to follow and examples of multiple ratio schedules of reinforcement.

student should receive depending on the daily score attained. Although a bit confusing, multiple ratio schedules of reinforcement do provide bonus points for extra effort and substantial improvement in academic performance. They should serve as an indication to students of how important reaching one's aim score really is. Of course, if the multiple ratio system seems too complicated, bonus points could be given in addition to the fixed ratio amount for surpassing a short-term aim score.

MAINTENANCE STAGE

In the maintenance stage of learning, discussed earlier in this chapter, the aim is for the student to retain the mastery levels of performance attained while direct intervention was in effect. In some cases, maintenance conditions are conducted without any intervention scheduled to determine whether the student can actually perform the task or skill without any help from the teacher. In other cases, during the maintenance conditions the student receives reinforcement for satisfactory performance, but infrequently. Unfortunately, not many academic and behavioral researchers have devoted their energies to the study of retention.

In the previous section, the influence of fixed schedules of reinforcement on students gaining proficient levels of performance was discussed. Once mastery levels are achieved, it is important that students maintain them. For example, once a youngster reaches a mastery level of performance in oral reading, in order to keep up with the peer group, fluency must be retained. Of course, merely practicing oral reading skills should help to retain satisfactory reading levels. Certainly, if once reading is "mastered" it is dropped from the curriculum and no longer receives attention from the teacher or student, performance levels will decrease. Academic learning, particularly for those who have had difficulty mastering the skill in the first place, is not like riding a bike. Once students learn how, they might not remember. Therefore, one important key to retention is continued practice, although on a periodic basis. For many learning disabled students, however, practice alone is not enough. For them, direct though infrequent intervention is required for some time to insure that learning is retained. Following is a summary of some tactics that facilitate maintenance and retention.

Overlearning

This procedure has received little attention from researchers lately, but has merit and should be reinvestigated as a maintenance procedure. The concept of overlearning requires the learner to practice a task well beyond the level of mastery. Probably the concept of overlearning gave rise to the notion that three or even five consecutive scores be above a predetermined level before the student can move on to learn more difficult tasks. If a teacher were to incorporate overlearning into the teaching process, students would have to demonstrate mastery for a longer time than is typically used. Snell made the point that if overlearning is used, "repeated practice or review distributed over time rather than massed into a brief time period" should facilitate long-term retention (1978, p. 363). Smith (1968) felt that overlearning should be an integral part of the teaching routine for handicapped learners because it tends to improve retention and generalization.

Reinforcement Schedules

A number of reinforcement schedules have proven to be helpful in encouraging retention. They generally are referred to as *intermittent* schedules of reinforcement. Units of reinforcement are given to the student on a planned but irregular basis. In fixed schedules, reinforcement is delivered after a set number of correct responses or a set amount of time. Intermittent or variable schedules of reinforcement provide students with reinforcement in such a way that the student cannot predict when the opportunity for reinforcement will occur. This, in a sense, keeps the student on guard, performing as best as possible. Variable schedules usually lead to consistent performance with higher and more constant rates (Craighead, Kazdin, & Mahoney, 1976; Saudargas, Madsen, & Scott, 1977).

The *variable interval* (VI) schedule, as with most interval schedules, usually is used for social behavior. As with the fixed interval, reinforcement is delivered according to segments or amounts of time, but each time segment differs from the next.

One common application of a variable interval schedule is the "timer game" (described in detail in Chapter 7). A kitchen timer is set to ring *on the average* of every five minutes (a schedule of 5:1). Sometimes it will ring after one minute, sometimes after nine minutes, sometimes after three minutes, and so on. Anyone in his or her seat working on the assignment when the bell rings receives a point. Anyone not behaving appropriately when the bell rings does not receive a point. At the end of the period, the team or student with the most points wins. Because of the unpredictability of when reinforcement can be earned, students tend to behave consistently better throughout the entire period.

Variable ratio (VR) schedules of reinforcement are similar to fixed ratio schedules, but here once a ratio is determined an average of that number is applied per session. It is not advisable to use VR schedules of reinforcement directly on academic subjects, for it is confusing to students that one day's performance should be worth more units of reinforcement than another day's performance.

An interesting and useful application of a VR schedule can be made to academic situations, however. During a long-term maintenance phase, reinforcement can be given periodically over time. For example, Steve was a poor reader but finally achieved his long-term aim score. The teacher was afraid that he would not maintain his now proficient rate of oral reading. During intervention, Steve received reinforcement using a fixed ratio of 15:1 for correct rate. During long-term follow-up, the teacher read with Steve three days a week. She told him that they were going to play a game. Some days he would receive reinforcement for his reading assignment and some days he would not. He would never know in advance which days "counted." Initially, she applied a VR of 2:1 to his reading sessions, so on the average every other reading session earned him reinforcement (using the fixed ratio schedule of the intervention condition to determine the exact amount of reinforcement earned). Gradually, the VR scheduled was leaned. By the end of the school year, reinforcement was earned only periodically. Through the use of this technique, however, Steve not only maintained his proficient oral reading rate, but also continued to improve.

VR schedules for academic situations must be carefully applied. Using such schedules for cases such as Steve's, however, might facilitate the maintenance of desirable performances.

Social Reinforcement

Social reinforcement (the use of praise, teacher and peer approval) was discussed earlier. As mentioned, it is underutilized as a planned intervention. Often, after months and months of direct intervention on either a behavioral or academic target, once desired levels of performance are achieved the issue is forgotten and all intervention is discontinued. It is no wonder inappropriate behaviors often reappear or desired academic performance levels decrease.

Possibly the use of periodic social reinforcement from the teacher could alleviate this situation. Statements like: "Gee, you remembered to borrow here," or "The classroom is so much nicer now that you remembered to come in from recess quietly," would encourage the maintenance of desirable performances. The power of praise is well documented. This tactic might facilitate maintenance if used on a variable schedule. The periodic praise from the teacher, reminding the student of what the desired behavior actually is, might well be sufficient to keep a former target behavior within a youngster's repertoire. Also, maintenance of improvements noted at school must also be considered outside of the school situation. Parents can serve a vital role in this process. Through consultation and some training efforts, parents have facilitated maintenance of their children's gains through social reinforcement (Kelley, Embry, & Baer, 1979; Patterson & Fleischman, 1979; Walker, Hops, & Johnson, 1975).

Some interesting work utilizing peer social reinforcement has proven to maintain appropriate social behavior and reinforce appropriate actions of target students. Through what these researchers refer to as "peer reprogramming," maintenance of desirable behavior was achieved. Previously when intervention was withdrawn, inappropriate behavior rose almost to the levels of the initial baseline period. Often teachers forget that a student's peer group is present in the classroom situation also. If guided, classmates can be valuable resources in managing and maintaining desirable classroom behavior.

Intrinsic Reinforcement

The hope is that students will eventually maintain proficient levels of social and basic academic skills because they enjoy the product of those skills. All teachers hope that their students eventually will enjoy reading, that they will read without outside encouragement. The same is true for social behavior. The hope is that students will enjoy being "good citizens" and no longer have to be rewarded for appropriate actions or admonished for their lack.

Certainly this is the ultimate aim of the educational process. Unfortunately, many learning disabled students do not achieve this goal in all school related areas. Teachers must strive continually to help their students attain such proficient levels of performance that intrinsic reinforcement will in fact guarantee maintenance.

GENERALIZATION STAGE

Generalization, transferring knowledge and skills to new settings or situations, is an area of great deficiency for many learning disabled youngsters. For this population of learners, teachers should program for generalization rather than expect it to occur. Some (Buckley & Walker, 1978) suggest that by making the learning situation closely match those situations in which generalization should occur, transfer of learning might be enhanced. Stokes and Baer (1977) suggest that generalization could be facilitated through the use of instructions.

There are several guidelines about generalization that could be helpful: do not expect it to occur, extend the contingencies used in the teaching situation to the generalization settings also, and plan to implement the original, effective intervention procedure in the generalization situations if necessary. Unfortunately, generalization is almost an untapped area as far as educational research and the learning disabled population are concerned. Stokes and Baer (1977) postulate that generalization might well be a skill in and of itself that can be taught to those who are deficient in its application.

In their comprehensive review of generalization and maintenance of behavior change, Wehman, Abramson, and Norman (1977) have some valuable insights regarding the influence of specific tactics. One programming technique that has proven useful is varying stimulus conditions—introducing extraneous, irrelevant, or distracting stimuli; changing instructors and instructional settings; and changing class size. Teaching the student what to and what not to respond to, and reinforcing only correct responses in a variety of settings in the presence of different people also seems to promote generalization. Wehman et al., as well as Marholin, Siegel, and Phillips (1976), make the point that if those in the child's environment (parents, siblings, and other relatives) do not carry out remedial efforts through consistent application of those procedures used at school, little maintenance or generalization will occur. Through training, all those in a youngster's environment can be taught to systematically and consistently deal with academic and social behaviors. One idea involves reprogramming a student's environment (refer also to the Peer Management section of Chapter 5). In addition, these authors stress that self-management procedures also can encourage generalization (see that section in Chapter 5).

Generalization truly is a ubiquitous problem for all those who engage in instructional and remedial efforts. Clearly, much more research must be conducted, for some consider it a programming problem (Buckley & Walker, 1978; Wehman et al., 1977) while others believe that it could well be a cognitive function (Wildman & Wildman, 1975), and meanwhile teachers are left to ponder the problem.

A summary for Chapter 4 appears at the end of Chapter 5 as part of a combined review of these two closely related chapters.

REFERENCE NOTES

1. HARING, N. G. *An investigation of phases of learning and facilitating instructional events for the severely handicapped* (Project No. 443CN70564, Grant No. 443G00750093). Seattle, Wash.: College of Education, University of Washington, 1978.

2. WHITE, O., & LIBERTY, K. *Suggested changes for various patterns of performance* (Working Paper). Seattle, Wash.: Experimental Educational Unit, University of Washington, 1974.

3. BECK, R. *Math worksheets* (Title IV, Project C). Great Falls, Mont.: Great Falls Public Schools, 1979.

4. GAST, D. L., WILHOITE, B., & EVANS, L. S. *Four time delay studies.* Unpublished manuscript, University of Kentucky, 1979.

REFERENCES

AFFLECK, J. Q., LOWENBRAUN, S., & ARCHER, A. *Teaching the mildly handicapped in the regular classroom* (2nd ed.). Columbus, Ohio: Charles E. Merrill Publishing Co., 1980.

ALLEN, K. E., HART, B. M., BUELL, J. S., HARRIS, F. R., & WOLF, M. M. Effects of social reinforcement on isolate behavior of a nursery school child. *Child Development*, 1964, 35, 511–518.

ANDERSON, R. C., & FAUST, G. W. *Educational psychology: The science of instruction and learning.* New York: Dodd, Mead & Co., 1974.

AYLLON, T., & AZRIN, N. H. Reinforcement and instructions with mental patients. *Journal of the Experimental Analysis of Behavior*, 1964, 7, 327–331.

AYLLON, T., LAYMAN, D., & BURKE, S. Disruptive behavior and reinforcement of academic performance. *The Psychological Record*, 1972, 22, 315–323.

BANDURA, A. Behavioral modifications through modeling procedures. In L. Krasner & L. P. Ullmann (Eds.), *Research in behavior modification.* New York: Holt, Rinehart & Winston, 1965.

BANDURA, A. *Principles of behavior modification.* New York: Holt, Rinehart & Winston, 1969.

BIRNBRAUER, J. S., BIJOU, S. W., WOLF, M. M. & KIDDER, J. D. Programed instruction in the classroom. In L. P. Ullmann & L. Krasner (Eds.), *Case studies in behavior modification.* New York: Holt, Rinehart & Winston, 1965.

BRODEN, M., HALL, R. V., DUNLAP, A., & CLARK, R. Effects of teacher attention and a token reinforcement system in a junior high school special education class. *Exceptional Children*, 1970, 36, 341–349.

BROOKS, R. B., & SNOW, D. L. Two case illustrations of the use of behavior-modification techniques in the school setting. *Behavior Therapy*, 1972, 3, 100–103.

BUCKLEY, N. K., & WALKER, H. M. *Modifying classroom behavior: A manual of procedure for classroom teachers* (revised ed.). Champaign, Ill.: Research Press Co., 1978.

BUSS, A. H., BRADEN, W., ORGEL, A., & BUSS, E. H. Acquisition and extinction with different verbal reinforcement combinations. *Journal of Experimental Psychology*, 1956, 52, 288–295.

BUSS, A. H., & BUSS, E. H. The effect of verbal reinforcement combinations on conceptual learning. *Journal of Experimental Psychology*, 1956, 52, 283–287.

BUSS, A. H., WEINER, M., & BUSS, E. Stimulus generalization as a function of verbal reinforcement combinations. *Journal of Experimental Psychology*, 1954, 48, 433–436.

COWEN, R. J., JONES, F. H., & BELLACK, A. S. Grandma's rule with group contingencies—A cost-efficient means of classroom management. *Behavior Modification*, 1979, 3, 397–418.

CRAIGHEAD, W. E., KAZDIN, A. E., & MAHONEY, M. J. *Behavior modification: Principles, issues, and applications.* Boston: Houghton Mifflin Co., 1976.

CULLINAN, D., KAUFFMAN, J. M., & LaFLEUR, N. K. Modeling: Research with implications for special education. *The Journal of Special Education*, 1975, 9, 209–221.

EVANS, G. W., & OSWALT, G. L. Acceleration of academic progress through the manipulation of peer influence. *Behaviour Research and Therapy*, 1968, 6, 189–195.

GILCHRIST, E. P. The extent to which praise and reproof affect a pupil's work. *School and Society*, 1916, 4, 872–874.

HALL, R. V., LUND, D., & JACKSON, D. Effects of teacher attention on study behavior. *Journal of Applied Behavior Analysis*, 1968, 1, 1–12.

HARING, N. G., LOVITT, T. C., EATON, M. D., & HANSEN, C. L. *The fourth R: Research in the classroom.* Columbus, Ohio: Charles E. Merrill Publishing Co., 1978.

HELLER, M. S., & WHITE, M. A. Rates of teacher verbal approval and disapproval to higher and lower ability classes. *Journal of Educational Psychology*, 1975, 67, 796–800.

HOMME, L. E., deBACA, P. C., DEVINE, J. V., STEINHORST, R., & RICKERT, E. J. Use of the Premack principle in controlling the behavior of nursery school children. *Journal of the Experimental Analysis of Behavior*, 1963, 6, 544.

HOPKINS, B. L. Effects of candy and social reinforcement, instructions and reinforcement schedule leaning on the modification and maintenance of smiling. *Journal of Applied Behavior Analysis*, 1968, 1, 121–129.

HOPKINS, B. L., SCHUTTE, R. C., & GARTON, K. L. The effects of access to a playroom on the rate and quality of printing and writing of first and second-grade students. *Journal of Applied Behavior Analysis*, 1971, 4, 77–87.

KAUFFMAN, J. M., LaFLEUR, N. K., HALLAHAN, D. P., & CHANES, C. M. Imitation as a consequence for children's behavior: Two experimental case studies. *Behavior Therapy*, 1975, 6, 535–542.

KAZDIN, A. E. Role of instructions and reinforcement in behavior changes in token reinforcement programs. *Journal of Educational Psychology*, 1973, 64, 63–71.

KELLEY, M. L., EMBRY, L. H., & BAER, D. M. Skills for child management and family support: Training parents for maintenance. *Behavior Modification,* 1979, *3,* 373–396.

KENNEDY, W. A., & WILLCUTT, H. C. Praise and blame as incentives. *Psychological Bulletin,* 1964, *62,* 323–332.

KULHAVY, R. W. Feedback in written instruction. *Review of Educational Research,* 1977, *47,* 211–232.

KULHAVY, R. W., & ANDERSON, R. C. Delay-retention effect with multiple-choice tests. *Journal of Educational Psychology,* 1972, *63,* 505–512.

LANE, H. *The wild boy of Aveyron.* Cambridge, Mass.: Harvard University Press, 1976.

LOVITT, T. C. *Managing inappropriate behaviors in the classroom.* Reston, Va.: The Council for Exceptional Children, 1978.

LOVITT, T. C. GUPPY, T. E., & BLATTNER, J. E. The use of a free-time contingency with fourth graders to increase spelling accuracy. *Behaviour Research and Therapy,* 1969, *7,* 151–156.

LOVITT, T. C., & SMITH, D. D. Using withdrawal of positive reinforcement to alter subtraction performance. *Exceptional Children,* 1974, *40,* 357–358.

LOVITT, T. C., & SMITH, J. O. Effects of instructions on an individual's verbal behavior. *Exceptional Children,* 1972, *38,* 685–693.

MARHOLIN, D., II, SIEGEL, L. J., & PHILLIPS, D. Treatment and transfer: A search for empirical procedures. *Progress in Behavior Modification,* 1976, *3,* 293–342.

McGEE, J. E. Moderate failure as an instructional tool. *Exceptional Children,* 1970, *36,* 757–761.

O'LEARY, K. D., BECKER, W. C., EVANS, M. B., & SAUDARGAS, R. A. A token reinforcement program in a public school: A replication and systematic analysis. *Journal of Applied Behavior Analysis,* 1969, *2,* 3–13.

OSBORNE, J. G. Free-time as a reinforcer in the management of classroom behavior. *Journal of Applied Behavior Analysis,* 1969, *2,* 113–118.

PATTERSON, G. R., & FLEISCHMAN, M. J. Maintenance of treatment effects: Some considerations concerning family systems and follow-up data. *Behavior Therapy,* 1979, *10,* 168–185.

PREMACK, D. Toward empirical behavior laws: I. Positive reinforcement. *Psychological Review,* 1959, *66,* 219–233.

ROBERTS, M. B. The influences of increased correct and decreased error oral reading rates on the recall comprehension abilities of learning disabled children (Doctoral dissertation, George Peabody College for Teachers, 1977). *Dissertation Abstracts International,* 1977, *38,* 2706A. (Xerox University Microfilms No. 77-25, 125).

SAUDARGAS, R. W., MADSEN, C. H., JR., & SCOTT, J. W. Differential effects of fixed- and variable-time feedback on production rates of elementary school children. *Journal of Applied Behavior Analysis,* 1977, *10,* 673–678.

SCHULTZ, C. B., & SHERMAN, R. H. Social class, development, and differences in reinforcer effectiveness. *Review of Educational Research,* 1976, *46,* 25–59.

SCHUTTE, R. C., & HOPKINS, B. L. The effects of teacher attention on following instructions in a kindergarten class. *Journal of Applied Behavior Analysis,* 1970, *3,* 117–122.

SKINNER, B. F. *The technology of teaching.* New York: Appleton-Century-Crofts, 1968.

SMITH, D. D. The influence of instructions, feedback and reinforcement contingencies on children's abilities to acquire and become proficient at computational arithmetic skills (Doctoral dissertation, University of Washington, 1973). *Dissertation Abstracts International,* 1974, *35,* 290A–291A. (Xerox University Microfilms No. 74-15, 593).

SMITH, D. D. The influence of modeling on children's oral reading performance. In A. H. Fink (Ed.), *International prospectives in future special education.* Reston, Va.: The Council for Exceptional Children, 1978.

SMITH, D. D. The improvement of children's oral reading through the use of teacher modeling. *Journal of Learning Disabilities,* 1979, *12,* 172–175.

SMITH, D. D., & LOVITT, T. C. The use of modeling techniques to influence the acquisition of computational arithmetic skills in learning-disabled children. In E. Ramp & G. Semb (Eds.), *Behavior analysis: Areas of research and application.* Englewood Cliffs, N.J.: Prentice-Hall, 1975.

SMITH, D. D., & LOVITT, T. C. The differential effects of reinforcement contingencies on arithmetic performance. *Journal of Learning Disabilities,* 1976, *9,* 21–29.

SMITH, R. M. *Clinical teaching: Methods of instruction for the retarded.* New York: McGraw-Hill, 1968.

SNELL, M. E. (Ed.) *Systematic instruction of the moderately and severely handicapped.* Columbus, Ohio: Charles E. Merrill Publishing Co., 1978.

SNELL, M. E., & SMITH, D. D. Intervention strategies. In M. E. Snell (Ed.), *Systematic instruction of the moderately and severely handicapped.* Columbus, Ohio: Charles E. Merrill Publishing Co., 1978.

SOLOMON, R. W., & WAHLER, R. G. Peer reinforcement control of classroom problem behavior. *Journal of Applied Behavior Analysis,* 1973, *6,* 49–56.

STAATS, A. W., STAATS, C. K., SCHULTZ, R. E., & WOLF, M. M. The conditioning of textual responses using "extrinsic" reinforcers. *Journal of Experimental Analysis of Behavior*, 1962, *5*, 33–40.

STOKES, T. F., & BAER, D. M. An implicit technology of generalization. *Journal of Applied Behavior Analysis*, 1977, *10*, 349–367.

STRIKE, K. A. The logic of learning by discovery. *Review of Educational Research*, 1975, *45*, 461–483.

SURBER, J. R., & ANDERSON, R. C. Delay-retention effect in natural classroom settings. *Journal of Educational Psychology*, 1975, *67*, 170–173.

THOMAS, J. D., PRESLAND, I. E., GRANT, M. D., & GLYNN, T. L. Natural rates of teacher approval and disapproval in grade-7 classrooms. *Journal of Applied Behavior Analysis*, 1978, *11*, 91–94.

THURSTONE, T. G., & LILLIE, D. L. *Beginning to learn perceptual skills: A multileveled program for developing visual perception.* Chicago: Science Research Associates, Inc., 1972.

WALKER, H. M., & BUCKLEY, N. K. The use of positive reinforcement in conditioning attending behavior.

Journal of Applied Behavior Analysis, 1968, *1*, 245–252.

WALKER, H. M., HOPS, H., & JOHNSON, S. M. Generalization and maintenance of classroom treatment effects. *Behavior Therapy*, 1975, *6*, 188–200.

WEHMAN, P., ABRAMSON, M., & NORMAN, C. Transfer of training in behavior modification programs: An evaluative review. *The Journal of Special Education*, 1977, *11*, 217–231.

WHITE, M. A. Natural rates of teacher approval and disapproval in the classroom. *Journal of Applied Behavior Analysis*, 1975, *8*, 367–372.

WILDMAN, R. W., II, & WILDMAN, R. W. The generalization of behavior modification procedures: A review—With special emphasis on classroom applications. *Psychology in the Schools*, 1975, *12*, 432–448.

ZIMMERMAN, E. H., & ZIMMERMAN, J. The alteration of behavior in a special classroom situation. *Journal of the Experimental Analysis of Behavior*, 1962, *5*, 59–60.

5 INTERVENTION STRATEGIES:PART 2 VARIOUS STRATEGIES TO REDUCE OR INCREASE PERFORMANCES

In the preceding chapter, tactics aimed at causing increases in behavioral targets were presented. This chapter presents tactics used to reduce the frequency of specific behaviors, as well as tactics used to increase or decrease behavioral occurrences. A summary at the conclusion of the chapter reviews the information presented in both Chapters 4 and 5.

TEACHING TACTICS THAT REDUCE PERFORMANCES

Tactics that increase the occurrence of specific behaviors were discussed in Chapter 4 in terms of stages of learning (acquisition, proficiency, maintenance, and generalization). Although a comparable relationship might exist when the aim is to decrease the occurrences of specific behaviors, researchers have not directed their endeavors along these lines. Some relation to the stages of learning can be found when the aim is to reduce behavioral occurrences. Pupils who display excessive amounts of behavior already have acquired inappropriate or undesirable responses and are most likely too proficient in their execution. In these instances, the aim is to reduce or eliminate these performance repertoires because they interfere with positive learning. Although there probably are definite stages of unlearning that individuals pass through as inappropriate behavioral repertoires are decreased, only two stages have been researched: *reduction* and *maintenance*. Figure 5.1 illustrates these stages.

These stages are important to consider, for it is often vital to the learning situation that inappropriate, competing behavioral repertoires be controlled. Usually this is achieved through direct intervention. Also, it is

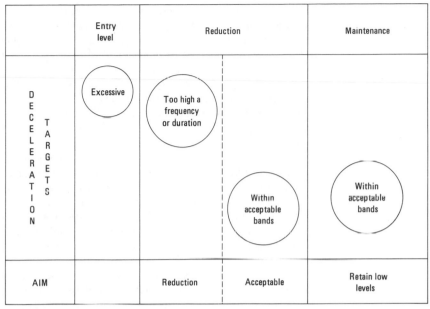

Figure 5.1   Stages that occur when the aim is deceleration or reduction in the frequency or duration of an undesirable behavior.

critical for maintenance to occur, for once the reduction has been achieved, the low levels of the treatment period must be maintained. Unfortunately, researchers have not clearly determined the influence of specific reduction tactics by stages of learning. Although of potential future use, this organizational scheme is not efficient for this chapter.

One common way to organize information about interventions that aim to decrease performance is to group tactics by the way they are presented. Some tactics involve removal: of the individual, of people's attention from the individual, or of reinforcing events. Other tactics require the delivery of the intervention: adding instructions, issuing reprimands, or scheduling unpleasant events contingent upon the inappropriate behavior's occurrence. Whether the intervention procedure requires the application to or removal of something from the educational situation, the intent is unchanged—all of the tactics described here decrease the frequency of undesirable behaviors. In the past all these tactics would have been called *punishers*. During recent years a number of punishment tactics have been developed, refined, and researched. For the sake of clarity each tactic is described under a separate heading, only one of which is (appropriately) called punishment.

Many learning disabled youngsters come to the school situation with a number of behavioral repertoires counterproductive to learning. Often these behavior patterns are the primary reasons for referral to special education. Inappropriate classroom behavior can disrupt the learning situation not only for the target student, but also for the entire class. Usually, some undesirable behaviors are exhibited by all class members. These become a problem when their intensity or frequency is so great that they become noticeable and, therefore, disturbing to the teacher and the peer group. In some cases, behavioral excesses are mild in nature and high frequency is the problem. Being out of one's seat and talking out of turn are very disruptive when the frequency is high. In other cases, the behavior of concern is not mild in nature and even a low frequency is undesirable. It might take only one aggressive act or one broken window a day to cause consternation from school officials. Whether the nature of the behavior of concern is mild or severe, of low or high frequency, if the learning situation is disturbed, remediation must be planned.

One caution must be added. Some learning disabled students have a variety of behavioral problems. When initial targets are selected for change, sometimes they all seem to fall into the behavioral excess category. In such cases teachers often are tempted to turn all their attention to decreasing these problems. White and Haring (1976) present a philosophy that has merit, and should be considered when the reduction of many behaviors is the target. They contend that for some students enrolled in special education, the entire remedial program is aimed at the reduction of a series of inappropriate behaviors, with no positive programs scheduled. The only view the student has of the teacher is negative. They suggest that a *fair pair* philosophy be adopted wherein for every negative behavior targeted for reduction, a positive behavior is targeted for improvement. In other words, an attempt at a balanced situation should be sought. This seems to be a wise educational philosophy based on common sense. The suggestion is for teachers to follow the fair pair philosophy when planning entire educational programs for their students.

When disruptive or undesirable behavior problems come to the attention of teachers, direct remediation is warranted. Before drastic actions are taken, it might be advisable to make some minor changes in the educational environment first. For example, Buckley and Walker (1978) suggest that simply changing the arrangement of student desks might be sufficient to reduce disruption to acceptable levels. Lovitt (1978) suggests that preventive measures can be taken so that classroom atmospheres are developed where disruptions are less likely to occur. Consistently stating and enforcing some simple classroom rules, for example, could prove to be effective preventative measures. He also believes that allowing children to participate in the development of decisions about the classroom organization can alleviate potential behavior problems. In addition, Lovitt offers some interesting observations about many classrooms: they are uninteresting and even boring. Possibly, if classrooms were by nature more fun and interesting, behavior problems might decrease.

A new trend in social research also adds information to literature about the remediation of inappropriate behavior. In several experiments, researchers (Ayllon, Layman, & Burke, 1972; Ayllon & Roberts, 1974) studied the relationship between improved academic performance and the amount of disruption. When children were reinforced for better academic achievement, their levels of disruption decreased to acceptable levels without direct intervention. Ayllon and Roberts (1974) conclude that "a reciprocal relationship may exist between academic performance and disruptive behavior, not the traditionally held 'make them sit still so they will learn better,' but rather a 'teach them better and they may be still' relationship" (p. 75).

The remainder of this section is a review of those tactics that reduce or eliminate undesirable student performances. Discussion is organized into two general areas: tactics that are actualized through the removal of something, and those requiring the application of an event.

Removal

Intervention strategies that functionally reduce the frequency of behaviors through their removal are described below. The mildest removal reduction tactics are discussed first and the most severe last, in the hope that teachers will try mild versions before they move to harsher tactics.

Extinction.   Extinction has been observed systematically in research for a number of years (Fuller, 1949). In many cases it is a procedure deliberately scheduled to cause a reduction in the frequency of a target behavior; in other cases it is a phenomenon teachers seek to avoid. When a desired behavior is reinforced, particularly on a continuous schedule, and the reinforcement is discontinued, the once increased behavior decreases rapidly and dramatically; this is referred to as extinction. It is the reason why teachers should move from continuous to intermittent schedules of reinforcement during the instructional process, thereby retaining appropriate behavior patterns where desired.

The most common form of an extinction procedure applied to reduce the frequency of classroom behaviors is *ignoring*. Allen, Hart, Buell, Harris, and Wolf (1964), in their landmark study, clearly demonstrated the power of adult attention on nursery school children's behavior. They showed that behavior correlates to the application and withdrawal of teacher attention. Sajwaj, Twardosz, and Burke (1972) also found ignoring to be a powerful intervention. When the teacher in their study ignored a student when he initiated speech to the teacher, speech to peers increased and initiations to teacher decreased.

Tantrums of young children also have been eliminated through the use of the ignoring procedure. Williams (1959) demonstrated that parents, by ignoring young children's tantrums, could cause their elimination; Zimmerman and Zimmerman (1962) eliminated tantrums in the classroom through ignoring. Lovitt, Lovitt, Eaton, and Kirkwood (1973) found that even when peers contingently ignored inappropriate behavior of their classmates, undesirable occurrences decreased.

Others (Hall, Fox, Willard, Goldsmith, Emerson, Owen, Davis, & Porcia, 1971; Roberts & Smith, 1977), however, found that ignoring inappropriate behavior was ineffective when used alone. In fact, several researchers (Becker, Madsen, Arnold, & Thomas, 1967; Madsen, Becker, & Thomas, 1968) noted that disruption actually increased during the condition that employed only ignoring.

When ignoring was paired with reinforcement procedures, such as praise, the tactic proved very effective. Inappropriate behavior decreased and desirable behavior increased through the combined use of ignoring and the reinforcement of approximations of the desired behavior (Birnbrauer, Bijou, Wolf, & Kidder, 1965).

Lovitt (1978) feels that ignoring is a good tactic for teachers to learn how to apply:

> *One advantage of using extinction is that it can be an extremely effective technique, particularly when a desired incompatible behavior is simultaneously reinforced. Another advantage is that the effects are long lasting, generally more so than when other decelerating tactics are arranged.* (p. 23)

Of course there are instances when ignoring is not the appropriate tactic to select. For example, when adult attention is not controlling the target behavior, ignoring it usually does not reduce its frequency. In such cases, some of the tactics suggested below might be more effective.

Withdrawal of reinforcement.   A number of tactics rely on the principles of withdrawal of reinforcement. As the words imply, these interventions involve taking away things that are reinforcing to the individual. Parents who deny their children privileges for misbehavior are applying a withdrawal of reinforcement procedure. Baer (1962), in a now classic laboratory study, used withdrawal of reinforcement to decrease thumbsucking. His five-year-old subject watched cartoons. When he sucked his thumb, the cartoons were turned off, and thumbsucking decreased.

Another form of withdrawal of positive reinforcement is referred to as *response cost*. Kazdin (1977) provides this definition: "Response cost refers to a procedure in which a positive reinforcer is lost or some penalty is involved. . . . The most commonly used form of response cost is the withdrawal of tokens or fines" (p. 69). Sometimes points, slips of paper, or sequentially numbered cards are given to students noncontingently, and are taken away when undesirable behavior occurs (Hall, Axelrod, Foundopoulos, Shellman, Campbell, & Cranston, 1971; Sajwaj, Culver, Hall, & Lehr, 1972; Sulzbacher & Houser, 1968). Response cost also was used to decrease errors made on academic assignments (Lovitt & Smith, 1972). Most commonly, response cost or fining is used in token economy programs (described later in this chapter), in which youngsters earn points through good behavior and lose points because of inappropriate actions. For example, response cost was used in a model residential program, Achievement Place, for predelinquent youths (Phillips, 1968) to modify many behaviors such as punctuality and aggressive verbal statements.

When response cost situations are arranged, students are not required to leave the educational situation, and the consequences of their actions more closely approximate real life. For response cost to work, however, the fine must be significant.

Timeout.   Gast and Nelson (1977a) provide the following definition of timeout: "Operationally defined, timeout refers to the contingent withdrawal of

The youngster in the foreground did not participate in the group activity appropriately. He was asked to leave the group for a few minutes. This is an example of the least severe form of timeout: contingent observation.

those reinforcing stimuli thought to be maintaining the behavior of interest" (p. 461). They indicate that there are at least three major variations of timeout. The first, *contingent observation*, is the mildest form and involves a combination of timeout and modeling. The student is removed from a group activity, but remains in close proximity so that he or she can observe students interacting and participating appropriately. A student misbehaving during a circle time activity might be requested to return to his or her desk for a short period of time and watch classmates participating in the desired manner.

The next form of timeout is referred to as *exclusion timeout* and requires that the student be removed from the learning activity. The educational components are missing, for the student cannot observe the appropriate performance of his or her peers. A disruptive student might be excused from music and requested to return to homeroom.

The most severe variation of timeout (and the one most publicized), *seclusion timeout*, necessitates the use of an isolation room. The misbehaving student is removed from the classroom and spends a specified amount of time alone. Upon each act of aggression, for example, a student was instructed to go to the timeout room for a period of three minutes. When seclusion timeout is used, several important precautions must be taken. First, an appropriate place or room must be found. It should be well-lighted, properly ventilated, sizable (at least six feet by six feet), safe, unlocked, and preferably having a window so the student can be observed periodically (Gast & Nelson, 1977a, 1977b). Also, the duration of timeout should be predetermined (anywhere from one to five minutes is usually sufficient[1]). It is advisable for release to be contingent upon good behavior. Some (Clark, Rowbury, Baer, & Baer, 1973; Plummer, Baer, & LeBlanc, 1977) advocate an extension release clause. Sometimes referred to as a *changeover delay* procedure, this extends timeout for fifteen seconds if the student is misbehaving when timeout is scheduled to end: to be released the student must act appropriately for at least the last fifteen seconds of the timeout experience.

Although timeout has received a substantial amount of attention recently, it is not a new or novel intervention. The first documented use of timeout was by Itard in the early 1800s as he attempted to train the *enfant sauvage*, Victor (Lane, 1976). An isolation technique also is described by Olson (1935):

> *In general, the careful teacher attempts to avoid situations in which a child is given the feeling of being cut off from a group. An occasional child, however, may "go to pieces" so completely as to disrupt either the comfort or activities of his associates in a room. Nursery school teachers, in particular, have found it highly advantageous to remove such a child from the group to a place where he may relax and acquire control without being a distracting influence or attracting the attention he may be seeking. In some instances special rooms have been set aside for this purpose. The isolation technique must be used skillfully in order to be an educational experience for the child, gradually modifying him in the direction of greater control. This goal may be defeated if the child regards the treatment simply as punishment and develops a feeling of antagonism toward the teacher.* (pp. 378–379)

More recently, timeout has proven to be an effective intervention procedure when scheduled to reduce or eliminate a variety of undesirable behaviors. For example, stealing food (Ayllon, 1963; Barton, Guess, Garcia, & Baer, 1970), tantrumming (Wolf, Risley, & Mees, 1964), physical aggression and verbal abusiveness (Bostow & Bailey, 1969; Hewett, 1967), general disruptiveness (Clark et al., 1973; Ramp, Ulrich, & Dulaney, 1971), and talking out of turn (Luiselli, Helfen, & Anderson, 1976) were reduced substantially through the use of timeout. Timeout was even effective for peers who had not received it. Wilson, Robertson, Herlong, and Haynes (1979) found that the untargeted aggressive behavior of the classmates of an aggressive kindergartner showed concomitant changes that paralleled those of the child who received timeout.

Timeout, however, is not always effective. Solnick, Rincover, and Peterson (1977), for example, found that an autistic girl's self-stimulatory responses increased when timeout was scheduled. Apparently, timeout served as a reinforcer for her autistic-like behaviors. When in timeout, she

---

[1]White, Nielsen, & Johnson (1972) compared different durations of timeout and found that one minute of timeout was as effective as five or thirty minutes if the student had not been exposed to longer durations of timeout previously.

was free to engage in these undesirable behaviors without correction. Plummer et al. (1977) also found that timeout can serve as a reinforcer; in their study, disruptive behavior persisted even when timeout was scheduled. The instructional situation was not reinforcing to the students and timeout provided a possible escape. This phenomenon also was observed by Solnick et al. (1977) in their second experiment, in which they found that when the classroom environment is impoverished and not of reinforcing value, timeout is ineffective.

Teachers who work with learning disabled students must be cognizant of these findings. For students who find the academic situation frustrating and even punishing at times, timeout may prove to cause increases rather than decreases in the target behaviors. Inappropriateness may increase when timeout is scheduled because it allows the student to escape an aversive situation. When the learning process is not enjoyable and teachers do not compensate for the often boring and repetitive activities they plan for their students, even timeout, a tactic designed to be unpleasant, can become a more attractive alternative to students.

Timeout, particularly seclusion timeout, has received considerable attention from the press and public recently. There are some very undesirable features of seclusion timeout, and careful consideration must be given to the seriousness of the behavioral infraction before it is scheduled. Frequently it is misused and abused. The implementation of timeout is costly to both student and teacher. The student loses valuable instructional time, and the teacher is forced to schedule an intervention that can be difficult to manage.

Because of the furor over seclusion timeout and because of several court actions placed against residential facilities for the handicapped, a number of precautions must be taken before it is implemented. First, an appropriate and safe place must be located. If a room cannot be found where an adult can monitor the actions of the student, another intervention should be scheduled. For the protection of the teacher, the school principal should be consulted next. If the school administration agrees that seclusion timeout is necessary, the parents should be contacted and their permission obtained. Once timeout is initiated, precise records on its use should be kept. A sample data sheet is provided in Figure 5.2. On that sheet the number of times a student goes to the timeout room and the amount of time spent there are noted.

Timeout and its variations can be very effective tools for teachers who are trying to eliminate or greatly reduce behavioral repertoires that interfere with the learning process. Implementation should occur with care and caution. The student's performance should warrant timeout either because it was unaltered by other tactics or because the transgressions are serious.

Application   A vast number of tactics, when applied, reduce the occurrences of inappropriate or undesirable behaviors. These can be as mild as specifying classroom rules, softly reprimanding disruptive students, or reinforcing students for behaviors incompatible with the undesirable one. For many learning disabled students, more direct and even punitive tactics are needed if nonproductive behaviors that inhibit learning are to be eliminated.

| | | Student's name | | Target behavior |

Day	Date	Time Timeout Initiated	Total Time in Timeout	Description of Behavior in Timeout

Figure 5.2   Sample record sheet to be posted near the door of seclusion timeout room.

Rules.   Of course, it is advisable to first use instructions to inform students of the expected standards of classroom behavior. Students can even be active participants in the formation of the rules for their classroom environments. In some cases, this is sufficient to produce the desired results; but, unfortunately, frequently it is not. A number of studies have investigated the influence of rules and instructions on general disruption. In most cases, rules have proven ineffective and other interventions had to be employed (Greenwood, Hops, Delquadri, & Guild, 1974; Long & Williams 1973; Madsen et al., 1968; O'Leary, Becker, Evans, & Saudargas, 1969). One minor addition to rules was offered by O'Leary, Kaufman, Kass, & Drabman (1970). In their study, softly reprimanding students who violated classroom rules was effective in reducing disruption. In fact, reprimands audible only to the disruptive student were more effective than using a tone of voice audible to the whole class. Certainly instructions, rules, and reprimands should all be tried before more drastic measures are taken.

Counterconditioning.   When this procedure is applied, a behavior incompatible with the undesirable one is reinforced. Disruption was modified by ignoring inappropriate actions and reinforcing desirable behavior (Becker et al., 1967; Madsen et al., 1968). Many situations occur in classrooms in which an alternate behavior can be reinforced. For instance, one cannot be in seat and out of seat at the same time; one cannot be talking out of turn and be quiet concurrently. Teachers should try to reinforce positive behavior before they implement unpleasant tactics. In many instances, direct intervention on the inappropriate or undesirable behavior is necessary. It is advisable, however, to first use a positive procedure, such as counterconditioning, so the classroom atmosphere can be as free from negative occurrences as possible.

Schedules of Reinforcement

Various reinforcement schedules can be applied to decrease inappropriate behavior of students. One such arrangement is referred to as *differential reinforcement for lower rates of performance* (DRL). Students receive no reinforcement when the frequency of their inappropriate behavior is above a certain level. Sajwaj et al. (1972), for example, reduced talking out of turn and being out of seat through a DRL procedure. No more than two disruptive behaviors were allowed a day. On days when the student met the criterion, he was allowed to wear a five-star general badge, which merited special privileges. When the badge was earned for two consecutive days, a letter of commendation was sent to the principal. Others (Dietz & Repp, 1973; Hall, Fox et al., 1971) used DRL schedules of reinforcement to reduce talking out of turn for elementary as well as secondary students.

The DRL schedule can be applied gradually. If a teacher wants to encourage a reduction in a student's error rate in oral reading, the criterion could be gradually lowered until the student's rate is at the desired level. For example, reinforcement would be given at first if the student's error rate fell below ten. After several days of meeting that criterion, the criterion could be lowered to eight. Once the error rate scores reach this level for several days, the criterion could be lowered again. This gradual reduction would occur until the student reached the aim score for error rate in oral reading.

Another reinforcement schedule used to reduce target behaviors is referred to as *differential reinforcement of other behaviors* (DRO). According to Axelrod (1977), "a DRO schedule is one in which reinforcement is delivered only if a particular behavior does not occur for a specified period of time" (p. 29). Schmidt and Ulrich (1969) used a DRO procedure to reduce excessive classroom noise. For every ten minutes that the noise was below a specified level, the class received two extra minutes of gym and a two-minute break. Lovitt (1978) describes a DRO schedule as one in which a range of behaviors is reinforced, but the targeted inappropriate behavior is neither directly punished nor reinforced. One must be careful to specify which actions receive reinforcement and which do not. Counterconditioning can involve the use of a DRO schedule, for the inappropriate behavior is not reinforced while its positive counterpart is.

Group contingencies.   Although group contingency systems can be used to stimulate increases in behavior (Evans & Oswalt, 1968), they are most frequently applied as reduction intervention packages. In group contingencies, a group of students either receives or loses reinforcement. The intervention can be dependent on the behavior of the whole group or of an individual.

Litow and Pumroy (1975) offer a convenient way of viewing major variations of group contingencies. They categorize group contingencies into three types: dependent, independent, and interdependent. In the dependent group contingency situation, the class receives reinforcement if a classmate earns it for them. When the independent version is used, a group goal is stated, but students earn reinforcement for themselves as they meet the goal set for the group. When interdependent group contingencies are applied, the behavior of the whole class determines whether reinforcement is received.

Evans and Oswalt (1968) used dependent group contingencies in a series of experiments aimed at improving students' academic performance. In one experiment, for example, if the target student correctly spelled specified words, the whole class was dismissed for recess five minutes early. In another experiment, the teacher read a story to the class for five minutes if the target student computed specific math problems accurately.

Brooks and Snow (1972) also used a dependent group contingency, but in this case their aim was to modify a ten-year-old boy's stealing. When he remained with the group he did not steal. The class was given points when he stayed with the group, finished his work on time, and evidenced appropriate behavior; they lost points when he violated rules.

Dependent group contingencies have proven to be effective strategies to employ if the behavior of one student is in need of modification. Several precautions should be taken, however, before this contingency system is employed. Target individuals should be capable of earning reinforcement for the group, for if they are not, their peers might inflict severe penalties on them because they failed and the group was denied its due reward.

Independent group contingencies have not been submitted to as much research as either dependent or interdependent group contingencies, but they are feasible for many classroom situations. Independent contingencies eliminate the competitive element present in many group contingency situations. Students can, with the assistance of the teacher, keep track of their own inappropriate behavior during an academic period. Students whose daily score is below the goal can leave for recess five minutes early; those who exceed the goal must stay in the classroom and continue working. An independent group contingency aimed at reducing errors is frequently applied to spelling, where the goal is for all students to make no errors. Spelling tests are given daily: as soon as a student makes a score of 100 percent he or she is dismissed from spelling for the rest of the week. For all those who meet the criterion a special Friday activity is arranged.

The most commonly used group contingencies are interdependent, in which the behavior of the group determines whether the group receives reinforcement. In one of the first published reports about the effectiveness of an interdependent contingency, Sulzbacher and Houser (1968) demonstrated its simplicity and power. This intervention was selected because the children engaged in acts that greatly bothered the teacher (using and talking about what these researchers referred to as the "naughty finger"). During intervention, the teacher placed a flip chart at the front of the room. On it

By flipping a card, the teacher is indicating to the class that they have lost one minute of freetime. This system is similar to the one used by Sulzbacher and Houser (1968).

were cards with the numbers 10 to zero. The first card showing was the number 10. This indicated that the students had 10 minutes of a special recess at the end of the day. For each transgression a card was flipped, revealing a lower number and indicating that the class lost one minute from their special recess time. Even on the first day of intervention a substantial reduction in the frequency of this behavior was noted. A variation of this tactic also was effective in modifying general disruptive behavior of middle school students (Long & Williams, 1973). The nice feature of this technique is that the teacher is not required to spend much time managing a complex record keeping system.

Interdependent group contingencies have effectively reduced classroom noise (Schmidt & Ulrich, 1969; Wilson & Hopkins, 1973), general classroom disruption (Greenwood et al., 1974; Herman & Tramontana, 1971), and classroom attention (Packard, 1970). Some (Speltz, Moore, & McReynolds, 1979) suggest that interdependent group contingencies are far superior to other forms of this tactic. A number of interesting variations of interdependent group contingencies have been employed. Wilson and Hopkins (1973), for example, used contingent popular music to modify excessive noise from junior high school students during home economics class. Rettig and Paulson (1975) suggest several novel variations. In one situation, the children wasted a substantial amount of time moving from one class to another. The teacher kept track of the amount of time wasted each day (average seven minutes). During intervention condition the teacher established a free activity period on Friday afternoons, but subtracted from that free period any time wasted in transition. Time spent in transition dropped to twenty-one seconds each day. In another situation, these researchers decreased inappropriate comments made during discussion time by making a blue pencil mark for each appropriate comment and a red mark for each inappropriate or off-topic comment. At the end of a discussion session, the teacher subtracted the red from the blue marks. The difference earned the students extra minutes of physical education time (which they enjoyed).

Interdependent group contingencies can be useful to teachers because the entire class is responsible for its collective actions. The procedure can be simple to manage and require little teacher time to implement. It is important, however, for the teacher to be certain that the children involved are capable of the requisite behavior. If not, undue pressure could be placed on the individual who causes the group to lose its opportunity for reinforcement. When one child consistently ruins the chances for the group, an individual contingency program could be arranged for that pupil, while the others participate in the group contingency. Also, the teacher must plan for the possibility that several students might actually enjoy subverting the program for the group. If this occurs, the teacher must make special arrangements for the subversive students. Interdependent group contingency programs can be very effective, particularly when the peer group's attention and reactions are the reasons that undesirable behavior occurs.

Overcorrection. The rationale of overcorrection, a relatively new intervention package, is for the offenders to assume responsibility for disruptions they have caused (Axelrod, Brantner, & Meddock, 1978). Overcorrection was developed and refined by Foxx and Azrin (1972)[2]; their aim was to find a reduction strategy that reeducates the offender but does not have the negative aspects of punishment. Most reduction tactics do not include an educational aspect. Contingent observation timeout includes a modeling component, but other forms of timeout not only exclude an educational component but, in fact, remove the individual from the educational situation. Overcorrection does not do this.

There are two forms of overcorrection: restitution and positive practice. The intent of *restitution overcorrection* is for an individual who destroys or alters an environment to assume the responsibility for not only rectifying the situation but also improving it so that it is better than its original state.

Foxx and Azrin (1972) feel that the restitution tactic should be applied immediately after a transgression and should be directly related to the act. Also, a substantial amount of effort should be required to remedy the situation. Restitution requires that all objects in a disturbed area be replaced or all persons offended receive an apology (Rusch & Close, 1976). The intent is to teach socially appropriate behaviors along with applying a procedure designed to decrease the inappropriate ones. According to Rusch and Close, overcorrection usually is composed of the following: stop the person from the ongoing, undesirable activity; verbal reprimand; verbal instructions to guide restitution or positive practice; physical guidance (if necessary); and return to the appropriate activity. Examples of behaviors that might be modified

---

[2]There is some indication, however, that it was used before the Foxx and Azrin work. One notable example is the walking (gait) instructional program developed at Parsons State Training School and State Hospital's Mimosa Cottage Project during the 1960s. A film on this project has been produced (University of Kansas, 1967).

This student wrote on his desk. The teacher scheduled a restitution overcorrection procedure by having him clean all of the desks in the room.

through restitution overcorrection and possible forms of the intervention are shown in Table 5.1.

The other form of overcorrection is referred to as *positive practice overcorrection*. Forced practice of desired forms of the target behavior are encouraged. One variation of positive practice overcorrection is required relaxation for agitation. Webster and Azrin (1973) used this tactic to reduce the agitated behavioral repertoires of adult mental patients. The procedure involved teaching the patients to be calm, composed, and relaxed by having them spend a fixed amount of time in bed for each agitated episode. It is possible, as in this case, to consider overcorrection as a calming down period. Of course, this was developed for extreme cases and is not practical for typical school problems. With some alterations, however, teaching children who become distressed quickly to gain self-control by learning to relax and be quiet might be beneficial.

In a more common situation, Azrin and Powers (1975) studied the effects of delayed positive practice overcorrection in modifying youngsters'

Table 5.1 **Examples of restitution overcorrection**

Undesirable Act	*Restitution Procedure*
1. Throw and overturn furniture	Restore whole room to a pleasant appearance, straighten furniture, dust and clean whole room
2. Bite others	Assist with medical attention to victim and clean mouth with antiseptic for 10 minutes
3. Write on desk	Clean all desks in class
4. Write obscenities on wall	Paint whole wall
5. Steal	Return item stolen and an additional item
6. Chew objects	Cleanse mouth with antiseptic
7. Throw rocks on playground	Pick up litter and rocks to clear ground

SOURCE: Some of the examples in this table were taken from Foxx (1976), and Foxx and Azrin (1972).

talking out of turn. When the teacher delayed the positive practice of hand-raising until the next recess time (a time more convenient for her), talking out during class time was reduced. The students were required to practice appropriate behavior to gain permission to speak without disrupting the class routine.

Positive practice overcorrection has been used frequently to decrease autistic-like behavior (Epstein, Doke, Sajwaj, Sorrell, & Rimmer, 1974; Foxx and Azrin, 1973; Kissel & Whitman, 1977; Newman, Whorton, & Simpson, 1977; Simpson & Sasso, 1978). Examples of situations in which positive practice might be applied successfully can be found on Table 5.2.

It is important that the reader not confuse positive practice overcorrection with negative practice. In negative practice (a tactic recommended to reduce stuttering), the student practices the undesirable behavior over and over (Dunlap, 1942; Rutherford, 1940). Positive practice, on the other hand, requires the individual to practice a desired form of the target behavior.

Since overcorrection is a new tactic and not fully researched or refined, researchers have not determined whether there are side effects, whether maintenance and generalization are facilitated, or what the optimum duration of the overcorrection procedure should be. Further, it has been researched and field tested primarily with the moderately retarded and severely handicapped populations. It does, however, hold promise for the learning disabled student as well.

Punishment.   Punishment is the most severe reduction tactic. As with reinforcement, punishment is functionally related to the frequency of the target behavior, but in this case the behavior is meant to decrease. Although all tactics in this section could be referred to as punishment, for the sake of clarity *punishment* here includes those tactics involving the application of aversive consequences.

Punishment has been long and commonly used by both parents and teachers to modify children's behavior (Hewett, 1967). One reason for the widespread use of punishment is its effectiveness. If often yields the desired

Table 5.2   **Examples of positive practice overcorrection**

Undesirable Act	*Positive Practice Procedure*
1. Nailbiting	Hold hands at side for one minute
2. Autistic-like gestures	Hold hands stiff for 15 seconds
3. Inappropriate jargon-like verbalization	Hand over mouth for 30 seconds; then repeat words, phrases, and appropriate sounds
4. Poor spelling on a composition assignment	Look up all words spelled incorrectly in dictionary and write a paragraph about each word
5. Use of slang words	Practice using correct words in phrases
6. Agitation and disruption	Required relaxation
7. Talking out of turn	Raise hand and wait for teacher to call on student during five-minute practice sessions

SOURCE: Some of the examples in this table were taken from Azrin and Powers (1975), Epstein et al. (1974), Freeman, Graham, and Ritvo (1975), Newman et al. (1977), Phillips (1968), Webster and Azrin (1973).

results faster than other tactics (Azrin & Holz, 1966; Baer, 1970; Lovitt, 1978). Heron (1978) comments on the popularity of this procedure:

> *The use of punishment procedures to reduce, suppress, or eliminate inappropriate classroom behavior has had a long and controversial history. In the past the capricious use of punishment by the teacher was seldom, if ever, challenged. The "hickory stick," dunce caps, and the like were commonly used to control a child's inappropriate behavior and to demonstrate the power and authority of the teacher.* (p. 243)

Why many people have a propensity to select punishment as a first choice tactic rather than as a last resort is not clear. When deciding on its use, its negative aspects should be considered.

Many researchers (Baer, 1970; Heron, 1978; Johnston, 1972; Lovitt, 1978; Risley, 1968) caution teachers about some negative ramifications of punishment. Children often associate the aversive technique with the person who administers it. Punishment increases the likelihood of the student trying to escape the situation. Its influence does not usually generalize across settings, so often it needs to be applied in all situations in which the behavior occurs. It can even result in overgeneralization, thus decreasing positive behavior. Punishment is not a behavior-building technique, for new skills are not taught through this method.

In a study by Risley (1968), autistic rocking was the target; when punishment was applied, another undesirable behavior appeared. Whether symptom substitution is a common problem is not definitely known, but for this child it certainly was an undesirable side effect.

Hewett (1968) makes a good and interesting point about punishment in the schools. He feels that punishment is a nonproductive tactic because it puts fear into a classroom. Children perform because they are afraid not to, or do not perform because they are afraid to. This, he posits, does not foster a good learning environment.

If punishment is to be used as an intervention strategy in a classroom, teachers should follow some steps and precautions. First, the nature of the behavior must be considered. Is it dangerous? Could the student be hurt? Could others be hurt? Also, is it frequent? Is less serious behavior causing problems because of repetition? Could property be damaged? Data should be collected to determine whether the behavior is severe or frequent enough to warrant the use of punishment. Other, nonaversive or less aversive tactics should be tried first; data indicating the ineffectiveness of milder tactics should represent need for more serious measures before punishment is used. Although consent from the principal and parents is not legally required, it is suggested that permission be granted in writing before punishment is applied in classroom situations (Repp & Deitz, 1978). Some (Buckley & Walker, 1978; Johnston, 1972) feel that rules should be specified clearly to the student *before* the infraction occurs. The student should understand why he or she is being punished. When unacceptable (inappropriate) behavior is noted, no threat or warning should be given. MacMillan, Forness, and Trumbull (1973) suggest that punishment should be delivered early in the response sequence; the student should not be allowed to complete the undesirable behavior. Each and every time the target behavior occurs, the punishment procedure should be applied. Although little research has investigated the effects of different schedules of punishment, in one study (Kircher, Pear, & Martin, 1971) a ratio of 1:1 (every time the behavior occurs, punishment is delivered) was most effective. There does seem to be substantial agreement (Azrin & Holz, 1966; Buckley & Walker, 1978; Heron, 1978; Johnston, 1972; MacMillan et al., 1973) that teachers should select a punishment tactic of great enough intensity—it is not advisable to start with a low intensity level and have to increase it gradually, because students get used to it. This results in the tactic losing its power.

Buckley and Walker (1978) offer some sound advice about the punishment situation. They feel that when teachers use punishment, they should make a concentrated effort to reinforce many other behaviors of the student. Teachers should develop good, positive relationships with all of their students; however, this seems to be even more crucial when punishment procedures have to be used.

Professionals have shown a considerable amount of concern about punishment. There are few laws or rules against the use of punishment in the schools. In fact, Smith, Polloway, and West (1979) cite a recent Supreme Court ruling that supports the use of corporal punishment in schools because schools act *in loco parentis*. Baer (1970) posits that because punishment is so effective, it could become a reinforcer for those who use it, resulting in higher frequencies of its use. Smith et al. are afraid that the more severely handicapped students are, the more likely that punishment will be selected as an intervention. Since there are few constraints against the use of the procedure, the worst fears of some could be realized.

It is important to note that punishment can be mild as well as severe. For example, the quantity of seatwork assignments increased when students were required to stay in from recess when they did not complete enough work (Catera & Heron, 1978). Teachers have long used stern facial expressions to control classroom behavior. Hall, Axelrod et al. (1971) made students stay after school contingent upon being out of their seats. Light shock was used for nonattention (Kircher et al., 1971) and for autistic-like behavior (Risley, 1968).

The controversy over punishment has raged for years. Olson (1935) stated that punishment has no real place in "modern" schools. He believed that the use of punishment by a teacher was a sign of incompetence and inefficiency, and that direct and rewarding consequences are more effective. Baer (1970), on the other hand, feels that punishment might well be a worthwhile tactic, particularly when the target behavior is harmful.

TEACHING TACTICS THAT EITHER INCREASE OR DECREASE PERFORMANCES

Chapter 4 and the previous part of this chapter dealt with intervention strategies that either increase or decrease students' performance levels. Some intervention strategies, however, are used in *both* of these situations.

Usually they incorporate a number of tactics and form packages of procedures that aim to remediate an individual's overall abilities. In some cases,
they are scheduled only during a specific time of the day or for a specific skill;
in other cases, they are in effect during the entire school day and comprise the
entire treatment program. Three distinctively different package intervention
strategies are discussed here: *token economies, peer management,* and
self-management.

Token Economies   Only a brief description of token economies is provided here because token
programs can be quite intricate in design and application.[3] Token economies
incorporate almost all of the principles and procedures described in both
Chapters 4 and 5. For example, procedures described as priming, programming, and refinement tactics have all been incorporated into token programs.

A wide variety of reinforcing events (edibles, concrete items, and free
time) can be and have been used. The various schedules of reinforcement
were tested and refined in token economies. In addition, most of the reduction tactics (ranging from response cost to punishment) are salient features of
token programs. The unique feature of token economies is the use of a
tangible item to represent the amount of reinforcement earned or lost due to
the occurrence of specific behavior. The tangible item can be a mark (point)
placed on a card, or chips (such as poker chips), or the Peabody Language
Development Kits tokens (PLDK-AGS, 1965). These tangible items are
referred to as tokens, and serve as a concrete representation of achievement.
They, like money, are generalized reinforcers, for they allow the individual
to "purchase" an almost infinite number of things or privileges.

The use of token economies to encourage the improvement of individuals' skills is not new. They were developed and refined during the early
1960s, and were implemented across a variety of settings and groups of
people. There were several early demonstration token cottage programs (a
twenty-four-hour-a-day remedial program using a token economy). Ayllon
and Azrin (1964) clearly demonstrated the effectiveness of such programs
with severely disturbed women. Girardeau and Spradlin (1964) initiated the
now famous token cottage program for retarded girls, Mimosa Cottage. Concurrently, successful efforts were made to use a token economy for classroom
activities in the educational component at Ranier State School (Birnbrauer et
al., 1965). In the ambitious Santa Monica Project, Hewett, Taylor, and
Artuso (1969) applied these procedures to an entire school district's special
education program. Possibly the first effort to test the influence of token
economies in a classroom for learning disabled students was made by
McKenzie, Clark, Wolf, Kothera, and Benson (1968). Academic work was
rewarded through tokens and the students' parents managed the delivery of
the rewards. Since these early demonstration projects, the number of token
programs has expanded greatly. They have been used in residential programs, special education classrooms, regular education classrooms, after-

[3] A number of fine texts and chapters are available that deal exclusively with the implementation
of token economies. Interested readers are referred to Drabman (1976); Kazdin (1977); and
Stainback, Payne, Stainback, and Payne (1973).

PLDK-AGS tokens are often used in token economies as concrete representations of achievement.

school remedial classes, and more. After twenty years of use and refinement, the clear power and effectiveness of token programs is well documented.

Token programs have several advantages worth noting. After some practice with the system, teachers find tokens easy to dispense, causing little disruption in the teaching routine. Tokens can be given or taken away immediately after a behavior occurs, while the actual receipt of reinforcement occurs at a later, convenient time. If privileges (rather than costly items) are used as the reinforcers, the economic costs can be low. Because token systems can increase and reduce student performances, only one overall intervention plan is necessary. This seems to make the general classroom operation run efficiently, since both teacher and students clearly understand the contingencies operating during the entire day.

Another advantage of token programs was found by Iwata and Bailey (1974), who compared token and response cost interventions. Although no differences in student performance were noted, the teachers' praise rates were substantially higher while positive, token programs were in effect. When the response cost intervention was scheduled, the teachers' verbal disapproving statements were considerably higher.

Several cautions about the use of overall token economies in classroom situations must be noted, however. First, children must always have the opportunity to earn more tokens than they can realistically lose. Broden, Hall, Dunlap, and Clark (1970) found that when students end up owing points, the general effectiveness of the program is seriously affected. In that situation timeout had to be included. Back-up procedures should be planned for those rare instances when neither positive reinforcement nor response cost controls disruptive behavior. A more serious problem is discussed by Kazdin and Bootzin (1972). In their review of the literature, they found that in many cases the positive changes noted while token programs are in effect deteriorate once the tokens are withdrawn. In other words, maintenance is not guaranteed and direct intervention often is necessary to maintain the positive changes encouraged during the treatment program.

Although this caution has not been researched, many teachers who have used token programs in their self-contained or resource programs have observed that some students have a more difficult time in the regular program because tokens are not earned there. Many of those teachers work cooperatively with the regular class teachers who receive their students, so that program continuity can be established and reintegration can occur smoothly.

Because of these disadvantages, one recommendation is to implement entire token programs only when the educational situation definitely warrants such drastic measures. For students who need concrete representations of their academic and social improvement, token programs can be beneficial. They are more positive in nature than programs consisting entirely of reduction tactics. When they are implemented, teachers must spend time (at the end of the remedial program) helping students learn the reinforcing value of such intrinsic, intangible reinforcement as praise and the reward of self-achievement. Deliberate efforts have to be made so that these students can cope successfully in regular educational situations.

The following two combination packages are less artificial, and possibly could be tried before implementing entire token programs. If token economies are scheduled, both peer management and self-management procedures can be instrumental in maintaining gains made during the treatment program. They definitely should be implemented after a token program and before a student is mainstreamed.

Peer Management   The use of children to teach other children is not a new concept. Gartner, Kohler, and Riessman (1971) point out that as early as the first century, Roman teachers indicated that younger children could profit from instruction from older classmates. Across time, it seems evident that students who tutor and those who receive tutoring both benefit from the learning situation (Paolitto, 1976). Three distinct areas in which peer management has proven beneficial are tutoring, behavioral management, and peer management to maintain.

Tutoring.   Many tutoring systems have been explored in schools. Probably the most common arrangement is *cross-age tutoring*, in which an older student tutors a younger one. Cross-age tutoring has positively altered students' written expression (Drass & Jones, 1971), arithmetic performance (Greenwood, Sloane, & Baskin, 1974; Harris & Sherman, 1973; Johnson & Bailey, 1974), reading (Howell & Kaplan, 1978; Trovato & Bucher, 1980; Willis, Crowder, & Morris, 1972), and spelling (Jenkins, Mayhall, Peschka, & Jenkins, 1974). Other researchers have found *same-age* or *classmate tutoring* also to be an effective and efficient use of resources. Classmate tutors have taught their peers to name geometric figures (Starlin, 1971), to spell better (Harris, Sherman, Henderson, & Harris, 1972), to read sight words (Parson & Heward, 1979), and to calculate arithmetic problems (Conlon, Hall, & Hanley, 1972; Kane & Alley, 1980).

If peer tutoring is to be employed successfully, several things must be considered. First, the tutors must be carefully selected. There should be a good fit between the two individuals who work together (Bloom, Note 1). The tutors must be trained (Howell & Kaplan, 1978; McGee, Kauffman, & Nussen, 1977). Tutors should be proficient in the skill they are assigned

Here, one student in the class is helping a classmate complete a workbook assignment. Peer tutoring can benefit both students and free a busy teacher to work with other students.

to teach as well as in teaching skills. It is beneficial to have tutors participate in training programs to learn how to use instruction, feedback, praise, and reinforcement efficiently. Bloom also feels that the tutors should be given defined space and specific materials.

There are other findings teachers should be aware of when they schedule tutoring in their classrooms. Patterson and Anderson (1964), for example, found that tutoring was more effective after second grade: third and fourth graders profited more from the tutoring experience than younger students. Devin-Sheehan, Feldman, and Allen (1976), through their work with the Ontario-Montclaire Demonstration Program, found that one-to-one cross-age tutoring was far superior to small-group tutoring. They also found that low achievers benefit from tutoring younger students, both academically and socially.

Tutors tend to retain their interest in tutoring and get better results from their pupils when they receive reinforcement for tutoring. Willis et al. (1972) divided their tutors into teams (the Fantastic Four, Mod Squad). The team with the highest efficiency rating (most changes in pupils) received a large trophy. In another study, Willis, Morris, and Crowder (1972) praised the tutors and rewarded them with gold pins after several weeks of work.

For teachers who have a wide discrepancy in the abilities of their students or a large number of students in their class, tutoring might be advantageous. Since one-to-one and individualized instruction is beneficial to most students, it may be important to implement individualization for particular students in particular areas. For already busy teachers, sometimes the only way to individualize instruction is to employ others who might be available. One ready resource to deploy is the students.

Behavioral managers.   Peers have helped classmates improve their social behavior. For example, peers residing in group homes for delinquent boys have managed total contingency systems, including token dispensing and fining (Graubard, 1969; Phillips, 1968). Several studies on the effectiveness of using peer behavioral managers in classroom situations indicate that peers can modify aggression (Grieger, Kauffman, & Grieger, 1976, Lazor son, 1980; Wahler, 1967), general classroom disruption (Solomon & Wahler, 1973), study behavior (Surratt, Ulrich, & Hawkins, 1969), and independent working and compliance (Siegel & Steinman, 1975).

Peers can be used as managers of their classmates to modify inappropriate social behavior. As with peer tutoring, behavioral managers should receive instruction about the role they are to play and reinforcement for executing their assignments properly. One clever use of a classmate as a behavioral engineer was conducted by Lovitt et al. (1973). The students, two nine-year-old learning disabled youngsters, were classmates and usually sat near each other in class. One of the students tended to engage in inappropriate and distracting verbal behavior, which the authors generically referred to as "bathroom language." During the intervention condition, the peer manager, upon inappropriate language from his classmate, said, "I don't like you when you say _____." Then he picked up his schoolwork and moved to another desk, away from the other child. Within a short period of time, the frequency of this type of language dropped to zero and remained at that level. Most likely the use of a classmate as the behavioral manager (rather than the teacher) created a positive atmosphere for both boys, and released the teacher from interfering in the situation.

When carefully monitored, peers can effectively be used as behavioral managers to help develop a more positive classroom environment. Since in many situations peers encourage inappropriate behavior, it seems worthwhile to encourage them to develop more positive behavior in each other.

Peer management to maintain.   In many situations, inappropriate behavior occurs because the peer group encourages it and reinforces its maintenance. If, after a treatment program, the environment that originally reinforced undesirable behavior is not altered, the likelihood of that behavior reoccurring is increased. Since "the peer group is likely to provide immediate and powerful social reinforcers for the maintenance of deviant behavior" (Patterson, Littman, & Bricker, 1967, p. 37), it seems that the peer group must be reprogrammed if maintenance of treatment effects is to occur.

Several efforts to change classroom environments by teaching peers to reinforce positive rather than negative behavior in their classmates have been successful (Buehler, Patterson, & Furniss, 1966; Patterson & Brodsky, 1966). Unfortunately, the theme of this 1960s research has not been expanded upon. As the importance of maintenance of treatment effects becomes more and more obvious to teachers and researchers, perhaps the use of peer management to facilitate maintenance of desirable behavior will be studied carefully.

Self-management[4]   Some authors (Fagen, Long, & Stevens, 1975) believe that self-management is a part and priority of the American way of life; that self-control, for example, is an integral part of the American democratic value system. Despite these values, many special and regular education classrooms allow students

[4]Those interested in more detail about self-management procedures and their influence should refer to the following comprehensive reviews: O'Leary and Dubey (1979), and Rosenbaum and Drabman (1979).

little, if any, freedom of choice. This has implications far beyond the classroom. As Fagen, Long, and Stevens pointed out:

> *While the value for self-control is profound and enduring, insufficient attention has been given to developing the personal skills or educational opportunities which foster the responsible and fulfilling expression of self-control.* (p. 13)

Because our educational system allows little opportunity for children to make choices, and because we do not teach children how to manage their own lives, it may be concluded that "the graduates of our educational systems have been less competent in their capacity to willingly seek and freely choose among available alternatives" (Fagen et al., p. 29).

When students present behavioral and academic problems at school, teachers employ direct remediation activities to these difficulties. Usually, after considerable effort, undesirable behavioral incidents come under the teacher's control. If, however, students do not learn to regulate their own behavioral patterns, once out of the control of their parents and the educational system, serious problems can reemerge. O'Leary and O'Leary (1977) state that "knowing how a teacher can influence a child is extremely useful, but the problems of self-management must be addressed if one is interested in long-term behavioral change" (p. 301).

It is also important, as adults, for individuals to be able to schedule their own activities, determine how they will spend leisure time, and set priorities for the expenditure of their own time and resources. Unfortunately, these skills often are not part of the educational curriculum and many learning disabled students seem inept when out of the influence of their adult monitors.

Recently, tactics collectively referred to as self-management strategies have come to the attention of researchers and teachers. This line of investigation and practice is relatively new, and a clear delineation of these diverse procedures and their influence is not available. Also, agreement about the specific names of each variation has not been reached. For the sake of clarity, an attempt was made here to divide the vast number of options and discuss them under separate headings.

Self-control.   The aim of self-control tactics is for individuals to monitor their own behavior. For example, in some instances students determine when and how much study time they need to increase academic performance. In other instances they do not engage in inappropriate behavior because they know which situations precipitate those events and seek to avoid them.

These procedures sometimes are referred to as *self-regulation procedures*. They are usually employed when the target is to reduce undesirable behavior patterns. A series of activities are employed, with controlled relaxation as one of the usual components. One example of a self-control strategy for aggression is called the "Turtle Technique" (O'Leary & O'Leary, 1977; Robin, Schneider, & Dolnick, 1977). The student delays responding or reacting and assumes the turtle position (eyes closed, fists clenched, and head on desk), which relaxes him or her and restrains the aggression. The child then relaxes and thinks of alternative ways to deal with the situation.

Fagen et al. (1975) describe an entire curriculum that aims to develop self-control. Selected instructional targets include anticipating consequences, appreciating feelings, managing frustration, inhibition, and delay, and relaxing. Interested readers should find this total curriculum useful in helping students develop self-control in interpersonal situations.

Self-instruction.   Little detail is offered here about self-instruction because it is incorporated into programmed instruction and is too difficult for teachers, who would have to create new instructional materials without release time and help from additional personnel.[5] Self-instruction however, is available in commercially available instructional materials. Programmed workbooks such as the *BRL Sullivan Reading Program* (Sullivan, 1972) and the *Monterey Math Program* (Gray & McLain, 1975) allow students to proceed through materials at their own pace, learning different but related concepts as they move through the materials.

In one recent study, a comparison was conducted between a self-instructional format and a traditional group instructional approach to teaching computational arithmetic. Leon and Pepe (Note 2) found that students using a self-instructional format learned more efficiently. The self-instructional students passed through more modules and required less direct training than those participating in the traditional approach.

Self-evaluation.   There are many components of self-evaluation. Sometimes they are used together as an intervention package, and sometimes only one component is utilized. The first level of self-evaluation allows students to correct their own work. The *self-correction* feature, though not thoroughly researched, can be useful to busy teachers (because teacher time is saved) and students receive useful and immediate feedback. Crow and Mayhew (1976), however, found that accuracy of correcting arithmetic assignments increased when the teacher periodically checked the students' papers. In their study, student performance did not deteriorate when the students rather than the teacher corrected schoolwork.

Some studies have investigated the influence of *self-recording* on students' behavior. When this strategy is implemented, students keep records regarding the frequency of their target behaviors. For example, students have kept records of the amount of time spent studying and number of talkouts (Broden, Hall, & Mitts, 1971). Merely taking data on their own behavior was sufficient to cause the desired changes.

A variation of self-recording requires students to *self-report* to the teacher and sometimes to the class about their performances (Crow & Mayhew, 1976; Drabman, Spitalnik, & O'Leary, 1973; Hundert & Bucher, 1978). In most of these studies the authors were concerned about the honesty of the children and the reliability of their reports. In some studies the children were periodically checked by a teacher, and these authors feel that

[5]Interested readers should refer to Espich and Williams (1967), Popham and Baker (1970), Rowntree (1966), Skinner (1968), Smith, Smith, and Haring (1977), and Thiagarajan, Semmel, and Semmel (1974).

this insured accuracy of reporting. In several cases, it was recommended that teachers give rewards for accurate self-reports.

Along this line, interesting research has been conducted specifically with learning disabled students. Deshler, Ferrell, and Kass (1978) compared learning disabled youngsters' ability to recognize errors in their school work with that of normal students. Both groups were asked to find the errors in their written work. The learning disabled students made more errors, were proportionally unable to detect errors, were more sensitive about the errors they made, and seemed less willing (or possibly less able) to call an incorrect element an error. This information has vast implications about the use of self-reporting techniques with the learning disabled population. First, it seems that these youngsters have to be taught how to monitor for errors (as they are being produced and checked). Also, they must learn to deal with errors neutrally so they can profit from their mistakes. Certainly teachers must be cognizant of this potential deficiency in their learning disabled students and program for it.

In some studies (Dickie & Finegan, 1977; Lowe & Smith, Note 3), *self-graphing* has proven to be effective in producing positive changes in behavior. Teachers have used self-graphing to help modify both social and academic performance. In some cases the teachers help the students calculate the data, but with or without teacher assistance the students plot daily scores on a graph. Of course, a nice by-product of this tactic is that the students learn additional math skills (graphing), and, it is hoped, improve in the target area.

Self-imposed contingencies. A case has even been made that students should be allowed to determine and apply reinforcement to their own classroom behavior (Lovitt, 1973). Some research has compared the effectiveness of teacher-imposed contingencies and self-imposed contingencies. Evidently, self-determined reinforcement influenced substantial gains in arithmetic (Karraker, 1977; Lovitt & Curtiss, 1969). In several reading studies, however, self- and teacher-imposed reinforcement were clearly superior to no reinforcement, but were not significantly different from each other (Billingsley, 1977; Felixbrod & O'Leary, 1973; Glynn, 1970). In attempting to account for these equivocal results, Billingsley found that some students perform better when they set the contingencies, and others do not. He feels that teachers cannot, *a priori*, assume that one way of determining reinforcement delivery is superior to another. Since, however, some students do make even greater gains when they determine the reinforcement schedule, he suggests that teachers spend some time determining which system works best for each student.

Self-management to maintain. An important aspect of self-management procedures is their potential power to influence the maintenance of desired behavior changes. As discussed in Chapter 4, tactics that facilitate maintenance of skills must be identified if the benefits of remedial programs are to be long term. As mentioned in the token economy section, substantial amounts of gain when the direct intervention procedures were in effect often are lost when the program is withdrawn. Some research indicates that self-management packages can facilitate maintenance (O'Leary & Dubey, 1979). When maintenance of treatment effects was the aim, the self-management tactics were scheduled to follow earlier successful direct intervention conditions. For example, Kaufman and O'Leary (1972) found that general classroom disruption could be reduced through rewards and response cost procedures. A self-evaluation condition was instituted to maintain the gains made earlier: the students stated why they earned rewards and decided how many tokens they should receive.

Self-evaluation tactics maintain changes regardless of the desired direction—to increase or decrease student performance. For example, they have kept levels of disruption low (Drabman et al., 1973) and levels of room cleaning high (Wood & Flynn, 1978). Moreover, according to the research literature, self-management techniques do make behavior changed during direct intervention conditions more resistant to extinction (Bolstad & Johnson, 1972; Drabman, Spitalnik, & O'Leary, 1973; McLaughlin, 1976; O'Leary & Dubey, 1979). Therefore, when students enter into maintenance stages and concern is on retaining satisfactory levels of performance, teachers might consider scheduling self-management procedures.

An appraisal.   Self-management tactics have at least two distinct functions. In some cases, these procedures serve as direct intervention strategies that influence a variety of target behaviors. They can reduce disruption, aggression, and other undesirable behavior, and they can increase academic performance. In many cases, one kind of self-management procedure (self-graphing, self-rating) was employed, and in other cases a combination of recording, evaluating, and rewarding (Wasserman, Brown, & Reschly, 1974) was presented as an intervention package.

In most of the work done in this area, some concern focused on student accuracy and honesty. Periodic teacher checks and reinforcement for accurate reporting seem to be sufficient to guarantee reliability of the data. For those who select self-management procedures, however, it is advisable to use some caution. Some students could take advantage of the opportunity to set their own reward schedules if not monitored by the teacher. Also, as Friedling and O'Leary (1979) point out, if self-management procedures are to be expected to influence an individual's performance, that individual should have a desire to change problematic behavior.

A second function of self-management tactics aims not at producing desired changes in student performance but rather maintaining those changes observed during earlier intervention conditions. This seems to be an area of extreme promise. Few tactics have proven successful in the maintenance stage of learning; one reason for this is that few researchers have concentrated their energies on the maintenance stage. Also, some tactics (token economies) have not been successful in this stage. For teachers who are presented with students who do not seem to maintain adequate levels of performance, self-management procedures might be useful.

Since adults need to manage their own affairs in all areas, it is important for the educational system to teach students how to be independent. Youngsters must learn to self-monitor their behavior, schedule their daily,

Table 5.3 Tactics by stage of learning

	Acquisition		Proficiency		Maintenance	Generalization
	Initial	*Advanced*	*Early* *(low rate behaviors)*	*Advanced* *(high rate behaviors)*		
Social and Academic	*Priming* physical guidance shaping modeling match-to-sample telling cueing and prompting *Programming* chaining (backward and forward) errorless learning	*Refinement* feedback directions error drill reward for accuracy response cost	*Reinforcement Schedules* CRF *Contingency Management* token economies *Premack Principle* *Social Reinforcement* praise teacher attention modeling feedback	*Reinforcement Schedules* FI FR DRH and DRL *Contingency Management* multiple ratios *Premack Principle* *Social Reinforcement* praise teacher attention peer approval	*Programming* overlearning feedback *Reinforcement* *Schedules* intermittent reinforcement VI VR DRH and DRL *Social Reinforcement* peer management *Intrinsic Reinforcement* Self-management	*Programming* instructions reinforcement varying stimulus conditions
Academic			*Drill* new response drill error drill general (flashcard) speed drill	*Reinforcement* go/no-go contingencies multiple ratio *Peer Management* peer tutoring *Self-management* self-instruction self-evaluation		
Social			*Peer Management* peer modeling behavioral management	*Contingency Management* group contingencies good behavior games timer games *Self-management* self-control		

monthly, and yearly activities, and select appropriate reinforcers and apply them at appropriate times. Possibly the incorporation of self-management procedures into classrooms will serve a third purpose: the development of independent life skills.

SUMMARY

As students learn new skills they pass through several stages of learning. Many instructional procedures are effective in only one of these stages and are ineffective in the others. Table 5.3 lists tactics that tend to be most effective in each stage of learning. In addition, it indicates whether social or academic targets are most responsive to each tactic. Since little research has been conducted on the adaption stage of learning and few guidelines exist about which tactics might encourage behavior changes in that area, that stage was omitted from Table 5.3.

In Table 5.4, a summary of deceleration tactics is provided. Tactics that decrease behavioral occurrences are listed according to academic and social areas. In addition, a further delineation is made as to whether the tactic utilizes an application or a removal of an event.

Although discussion of specific intervention strategies was organized according to tactics that increase performances and those that reduce behavioral occurrences, this is a simplistic view of the educational process. Unfortunately, teachers cannot simply match their students' behavioral descriptions to the categories provided in Tables 5.3 and 5.4 and be guaranteed successful remediation programs. All students are individuals, and what is effective for one student might not be for another. The purpose of these chapters was to help teachers better select those procedures with the highest *probability* of effecting desired changes. For some students, direct interven-

Table 5.4	**Deceleration tactics**

Academic and Social	Removal:
	    withdrawal of positive reinforcement
	    response cost (fines)
	    extinction (ignoring)
	Application:
	    positive practice overcorrection
	    DRL
	    instructions
	    feedback

Social Only	Removal:
	    timeout
	Application:
	    restitutional overcorrection
	    punishment
	    DRO
	    reprimands

tion for academic improvement causes concomitant improvement (reduction) in disruption. For others, direct remedial efforts are necessary for social as well as academic behavior.

One major purpose of these chapters was to review the basic, generic intervention procedures that can be useful across a variety of social and academic skills. Tactics specifically applied to only one particular area (reading, writing) are described in later chapters. Because the basic jargon, terms, and related definitions were presented here, the remainder of this book should be more coherent and understandable.

REFERENCE NOTES

1. BLOOM, S. *Peer and cross-age tutoring in the schools: An individualized supplement to group instruction* (Handbook published under a contract from the National Institute of Education, Department of HEW). Chicago, undated.

2. LEON, J. A., & PEPE, H. *Self-instructional training: Cognitive behavior modification as a resource room strategy* (Research paper, BEH Grant No.

G007701911). Albuquerque, N.M.: University of New Mexico, 1979.

3. LOWE, J., & SMITH, D. D. *Self-management techniques to improve middle school students' math proficiency* (Working paper). Albuquerque, N.M.: Department of Special Education, University of New Mexico, 1979.

REFERENCES

ALLEN, K. E., HART, B. M., BUELL, J. S., HARRIS, F. R., & WOLF, M. M. Effects of social reinforcement on isolate behavior of nursery school child. *Child Development*, 1964, 35, 511–518.

AXELROD, S. *Behavior modification for the classroom teacher*. New York: McGraw-Hill, 1977.

AXELROD, S., BRANTNER, J. P., & MEDDOCK, T. D. Overcorrection: A review and critical analysis. *The Journal of Special Education*, 1978, 12, 367–391.

AYLLON, T. Intensive treatment of psychotic behaviour by stimulus satiation and food reinforcement. *Behaviour Research and Therapy*, 1963, 1, 53–61.

AYLLON, T., & AZRIN, N. H. Reinforcement and instructions with mental patients. *Journal of the Experimental Analysis of Behavior*, 1964, 7, 327–331.

AYLLON, T., LAYMAN, D., & BURKE, S. Disruptive behavior and reinforcement of academic performance. *The Psychological Record*, 1972, 22, 315–323.

AYLLON, T., & ROBERTS, M. D. Eliminating discipline problems by strengthening academic performance. *Journal of Applied Behavior Analysis*, 1974, 7, 71–76.

AZRIN, N. H., & HOLZ, W. C. Punishment. In W. K. Honig (Ed.), *Operant behavior: Areas of research and application*. New York: Appleton-Century-Crofts, 1966.

AZRIN, N. H., & POWERS, M. A. Eliminating classroom disturbances of emotionally disturbed children by

positive practice procedures. *Behavior Therapy*, 1975, 6, 525–534.

BAER, D. M. Laboratory control of thumbsucking by withdrawal and re-presentation of reinforcement. *Journal of the Experimental Analysis of Behavior*, 1962, 5, 525–528.

BAER, D. M. A case for the selective reinforcement of punishment. In C. Neuringer & J. L. Michael (Eds.), *Behavior modification in clinical psychology*. New York: Appleton-Century-Crofts, 1970.

BARTON, E. S., GUESS, D., GARCIA, E., & BAER, D. M. Improvement of retardates' mealtime behaviors by timeout procedures using multiple baseline techniques. *Journal of Applied Behavior Analysis*, 1970, 3, 77–84.

BECKER, W. C., MADSEN, C. H., ARNOLD, C. R., & THOMAS, D. R. The contingent use of teacher attention and praise in reducing classroom behavior problems. *The Journal of Special Education*, 1967, 1, 287–307.

BILLINGSLEY, F. F. The effects of self- and externally-imposed schedules of reinforcement on oral reading performances. *Journal of Learning Disabilities*, 1977, 10, 549–559.

BIRNBRAUER, J. S., BIJOU, S. W., WOLF, M. M., & KIDDER, J. D. Programmed instruction in the classroom. In L. P. Ullmann & L. Krasner (Eds.), *Case studies in behavior modification*. New York: Holt, Rinehart & Winston, 1965.

BOLSTAD, O. D.; & JOHNSON, S. M. Self-regulation in the modification of disruptive classroom behavior. *Journal of Applied Behavior Analysis*, 1972, *5*, 443–454.

BOSTOW, D. E., & BAILEY, J. B. Modification of severe disruptive and aggressive behavior using brief time-out and reinforcement procedures. *Journal of Applied Behavior Analysis*, 1969, *2*, 31–37.

BRODEN, M., HALL, R. V., DUNLAP, A., & CLARK, R. Effects of teacher attention and a token reinforcement system in a junior high school special education class. *Exceptional Children*, 1970, *36*, 341–349.

BRODEN, M., HALL, R. V., & MITTS, B. The effect of self-recording on the classroom behavior of two eighth-grade students. *Journal of Applied Behavior Analysis*, 1971, *4*, 191–199.

BROOKS, R. B., & SNOW, D. L. Two case illustrations of the use of behavior-modification techniques in the school setting. *Behavior Therapy*, 1972, *3*, 100–103.

BUCKLEY, N. K., & WALKER, H. M., *Modifying classroom behavior: A manual of procedure for classroom teachers* (revised ed.). Champaign, Ill.: Research Press Co., 1978.

BUEHLER, R. E., PATTERSON, G. R., & FURNISS, J. M. The reinforcement of behavior in institutional settings. *Behaviour Research and Therapy*, 1900, *4*, 157–167.

CATERA, R., & HERON, T. E. Comparison of punishment and reinforcement contingencies. *The Directive Teacher*, 1978, *1*, 7–9.

CLARK, H. B., ROWBURY, T., BAER, A. M., & BAER, D. M. Timeout as a punishing stimulus in continuous and intermittent schedules. *Journal of Applied Behavior Analysis*, 1973, *6*, 443–455.

CONLON, M. F., HALL, C., & HANLEY, E. M. The effects of a peer correction procedure on the arithmetic accuracy for two elementary school children. In G. Semb (Ed.), *Behavior analysis and education—1972*. Lawrence, Kans.; University of Kansas, 1972.

CROW, R., & MAYHEW, G. Reinforcement effects on accuracy of self-reporting behavior of elementary students. In T. A. Brigham, R. Hawkins, J. W. Scott, & T. F. McLaughlin (Eds.), *Behavior analysis in education: Self-control and reading.* Dubuque, Iowa: Kendall & Hunt Publishing Co., 1976.

DESHLER, D. D., FERRELL, W. R., & KASS, C. E. Error monitoring of schoolwork by learning disabled adolescents. *Journal of Learning Disabilities*, 1978, *11*, 401–414.

DEVIN-SHEEHAN, L., FELDMAN, R. S., & ALLEN, V. L. Research on children tutoring children: A critical review. *Review of Educational Research*, 1976, *46*, 355–385.

DICKIE, R. F., & FINEGAN, S. The long-term effects of self-recording on academic behavior rate in an "emo-tionally disturbed" boy. *School Applications of Learning Theory*, 1977, *9*, 38–48.

DIETZ, S. M., & REPP, A. C. Decreasing classroom misbehavior through the use of DRL schedules of reinforcement. *Journal of Applied Behavior Analysis*, 1973, *6*, 457–463.

DRABMAN, R. S. Behavior modification in the classroom. In W. E. Craighead, A. E. Kazdin, & M. J. Mahoney (Eds.), *Behavior modification: Principles, issues, and applications.* Boston: Houghton Mifflin Co., 1976.

DRABMAN, R. S., SPITALNIK, R., & O'LEARY, K. D. Teaching self control to disruptive children. *Journal of Abnormal Psychology*, 1973, *82*, 10–16.

DRASS, S. D., & JONES, R. L. Learning disabled children as behavior modifiers. *Journal of Learning Disabilities*, 1971, *4*, 418–425.

DUNLAP, K. The technique of negative practice. *American Journal of Psychology*, 1942, *55*, 270–273.

EPSTEIN, L. H., DOKE, L. A., SAJWAJ, T. E., SORRELL, S., & RIMMER, B. Generality and side effects of overcorrection. *Journal of Applied Behavior Analysis*, 1974, *7*, 385–390.

ESPICH, J. E., & WILLIAMS, B. *Developing programmed instructional materials: A handbook for program writers.* Palo Alto, Calif.: Fearon Publishers, 1967.

EVANS, G. W., & OSWALT, C. L. Acceleration of academic progress through the manipulation of peer influence. *Behaviour Research and Therapy*, 1968, *6*, 189–195.

FAGEN, S. A., LONG, N. J., & STEVENS, D. J. *Teaching children self-control: Preventing emotional and learning problems in the elementary school.* Columbus, Ohio: Charles E. Merrill Publishing Co., 1975.

FELIXBROD, J. J., & O'LEARY, K. D. Effects of reinforcement on children's academic behavior as a function of self-determined and externally imposed contingencies. *Journal of Applied Behavior Analysis*, 1973, *6*, 241–250.

FOXX, R. M. Increasing a mildly retarded woman's attendance at self-help classes by overcorrection and instruction. *Behavior Therapy*, 1976, *7*, 390–396.

FOXX, R. M., & AZRIN, N. H. Restitution: A method of eliminating aggressive-disruptive behavior of retarded and brain damaged patients. *Behaviour Research and Therapy*, 1972, *10*, 15–27.

FOXX, R. M., & AZRIN, N. H. The elimination of autistic self-stimulatory behavior by overcorrection. *Journal of Applied Behavior Analysis*, 1973, *6*, 1–14.

FREEMAN, B. J., GRAHAM, V., & RITVO, E. R. Reduction of self-destructive behavior by overcorrection. *Psychological Reports*, 1975, *37*, 446.

FRIEDLING, C., & O'LEARY, S. G. Effects of self-instructional training on second- and third-grade hyperactive children: A failure to replicate. *Journal of Applied Behavior Analysis*, 1979, *12*, 211-219.

FULLER, P. R. Operant conditioning of a vegetative human organism. *American Journal of Psychology*, 1949, *62*, 587-590.

GARTNER, A., KOHLER, M. C., & RIESSMAN, F. *Children teach children: Learning by teaching.* New York: Harper & Row, 1971.

GAST, D. L., & NELSON, C. M. Time out in the classroom; Implications for special education. *Exceptional Children*, 1977, *43*, 461-464. (a)

GAST, D. L., & NELSON, C. M. Legal and ethical considerations for the use of timeout in special education settings. *The Journal of Special Education*, 1977, *11*, 457-467. (b)

GIRARDEAU, F. L., & SPRADLIN, J. E. Token rewards in a cottage program. *Mental Retardation*, 1964, *2*, 345-351.

GLYNN, E. L. Classroom applications of self-determined reinforcement. *Journal of Applied Behavior Analysis*, 1970, *3*, 123-132.

GRAUBARD, P. S. Utilizing the group in teaching disturbed delinquents to learn. *Exceptional Children*, 1969, *36*, 267-276.

GRAY, B., & McLAIN, L. *Monterey arithmetic program.* Monterey, Calif.: Monterey Learning System, 1975.

GREENWOOD, C. R., HOPS, H., DELQUADRI, J., & GUILD, J. Group contingencies for group consequences in classroom management: A further analysis. *Journal of Applied Behavior Analysis*, 1974, *7*, 413-425.

GREENWOOD, C. R., SLOANE, H. N., JR., & BASKIN, A. Training elementary aged peer-behavior managers to control small group programmed mathematics. *Journal of Applied Behavior Analysis*, 1974, *7*, 103-144.

GRIEGER, T., KAUFFMAN, J. M., & GRIEGER, R. M. Effects of peer reporting on cooperative play and aggression of kindergarten children. *Journal of School Psychology*, 1976, *14*, 307-312.

HALL, R. V., AXELROD, S., FOUNDOPOULOS, M., SHELLMAN, J., CAMPBELL, R. A., & CRANSTON, S. S. The effective use of punishment to modify behavior in the classroom. *Educational Technology*, 1971, *11*, 24-26.

HALL, R. V., FOX, R., WILLARD, D., GOLDSMITH, L., EMERSON, M., OWEN, M., DAVIS, F., & PORCIA, E. The teacher as observer and experimenter in the modification of disputing and talking-out behaviors. *Journal of Applied Behavior Analysis*, 1971, *4*, 141-149.

HARRIS, V. W., & SHERMAN, J. A. Effects of peer tutoring and consequences on the math performance of elementary classroom students. *Journal of Applied Behavior Analysis*, 1973, *6*, 587-597.

HARRIS, V. W., SHERMAN, J. A., HENDERSON, D. G., & HARRIS, M. S. Effects of peer tutoring on the spelling performance of elementary classroom students. In G. Semb (Ed.), *Behavior analysis and education—1972.* Lawrence, Kans.: University of Kansas, 1972.

HERMAN, S. H., & TRAMONTANA, J. Instructions and group versus individual reinforcement in modifying disruptive group behavior. *Journal of Applied Behavior Analysis*, 1971, *4*, 113-119.

HERON, T. E. Punishment: A review of the literature with implications for the teacher of mainstreamed children. *The Journal of Special Education*, 1978, *12*, 243-252.

HEWETT, F. M. Educational engineering with emotionally disturbed children. *Exceptional Children*, 1967, *33*, 459-467.

HEWETT, F. M. *The emotionally disturbed child in the classroom.* Boston: Allyn & Bacon, 1968.

HEWETT, F. M., TAYLOR, F. D., & ARTUSO, A. A. The Santa Monica project: Evaluation of an engineered classroom design with emotionally disturbed children. *Exceptional Children*, 1969, *35*, 523-529.

HOWELL, K. W., & KAPLAN, J. S. Monitoring peer tutor behavior. *Exceptional Children*, 1978, *45*, 135-137.

HUNDERT, J., & BUCHER, B. Pupils' self-scored arithmetic performance: A practical procedure for maintaining accuracy. *Journal of Applied Behavior Analysis*, 1978, *11*, 304.

IWATA, B. A., & BAILEY, J. S. Reward versus cost token systems: An analysis of the effects on students and teacher. *Journal of Applied Behavior Analysis*, 1974, *7*, 567-576.

JENKINS, J. R., MAYHALL, W. F., PESCHKA, C. M., & JENKINS, L. M. Comparing small group and tutorial instruction in resource rooms. *Exceptional Children*, 1974, *40*, 245-250.

JOHNSON, M., & BAILEY, J. S. Cross-age tutoring: Fifth graders as arithmetic tutors for kindergarten children. *Journal of Applied Behavior Analysis*, 1974, *7*, 223-232.

JOHNSTON, J. M. Punishment of human behavior. *American Psychologist*, 1972, *27*, 1033-1054.

KANE, B. J., & ALLEY, G. R. A peer-tutored, instructional management program in computational mathematics for incarcerated, learning disabled juvenile delinquents. *Journal of Learning Disabilities*, 1980, *13*, 148-151.

KARRAKER, R. J. Self versus teacher selected reinforcers in a token economy. *Exceptional Children*, 1977, *43*, 454-455.

KAUFMAN, K. F., & O'LEARY, K. D. Reward, cost, and self-evaluation procedures for disruptive adolescents in a psychiatric hospital school. *Journal of Applied Behavior Analysis*, 1972, 5, 293–309.

KAZDIN, A. E. *The token economy: A review and evaluation*. New York: Plenum Press, 1977.

KAZDIN, A. E., & BOOTZIN, R. R. The token economy: An evaluative review. *Journal of Applied Behavior Analysis*, 1972, 5, 343–372.

KIRCHER, A. S., PEAR, J. J., & MARTIN, G. L. Shock as punishment in a picture-naming task with retarded children. *Journal of Applied Behavior Analysis*, 1971, 4, 227–233.

KISSEL, R. C., & WHITMAN, T. L. An examination of the direct and generalized effects of a play-training and overcorrection procedure upon the self-stimulatory behavior of a profoundly retarded boy. *American Association for the Education of the Severely and Profoundly Handicapped Review*, 1977, 2, 131–146.

LANE, H. *The wild boy of Aveyron*. Cambridge, Mass.: Harvard University Press, 1976.

LAZERSON, D. B. "I must be good if I can teach!"—Peer tutoring with aggressive and withdrawn children. *Journal of Learning Disabilities*, 1980, 13, 152–157.

LITOW, L., & PUMROY, D. K. A brief review of classroom group-oriented contingencies. *Journal of Applied Behavior Analysis*, 1975, 8, 341–347.

LONG, J. D., & WILLIAMS, R. L. The comparative effectiveness of group and individually contingent free time with inner-city junior high school students. *Journal of Applied Behavior Analysis*, 1973, 6, 465–474.

LOVITT, T. C. Self-management projects with children with behavioral disabilities. *Journal of Learning Disabilities*, 1973, 6, 138–150.

LOVITT, T. C. *Managing inappropriate behaviors in the classroom*. Reston, Va.: The Council for Exceptional Children, 1978.

LOVITT, T. C., & CURTISS, K. A. Academic response rate as a function of teacher- and self-imposed contingencies. *Journal of Applied Behavior Analysis*, 1969, 2, 49–53.

LOVITT, T. C., LOVITT, A. O., EATON, M. D., & KIRKWOOD, M. The deceleration of inappropriate comments by a natural consequence. *Journal of School Psychology*, 1973, 11, 148–154.

LOVITT, T. C., & SMITH, J. O. Effects of instructions on an individual's verbal behavior. *Exceptional Children*, 1972, 38, 685–693.

LUISELLI, J. K., HELFEN, C. S., & ANDERSON, D. F. The application of brief time-out to control classroom talk-out behavior. *School Applications of Learning Theory*, 1976, 9, 16–24.

MACMILLAN, D. L., FORNESS, S. R., & TRUMBULL, B. M. The role of punishment in the classroom. *Exceptional Children*, 1973, 40, 85–97.

MADSEN, C. H., JR., BECKER, W. C., & THOMAS, D. R. Rules, praise, and ignoring: Elements of elementary classroom control. *Journal of Applied Behavior Analysis*, 1968, 1, 139–150.

MCGEE, C. S., KAUFFMAN, J. M., & NUSSEN, J. L. Children as therapeutic change agents: Reinforcement intervention paradigms. *Review of Educational Research*, 1977, 47, 451–477.

MCKENZIE, II. S., CLARK, M., WOLF, M. M., KOTHERA, R., & BENSON, C. Behavior modification of children with learning disabilities using grades as tokens and allowances as back up reinforcers. *Exceptional Children*, 1968, 34, 745–752.

MCLAUGHLIN, T. F. Self-control in the classroom. *Review of Educational Research*, 1976, 46, 631–663.

NEWMAN, R., WHORTON, D. & SIMPSON, R. The modification of self-stimulatory verbalizations in an autistic child through the use of an overcorrection procedure. *American Association for the Education of the Severely and Profoundly Handicapped Review*, 1977, 2, 157–163.

O'LEARY, K. D., BECKER, W. C., EVANS, M. B., & SAUDARGAS, R. A. A token reinforcement program in a public school: A replication and systematic analysis. *Journal of Applied Behavior Analysis*, 1969, 2, 3–13.

O'LEARY, S. G., & DUBEY, D. R. Applications of self-control procedures by children: A review. *Journal of Applied Behavior Analysis*, 1979, 12, 449–465.

O'LEARY, K. D., KAUFMAN, K. F., KASS, R. E., & DRABMAN, R. S. The effects of loud and soft reprimands on the behavior of disruptive students. *Exceptional Children*, 1970, 37, 145–155.

O'LEARY, K. D., & O'LEARY, S. G. *Classroom management: The successful use of behavior modification* (2nd ed.). Elmsford, N.Y.: Pergamon Press, 1977.

OLSON, W. C. The diagnosis and treatment of behavior disorders of children. In the Thirty-Fourth Yearbook of the National Society for the Study of Education (Eds.), *Educational diagnosis*. Bloomington, Ill.: Public Schools Publishing Co., 1935.

PACKARD, R. G. The control of "classroom attention": A group contingency for complex behavior. *Journal of Applied Behavior Analysis*, 1970, 3, 13–28.

PAOLITTO, D. P. The effect of cross-age tutoring on adolescence: An inquiry into theoretical assumptions. *Review of Educational Research*, 1976, 46, 215–237.

PARSON, L. R., & HEWARD, W. L. Training peers to tutor: Evaluation of a tutor training package for primary learning disabled students. *Journal of Applied Behavior Analysis*, 1979, 12, 309–310.

PATTERSON, G. R., & ANDERSON, D. Peers as social reinforcers. *Child Development*, 1964, 35, 951–960.

PATTERSON, G. R., & BRODSKY, G. A behavior modification programme for a child with multiple problem behaviours. *Journal of Child Psychology and Psychiatry*, 1966, *7*, 277–295.

PATTERSON, G. R., LITTMAN, R. A., & BRICKER, W. Assertive behavior in children: A step toward a theory of aggression. *Monographs of the Society for Research in Child Development*, 1967, *32* (5, Serial No. 113).

Peabody Language Development Kits—American Guidance Service. *Tokens.* Circle Pines, Minn.: American Guidance Service, 1965.

PHILLIPS, E. L. Achievement place: Token reinforcement procedures in a home-style rehabilitation setting for "pre-delinquent" boys. *Journal of Applied Behavior Analysis*, 1968, *1*, 213–223.

PLUMMER, S., BAER, D. M., & LeBLANC, J. M. Functional considerations in the use of procedural timeout and an effective alternative. *Journal of Applied Behavior Analysis*, 1977, *10*, 689–705.

POPHAM, W. J., & BAKER, E. L. *Planning an instructional sequence.* Englewood Cliffs, N.J.: Prentice-Hall, 1970.

RAMP, E., ULRICH, R., & DULANEY, S. Delayed timeout as a procedure for reducing disruptive classroom behavior: A case study. *Journal of Applied Behavior Analysis*, 1971, *4*, 235–239.

REPP, A. C., & DIETZ, D. E. D. On the selective use of punishment—Suggested guidelines for administrators. *Mental Retardation*, 1978, *16*, 250–254.

RETTIG, E. B., & PAULSON, T. L. *ABC's for teachers: An inservice training program in behavior modification skills.* Van Nuys, Calif.: Associates for Behavior Change, 1975.

RISLEY, T. R. The effects and side effects of punishing the autistic behaviors of a deviant child. *Journal of Applied Behavior Analysis*, 1968, *1*, 21–34.

ROBERTS, M. B., & SMITH, D. D. The influence of contingent instructions on the social behavior of a young boy. *School Applications of Learning Theory*, 1977, *9*, 24–42.

ROBIN, A., SCHNEIDER, M., & DOLNICK, M. The turtle technique: An extended case study of self-control in the classroom. In K. D. O'Leary & S. G. O'Leary (Eds.), *Classroom management: The successful use of behavior modification* (2nd ed.). New York: Pergamon Press, 1977.

ROSENBAUM, M. S., & DRABMAN, R. S. Self-control training in the classroom: A review and critique. *Journal of Applied Behavior Analysis*, 1979, *12*, 467–485.

ROWNTREE, D. *Basically branching: A handbook for programmers.* London: Macdonald & Co., 1966.

RUSCH, F. R., & CLOSE, D. W. Overcorrection: A procedural evaluation. *American Association for the Education of the Severely and Profoundly Handicapped Review*, 1976, *1*, 32–45.

RUTHERFORD, B. R. The use of negative practice in speech therapy with children handicapped by cerebral palsy, athetoid type. *Journal of Speech and Hearing Disabilities*, 1940, *5*, 259–264.

SAJWAJ, T., CULVER, P., HALL, C., & LEHR, L. 3 simple punishment techniques for the control of classroom disruptions. In G. Semb (Ed.), *Behavior analysis and education—1972.* Lawrence, Kans.: University of Kansas, 1972.

SAJWAJ, T., TWARDOSZ, S., & BURKE, M. Side effects of extinction procedures in a remedial preschool. *Journal of Applied Behavior Analysis*, 1972, *5*, 163–175.

SCHMIDT, G. W., & ULRICH, R. E. Effects of group contingent events upon classroom noise. *Journal of Applied Behavior Analysis*, 1969, *2*, 171–179.

SIEGEL, L. J., & STEINMAN, W. M. The modification of a peer-observer's classroom behavior as a function of his serving as a reinforcing agent. In E. Ramp & G. Semb (Eds.), *Behavior analysis: Areas of research and application.* Englewood Cliffs, N.J.: Prentice-Hall, 1975.

SIMPSON, R. L., & SASSO, G. M. The modification of rumination in a severely emotionally disturbed child through an over-correction procedure. *American Association for the Education of the Severely and Profoundly Handicapped Review*, 1978, *3*, 145–150.

SKINNER, B. F. *The technology of teaching.* New York: Appleton-Century-Crofts, 1968.

SMITH, J. D., POLLOWAY, E. A., & WEST, G. K. Corporal punishment and its implications for exceptional children. *Exceptional Children*, 1979, *45*, 264–268.

SMITH, J. O., SMITH, D. D., & HARING, N. G. A model for the development of instructional materials for the handicapped. *Peabody Journal of Education*, 1977, *54*, 174–180.

SOLNICK, J. V., RINCOVER, A., & PETERSON, C. R. Some determinants of the reinforcing and punishing effects of timeout. *Journal of Applied Behavior Analysis*, 1977, *10*, 415–424.

SOLOMON, R. W., & WAHLER, R. G. Peer reinforcement control of classroom problem behavior. *Journal of Applied Behavior Analysis*, 1973, *6*, 49–56.

SPELTZ, M. L., MOORE, J. E., & McREYNOLDS, W. T. A comparison of standardized and group contingencies in a classroom setting. *Behavior Therapy*, 1979, *10*, 219–226.

STAINBACK, W. C., PAYNE, J. S., STAINBACK, S. B., & PAYNE, R. A. *Establishing a token economy in the classroom.* Columbus, Ohio: Charles E. Merrill Publishing Co., 1973.

STARLIN, C. Peers and precision. *Teaching Exceptional Children*, 1971, *33*, 129–140.

SULLIVAN, M. W. *The BRL Sullivan reading program.* Palo Alto, Calif.: Behavioral Research Laboratories, 1972.

SULZBACHER, S. I., & HOUSER, J. E. A tactic to eliminate disruptive behaviors in the classroom: Group contingent consequences. *American Journal of Mental Deficiency,* 1968, 73, 88–90.

SURRATT, P. R., ULRICH, R. E., & HAWKINS, R. P. An elementary student as a behavioral engineer. *Journal of Applied Behavior Analysis,* 1969, 2, 85–92.

THIAGARAJAN, S., SEMMEL, D. S., & SEMMEL, M. I. *Instructional development for training teachers of exceptional children: A sourcebook.* Reston, Va.: The Council for Exceptional Children, 1974.

TROVATO, J., & BUCHER, B. Peer tutoring with or without home-based reinforcement for reading remediation. *Journal of Applied Behavior Analysis,* 1980, 13, 129–141.

University of Kansas Bureau of Child Research (Producer). *Operation behavior modification.* Lawrence, Kans.: University of Kansas Bureau of Child Research, 1967. (Film)

WAHLER, R. G. Child-child interactions in free field settings: Some experimental analyses. *Journal of Experimental Child Psychology,* 1967, 5, 278–293.

WASSERMAN, H., BROWN, D., & RESCHLY, D. Application of self-management procedures for the modification of academic and classroom behaviors of two "hyperactive" children. *School Applications of Learning Theory,* 1974, 7, 17–24.

WEBSTER, D. R., & AZRIN, N. H. Required relaxation: A method of inhibiting agitative disruptive behavior of retardates. *Behaviour Research and Therapy,* 1973, 11, 67–78.

WHITE, G. F., NIELSEN, G., & JOHNSON, S. M. Time-out duration and the suppression of deviant behavior in children. *Journal of Applied Behavior Analysis,* 1972, 5, 111–120.

WHITE, O. R., & HARING, N. G. *Exceptional teaching: A multi-media training package.* Columbus, Ohio: Charles E. Merrill Publishing Co., 1976.

WILLIAMS, C. D. The elimination of tantrum behavior by extinction procedures. *Journal of Abnormal and Social Psychology,* 1959, 59, 269.

WILLIS, J., CROWDER, J., & MORRIS, B. A behavioral approach to remedial reading using students as behavioral engineers. In G. Semb (Ed.), *Behavior analysis and education—1972.* Lawrence, Kans.: University of Kansas, 1972.

WILSON, C. W., & HOPKINS, B. L. The effects of contingent music on the intensity of noise in junior high home economics classes. *Journal of Applied Behavior Analysis,* 1973, 6, 269–275.

WILLIS, J. W., MORRIS, B., & CROWDER, J. A remedial reading technique for disabled readers that employs students as behavioral engineers. *Psychology in the Schools,* 1972, 9, 67–70.

WILSON, C. C., ROBERTSON, S. J., HERLONG, L. H., & HAYNES, S. N. Vicarious effects of time-out in the modification of aggression in the classroom. *Behavior Modification,* 1979, 3, 97–111.

WOLF, M. M., RISLEY, T., & MEES, H. Application of operant conditioning procedures to the behaviour problems of an autistic child. *Behaviour Research and Therapy,* 1964, 1, 305–312.

WOOD, R., & FLYNN, J. M. A self-evaluation token system versus an external evaluation token system alone in a residential setting with predelinquent youth. *Journal of Applied Behavior Analysis,* 1978, 11, 503–512.

ZIMMERMAN, E. H., & ZIMMERMAN, J. The alteration of behavior in a special classroom situation. *Journal of the Experimental Analysis of Behavior,* 1962, 5, 59–60.

6 PROBLEM SOLVING: A GENERAL APPROACH TO REMEDIATION

C. JUNE MAKER

University of New Mexico

Children must have certain skills to enable them to learn effectively in school, such as ability to pay attention to relevant information, ability to discriminate sounds and shapes, and knowledge of appropriate ways to approach academic tasks. Many learning disabled children do not have all of these skills when they enter school, so the teacher must assess each child's level of proficiency and plan appropriate strategies for developing them.

In the field of learning disabilities, there is considerable controversy over the nature of these prerequisite abilities, their actual effect on later learning, the nature of the disabilities children may have, and the actual effect of a particular disability on later learning. This chapter does not attempt to resolve any of these conflicting points of view, but presents information, both suggestive and well-documented, that may be helpful to teachers in dealing with children who are having learning problems.

In an attempt to integrate the diverse points of view and to bring some structure to the discussion of these prerequisite skills, the chapter is organized according to the steps in a problem-solving process, and shows the possible influence of certain disabilities or inefficient learning strategies on children's performance in some aspect of the problem-solving process. The focus is on how these skills can be recognized and how they can be developed if they are not present. The chapter contains the following elements: an overview of the problem-solving process; a description of a general approach to remediation; a discussion of each step in the process; an analysis of the possible specific disabilities influencing performance at each step; and a discussion of some of the factors having a more general effect on the whole process

THE NEED FOR PROBLEM-SOLVING STRATEGIES

If children are to succeed in academic tasks, they must:

be able to understand the requirements of a task.

be aware of an appropriate strategy to use in solving the problem or in doing the task.

possess the underlying skills or abilities involved in doing the task.

be aware of their own skills or abilities as they relate to performance on the task.

use the appropriate strategy in an organized rather than random fashion.

assess their own performance in relation to the requirements of the task or problem.

In the past, research on learning disabilities has focused only on whether or not children possess the underlying skills or abilities involved in academic tasks. Learning disabled children have been characterized as having visual and auditory perceptual deficits (Cruickshank & Hallahan, 1975; Frostig & Horne, 1964; Getman, 1965; Hallahan & Cruickshank, 1973; Kirk & Kirk, 1971; Lahey & Lefton, 1976; Lahey & McNees, 1975; Wepman, 1958), perceptual-motor deficiencies (Barsch, 1967; Hallahan & Cruickshank, 1973; Kephart, 1971; Roach & Kephart, 1966; Wedell, 1968, 1973; Werner & Strauss, 1939), deficits in attention (Hallahan, Kauffman, & Ball, 1973; Tarver & Hallahan, 1974; Tarver, Hallahan, Cohen, & Kauffman, 1977; Tarver, Hallahan, Kauffman, & Ball, 1976), and memory deficits (Das, Leong, & Williams, 1978; Smiley, Oakley, Worthen, Campione, & Brown, 1977; Swanson, 1979; Torgesen, 1976).

Recently, reviews have shown that research has failed to substantiate some of the most basic assumptions of the perceptual and perceptual-motor theories. For example:

1. Training in visual-perceptual skills does not seem to increase academic achievement (Larsen & Hammill, 1975).

2. Many children's failure in school cannot be attributed to poor visual-perceptual skills (Larsen & Hammill, 1975).

3. Certain perceptual and perceptual-motor tests do not differentiate between learning disabled and normally achieving children (Harber, 1979; Larsen, Rogers, & Sowell, 1976).

4. A strong relationship does not exist between auditory perceptual abilities and reading achievement (Hammill & Larsen, 1974).

Because of the confusing results of research, many researchers and practitioners have begun to focus on other possible reasons for these children's academic failure. Recent findings have suggested that, although some children do have perceptual or other disabilities, others do not, but are unable or unwilling to *apply the appropriate strategy or strategies* for solving a problem. For example, Hall (1979) reviews studies showing that learning disabled children have the ability to acquire and store information, but lack spontaneous access to these processes. In other words, these children can perform as well as normally achieving children on memory tasks if taught to use appropriate recall, retrieval, or rehearsal strategies in solving the problem. Other studies (Hallahan, Lloyd, Kosiewicz, Kauffman, & Graves, 1979; Hallahan, Lloyd, Kosiewicz, & Kneedler, 1979) show that students taught to evaluate whether they were attending to a task when they hear a tape-recorded tone during seatwork activities improved in on-task behavior. An added effect was improved academic productivity on measures of handwriting and arithmetic. Finally, some investigators have attempted to modify children's impulsive responding (see section on cognitive tempo in this chapter) in the hopes that altering response style would improve general performance. Unfortunately, they have had little or no success (Messer, 1976; Zelniker & Jeffrey, 1976; McKinney, Haskins, & Moore, Note 1). On the other hand, when taught directly to do so, impulsive children respond less quickly and make fewer errors (Egeland, 1974; Finch & Spirito, 1980; McKinney & Haskins, 1980; Meichenbaum & Goodman, 1971; Moore & Cole, 1978). Taken together, these studies indicate that rather than being unable to inhibit responding, these children fail to use systematic or organized strategies for solving the problem. Rather than focusing on the disabilities children may have, the approach in these new studies has been to look at their abilities and how the children can be taught to use them in problem-solving situations.

A growing body of research indicates that learning disabled children, as well as younger, more immature children, do not use *active* strategies for learning or solving problems (Hall, 1980; Hallahan & Reeve, in press; Lloyd, 1980; Loper, 1980; Torgesen, 1977). Their passive, rather than active, participation in the learning process could be caused by or related to a number of factors (Loper, 1980). Their level of awareness of task and strategy variables might be insufficient. For example, they might be unable to understand when situations require their active, personal involvement or be unable to understand their own abilities and either predict future performance or evaluate present performance. Their use of a strategy that does not generalize might inhibit learning. An inability to understand internal variables that may influence performance in addition to external variables could also affect satisfactory performance. Lloyd (1980) suggests that learning disabled children's use of appropriate attack strategies (using a set of rote subskills and knowing the rules for combining them so that a strategy can be applied to all the items in a class of problems) might be faulty. Also, an inability to generalize a previously learned problem-solving strategy to a new problem (Hall, 1979, 1980; Lloyd, 1980; Loper, 1980; McKinney & Haskins,

1980) or to produce spontaneous problem-solving plans (Hall, 1979) could contribute to inefficient learning.

Finally, research into problem-solving strategies used by learning disabled adolescents also suggests a practical approach for teachers to use in their assessment of children's problem-solving abilities. In one study (Havertape & Kass, 1978), learning disabled and normally achieving students verbalized self-directions and were recorded while they were attempting to solve problems. These recordings were analyzed and classified according to components and levels of proficiency within the components (see Table 6.1), and the two groups (learning disabled and normally achieving) were compared. Except for Level 4 in Step 3, the learning disabled students were less proficient than normally achieving students in every step and level of proficiency. These researchers conclude that in many cases, learning disabled

Table 6.1   **Illustration of classification system with proportions of response and z values for each level of proficiency within each step of problem solving by LD and NLD students**

Step 1: Getting the Information	Proportion LD	Proportion NLD	z^*
5 Reads problem correctly	.33	.88	18.3
4 Reads problem correctly with effort	.14	.01	8.12
3 Rereads problem several times	.25	.08	8.5
2 Reads only parts of the problem	.25	.01	10.5
1 Does not read the problem	.06	.01	7.14
Step 2: Understanding the Problem			
3 Verbalizations show understanding of problem with correct solution	.30	.65	11.6
2 Verbalizations show understanding of problem with incorrect solution	.10	.15	2.5
1 Verbalizations show lack of understanding with incorrect solution	.60	.20	3.3
Step 3: Solving the Problem			
7 Uses logical and efficient steps with no error	.16	.57	13.6
6 Uses logical and efficient steps but with error(s)	.02	.08	4.6
5 Uses logical and inefficient steps with no error	.14	.08	3.0
4 Uses logical and inefficient steps with error(s)	.16	.17	.43
3 Begins logical procedure but does not finish problem	.06	.004	5.6
2 Verbalizes inability to solve problem and does not guess	.07	.03	3.07
1 Answers problems or proceeds in solution randomly or impulsively	.40	.06	13.0

SOURCE: J. F. Havertape & C. E. Kass, Examination of problem solving in learning disabled adolescents through verbalized self-instructions. *Learning Disability Quarterly*, 1978, *1*, p. 98. Reprinted by permission.

*   *z greater than 2.58 has p less than .01; z greater than 1.96 has p less than .05*

students have few attack strategies to apply to problem solution. Those who possess some strategies do not use them effectively. According to Havertape and Kass, "The most striking result was that 40% of the learning disabled group's responses consisted of random or impulsive answers without any relationship to the problem requirements. Typical comments were: 'Gee, I don't know. . . . I'll say _____," or 'I don't understand; it must be _____'" (p. 98).

COGNITIVE MODIFICATION

*Definition and
Important
Elements*

In many studies, and in some classrooms, one approach that is successful in developing problem-solving skills is *cognitive modification* (CM).[1] Several approaches are similar (cognitive-behavior modification, cognitive therapy, cognitive-functional approach, cognitive training, cognitive control training), and are discussed together under the general heading of cognitive modification. Cognitive modification combines the successful techniques of behavior therapy with those of cognitive therapy into an approach using a person's inner speech as a means of guiding behavior. A basic premise of this approach is that cognitions (of which inner speech is one aspect) influence behavior; therefore, by changing cognitions, behavior can be changed. Essentially, inner speech is viewed as a behavior subject to the same principles of learning as overt behavior. Keogh and Glover (1980), in their discussion of the characteristics of cognitive behavior modification, compare this approach with cognitive therapy and behavior therapy:

> *It is* behavioral *in that it is structured, utilizes reinforcement techniques, is usually focused on particular problems or complaints, and is not concerned with antecedents or etiology of the problem. It is* cognitive *in that its goal is to produce change in the individual by modifying his thinking.* (p. 5)

Consider this example of the use of cognitive modification techniques in a task requiring the copying of line patterns (Meichenbaum, Note 2).

1.   An adult model performs the task while describing the procedure aloud.

> *Okay, what is it I have to do? You want me to copy the picture with the different lines. I have to go slowly and carefully. Okay, draw the line down, down, good; then to the right, that's it; now down some more and to the left. Good, I'm doing fine so far. Remember, go slowly. Now back up again. No, I was supposed to go down. That's okay. Just erase the line carefully. Good. Even if I make an error I can go on slowly and carefully. I have to go down now. Finished. I did it!* (p. 17)

[1]For a full explanation of this approach see Meichenbaum (1977). For a review of research with learning disabled and other special populations, see the special issue of *Exceptional Education Quarterly* (Vol. 1, No. 1, 1980) devoted to this topic. See also the journal devoted to cognitive modification, *Cognitive Therapy and Research.*

2. The child performs the same task while the model repeats the directions.

3. The child whispers the instructions as the task is performed.

4. The child performs the task, guiding the performance through private speech.

In this and other similar approaches (Lloyd, 1980), modeling is a primary means of instruction. Students act as their own therapists or trainers (self-control, self-reinforcement, self-assessment) and verbalization, or self-talk, is a major component, beginning with overt speech and then fading into more covert self-talk. Students guide themselves through several steps in solving a problem or doing a task by asking themselves questions such as:

> ... (1) problem definition ("What is it I have to do?"); (2) focusing attention plus response guidance ("Be careful... draw the line down."); (3) self-reinforcement ("Good, I'm doing fine."); and (4) self-evaluation coping skills plus error-correcting options ("That's okay ... even if I make an error I can go slowly.") (Meichenbaum, Note 2, p. 17)

Use with Learning Disabled Children

Several educators (Abikoff, 1979; Kauffman & Hallahan, 1979; Keogh & Barkett, 1979; Keogh & Glover, 1980; Lloyd, 1980; Mahoney, 1974; Meichenbaum, Note 2) have suggested that cognitive modification procedures offer particular promise as a way to remediate the academic and behavioral problems of children with learning difficulties. Evidence to support this comes from several sources. First, as discussed earlier in this chapter, cognitive modification and other similar procedures have shown success in producing academic or behavioral changes in children who are hyperactive,[2] children who tend to be impulsive rather than reflective in responding,[3] and children who have difficulties in attending to school tasks (Lloyd, 1980). The particular procedures used and their effectiveness are discussed in more detail in subsequent sections of this chapter.

A second source of evidence comes from studies showing that cognitive modification approaches seem to have more generalizable and durable effects than other approaches (Keogh & Barkett, 1979; Keogh & Glover, 1980). For example, in a review of the effects of three intervention strategies—medication, behavior modification, and cognitive training—Keogh and Barkett (1979) conclude that although different interventions generally influence different aspects of performance, cognitive training appears to offer the greatest possibility of transfer or generalization. Perhaps this is due to the focus on general and specific strategies for problem solving, which would enhance overall performance on cognitive tasks.

---

[2]Readers interested in research literature on the use of cognitive modification on hyperactivity are referred to Abikoff (1979), Keogh and Barkett (1979), and Meichenbaum (1977) for reviews.

[3]For reviews of the research literature on the use of cognitive modification on impulsivity, interested readers should see Abikoff (1979), Lloyd (1980), and Meichenbaum (1977).

Finally, another source of evidence comes from the characterization of learning disabled youngsters as "passive" learners (Hallahan & Reeve, in press; Torgesen, 1977). If these students do not take an active role in their own learning or do not know when a learning situation needs active strategies, training procedures requiring them to be active participants in their own treatment as well as providing them with active strategies should serve as direct remediators of their learning problems (Lloyd, 1980).

Application to
Problem Solving
In the related area of development of general problem-solving skills, cognitive modification techniques have also been successful (Keogh & Glover, 1980; Lloyd, 1980; McKinney & Haskins, 1980). For a cognitive modification program to be successful, certain elements seem necessary (Keogh & Glover, 1980). Programs should be comprehensive (involve teachers as well as parents in the modeling and training procedures, address social as well as academic situations), use a variety of procedures (modeling, self-verbalization, self-instruction), and last long enough to insure that children have learned the strategies. It also seems important that the programs be directed toward the development of specific problem-solving strategies as well as learning the rules for applying the most effective approaches to different kinds of problems (Lloyd, 1980; McKinney & Haskins, 1980). For example, the problem-solving steps identified by Havertape and Kass (1978) are very general, and include getting the information, understanding the problem, and solving the problem (see Table 6.1). Within each of these general steps, specific problems require the use of different strategies. In a match-to-sample problem, solving the problem would involve systematic comparison of each variant with the sample. On the other hand, in solving a memory task, solving the problem would involve such strategies as grouping similar items together or verbally rehearsing each item in a series. More complicated problems such as the Twenty-Question Problem (Mosher & Hornsby, 1966) require sophisticated focusing strategies (as opposed to simple scanning strategies), in which the different choices are systematically eliminated. In this kind of problem, the most efficient problem-solving strategy involves the development of hypotheses and asking questions to test them. A particular problem-solving strategy, then, could be applied to a certain class of problem, but would not work with other types of problems. Children would also need to be taught rules for deciding which strategies to use as well as how to combine several techniques to solve a particular class of problems.

Also important to the success of a cognitive modification approach is a consideration of the age and maturity of the children involved. While younger children may lack the verbal or physical competencies needed to use the strategies, *overt* self-instruction may interfere with the performance of older or high IQ children (Kendler, Kendler, & Carrick, 1966; Meichenbaum & Goodman, 1969; Ridberg, Parke, & Hetherington, 1971). According to Keogh and Glover (1980), it seems that "once a behavior has been mastered and is regulated by private speech, imposition of overt verbalization interferes with performance" (p. 15). This conclusion is consistent with

Luria's (1961) model of the function of self-talk in mediating behavior, which postulates that a child goes through three stages in developing internalized control of this behavior: control by verbal instructions and reactions of external agents (parents); regulation by audible self-talk; and, finally, with increasing age or proficiency on a task, private speech shortened into single words and fragments of words. The goal of cognitive modification approaches, then, is to assist the child in developing appropriate overt self-regulatory speech which later becomes covert and guides behavior on academic tasks more effectively.

Some critics have argued that teaching specific problem-solving strategies is unwieldly in classroom situations (Ledwidge, 1978), since the number of strategies and rules for using them is almost infinite. However, certain types of strategies are absolutely essential to school success, given our heavy reliance on paper-and-pencil tasks in the early years of school. How often, for example, must a child compare a series of samples with a standard, copy shapes accurately, or remember a series of items?

THE PROBLEM-SOLVING PROCESS

As noted earlier, a child's substandard performance on an academic task can be due to a variety of factors, including deficits in underlying skills and in knowledge of appropriate strategies. Although current evidence does not support the assumption that all learning disabled children lack certain underlying abilities (visual perception, visual-motor abilities, auditory discrimination, selective attention), ample evidence certainly shows that *some* learning disabled children do not have these skills. To enable children to perform academic tasks, teachers must assess the levels of proficiency on specific skills and, if needed, plan remedial instruction. The following sections present a brief analysis of some of these disabilities and their possible influence on academic achievement, as well as some suggestions for their assessment and possible remedial approaches.

Step 1: Getting the Information

Since the steps in a problem-solving process are sequential, the first is absolutely essential to eventual solution. Children must first be able to get the information required to solve the problem. They must be able to encode or decode the instructions (usually presented orally or visually) and focus on the relevant aspects of the task. The disabilities most frequently influencing this process are visual perception and auditory discrimination. Children who are unable to distinguish forms, positions in space, or differentiate between a figure and its background have difficulties in many school tasks. In reading, for example, they must distinguish between the shapes of letters. In the beginning stages of math, they often are asked to combine groups of concrete objects (If we add one orange and three oranges, how many will we have?). Later, they are asked to complete computations involving the perception of figures and symbols. Children also must be able to discriminate sounds, since instructions often are given orally. Children who have difficulty discriminating sounds not only have trouble understanding directions presented verbally, but also have difficulty associating letters with speech sounds, thus causing difficulty in learning to read.

Assessment. Usually, when a child is tested for placement in a learning disabilities program, standardized tests of visual and visual-motor perception are included as a part of the diagnostic battery. These tests may include the *Frostig Developmental Test of Visual Perception* (Frostig, Lefever, Whittlesey, & Maslow, 1964), the *Bender Gestalt Test for Young Children* (Koppitz, 1964), the Visual Sequential Memory and Visual Reception subtests of the *Illinois Test of Psycholinguistic Abilities (ITPA)* (Kirk, McCarthy, & Kirk, 1968), the Draw-a-Design and Draw-a-Child subtests from the *McCarthy Scales of Children's Abilities* (McCarthy, 1972), and the Visual Achievement Forms from the *Purdue Perceptual-Motor Survey* (Roach & Kephart, 1966). In addition, certain items or subtests from intelligence tests can indicate visual perceptual abilities. Some examples of this are Discrimination of Forms, Rectangles, and Mutilated Pictures tests from the *Stanford-Binet* (Terman & Merrill, 1960) and the Picture Completion subtest from the *Wechsler Intelligence Scales for Children—Revised (WISC-R)* (Wechsler, 1974). In interpreting the results from these tests, however, the teacher must be careful to get enough information on the children's performance. For example, children who perform poorly on tasks such as those included in the *Bender Gestalt Test for Young Children* (in which a figure must be copied) may do so because of poor visual-perceptual skills or because of poor motor skills. To help in determining children's problems when they copy figures incorrectly, a teacher can later show them both the correct figure as a standard and the incorrect figure, and ask them to make the correct match. If the match can be made correctly, there is evidence that the problem is visual-motor. If a correct match is not made, there is evidence of a visual-perceptual problem (Hallahan & Kauffman, 1976). Items similar to those included on these tests or in reading readiness workbooks can be used for informal assessment of visual-perceptual abilities.

Standard test batteries often include tests of auditory discrimination or reception such as the *Auditory Discrimination Test* (Wepman, 1958), the *Goldman-Fristoe-Woodcock Test of Auditory Discrimination* (Goldman, Fristoe, & Woodcock, 1970), and the Auditory Reception, Auditory Closure, and Sound Blending subtests of the *ITPA*. Other more general tests of receptive skills are the *Peabody Picture Vocabulary Test (PPVT)* (Dunn, 1981), the *Durrell Listening-Reading Series* (Durrell, Hayes, & Brassard, 1969), the *Brown-Carlsen Listening Comprehension Test* (Brown & Carlsen, 1955), the Listening subtest of the *Sequential Tests of Educational Progress* (STEP) (Greenberger, 1977), and the Auditory Attention Span and Oral Directions subtests from the *Detroit Tests of Learning Aptitude* (Baker & Leland, 1959). When interpreting results from these and similar tests, it is important to consider what abilities (in addition to auditory discrimination) are required by the tests and may be causing poor performance. In the *PPVT*, for example, children are shown four pictures and given the name of an item or concept and asked to choose from the four pictures the one that goes best with the word given by the examiner. Performance on this test involves visual perception, memory, and vocabulary development as well as auditory skills. On many auditory tasks, children are asked to repeat a series of items presented orally. In addition to discrimination, such tasks involve memory. Teachers also can devise activities that informally assess the ability to discriminate speech sounds.

Remediation. As noted earlier, Larsen and Hammill's (1975) review of research on the relationship of visual-perceptual abilities to school learning showed that training in visual-perceptual skills did not cause increases in children's academic performances. According to other educators, the lack of academic improvement may be due to problems in research design, such as providing visual-perceptual training whether a child needs it or not, having training programs of short duration, or assessing immediate rather than long-term effects of the training.

Regardless of these controversies, some children clearly have visual-perceptual disabilities. Several approaches can be used to remediate these deficits, including commercially available programs, applied behavior analysis, and cognitive modification. Of the commercially available programs, Frostig and Horne's (1964) is probably the most widely used. It is designed to remediate the abilities assessed by the *Frostig Developmental Test of Visual Perception.* One other visual-perceptual program was designed to be used with a test. Kirk and Kirk (1971) present activities that can be used to remediate deficits identified by the *ITPA.* For a review of other such approaches, see Wallace and Kauffman (1973).

In using applied behavior analysis to enhance visual-perceptual skills,

This teacher is pointing out to the student the distinctive features of his seatwork assignment to help him gain a strategy for correctly answering the problems.

one effective approach is based on Gibson's (1969) theory of distinctive features. In her research, Gibson found that people concentrate on particular features of visual stimuli to make discriminations. For example, in discriminating a circle from a square, the distinctive features used are corners and straight lines, while in discriminating a square from a triangle, one must pay attention to the number of the sides. Children can be taught to attend to the distinctive features of visual stimuli through the use of reinforcement procedures. Tawney (1972), for example, found that when children were reinforced for discriminating on the basis of distinctive features, their performance improved more than those reinforced for discriminating on the basis of simple features that were not critical to discriminating the forms. When children have special difficulties, prompting procedures can be used to highlight the distinctive features. For young children, color such as red ink could be used to highlight the distinctive features and gradually faded and eliminated. When combined with reinforcement, prompting can be an effective technique for teaching even difficult discriminations (Bijou, 1968; Corey & Shamow, 1972).

A cognitive modification approach to learning visual discriminations might involve the addition of self-talk, self-reinforcement, and modeling techniques to the basic applied behavior analysis procedures, as in the example below.

1.   An adult model performs a discrimination task while talking out loud.

> *"Okay, what is it I have to do? You want me to figure out which of these shapes on the right is like the one on the left. I have to look carefully at each shape to see what makes it different from the model. Let's see, this one has corners, but the model doesn't. That one isn't right. Good, I'm doing fine so far. Let's see, the next one looks the same. No, I must look carefully. It isn't the same. It has straight lines. . . . That's okay, I can get them correct if I look at each one carefully. Finished. I did it!"*

2.   The child performs the same discrimination task while the model repeats the directions.

3.   The child whispers the instructions while going through the task.

4.   The child performs the task, guiding the performance through private speech.

When remediating auditory discrimination disabilities or listening problems, many of the same principles used to remediate visual perception and discrimination apply. The remedial procedures described by Kirk and Kirk (1971) include activities for developing auditory as well as visual perceptual abilities based on assessment using the *ITPA*. Others (Karnes, 1968; Minskoff, Wiseman, & Minskoff, 1974) have developed exercise books based on the *ITPA* as well. Johnson and Myklebust (1967) present remedial techniques for both receptive and expressive language problems, including activities for auditory discrimination training. It should be noted here that auditory discrimination training suffers from the same lack of connection with academic success as does visual discrimination (Hammill & Larsen, 1974). Considerable controversy exists over the use of the *ITPA* to assess these abilities and disabilities. For example, Hallahan and Cruickshank (1973) conclude from their review of the research on its use that the subtests are not completely independent, especially at the younger ages, and some of the abilities assessed may not correspond with the subtest names.

Applied behavior analysis approaches use reinforcement for making appropriate auditory discriminations. Other techniques involve the teacher modifying the presentation of instructions, keeping them simple, direct, and brief. Distracting or irrelevant directions should be avoided. When children follow instructions, they should be reinforced. When they do not follow instructions, reinforcement should be withheld. Cognitive modification procedures such as the example for visual perception also could be used for auditory discrimination.

Step 2: Understanding the Problem

The second step in a problem-solving process is understanding what is to be solved. In addition to reading comprehension (discussed in Chapter 9) and receptive and expressive language abilities (discussed in Chapter 8), this part of the process involves the general information-processing abilities usually referred to as memory (see Gagné and White, 1978, for a review of research and theory on the relationship between memory structures and learning outcomes). The abilities included in this cluster are sometimes referred to as listening skills or serial learning—acquiring, retaining, and retrieving information. Poor performance could result from disabilities or inadequate learning strategies in any one of the three areas: individuals could learn poorly what they are expected to remember, they could retain poorly what they had learned, or they could incompletely recall or retrieve what they had learned and retained (Butterfield, Wambold, & Belmont, 1973). Most recent research seems to indicate that learning disabled children can perform all the processes needed for acquisition, storage, and recall of information, but lack the knowledge of when and how to use the strategies (Hall, 1980).

It is also possible that some learning disabled children lack the underlying abilities needed to perform these tasks (Das et al., 1978; Smiley et al., 1977; Swanson, 1979). Disabilities or poor performance in any of these areas adversely affect academic achievement. For example, children who are unable to organize incoming information so that it is easier to remember have difficulty remembering items and developing abstract concepts. Miller (1956) proposes that people recode items by forming "chunks" of information that can be stored in memory in a single category (chair, desk, table, and couch are all *furniture* and can be more easily remembered as part of the category furniture than if one attempts to remember each item separately). In order to develop an accurate concrete or abstract concept, a person must know both those items that are examples of the concept and those that are not. In developing the concept of furniture, for instance, children must be able to compare a new possibility (a stove or refrigerator) with the existing examples of the concept to determine whether it differs on the relevant dimensions or whether it is similar enough to be included as a sample of the concept. If other examples are not available for comparison, this process is difficult, if not impossible. Similarly, children who cannot retrieve stored information have the same difficulties in remembering previous solutions to a problem or in using information contained in the present one.

Assessment.   Most procedures for assessing acquisition, storage, and retrieval of information are experimental, although some of the instruments discussed earlier can be used for this purpose: the *Brown-Carlsen Listening Comprehension Test*, the *Sequential Tests of Educational Progress (STEP)*, and the *Durrell Listening-Reading Series*. One subtest of the *WISC-R*, the Digit Span (including digits forward and digits backward), can be used as an indicator of a child's short-term memory ability. Experimental tasks also can be used as an informal indication of children's use of strategies for processing information. Bousfield's (1953) task, for example, can be used easily. A list of words drawn from several conceptual categories is presented randomly. The student is required to recall as many items as possible. Both the total number of items recalled and the extent to which children organize items in recall are recorded. Other informal strategies can be found in reading readiness materials or in listening skills training programs.

Remediation.   Several programs and books of activities are available that teach listening skills to normal children (Barker, 1971; Cunningham & Cunningham, 1976; Taylor, 1973), but few programs have been designed for learning disabled children. Activities designed to be used with the *ITPA*, however, do include memory strategies (Karnes, 1968; Kirk & Kirk, 1971; Minskoff, Wiseman, & Minskoff, 1974). Teachers can enhance the effectiveness of these and other approaches if they insure the appropriateness of their own speaking characteristics. Russell and Russell (1959) provide questions for teachers to use.

1.   In the classroom am I usually talking or do I often listen?

2.   When I give oral directions, do I prepare the pupils for what is to come and then avoid repetition?

3.   Do I make sure that the purposes for listening are clear to each student? (pp. 18–19)

Alley and Deshler (1979) also indicate areas for assessing speaking characteristics of teachers of learning disabled children.

1.   *Nonlinguistic communication.* Does the teacher make effective use of gestures, eye contact, pauses?

2.   *Preorganizers.* Does the teacher present an overview that stresses the major points of the material to be covered?

3.   *Organization.* Does the teacher present information in a logical, organized fashion?

4.   *Pace.* Does the teacher present the information at varied paces— slowing down for important points and repeating them for emphasis?

5. *Examples.* Does the teacher use examples to illustrate points and give concrete examples of abstract information? (p. 289)

To make any listening or memory skill development program more effective, teachers should provide the added dimensions of reinforcement for correct responses and for use of active strategies. If learning disabled children are "inactive" learners who, as some writers suggest (Hall, 1979, 1980; Torgesen, 1977; Wong, Wong, & Foth, 1977), possess the underlying structural abilities but lack the appropriate strategies, it is imperative that they be taught active memory strategies such as clustering and verbal rehearsal. In a study of the differential effects of three approaches, Bussell, Huls, and Long (1975) found that the most effective method for developing listening skills in learning disabled children was a combination of listening skills training, token reinforcement, and teacher enrichment. In a series of studies investigating the performance of learning disabled boys, Tarver and her associates (Hallahan, Tarver, Kauffman, & Graybeal, 1978; Tarver, Hallahan, Cohen, & Kauffman, 1977) significantly increased performance in remembering important information through the use of verbal rehearsal strategies.

In addition to encouraging children to use appropriate strategies by reinforcement, a cognitive modification approach suggests that some children need to be taught how and when to use these strategies. This approach has particular appeal, since in some studies learning disabled children who

Table 6.2   **Strategies for improving memory and information-processing skills**

I. Strategies Used Prior to the Task:
   A. Teacher presents questions to be answered (highlighting important information to be learned);
   B. Teacher presents an outline of important points;
   C. Teacher presents information so that the organization is clear (when presenting a list of words to be remembered, present them in categories with the category label at the top rather than presenting them randomly and expecting children to figure out their own organization).
II. Strategies Used During the Task:
   A. Student is encouraged to ask questions when information is unclear or the task is unclear;
   B. Student is taught how to look or listen for organizing cues such as "There are three steps in the process . . .";
   C. Student is taught how to develop an organization or clustering and coding system if there is none (lists of items can be grouped according to such similarities as function or use; abstract category; descriptive characteristics, including color and shape; degree of importance; and chronological order);
   D. Student is taught to look and listen for verbal as well as nonverbal cues;
   E. Student is taught to look and listen for main and supporting ideas;
   F. Student is taught to rehearse or repeat items to himself or herself as he or she hears or sees them;
   G. Student is taught to use visual imagery (usually best if the task is somewhat concrete);
   H. Student is taught to use mnemonic devices, such as remembering the first letters of the words in a series instead of the whole word;
   I. Older students can be taught how to take notes effectively.
III. Strategies Used After the Task:
   A. Teacher asks questions requiring students to summarize main ideas;
   B. Student is taught to review information from the task in the context of organizers or questions presented prior to the task;
   C. Student is taught to review the task *immediately* afterwards instead of waiting.

were taught such strategies as verbal rehearsal (repeating items in a series to oneself), associative clustering (grouping like items together), attention-directing cues such as highlighting important information, or other mnemonic devices, performed as well as normally achieving children in tasks in which they previously had shown inferior performance (Bauer, 1977a, 1977b, 1979; Hall, 1979; Torgesen, 1978; Torgesen & Goldman, 1977; Wong, Wong, & Foth, 1977). Specific strategies that might be effective for use in a cognitive modification approach are shown in Table 6.2. With the addition of self- and external reinforcement, modeling, and self-talk, strategies such as those presented in Table 6.2 can be used effectively by learning disabled children to improve their information-processing ability.

Step 3: Solving the Problem

The third step, actually solving the problem, has three general substeps and an infinite number of specific parts, depending on the type and complexity of the problem to be solved. The general substeps are generating hypotheses, evaluating hypotheses, and implementing the solution. Included in the sub-step called generation of hypotheses is the use of systematic, organized strategies versus random or impulsive ones, and generation of unique or varied hypotheses as opposed to generating only one or only very common solutions.

Instead of using systematic, organized strategies, many learning disabled children seem to solve problems in a random or impulsive manner (see the Cognitive Style section of this chapter). In one study, discussed earlier (Havertape & Kass, 1978), the authors conclude that the most striking result of their study was finding that 40 percent of the learning disabled students' responses consisted of random or impulsive answers without any relationship to the problem requirements. Using inappropriate or random methods for problem solution has a general and pervasive effect on achievement in academic tasks, resulting in the inconsistent, almost random performance of some learning disabled children.

The picture is more positive for the generation of unique and varied hypotheses. Although the creative and divergent thinking abilities of learning disabled children have not been investigated in many studies, the results of two studies are encouraging. Argulewicz, Mealor, and Richmond (1979) found that the learning disabled children were average or above the norm group in fluency, abstract titles, resistance to quick closure, and originality. The only area in which their performance was lower than the norm group was in elaboration, the addition of details to the basic idea. Tarver, Buss, and Maggiore (1979), in an investigation of the relationship between creativity and selective attention, found a significant positive relationship between certain creativity measures (originality and uniqueness) and incidental recall (remembering information incidental to the main task). This finding was consistent with the authors' hypothesis that these two aspects of creativity are facilitated by broad rather than selective attention. These particular studies are important not only for their demonstration of the particular abilities that learning disabled children possess, but also for calling attention to the possibility that some characteristics contributing to performance deficits in certain kinds of academic tasks can actually contribute to better performance in other types of tasks. Perhaps future research will concentrate on the identification of strengths and talents of these children rather than only on their deficiencies.

Other research and writing related to generating, evaluating, and implementing hypotheses is discussed in later sections of this chapter because of their more general nature.

Assessment. The methods used by Havertape and Kass (1978) to assess whether students employ systematic or random strategies (classifying recorded self-verbalizations of students while solving problems) also could be used in a classroom setting (see Table 6.1). With younger children, the teacher may supervise their verbalizing what they are doing while solving a problem or could ask them to explain how they solved a particular problem or approached a particular task. Other informal procedures could be implemented. Children could be observed while performing a series of concrete tasks and a record could be kept of the strategies used and the types of errors made (are errors due to lack of knowledge, lack of understanding of the task, or inefficient strategies). Also, a series of tasks could be presented and the children asked how they would go about solving each of them. Experimental tasks such as those described by McKinney and Haskins (1980), the *Pattern Matching Problem* (Neimark & Lewis, 1967), and Twenty-Questions (Mosher & Hornsby, 1966) could also be used. Children's strategies in problems such as these can be determined by the way in which incorrect choices are eliminated.

In assessing children's abilities to produce unique and varied hypotheses, numerous standardized and informal procedures are available. There is considerable controversy regarding whether these tests can be considered measures of the global construct of creativity. Critics argue that they simply measure a small part of creativity—the ability to produce many (fluency), many types (flexibility), unique (originality), and detailed (elaboration) ideas or solutions. If they are considered only as tests of these four abilities, their interpretation is valid. Some of the other more common standardized tests are: *The Torrance Tests of Creative Thinking* (Torrance, 1972), *Verbal and Figural Forms; Thinking Creatively with Sounds and Words* (Khatena & Torrance, 1973); and the *Tests of Creativity* (Guilford, 1971). In addition, informal checklists are available for the assessment of creative abilities. Some examples are Torrance's (1973) *Checklist of Creative Positives*, and the *Scales for Rating Behavioral Characteristics of Superior Students* (Renzulli, Smith, White, Callahan, & Hartman, 1977).

Remediation. If children have demonstrated their knowledge of appropriate problem-solving strategies but seldom or inconsistently use them, applied behavior analysis techniques can be used to encourage more frequent and consistent use of appropriate methods. Children should be provided with verbal and other reinforcement for any appropriate strategies or parts of strategies used. No studies are available comparing applied behavior analysis approaches with cognitive modification approaches in the development of problem-solving skills. However, Keogh and Barkett (1979), in a review of the effectiveness of three types of interventions—medication, applied behavior analysis, and cognitive modification—used with hyperactive children, conclude that different interventions influence different aspects of children's performances. Generally, medication changed overt activity level and modified such processes as visual perception and sustained attention. Applied behavior analysis increased specific on-task behavior for school assignments and decreased extraneous motor activity, while cognitive modification improved performance on problem-solving tasks, reduced impulsivity, and increased ability to attend to task. Abikoff (1979) arrived at similar conclusions about the effect of cognitive modification.

In one comparison study, McKinney and Haskins (1980) evaluated the effectiveness of three different approaches to developing more efficient problem-solving strategies on the *Pattern Matching Problem*. In the first procedure, children were simply given a rule for avoiding errors. The second involved direct instruction in the most sophisticated strategy for that task. In the third, impulsive children were either provided with strategy training or delay training, or assigned to a control group. From these results, the authors conclude that strategy training was superior to procedures that attempted to modify either task requirements or cognitive style during problem solving.

Others (Camp, Blom, Herbert, & Van Doorninck, 1977; Spivack, Platt, & Shure, 1976; Spivack & Shure, 1974) developed general problem-solving training programs that were successful when used with children who had learning problems. The most comprehensive of these seems to be the *"Think Aloud" Program* (Camp et al., 1977). Designed to enhance self-control in aggressive boys, the program also includes general problem-solving training. Through modeling, verbal self-instruction procedures, psychological processing tasks, and interpersonal problem-solving games, children are taught to use a general process involving four basic questions: "What is my problem?" "What is my plan?" "Am I using my plan?" "How did I do?" First, children are introduced to a "copy-cat" game introducing them to the four questions (see Figure 6.1). The copy-cat is then faded and cue cards are introduced to signal the child to self-verbalize.

Posttest comparisons showed significant differences between experimental and control groups on measures such as *Porteus Maze, Matching Familiar Figures*, performance IQ on the *WISC-R*, and academic achievement. Other programs and approaches are discussed later.

Several types of programs exist for the development of divergent thinking or the ability to produce a variety of ideas and solutions. Although their effectiveness in developing the overall characteristic of creativity is questionable, it seems clear that they do develop divergent thinking. According to a review by Mansfield, Busse, and Krepelka (1978), the most effective program seems to be the *Parnes Creative Problem Solving Program* (Parnes, 1967). Others that have been effective to a certain extent are the *Purdue Creative Thinking Program* (Feldhusen, Speedie, & Treffinger, 1971) and the *Productive Thinking Program* (Covington, Crutchfield, Davies, & Olton, 1972). All of these programs are made more effective if the teacher has had inservice training and is willing to foster a climate of psychological safety for the expression of unique or "wild" ideas (Torrance, 1967).

1	2
What is my problem?	How can I do it?
3	4
Am I using my plan?	How did I do?

Figure 6.1   An illustration from a comprehensive problem-solving program. (B. Camp & M. Bash, *Think aloud program: Group manual, revised.* Denver, Colo.: University of Colorado Medical School, 1975. ERIC Document Reproduction Service No. ED 142 024. Reprinted by permission of the authors.)

A somewhat different approach to remediation was taken by Carlson (1974), who, in a multiple baseline/successive treatments model, used a child's creative strengths in fluency and elaboration to increase academic achievement and evaluative efforts. The child improved in goal-directedness, self-evaluation, and several areas of academic achievement. Torrance (Note 3) also reported the successful use of creative strengths in fluency and flexibility to develop originality as well as to enhance academic achievement. These studies suggest that it may be effective, at least in this area, to put into practice the principle of working through a child's strengths to develop weak areas. (For additional suggestions and rationale for this approach, see Maker, 1979.)

An applied behavior analysis approach also can be used effectively to develop divergent thinking abilities. In fact, one criticism of studies evaluating the effectiveness of creativity training programs such as those discussed earlier is that experimenters may actually be assessing the effectiveness of reinforcement in producing the desired changes rather than the materials themselves. In many of these studies, reinforcement is unintentionally or inconsistently used (Campbell & Willis, 1978), and is treated as an error variable—a nuisance. Others (Goetz & Salmonson, 1972) recognized the importance of social reinforcement and found it useful for increasing form diversity in easel paintings by preschoolers, for increasing variability of block forms built by young children (Goetz & Baer, 1973), for producing changes in sentence structure and rate of using certain parts of speech in intermediate students' essay writing, and for increasing the components of creative behavior on lists of unusual uses (Glover & Gary, 1976). Using a multiple baseline design with a classroom of fifth graders, Campbell and Willis (1978) showed that a combination of social and token reinforcement could be used to develop the components of fluency, flexibility, and elaboration in children's story writing. Children's performances on the *Torrance Tests of Creative Thinking* also improved significantly after the program. In this study, an interesting result occurred: the target skills remained high after reinforcement was discontinued. As Campbell and Willis noted, the children thoroughly enjoyed the task and as they became more proficient, less external reinforcement was needed for maintenance.

Some classical studies of the differences between creative and noncreative or more creative and less creative individuals have shown that the less creative person often expresses highly self-critical thoughts that inhibit performance (see Barron, 1957; MacKinnon, 1962; Patrick, 1935). These results suggested to Meichenbaum (1975) that one way to enhance performance would be to alter self-statements and thoughts. Using a cognitive modification approach, he taught subjects to verbalize more appropriate statements. He noted that subjects' originality and flexibility on tests of divergent thinking increased and that positive changes in self-concept and preference for complexity also occurred. A side effect, important to this discussion, was that the self-instructional training developed a generalized set to apply a more creative approach to a variety of personal and academic performances. As an example of the self-statements that could be used, Meichenbaum (1977) gives the following example from the earlier study, which was used in a task

Table 6.3 Examples of self-statements practiced by students in a cognitive modification approach

---

Self-Statements Arising from an Attitudinal Conceptualization of Creativity

---

Set inducing self-statements
What to do:
  Be creative, be unique.
  Break away from the obvious, the commonplace.
  Think of something no one else will think of.
  Just be free wheeling.
  If you push yourself you can be creative.
  Quantity helps breed quality.

What not to do:
  Get rid of internal blocks.
  Defer judgments.
  Don't worry what others think.
  Not a matter of right or wrong.
  Don't give the first answer you think of.
  No negative self-statements.

Self-Statements Arising from a Mental Abilities Conceptualization of Creativity

---

Problem analysis—what you say to yourself before you start a problem
  Size up the problem; what is it you have to do?
  You have to put the elements together differently.
  Use different analogies.
  Do the task as if you were Osborn brainstorming or Gordon doing Synectics training.
  Elaborate on ideas.
  Make the strange familiar and the familiar strange.

Task execution—what you say to yourself while doing a task
  You're in a rut—okay try something new.
  Take a rest now; who knows when the ideas will visit again.
  Go slow—no hurry—no need to press.
  Good, you're getting it.
  This is fun.
  That was a pretty neat answer; wait till you tell the others!

Self-Statements Arising from a Psychoanalytic Conceptualization of Creativity

---

Release controls; let your mind wander.
Free-associate; let ideas flow.
Relax—just let it happen.
Let your ideas play.
Refer to your experience; just view it differently.
Let your ego regress.
Feel like a bystander through whom ideas are just flowing.
Let one answer lead to another.
Almost dreamlike, the ideas have a life of their own.

SOURCE: D. Meichenbaum, *Cognitive-behavior modification: An integrative approach.* New York: Plenum Press, 1977, p. 63. Reprinted by permission of the publisher.

This youngster is experimenting with the monkey from the *Torrance Tests of Creative Thinking,* and expanding his creative thinking abilities.

involving the development of clever, interesting, and unusual ways of improving a toy monkey so that children would have more fun playing with it.

> *I want to think of something no one else will think of, something unique. Be freewheeling, no hangups. I don't care what anyone thinks; just suspend judgment. I'm not sure what I'll come up with; it will be a surprise. The ideas can just flow through me. Okay, what is it I have to do? Think of ways to improve a toy monkey. Toy monkey. Let me close my eyes and relax. Just picture a monkey. I see a monkey; now let my mind wander; let one idea flow into another. I'll use analogies. Let me picture myself inside the monkey. . . . Now let me do the task as if I were someone else. (After inducing this general set, the experimenter then thought aloud as he tried to come up with answers.) (p. 62)*

Table 6.3 gives some other examples of self-statements developed for the study that could be modeled and practiced by students in a cognitive modification approach.

Certain other disabilities and characteristics often attributed to learning disabled children have a more general effect on their performances in problem-solving situations. These general influences (attention, cognitive style, motivation, modality preferences, developmental readiness) are discussed in the following section.

GENERAL INFLUENCES ON PROBLEM SOLVING

Attention

Hallahan and his associates (Hallahan & Cruickshank, 1973; Hallahan & Kauffman, 1975, 1976; Hallahan, Kauffman, & Ball, 1973; Tarver & Hallahan, 1974) have conducted and reviewed numerous studies showing that many learning disabled children are highly distractible, unable to filter out extraneous stimuli and focus selectively on a task. Using an experimental task designed by Hagen (1967), this group of researchers has demonstrated repeatedly that children who are classified as learning disabled or under-

152

achievers show a deficit (when compared to normally achieving children) in "selective attention." Selective attention is in many ways an efficient learning strategy. Sophisticated learners and older students showed an increased ability to recall items in a series when they were told that they would be asked to recall the items. They also had a corresponding decrease in their ability to recall items incidental to the main task. The ratio of central recall (items students are told to recall) to incidental recall gives an index of attention efficiency, or selective attention. In discussing distractibility as an overriding disability, Hallahan and Kauffman (1976) list several areas (serial learning or memory tasks, tasks involving eye-hand coordination, and match-to-sample tasks) in which an attentional deficit can cause academic difficulties or make the child appear to have other learning problems. The ability to select and concentrate on the relevant aspects of a task or a stimulus is important in every step of the problem-solving process and is impossible to separate from some of the other disabilities learning disabled children are characterized as having (Koppell, 1979). For example, in the first step of problem-solving, getting the information, one must be able to focus on the material necessary for understanding and solving the problem. To be efficient, one must be able to select this material quickly and avoid being distracted by irrelevant instructions or details. Furthermore, on a task involving, for instance, visual perception (match-to-sample), it is impossible to determine whether a child's poor performance stems from some perceptual disturbance making him or her unable to "see" the likenesses and differences, or whether this poor performance is due to inability to focus on the distinctive features of the figures. As for solving more complicated problems, this inability to focus on the relevant and to ignore irrelevant cues may contribute to the random, impulsive strategies observed in studies such as the one by Havertape and Kass (1978). If for some reason the cues for solving a problem cannot be discerned, the problem will make no sense and the student might give up or respond in a random fashion.

Assessment.   Even though selective attention seems to be so important to academic success, there are no commonly used standardized tests for assessment. Experimental measures such as the central-incidental task devised by Hagen (1967) and dichotic listening tasks (Maccoby, 1967) may be helpful. In addition, three subtests of the *WISC-R* (arithmetic, coding, and digit span) are often considered measures of a child's attentional abilities (Hallahan & Kauffman, 1976). Information procedures, such as counting the instances of on-task versus off-task behavior, are easy to use. A teacher could involve children in the monitoring of their own behavior using procedures similar to those employed in the experimental studies by Hallahan and associates (Hallahan, Lloyd, Kosiewicz, Kauffman, & Graves, 1979; Hallahan, Lloyd, Kosiewicz, & Kneedler, 1979).

Remediation.   The first program developed to educate distractible children was the structured classroom with reduced environmental stimuli and stimulus-rich teaching materials (Cruickshank, Bentzen, Ratzeburg, & Tannhauser, 1961). Elements of this approach include few if any decisions about classroom management or demeanor made by the child, explicit expectations and instructions, sound-treated walls and ceilings in classrooms, cubicles as work areas for children, no decorations on bulletin boards or walls, and opaque windows so that children cannot see activities outside. In contrast to the bleakness of the classroom, instructional materials were designed to attract a child's attention. For example, for a child to learn to read a particular word, that word might be presented in bold colors on a single page. Studies of the effectiveness of the total Cruickshank program, however, have shown no consistently conclusive results (Hallahan & Kauffman, 1975). Two elements of the program, stimulus-rich teaching materials and the use of cubicles, do have support from research, particularly when cues such as color (a stimulus dimension preferred by young children) are used to highlight the relevant aspects of a task (Hallahan & Kauffman, 1975). Shores and Haubrich (1969) found that cubicles were effective in increasing the attending behavior of emotionally disturbed children. Other strategies for developing attention are described by Bricker and Dennison (1978), and Allington (1975). The methods described by Allington are of particular interest since they involve teaching children to look for distinctive features.

Applied behavior analysis techniques have been used extensively in the remediation of distractibility, and the results are highly positive (Hallahan & Kauffman, 1975). By providing teacher attention for on-task behavior with no attention during off-task behavior (Hall, Lund, & Jackson, 1968; Hallahan & Kauffman, 1975) or rewards for attending to task (Ferritor, Buckholdt, Hamblin, & Smith, 1972; Walker & Buckley, 1968), children's attending can be increased. In an interesting study, Kazdin (1973) found that reinforcement of either attending or nonattending in one child increased attending of adjacent (nonreinforced) peers. In another study, Hallahan, Tarver, Kauffman, and Graybeal (1978) found that while reinforcement facilitated both selective attention and verbal rehearsal, response cost procedures did not. The authors hypothesized that in the response cost condition, the subject's attention was focused on the loss of the money rather than on the task. As with other underlying abilities, however, research has not demonstrated that children's academic achievement shows significant increases after their attending has improved (Kirby & Shields, 1972; Ferritor et al., 1972). When academic achievement is to be improved, reinforcement must be provided for academic achievement. On the other hand, in order to learn, a child must attend to the task. This can be improved by providing reinforcement for attention.

A potentially more effective approach to develop attention is cognitive modification. Due to the addition of training in the use of specific strategies, particularly verbalization and self-monitoring, students' performances have been enhanced. Hallahan and Reeve (in press) effectively increased children's on-task, arithmetic, and handwriting performance. In other studies (Tarver, Hallahan, Kauffman, & Ball, 1976), learning disabled children's selective attention improved significantly when they were taught to use verbal rehearsal strategies.

Cognitive Style   Another general influence on the problem-solving process is cognitive style, or more specifically, cognitive tempo. Research on the construct of reflectivity-impulsivity consistently has shown that children with learning problems usually can be classified as impulsive rather than reflective, while normally

achieving children are more often reflective than impulsive (Epstein, Hallahan, & Kauffman, 1975). The reflectivity-impulsivity dichotomy (Kagan,
1966) is defined as the tendency, in situations where there is uncertainty
about the correct answer, to respond quickly with a high rate of error (impulsive) or to respond more slowly and make fewer errors (reflective). Individuals who are above the mean of the group on response time (take more time to
respond) but below the mean on number of errors (make fewer errors) are
classified reflective, while those who are below the mean on response time
but above the mean on number of errors are classified impulsive. The two
remaining groups, the fast-accurate and slow-inaccurate, usually are not
studied due to the small numbers in these groups as well as the lack of
interest in studying their characteristics. An impulsive response style has
been linked to a variety of behavioral and learning problems in a variety of
populations. Considerable controversy also exists regarding this dimension
of performance, mainly focusing on measurement problems, because only
one instrument, the *Matching Familiar Figures Test* (*MFFT*) (Kagan, 1966),
or a variation of it, has been used (see Becker, Bender, & Morrison, 1978, for
a review).

Regardless of the criticisms of its measurement, there is a growing
body of research documenting the performance of underachieving children
on the *MFFT*. When considered with evidence from studies of selective
attention and hyperactivity as well as evidence that learning disabled children do respond randomly or unsystematically in problem-solving situations,
it seems important to at least consider this dimension of performance. A
tendency to respond quickly rather than making a more considered decision
can affect performance in all stages of problem-solving. When reading or
listening to directions, an impulsive individual may have a tendency to
ignore important information, and thus get an incomplete or incorrect concept of the requirements of the task. In solving a problem this same tendency may result in the choice of the first solution that appears even re-
motely plausible, to the exclusion of a more appropriate choice. In academic
situations, impulsive children are usually poor readers, low achievers in
math, deficient in selective attention, and retained more often (Epstein et
al., 1975).

Assessment.   As discussed earlier, the major means of assessment has been
through use of the *Matching Familiar Figures Test* (Kagan, 1966). In this
test, individuals are shown a collection of pictures of easily recognizable
objects, such as a lamp, a house, and a pair of glasses. They are instructed to
choose which of several alternative pictures exactly matches the standard.
Some other instruments used in such situations are the *Porteus Maze Test*
(Porteus, 1965) and the Block Design, Picture Arrangement, and Coding
subtests of the *WISC-R* (Wechsler, 1974). Informal assessment could be
accomplished simply by measuring response time and number of errors in
academic tasks.

Remediation.   Different methods have been used to modify the response
styles of students considered impulsive. Instructions to delay responding
(Heider, 1971; Kagan, Pearson, & Welch, 1966), observation of a filmed or
live reflective model (Denney, 1972; Ridberg, Parke, & Hetherington,

1971), matching reflective teachers with impulsive children (Nagle & Thwaite, 1979; Yando & Kagan, 1968), and reinforcement contingencies for delayed responding (Kendall & Finch, 1978; Nelson, Finch, & Hooke, 1975) have been used. Except for the placement of children with reflective teachers, these procedures have not consistently made impulsive children more reflective (Messer, 1976). In general, they have modified response time, but have not reduced the number of errors made or facilitated generalization to academic performance. Since research has indicated that impulsive children generally are inefficient in using problem-solving strategies (visual scanning strategies, analysis of distinctive features of stimuli, use of an organized approach, problem-focusing), one approach used has been to teach children to employ more effective strategies. This has been successful in modifying response time, reducing the number of errors on experimental tasks, and, when training is of sufficient duration, in generalizing to improved classroom and academic performance (see reviews by Abikoff, 1979; Finch & Spirito, 1980; Keogh & Glover, 1980; McKinney & Haskins, 1980; Messer, 1976). When applied behavior analysis procedures have been compared with training that includes self-talk or strategy training, cognitive modification techniques have been shown to be more durable and generalizable (Abikoff, 1979; Finch & Spirito, 1980; Keogh & Glover, 1980; Pressley, 1979).

Digate, Epstein, Cullinan, and Switzky (1978) review several procedures used to modify impulsive behavior, including required delay, direct instruction, self-verbalization, differentiation training, modeling, and response consequences. They also present teaching techniques useful for implementing each of these procedures. For example, in using differentiation training, they suggest that the teacher instruct pupils to

> *look at* all *the alternatives and the standard, divide the alternatives into component parts, select one distinguishing feature and search all alternatives looking for similarities and differences, evaluate the standard to determine the correct form of the component part, and successively eliminate alternatives that deviate from the distinguishing feature of the standard.* (p. 463)

In the section on modeling, it was suggested that the model should display physical movements that correspond to an efficient visual scanning pattern, point first to a standard and then carefully eliminate alternative choices; verbalize self-instructions related to responding slowly, avoid picking the first alternative without reviewing the others; and describe the scanning strategy. Impulsive children can benefit from placement close to reflective peers and observation of a reflective teacher.

Motivation   Teachers of learning disabled children often observe that these children no longer believe that they can learn, making it necessary to direct initial effort toward structuring tasks and activities through which children can experience success. In the experimental literature, a phenomenon similar to this was observed in individuals exposed to repeated failure in which they seemed to have no control over the outcome (Seligman, 1975). In these situations, individuals previously competent in a certain task became passive, lethargic, much less persistent, and suffered from a general lowering of self-esteem. This phenomenon is called *learned helplessness*, and is closely related to the ideas expressed by attribution theorists (see Shaver, 1975, for an introduction to attribution theory). Briefly, the basic assumption is that beliefs about what causes one's own behavior serve as "cognitive mediators," and thus influence subsequent behavior, such as willingness to attempt a new or difficult task, persistence, effort, and expectations for success. According to Weiner (Weiner, Frieze, Kukla, Reed, Rest, & Rosenbaum, 1971), children attribute their academic success or failure most frequently to either effort, ability, task difficulty, or luck. If, for example, children believe that success is due to effort, they are likely to expend effort on similar tasks in the future. On the other hand, if they believe that success is due to luck, to expend a great deal of effort in the future would seem useless, as they would not expect it to increase their chances for success.

Although little research has linked the experimental construct of learned helplessness with the performance of learning disabled children, the ideas seem promising because of their relevance to real classroom problems (Thomas, 1979). Henker, Whalen, and Hinshaw (1980) even suggest that the labeling process may influence attributions and subsequent performance. After children are labeled learning disabled, they may begin to attribute reading errors to factors beyond their control, such as lack of ability. Unlabeled children may see the same problem as caused by insufficient effort or concentration. If labeled children believe that failure is beyond their control, they may stop trying. Children who believe that they have control over success continue to try. The theory also suggests that some unlabeled children consistently experience repeated failure and change their attributions to exhibit characteristics of learned helplessness.

Some new programs using cognitive modification approaches in designing intervention strategies are beginning to consider the implications of a person's beliefs about personal control over success and failure (Henker et al., 1980). Initial support for the effectiveness of the approach was obtained in a study of hyperactive boys (Bugental, Whalen, & Henker, 1977). Children who tended to attribute school performance to their own efforts made greater improvements when self-control procedures were used. Children who believed academic success and failure were caused more by such factors as luck and other people responded better to social reinforcement. In a newly designed program at the University of California at Los Angeles, children's beliefs about the causes of their behavior are assessed prior to developing treatment programs, and part of the treatment is designed to foster attributions for success and failure that preclude learned helplessness. The methods used in that program may be useful to teachers in dealing with these "helpless" children. Some of these techniques are summarized below:

1. Encourage attributions to self through cognitive modification techniques emphasizing self-control over behavior.[4]

---

[4]See also the section on implications of attributional style in Meichenbaum's (1977) general discussion of cognitive modification techniques.

2. Minimize (but do not eliminate) the occurrence of failure.

3. In instances of failure, encourage specific rather than general attributions (errors are due to a specific error pattern mistake rather than being a bad person).

4. Involve children in selecting target behaviors for change, and in generating solutions for problem behaviors.

5. Emphasize strategies for coping with academic mistakes or failures rather than explaining problem sources. In other words, rather than emphasizing why children fail, concentrate on developing ways to use that failure to plan more effective problem-solving strategies for the future.

6. Have children engage in self-evaluation of performance, in which they must try to match the ratings given them by someone else.

Modality Preferences

Teachers of learning disabled children frequently are told to assess the child's preferred or strong learning modality (does he or she learn best through visual, auditory, or tactile presentation of information), and to plan instruction so that use of a weak modality is minimized. Instruction, then, uses the strong modality and remedial procedures are developed to strengthen the weak areas. Even though the results of research are clear and consistent in showing that these approaches are not successful in improving children's academic performance (see Tarver & Dawson, 1978), teachers continue to believe in and employ a "modality-matching" model (Arter & Jenkins, 1977).

Since a modality and instructional matching approach does not seem to offer promise, it is not advocated here. However, if a child does have a severe deficit in some sensory, motor, or sensory-motor area, performance on tasks requiring use of that modality may be impaired. Such severe deficits should certainly be considered in planning instruction.

Developmental Readiness

Another general effect on children's performance in school is their developmental readiness for academic tasks. Many cognitive factors associated with the academic problems of learning disabled children could also be discussed in a developmental context. Indeed, in many studies, the performance of these children is more like their younger, normally achieving peers than like their age-mates. These results have led many individuals to advocate a developmental lag hypothesis as an overall explanation of the problems experienced by learning disabled children. Since those cognitive "deficits," of particular interest for this population, have been discussed and space does not permit general suggestions, the reader is referred to Case (1975) and Jackson, Robinson, and Dale (1976) for suggestions about adapting instruction to the developmental capacities of the learner.

One area, motor development, does need to be discussed briefly, since it has not been covered elsewhere. In an attempt to eliminate some of the confusion surrounding movement and its relationship to learning problems, Keogh (1978) proposes three types of movement outcomes intended to distinguish between how the child moves and how movement can help the child: movement control (skill), movement behavior, and movement experiences (see Figure 6.2). Movement control, or the ability to move in relation to situational requirements, includes, first, movement-for-self and then movement-with-others. Children must learn how to control their movements before they can learn to match movements or move in relation to other people. Movement behavior includes effort, cooperation, and confidence. Movement experiences are used by the child (or arranged by the teacher) to gather information or to develop social skills.

The most important movement problems related to learning disabilities seem to be clumsiness, hyperactivity, and perceptual-motor problems. Children who are clumsy may not have achieved the fine or gross motor skills enabling them to maintain adequate control. This not only causes problems in performance such as writing or copying, but also causes difficulties in peer relationships due to their inability to coordinate movement with that of others. In the area of movement behavior, the major problem is hyperactivity—a child moves too soon, too often, or at the wrong times. In addition to its contribution to difficulties in personal-social relationships (see Chapter 7), hyperactivity is closely related to distractibility and impulsivity in learning disabled children. Often the same child exhibits all three characteristics. An inability or unwillingness to inhibit movement adds to the difficulties a child may have in attending to a task or delaying impulsive responding on academic tasks. The motor part of perceptual-motor problems is as difficult to assess as the perceptual part. Motor responses are usually important as a way to create a product, which is then used to evaluate some aspect of a child's performance. Poor performance could result from inaccurate perception, inadequate motor control, or an inability to integrate the two. According to Keogh (1978), it is naive to expect that increased movement control or skill is a direct or simple link to improvement in academic areas. A more realistic view is that movement is a means for arranging learning experiences that are designed for specific academic purposes (to teach spatial directions such as up and down, it may

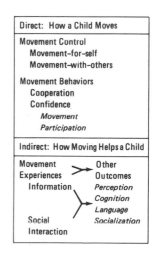

Figure 6.2

Keogh's Movement Outcome Scheme. (J. Keogh, Movement outcomes as conceptual guidelines in the perceptual-motor maze. *The Journal of Special Education*, 1978, *12*, p. 322. Reprinted by permission.)

be useful to have the child move up and down as the teacher verbalizes the words "up" and "down"). Assessment should be on the appropriate use of the concepts and not on the skill of moving up and down.[5]

SUMMARY

Some general observations might facilitate the use of information presented in this chapter. First, a variety of points of view has been presented, not to confuse the issues, but to provide the reader with the most complete and comprehensive range of information possible. There was no attempt to resolve the conflicting points of view regarding the subtle differences in manifestation of learning problems. This is left to those presently conducting related research. On the other hand, there was an attempt to resolve some of the conflicting points of view regarding teaching methods, to assist teachers in deciding what to try first. Differing points of view were presented to provide a wide range of alternatives should the "best" approach not work with a particular child. With regard to the teaching methods to use, in very simple terms the message of the chapter is find out (to the extent possible) the deficits children have that contribute to their learning problems, start at students' entry levels, and use whatever works for them—possibly trying a variety of approaches. Usually a combination of methods works best. Student performance data collected frequently help teachers to recognize the most effective methods for particular students.

[5]A discussion of specific techniques for the assessment and remediation of motor problems is beyond the scope of this chapter. The reader is referred to Poggio and Salkind (1979) for a review of instruments for assessing hyperactivity, to Keogh (1971) for a review of the literature relating hyperactivity to learning problems, Keogh and Barkett (1979) for a review of interventions and their effectiveness with hyperactive children, and Singer (1977) for a discussion of general considerations in the development of psychomotor skills. In addition, the cognitive modification techniques useful in modifying impulsivity and distractibility described in this chapter or in Meichenbaum (1977) are valuable in the treatment of hyperactive children.

REFERENCE NOTES

1. McKinney, J. D., Haskins, R., & Moore, M. G. *Problem solving strategies in reflective and impulsive children* (Final Report: NIE, Project No. 3-0344). Washington, D.C.: U.S. Government Printing Office, 1977.

2. Meichenbaum, D. *Cognitive factors as determinants of learning disabilities: A cognitive-functional approach.* Paper presented at the NATO conference on "The Neuropsychology of Learning Disorders: Theoretical Approaches," Korsor, Denmark, June, 1975.

3. Torrance, E. P. *Perspectives on the status of the gifted: Current perspectives.* Presentation to the 1977 Summer Institute on the Education of the Gifted/Talented, Teachers College, Columbia University, New York, June 20, 1977.

REFERENCES

Abikoff, H. Cognitive training interventions in children: Review of a new approach. *Journal of Learning Disabilities*, 1979, *12*, 123–155.

Alley, G., & Deshler, D. *Teaching the learning disabled adolescent. Strategies and methods.* Denver, Colo.: Love Publishing Co., 1979.

ALLINGTON, R. Attention and application: The oft forgotten steps in teaching reading. *Journal of Learning Disabilities*, 1975, *8*, 210–213.

ARGULEWICZ, E. N., MEALOR, D. J., & RICHMOND, B. O. Creative abilities of learning disabled children. *Journal of Learning Disabilities*, 1979, *12*, 21–24.

ARTER, J. A., & JENKINS, J. R. Examining the benefits and prevalence of modality considerations in special education. *The Journal of Special Education*, 1977, *11*, 281–298.

BAKER, H. J., & LELAND, B. *Detroit tests of learning aptitude*. Indianapolis: Bobbs-Merrill Co., 1959.

BARKER, L. L. *Listening behavior*. Englewood Cliffs, N.J.: Prentice-Hall, 1971.

BARRON, F. Originality in relation to personality and intellect. *Journal of Personality*, 1957, *25*, 730–742.

BARSCH, R. H. *Achieving perceptual-motor efficiency* (Vol. 1). Seattle, Wash.: Special Child Publications, 1967.

BAUER, R. H. Memory processes in children with learning disabilities: Evidence for deficient rehearsal. *Journal of Experimental Child Psychology*, 1977, *24*, 415–430. (a)

BAUER, R. H. Short-term memory in learning disabled and nondisabled children. *Bulletin of the Psychonomic Society*, 1977, *10*, 128–130. (b)

BAUER, R. H. Memory, acquisition, and category clustering in learning-disabled children. *Journal of Experimental Child Psychology*, 1979, *27*, 365–383.

BECKER, L. D., BENDER, N. N., & MORRISON, G. Measuring impulsivity-reflection: A critical review. *Journal of Learning Disabilities*, 1978, *11*, 626–632.

BIJOU, S. W. Studies in the experimental development of left-right concepts in retarded children using fading techniques. In N. R. Ellis (Ed.), *International review of research in mental retardation* (Vol. 3). New York: Academic Press, 1968.

BOUSFIELD, W. A. The occurrence of clustering in the recall of randomly arranged associates. *Journal of General Psychology*, 1953, *49*, 229–240.

BRICKER, D. D., & DENNISON, L. Training prerequisites to verbal behavior. In M. E. Snell (Ed.), *Systematic instruction of the moderately and severely handicapped*. Columbus, Ohio: Charles E. Merrill Publishing Co., 1978.

BROWN, J. I., & CARLSEN, G. R. *Brown-Carlsen listening comprehension test*. N.Y.: Harcourt Brace Jovanovich, 1955.

BUGENTAL, D. B., WHALEN, C. K., & HENKER, B. Causal attributions of hyperactive children and motivational assumptions of two behavior-change approaches: Evidence for an interactionist postion. *Child Development*, 1977, *48*, 874–884.

BUSSELL, C., HULS, B., & LONG, L. Positive reinforcers for modification of auditory processing skills in LD and EMR children. *Journal of Learning Disabilities*, 1975, *8*, 373–376.

BUTTERFIELD, E. C., WAMBOLD, C., & BELMONT, J. M. On the theory and practice of improving short-term memory. *American Journal of Mental Deficiency*, 1973, *77*, 654–669.

CAMP, B., & BASH, M. *Think aloud program: Group manual, revised*. Denver, Colo.: University of Colorado Medical School, 1975. (ERIC Document Reproduction Service No. ED 142 024)

CAMP, B. W., BLOM, G. E., HERBERT, F., & VAN DOORNINCK, W. J. "Think aloud": A program for developing self-control in young aggressive boys. *Journal of Abnormal Child Psychology*, 1977, *5*, 157–169.

CAMPBELL, J. A., & WILLIS, J. Modifying components of "creative behavior" in the natural environment. *Behavior Modification*, 1978, *2*, 549–564.

CARLSON, N. A. Using the creative strengths of a learning disabled child to increase evaluative effort and academic achievement (Doctoral dissertation, Michigan State University, 1974). *Dissertation Abstracts International*, 1975, *35*, 5962A–5963A. (University Microfilms No. 75-7135)

CASE, R. Gearing the demands of instruction to the developmental capacities of the learner. *Review of Educational Research*, 1975, *45*, 59–87.

COREY, J. R., & SHAMOW, J. The effects of fading on the acquisition and retention of oral reading. *Journal of Applied Behavior Analysis*, 1972, *5*, 311–315.

COVINGTON, M. V., CRUTCHFIELD, R. S., DAVIES, L., & OLTON, R. M. *The productive thinking program: A course in learning to think*. Columbus, Ohio: Charles E. Merrill Publishing Co., 1972.

CRUICKSHANK, W. M., BENTZEN, F. A., RATZEBURG, F. H., & TANNHAUSER, M. T. *A teaching method for brain-injured and hyperactive children*. Syracuse, N.Y.: Syracuse University Press, 1961.

CRUICKSHANK, W. M., & HALLAHAN, D. P. *Perceptual and learning disabilities in children* (Vol. 1): *Psychoeducational practices*. Syracuse, N.Y.: Syracuse University Press, 1975.

CUNNINGHAM, P. M., & CUNNINGHAM, J. W. Improving listening in content area subjects. *NASSP Bulletin*, 1976, *60*, 26–31.

DAS, J. P., LEONG, C. K., & WILLIAMS, N. H. The relationship between learning disability and simultaneous-successive processing. *Journal of Learning Disabilities*, 1978, *12*, 618–625.

DENNEY, D. R. Modeling effects upon conceptual style and cognitive tempo. *Child Development*, 1972, *43*, 105–119.

DIGATE, G., EPSTEIN, M. H., CULLINAN, D., & SWITZKY, H. N. Modification of impulsivity: Implications for improved efficiency in learning for exceptional children. *The Journal of Special Education,* 1978, *12,* 459–468.

DUNN, L. *Peabody picture vocabulary test* (rev. ed.). Circle Pines, Minn.: American Guidance Service, 1981.

DURRELL, D., HAYES, M. T., & BRASSARD, M. B. *Durrell listening-reading series: Primary and secondary levels.* New York: Harcourt, Brace & World, 1969.

EGELAND, B. Training impulsive children in the use of more efficient scanning techniques. *Child Development,* 1974, *45,* 165–171.

EPSTEIN, M., HALLAHAN, D., & KAUFFMAN, J. Implications of the reflectivity-impulsivity dimension for special education. *The Journal of Special Education,* 1975, *9,* 11–25.

FELDHUSEN, J. F., SPEEDIE, S. M., & TREFFINGER, D. J. The Purdue creative thinking program: Research and evaluation. *NSPI Journal,* 1971, *10,* 5–9.

FERRITOR, D. E., BUCKHOLDT, D., HAMBLIN, R. L., & SMITH, L. The noneffects of contingent reinforcement or attending behavior on work accomplished. *Journal of Applied Behavior Analysis,* 1972, *5,* 7–17.

FINCH, A. J., & SPIRITO, A. Use of cognitive training to change cognitive processes. *Exceptional Education Quarterly,* 1980, *1,* 31–39.

FROSTIG, M., & HORNE, D. *The Frostig program for the development of visual perception.* Chicago: Follett Publishing Co., 1964.

FROSTIG, M., LEFEVER, D. W., WHITTLESEY, J. R. B., & MASLOW, P. *The Marianne Frostig developmental test of visual perception.* Palo Alto, Calif.: Consulting Psychologists Press, 1964.

GAGNÉ, R. M., & WHITE, R. T. Memory structures and learning outcomes. *Review of Educational Research,* 1978, *48,* 187–222.

GETMAN, G. N. The visuomotor complex in the acquisition of learning skills. In J. Hellmuth (Ed.), *Learning disorders* (Vol. 1). Seattle, Wash.: Special Child Publications, 1965.

GIBSON, E. J. *Principles of perceptual learning and development.* New York: Appleton-Century-Crofts, 1969.

GLOVER, J. A., & GARY, A. L. Procedures to increase some aspects of creativity. *Journal of Applied Behavior Analysis,* 1976, *9,* 79–84.

GOETZ, E. M., & BAER, D. M. Social control of form diversity and the emergence of new forms in children's blockbuilding. *Journal of Applied Behavior Analysis,* 1973, *6,* 209–218.

GOETZ, E. M., & SALMONSON, M. M. The effect of general and descriptive reinforcement on "creativity" in easel painting. In G. Semb (Ed.), *Behavior analysis and education—1972.* Lawrence, Kans.: University of Kansas, 1972.

GOLDMAN, R., FRISTOE, M., & WOODCOCK, R. W. *Goldman-Fristoe-Woodcock test of auditory discrimination.* Circle Pines, Minn.: American Guidance Service, 1970.

GREENBERGER, S. M. *Sequential testing and educational programming* (STEP 1 & 2). San Rafael, Calif.: Academic Therapy Publications, 1977.

GUILFORD, J. P. *Creativity tests for children.* Beverly Hills, Calif.: Sheridan Psychological Services, 1971.

HAGEN, J. W. The effect of distraction on selective attention. *Child Development,* 1967, *38,* 685–694.

HALL, R. J. An information processing approach to the study of learning disabilities: The effects of cue elaboration on the maintenance and generalization of problem solving strategies (Doctoral dissertation, University of California, Los Angeles, 1979). *Dissertation Abstracts International,* 1980, *40,* 3948A–3949A. (University Microfilms International No. 8001376)

HALL, R. J. Information processing and cognitive training in learning disabled children: An executive level meeting. *Exceptional Education Quarterly,* 1980, *1,* 9–15.

HALL, R. V., LUND, D., & JACKSON, D. Effects of teacher attention on study behavior. *Journal of Applied Behavior Analysis,* 1968, *1,* 1–12.

HALLAHAN, D. P., & CRUICKSHANK, W. M. *Psychoeducational foundations of learning disabilities.* Englewood Cliffs, N.J.: Prentice-Hall, 1973.

HALLAHAN, D. P., & KAUFFMAN, J. M. Research on the education of distractible and hyperactive children. In W. M. Cruickshank & D. P. Hallahan (Eds.), *Perceptual and learning disabilities in children* (Vol. 2): *Research and theory.* Syracuse, N.Y.: Syracuse University Press, 1975.

HALLAHAN, D. P., & KAUFFMAN, J. M. *Introduction to learning disabilities: A psycho-behavioral approach.* Englewood Cliffs, N.J.: Prentice-Hall, 1976.

HALLAHAN, D. P., KAUFFMAN, J. M., & BALL, D. W. Selective attention and cognitive tempo of low achieving and high achieving sixth grade males. *Perceptual and Motor Skills,* 1973, *36,* 579–583.

HALLAHAN, D. P., LLOYD, J., KOSIEWICZ, M. M., KAUFFMAN, J. M., & GRAVES, A. W. Self-Monitoring of attention as a treatment for a learning disabled boy's off-task behavior. *Learning Disability Quarterly,* 1979, *2,* 24–32.

HALLAHAN, D. P., LLOYD, J., KOSIEWICZ, M. M., & KNEEDLER, R. D. *A comparison and self-assessment on the effects of self-recording and self-assessment on the on-task behavior and academic productivity of a learning disabled boy* (Technical Report #13). Charlottesville, Va.: University of Virginia Learning Disabilities Research Institute, 1979.

HALLAHAN, D. P., & REEVE, R. E. Selective attention and distractibility. In B. K. Keogh (Ed.), *Advances in special education* (Vol. 1). Greenwich, Conn.: J.A.I. Press, in press.

HALLAHAN, D. P., TARVER, S. G., KAUFFMAN, J. M., & GRAYBEAL, N. L. A comparison of the effects of reinforcement and response cost on the selective attention of learning disabled children. *Journal of Learning Disabilities*, 1978, *11*, 430–438.

HAMMILL, D., & LARSEN, S. The relationship of selected auditory perceptual skills and reading ability. *Journal of Learning Disabilities*, 1974, *7*, 429–435.

HARBER, J. R. Differentiating LD and normal children: The utility of selected perceptual and perceptual-motor tests. *Learning Disability Quarterly*, 1979, *2*, 70–75.

HAVERTAPE, J. F., KASS, C. E. Examination of problem solving in learning disabled adolescents through verbalized self-instructions. *Learning Disability Quarterly*, 1978, *1*, 94–103.

HEIDER, F. R. Information processing and the modification of an "impulsive conceptual tempo." *Child Development*, 1971, *42*, 1276–1281.

HENKER, B., WHALEN, C. K., & HINSHAW, S. P. The attributional contexts of cognitive intervention strategies. *Exceptional Education Quarterly*, 1980, *1*, 17–30.

HEWETT, F. M. *The emotionally disturbed child in the classroom.* Boston: Allyn & Bacon, 1968.

JACKSON, N. E., ROBINSON, H. B., & DALE, P. S. *Cognitive development in young children: A report for teachers* (NIE report). Washington, D.C.: U.S. Government Printing Office, 1976.

JOHNSON, D. J., & MYKLEBUST, H. R. *Learning disabilities: Educational principles and practices.* New York: Grune & Stratton, 1967.

KAGAN, J. Reflection-impulsivity: The generality and dynamics of conceptual tempo. *Journal of Abnormal Psychology*, 1966, *7*, 17–24.

KAGAN, J., PEARSON, L., & WELCH, L. Conceptual impulsivity and inductive reasoning. *Child Development*, 1966, 37, 583–594.

KARNES, M. B. *Helping young children develop language skills: A book of activities.* Reston, Va.: The Council for Exceptional Children, 1968.

KAUFFMAN, J. M., & HALLAHAN, D. P. Learning disability and hyperactivity (with comments on minimal brain dysfunction). In B. B. Lahey & A. E. Kazdin (Eds.), *Advances in clinical child psychology* (Vol. 2). New York: Plenum Press, 1979.

KAZDIN, A. E. The effect of vicarious reinforcement on attentive behavior in the classroom. *Journal of Applied Behavior Analysis*, 1973, *6*, 71–78.

KENDALL, P. C., & FINCH, A. J., JR. A cognitive behavioral treatment for impulsivity: A group comparison study. *Journal of Consulting and Clinical Psychology*, 1978, *46*, 110–117.

KENDLER, T. S., KENDLER, H. H., & CARRICK, M. A. Verbal labels and inferential problem solution of children. *Child Development*, 1966, 37, 749–763.

KEOGH, B. K. Hyperactivity and learning disorders: Review and speculation. *Exceptional Children*, 1971, *38*, 101–109.

KEOGH, B. K., & BARKETT, C. J. An educational analysis of hyperactive children's achievement problems. In C. Whalen & B. Henker (Eds.), *Hyperactive children: The social ecology of identification and treatment.* New York: Academic Press, 1979.

KEOGH, B. K., & GLOVER, A. T. The generality and durability of cognitive training. *Exceptional Education Quarterly*, 1980, *1*, 75–82.

KEOGH, J. Movement outcomes as conceptual guidelines in the perceptual-motor maze. *The Journal of Special Education*, 1978, *12*, 321–329.

KEPHART, N. C. *The slow learner in the classroom* (2nd ed.). Columbus, Ohio: Charles E. Merrill Publishing Co., 1971.

KHATENA, J., & TORRANCE, E. P. *Thinking creatively with sounds and words, research edition.* Columbus, Ohio: Personnel Press, 1973.

KIRBY, F. D., & SHIELDS, F. Modification of arithmetic response rate and attending behavior in a seventh-grade student. *Journal of Applied Behavior Analysis*, 1972, *5*, 79–84.

KIRK, S. A., & KIRK, W. *Psycholinguistic learning disabilities: Diagnosis and remediation.* Urbana, Ill.: University of Illinois Press, 1971.

KIRK, S. A., McCARTHY, J. J., & KIRK, W. D. *Illinois test of psycholinguistic abilities* (revised ed.). Urbana, Ill.: University of Illinois Press, 1968.

KOPPELL, S. Testing the attentional deficit notion. *Journal of Learning Disabilities*, 1979, *12*, 43–48.

KOPPITZ, E. M. *The Bender Gestalt test for young children.* New York: Grune & Stratton, 1964.

LAHEY, B. B., & LEFTON, L. A. Discrimination of letter combinations in good and poor readers. *The Journal of Special Education*, 1976, *10*, 205–210.

LAHEY, B. B., & McNEES, M. P. Letter-discrimination errors in kindergarten through third grade: Assessment and operant training. *The Journal of Special Education*, 1975, *9*, 191–199.

LARSEN, S. C., & HAMMILL, D. D. The relationship of selected visual-perceptual abilities to school learning. *The Journal of Special Education*, 1975, *9*, 281–291.

LARSEN, S. C., ROGERS, D., & SOWELL, V. The use of selected perceptual tests in differentiating between normal and learning disabled children. *Journal of Learning Disabilities*, 1976, *9*, 85–90.

LEDWIDGE, B. Cognitive behavior modification: A step in the wrong direction? *Psychological Bulletin*, 1978, *85*, 353–375.

LLOYD, J. Academic instruction and cognitive techniques: The need for attack strategy training. *Exceptional Education Quarterly*, 1980, *1*, 53–63.

LOPER, A. B. Metacognitive development: Implications for cognitive training of exceptional children. *Exceptional Education Quarterly*, 1980, *1*, 1–8.

LURIA, A. R. *The role of speech in the regulation of normal and abnormal behavior*. New York: Pergamon Press, 1961.

MACCOBY, E. E. Selective auditory attention in children. In L. P. Lipsitt & C. C. Spiker (Eds.), *Advances in child development and behavior* (Vol. 3). New York: Academic Press, 1967.

MACKINNON, D. W. The nature and nurture of creative talent. *American Psychologist*, 1962, *17*, 484–495.

MAHONEY, M. J. *Cognition and behavior modification*. Cambridge, Mass.: Ballinger Publishing Co., 1974.

MAKER, C. J. Developing multiple talents in exceptional children. *Teaching Exceptional Children*, 1979, *11*, 120–124.

MANSFIELD, R. S., BUSSE, T. V., & KREPELKA, E. J. The effectiveness of creativity training. *Review of Educational Research*, 1978, *48*, 517–536.

MCCARTHY, D. *McCarthy scales of children's abilities*. New York: Psychological Corp., 1972.

MCKINNEY, J. D., & HASKINS, R. Cognitive training and the development of problem solving strategies. *Exceptional Education Quarterly*, 1980, *1*, 41–51.

MEICHENBAUM, D. Enhancing creativity by modifying what subjects say to themselves. *American Educational Research Journal*, 1975, *12*, 129–145.

MEICHENBAUM, D. *Cognitive-behavior modification: An integrative approach*. New York: Plenum Press, 1977.

MEICHENBAUM, D., & GOODMAN, J. Reflection-impulsivity and verbal control of motor behavior. *Child Development*, 1969, *40*, 785–797.

MEICHENBAUM, D., & GOODMAN, J. Training impulsive children to talk to themselves: A means of developing self-control. *Journal of Abnormal Psychology*, 1971, *77*, 115–126.

MESSER, S. G. Reflection-impulsivity: A review. *Psychological Bulletin*, 1976, *83*, 1026–1052.

MILLER, G. A. The magical number seven, plus or minus two: Some limits on our capacity for processing information. *Psychological Review*, 1956, *63*, 81–97.

MINSKOFF, E. H., WISEMAN, D. E., & MINSKOFF, J. G. *The MWM program for developing language abilities*. Ridgefield, N.J.: Educational Performance Associates, 1974.

MOORE, S., & COLE, S. Cognitive self-mediation training with hyperkinetic children. *Bulletin of the Psychonomic Society*, 1978, *12*, 18–20.

MOSHER, F. A., & HORNSBY, J. R. On asking questions. In J. S. Bruner, R. R. Oliver, & P. M. Greenfield (Eds), *Studies in cognitive growth*. New York: John Wiley & Sons, 1966.

NAGLE, R. J., & THWAITE, B. C. Modeling effects on impulsivity with learning disabled children. *Journal of Learning Disabilities*, 1979, *12*, 331–336.

NEIMARK, E. D., & LEWIS, N. The development of logical problem-solving strategies. *Child Development*, 1967, *38*, 107–117.

NELSON, W. M. III, FINCH, A. J., JR., & HOOKE, J. F. Effects of reinforcement and response-cost on cognitive style in emotionally disturbed boys. *Journal of Abnormal Psychology*, 1975, *84*, 426–428.

PARNES, S. J. *Creative behavior guidebook*. New York: Charles Scribner's Sons, 1967.

PATRICK, C. Creative thought in poets. *Journal of Psychology*, 1935, *32*, 572–573.

POGGIO, J. P., & SALKIND, N. J. A review and appraisal of instruments assessing hyperactivity in children. *Learning Disability Quarterly*, 1979, *2*, 9–22.

PORTEUS, S. D. *The Porteus maze test* (3rd ed.). New York: Psychological Corp., 1965.

PRESSLEY, M. Increasing children's self-control through cognitive interventions. *Review of Educational Research*, 1979, *49*, 319–370.

RENZULLI, J. S., SMITH, L. H., WHITE, A. J., CALLAHAN, C. M., & HARTMAN, R. K. *Scales for rating behavioral characteristics of superior students*. Mansfield Center, Conn.: Creative Learning Press, 1977.

RIDBERG, E., PARKE, R., & HETHERINGTON, E. M. Modification of impulsive and reflective cognitive styles through observation of film mediated models. *Developmental Psychology*, 1971, *5*, 369–377.

ROACH, E., & KEPHART, N. *The Purdue perceptual-motor survey test*. Columbus, Ohio: Charles E. Merrill Publishing Co., 1966.

RUSSELL, D. H., & RUSSELL, E. E. *Listening aids through the grades*. New York: Teachers College, Columbia University, 1959.

SELIGMAN, M. E. *Helplessness.* San Francisco: W. H. Freeman & Co., 1975.

SHAVER, K. G. *An introduction to attribution processes.* Cambridge, Mass: Winthrop Publishers, 1975.

SHORES, R. E., & HAUBRICH, P. A. Effect of cubicles in educating emotionally disturbed children. *Exceptional Children,* 1969, *36,* 21–24.

SINGER, R. N. To err or not to err: A question for the instruction of psychomotor skills. *Review of Educational Research,* 1977, *47,* 479–498.

SMILEY, S. S., OAKLEY, D. D., WORTHEN, D., CAMPIONE, J. C., & BROWN, A. L. Recall of thematically relevant material by adolescent good and poor readers as a function of written versus oral presentation. *Journal of Educational Psychology,* 1977, *69,* 381–387.

SPIVACK, G., PLATT, J. J., & SHURE, M. B. *The problem-solving approach to adjustment.* San Francisco: Jossey-Bass, 1976.

SPIVACK, G., & SHURE, M. B. *Social adjustment of young children: A cognitive approach to solving real-life problems.* San Francisco: Jossey-Bass, 1974.

SWANSON, L. Auditory recall of conceptually, phonetically, and linguistically similar words by normal and learning disabled children. *The Journal of Special Education,* 1979, *13,* 63–67.

TARVER, S. G., BUSS, B. R., & MAGGIORE, R. P. The relationship between creativity and selective attention in LD boys. *Learning Disability Quarterly,* 1979, *2,* 53–59.

TARVER, S. G., & DAWSON, M. M. Modality preference and the teaching of reading. A review. *Journal of Learning Disabilities,* 1978, *11,* 5–17.

TARVER, S. G., & HALLAHAN, D. P. Attention deficits in children with learning disabilities: A review. *Journal of Learning Disabilities,* 1974, *7,* 560–569.

TARVER, S. G., HALLAHAN, D. P., COHEN, S. B., & KAUFFMAN, J. M. The development of visual selective attention and verbal rehearsal in learning disabled boys. *Journal of Learning Disabilities,* 1977, *10,* 491–500.

TARVER, S. G., HALLAHAN, D. P., KAUFFMAN, J. M., & BALL, D. W. Verbal rehearsal and selective attention in children with learning disabilities: A developmental lag. *Journal of Experimental Child Psychology,* 1976, *22,* 375–835.

TAWNEY, J. W. Training letter discrimination in four-year-old children. *Journal of Applied Behavior Analysis,* 1972, *5,* 455–465.

TAYLOR, S. E. *Listening* (revised ed.). Washington, D.C.: National Education Association, 1973.

TERMAN, L., & MERRILL, M. *Stanford-Binet intelligence scale* (revised I.Q. tables by S. R. Pinneau). New York: Houghton Mifflin Co., 1960.

THOMAS, A. Learned helplessness and expectancy factors: Implications for research in learning disabilities. *Review of Educational Research,* 1979, *49,* 208–221.

TORGESEN, J. K. Problems and prospects in the study of learning disabilities. In E. M. Hetherington, J. W. Hagen, R. Kron, & A. H. Stein (Eds.), *Review of child development research* (Vol. 5). Chicago: University of Chicago Press, 1976.

TORGESEN, J. K. The role of nonspecific factors in the task performance of learning disabled children: A theoretical assessment. *Journal of Learning Disabilities,* 1977, *10,* 27–34.

TORGESEN, J. K. Performance of reading disabled children on serial memory tasks: A selective review of recent research. *Reading Research Quarterly,* 1978, *14,* 57–87.

TORGESEN, J. K., & GOLDMAN, T. Verbal rehearsal and short-term memory in reading-disabled children. *Child Development,* 1977, *48,* 56–60.

TORRANCE, E. P. Creative teaching makes a difference. In J. C. Gowan, G. Demos, & E. P. Torrance (Eds.), *Creativity: Its educational implications.* New York: John Wiley & Sons, 1967.

TORRANCE, E. P. *The Torrance tests of creative thinking.* Lexington, Mass.: Ginn & Co., 1972.

TORRANCE, E. P. Non-test indicators of creative talent among disadvantaged children. *The Gifted Child Quarterly,* 1973, *17,* 3–9.

WALLACE, G., & KAUFFMAN, J. M. *Teaching children with learning problems.* Columbus, Ohio: Charles E. Merrill Publishing Co., 1973.

WALKER, H. M., & BUCKLEY, N. K. The use of positive reinforcement in conditioning attending behavior. *Journal of Applied Behavior Analysis,* 1968, *1,* 245–250.

WECHSLER, D. *Wechsler intelligence scale for children-Revised* (WISC-R). New York: Psychological Corp., 1974.

WEDELL, K. Perceptual-motor difficulties. *Special Education,* 1968, *57,* 25–30.

WEDELL, K. *Learning and perceptuo-motor disabilities in children.* New York: John Wiley & Sons, 1973.

WEINER, B., FRIEZE, I., KUKLA, A., REED, L., REST, S., & ROSENBAUM, R. M. *Perceiving the causes of success and failure.* Morristown, N.J.: General Learning Press, 1971.

WEPMAN, J. M. *Auditory discrimination test.* Chicago: Language Research Associates, 1958.

WERNER, H., & STRAUSS, A. A. Types of visuo-motor activity and their relation to high and low performance ages. *Proceedings of the American Association on Mental Deficiency,* 1939, *44,* 163–168.

WONG, B., WONG, R., & FOTH, D. Recall and clustering of verbal materials among normal and poor readers. *Bulletin of the Psychonomic Society,* 1977, *10,* 375–378.

YANDO, R. M., & KAGAN, J. The effect of teacher tempo on the child. *Child Development,* 1968, *39,* 27–34.

ZELNIKER, T., & JEFFREY, W. E. Reflective and impulsive children: Strategies of information processing underlying differences in problem solving. *Monographs of the Society for Research in Child Development,* 1976, *41* (5, Whole No. 168).

7 SOCIAL BEHAVIOR

Although this text emphasizes academically related areas, the social growth and development of learning disabled youngsters is of utmost importance. Although there are many ways of approaching the area of social behavior, one common way is to talk about behavioral excesses and deficiencies. Many educational professionals tend to be most concerned with youngsters who display behavioral excesses in classroom settings. Too much noise, too many fights, too many aggressive statements, and too much time spent wandering around the classroom are all examples of behavioral excesses adults find distressing in classroom situations. These youngsters' behavior patterns impair their own and their classmates' learning. Overly disruptive students draw attention to themselves, and usually school authorities quickly develop intervention plans for them. Tactics discussed in Chapter 5 and some discussed in this chapter were designed specifically to reduce occurrences of inappropriate or disruptive school behavior.

Many students do not draw attention to themselves and, therefore, do not receive the specialized services they require.[1] These students do not create undue disruption in the classroom or on the playground, but rather withdraw from social situations. Eventually, some become social isolates who cannot get along or interact in a positive way with either adults or peers. Many learning disabled students have a variety of difficulties in the social behavior area because they are "likely to be rejected or in conflict with parent, teacher, and peers alike" (Bryan & Bryan, 1975, p. 121). Clearly, learning disabled students should be considered a high risk for difficulties in the area of social development.

---

[1] Those particularly interested in the behavioral assessment and treatment of socially deficient children should refer to Van Hasselt, Hersen, Whitehill, and Bellack's (1979) excellent review.

This situation is easily understandable. It is amazing that even more of these students do not have serious emotional problems resulting from conflicts at school. For many, each day at school is a day filled with failure and frustration. Even for those who are assigned school tasks at which they can succeed, failure is implicit, for they know that they are not able to keep up with their age-mates. Day in and day out, school is not fun-filled, rewarding, or positive. Some students withdraw either emotionally or physically. Many have lower self-concepts (Smith, 1979). Truancy has long been observed in students who experience too much failure at school (Olson, 1935). Others become hostile and even aggressive.

Some learning disabled students do not have emotional or social problems resulting from their disabilities. Many remain well-behaved, forever trying to please their teachers and parents.

In this chapter both excessive and deficient social behaviors are discussed. Information is provided about controlling disruption and hyperactivity, as well as about developing appropriate classroom social skills.

CLASSROOM BEHAVIOR

To survive and succeed in typical classroom situations, students must behave relatively well (with a minimum amount of disruption) and have a good rapport with classmates and teachers. A number of social behaviors correlate highly with academic achievement. For example, independence, attention, persistence to task, self-control, compliance with teacher requests, and ability to follow instructions are prerequisites to school success (Cartledge &

Some learning disabled students have difficulty following standard classroom rules. This youngster had to be taught to raise his hand and wait until the teacher had time to come answer his question.

Milburn, 1978). Many social skills are implied in normal classroom rules (lack of disruption, volunteering, being on-task).

Bryan and Wheeler (1972) attempted to identify the components of learning disabled students' usual classroom social behavior. One of their concerns was that this behavior might affect the judgments teachers make about these students, thereby handicapping them even more. Their findings are most interesting. These youngsters did not, in fact, cause classroom disruptions and did not dominate teachers' time: they looked busy, but did not accomplish any school work.

These children can learn how to perform appropriately. Unfortunately, many teachers do not think of including these targets in the curriculum.

Classroom
Social Skills

Many social skills should be considered necessary for classroom survival. Without mastery of them, success in the classroom situation is impossible. For example, teachers are very concerned that students attend to the planned activities during the school day, a problem area for many learning disabled students. According to Bryan (1978), these youngsters spend less time on-task than their normal classmates, which not only could inhibit learning, but also transmits an undesirable social message to the teacher.

A few experts have tried to identify specific social skills students should possess. Roedell, Slaby, and Robinson (1976) believe that students should engage in prosocial behaviors at school. They feel that specific instances of cooperation, sharing, helping, and interacting positively are all important social behaviors that teachers should try to identify and reinforce in their pupils. More specific efforts have been made to identify social skills that should be mastered by all students. Many teachers have not known what to teach. Now, a comprehensive curriculum is available. The implications are tremendous for learning disabled students. Stephens (1978) offers a well-developed social skills list delineating important social skills that should be taught at school. A number of environmental behaviors (care for the environment, emergencies, lunchroom behavior), interpersonal skills (accepting authority, coping with conflict, gaining attention, greeting and helping others, making conversation, playing with others' property), self-related behaviors (accepting consequences, ethical behavior, expressing feelings), and task-related behaviors (asking and answering questions, attending, classroom discussion, completing tasks, following directions, group activities, independent work, on-task, performing before others) are included in instructional categories. In addition to the task analyses of these important social skills, Stephens has provided the teacher with assessment procedures and suggested teaching strategies and activities to facilitate the development and improvement of classroom social skills. This curriculum guide should become an invaluable tool to teachers of learning disabled students.

Disruptive
Classroom
Behavior

Since a comprehensive review of tactics that reduce disruptive classroom behavior can be found in Chapter 5, only a brief discussion is provided here.

A number of researchers and teachers have tried to identify specific intervention procedures that facilitate an environment conducive to learning, yet do not disrupt the environment during their implementation.

Some tactics producing these desired results are simple and are used commonly in many classrooms. One important reason for their success in research and classroom settings is consistency. Once a tactic is scheduled, every time it is supposed to be applied, it is. Also, the influence of the procedures is evaluated daily.

From research, the following guidelines are available to teachers as they arrange orderly and pleasant learning environments. For example, it is evident that, when classroom rules are clearly stated and pupils are praised for following them and ignored when they do not, disruption tends to decrease (Madsen, Becker, & Thomas, 1968). When students must be reprimanded for their disruptive incidents, it is best to do so quietly, in a tone inaudible to the other students (O'Leary, Kaufman, Kass, & Drabman, 1970). Sometimes one particular student has difficulty remembering the classroom rules and seems not to understand how students are expected to behave. In such cases, pairing two students together can be helpful, so that one student can model appropriate behavior for the other (Csapo, 1972).

Clearly, the use of specific praise statements helps youngsters understand what is expected for satisfactory classroom behavior. Ogburn (1974), in an attempt to combine humanism and behaviorism, shows how specific praise statements should be composed of four elements: the "I" message, behavioral description, reason, and positive consequences. For example, the following statement should help youngsters understand what is expected of them and why, and it also includes a reward for appropriate behavior: "I like the way Bill is doing his seatwork because he is not bothering anyone else and he is finishing his assignment. Bill may be the first in line for recess." The tactics suggested above are simple to use and do not require any substantial modifications in typical classroom routines. The following interventions require minor modifications, but teachers indicate that they are not difficult to implement.

When the majority of the class is participating in (or at least encouraging) the disruption, group contingencies have proven useful. A standardized classroom management program, the *Program for Academic Survival Skills* (PASS), is now available (Greenwood, Hops, Walker, Guild, Stokes, Young, Keleman, & Willardson, 1979). This data-based management system relies heavily on the use of group contingencies. The results of a two-site (Utah and Oregon) evaluation study clearly indicate the strength of these techniques to reduce classroom management problems. After only two days of training, a variety of personnel across diverse settings could successfully implement the group contingency procedures. Other examples of group contingency applications can be found in Chapter 5.

Incidents of classroom disruption have also been reduced through the use of games, one of which, the timer game, is easy to manage and popular with teachers and students. The teacher sets a common kitchen timer on a variable interval (VI) schedule. If, for example, a VI5 schedule were used, the timer bell would ring, on the average, every five minutes. Each student working appropriately (in seat, not talking or turning, working on the assignment) when the bell rings earns an extra minute of recess or a point toward the purchase of a special privilege. In the Dioden, Hall, Dunlap, and

Clark (1970) study, a VI8 was used and points earned for studying. Each point allowed the student to leave one minute earlier for lunch. In another study (Wolf, Hanley, King, Lachowicz, & Giles, 1970), a VI20 was used. When the bell rang, each student in seat earned points and each student out of seat lost points. Timer games are easy to adapt and implement in a variety of classroom situations.

Another game-like way of controlling disruption is the *good behavior game*. Its effectiveness was demonstrated in the first report of this technique (Barrish, Saunders, & Wolf, 1969). The class was divided into two teams. The winning team earned privileges (extra recess, lining up early for lunch). Any time a team member talked out or was out of seat, the team received a point. At the end of the day, the team with the fewest points was given a privilege. If both teams scored above a certain criterion, neither won. Since its first report in the literature, the good behavior game has grown in popularity and use. Its effectiveness has been reverified many times (Medland & Stachnik, 1972; Harris & Sherman, 1973; Warner, Miller, & Cohen, 1977). The game adds an element of fun to the classroom atmosphere and helps teachers avoid the potentially nagging aspects of classroom management.

Some interesting and important research results are available on the indirect management of classroom disruption. Usually, when classroom disruption is targeted for reduction and systematic procedures are applied, evaluation data reveal that the disruption decreases. Concomitant improvement in academic performance is not usually noted. Academic performance often improves when it becomes the target of direct instruction. This situation has led many to believe the statement, "You get what you go after." Ayllon and Roberts (1974), however, discovered an interesting reciprocal relationship between academic performance and disruption. They monitored both class disruption and written academic work. Initially, disruption occurred 34 percent of the time and the students' accuracy level was below 50 percent. Reinforcement procedures were initiated for improved academic performance, during which disruption dropped to below 15 percent and accuracy rose to 70 percent. Teachers should consider these results when planning a total educational program for their class of students. Elabo-

A simple kitchen timer can become a useful piece of classroom equipment. This timer is being used as part of a "good behavior game" to reduce general classroom disruption.

rate procedures for the reduction of classroom disruption are probably not necessary because satisfactory levels can be achieved through developing increased interest in improved academic performance.

HYPERACTIVITY

Hyperactivity is one behavioral characteristic observed in many learning disabled youngsters. Even in the earliest, concentrated efforts to remediate the academic and social problems associated with this group of learners, hyperactivity was recognized as a common characteristic (Strauss & Lehtinen, 1951; Cruickshank, Bentzen, Ratzeburg, & Tannhauser, 1961). Some estimated its prevalence to be between 4 percent and 10 percent of the school-age population (Neisworth, Kurtz, Ross, & Madle, 1976). Hyperactive youngsters are excessively distractible, inattentive, overactive, restless, or excitable. In devising a normative rating scale for hyperactivity, Spring, Blunden, Greenberg, and Yellin (1977) found that these youngsters were clearly separated from their normal counterparts by work fluctuations, excitability, distractibility, restlessness, and impulsivity. There is some agreement about what hyperactivity means: it has been operationally defined, but work toward a standard measurement system has not been completed (Sandoval, 1977).

Parents and teachers tend to be particularly concerned about hyperactive youngsters. One reason is the association between hyperactivity and learning problems. In a long-term follow-up study of hyperactive children (Minde, Lewin, Weiss, Lavigueur, Douglas, & Sykes, 1971), one prominent notion about hyperactivity was disproved. Many have thought that hyperactive children outgrow their difficulties during adolescence. This, however, was not substantiated in this research. Hyperactive youngsters consistently had more academic and conduct problems throughout school.

There is little consensus about such aspects of hyperactivity as its etiology, its relationship to learning problems, or its treatment. Block (1977) poses six different theories concerning the etiology of hyperactivity: central nervous system dysfunction, biochemical (neurochemical) imbalance, heredity, physical trauma, emotional disturbance, and sociocultural changes in the child's environment. Many professionals believe that hyperactivity is caused by brain damage. This, however, is not entirely supported in the research literature (Stewart, 1970; Keogh, 1971). The causes of hyperactivity probably vary from individual to individual. Since issues surrounding etiology are unresolved and cannot facilitate the selection of the most effective intervention for any particular youngster, teachers need not be overly concerned with causative factors.

In attempting to explain the relationship between hyperactivity and learning problems, Keogh (1971) presents three hypotheses. The first, which could be referred to as a medical-neurological syndrome explanation, stresses an underlying condition of distractibility, perceptual problems, and excessive motor activity as the cause for learning problems. The second posits that learning problems result from disruption of attention and excessive motor activity, which does not allow for accurate intake of information. The third places the blame on impulsivity and the ensuing disruption of the learning situation. Despite the formation of these three hypotheses over ten years ago, researchers have not resolved issues having to do with the relationship between hyperactivity and learning difficulties. Many years after the identification of hyperactivity, there still exists a substantial amount of myth and mystery about the problem and its manifestations.

Numerous suggestions about the remediation of hyperactivity have been offered. For example, some (Flynn & Rapoport, 1977) feel that hyperactive students function better and are less disruptive in open classroom situations. Mulholland (1973) suggests that biofeedback equipment might help hyperactive youngsters monitor and control their own behavior. Others (Rose, 1978; Rapp, 1978) propose that diet, particularly food dyes, is associated with hyperactive behavior, and that careful control of food intake might reduce the frequency and intensity of hyperactivity. Usually, however, there are two general treatment strategies used to control hyperactivity. Unfortunately, many professionals adhere to either one or the other, so that a polarized situation has developed. In the next two subsections discussions are provided about each method: medical and behavioral management.

Medical Management

Over forty years ago it was observed that stimulant drugs[2] cause a reduction in the excessive behavior patterns of hyperactive children (Bradley, 1937). Since that time, medical management of behavior problems has increased in popularity. Estimates of the number of children in America placed on medication for the purpose of controlling hyperactivity vary. Sroufe (1975) estimates that anywhere from 1 percent to 10 percent of America's children receive medication for behavior control. Murray (1976) reports that approximately 200,000 children yearly are medicated for the control of behavioral and cognitive disorders. Walker (1974) indicates that 10 percent to 15 percent of students in some school districts receive what he believes to be potentially dangerous drugs, prescribed by the family physician often on the urging of school officials, to control hyperactivity. Axelrod and Bailey (1979) believe that over half of all children referred to as learning disabled receive prescription medication for hyperactivity. What is most amazing about medical management of hyperactivity is that no one seems to really know how many youngsters receive medication for inappropriate social behavior or inadequate cognitive performance.

Some professionals firmly believe that only medical management (drugs) should be used in the treatment of hyperactivity. Research has indicated that attentional deficiencies (Dalby, Kinsbourne, Swanson, & Sobol, 1977), conduct and personality problems (Cunningham & Barkley, 1978; Greenwold & Jones, 1971), and even handwriting (Lerer, Artner, & Lerer, 1979) can be corrected through the use of methylphenidate (Ritalin). In one comprehensive study (Whalen, Henker, Collins, Finck, & Dotemoto, 1979),

[2]Readers wanting a more comprehensive review of stimulant drugs and learning problems should refer to Adelman and Compas (1977), Aman (1980), and O'Leary (1980).

an attempt was made to compare the classroom performance of hyperactive youngsters, both on and off medication, with their normal counterparts. When compared to their normal peers, hyperactive boys off of medication were less attentive and made more gross motor movements, verbalizations, disruptive noises, physical contacts with peers, social initiations, energetic responses, and inappropriate and unexpected acts. When on medication, these students behaved more like their peers and the classroom atmosphere was more conducive to learning.

Recently, both medical and education professionals have become increasingly concerned over the use of drugs to manage social behavior. The influence of stimulant drugs seems to be idiosyncratic, affecting individual children in different ways (Sulzbacher, 1972; Weithorn & Ross, 1975; Axelrod & Bailey, 1979). For some children, the influence of medication is affected by situational variables. In the Wulbert and Dries (1977) study, for example, behavioral improvements were noted in the home but not in the clinic, and vice versa. Some students experience unpleasant side effects (Eaton, Sells, & Lucas, 1976; Shafto & Sulzbacher, 1977; Axelrod & Bailey, 1979).

Many professionals are concerned about the inconsistent monitoring system used to assess the influence of drugs in the short and long term (Neisworth et al., 1976; Conners, 1973). Aman (1980), through his review of psychotropic drugs and learning problems, came to a conclusion that summarizes current professional opinion regarding medical management of hyperactivity:

> *There is presently little proof that medication is useful in treating learning problems in children. . . . Therefore when medication is provided for the treatment of learning problems, it should be administered in conjunction with an acceptable form of educational therapy.* (p. 94)

A number of sound suggestions are now available, and experience indicates that some changes in the old procedures are worthwhile. Applied behavior analysis evaluation data (see Chapter 3) can be collected before and after medication is prescribed (Sulzbacher, 1972; Carpenter & Sells, 1974; Neisworth et al., 1976; Eaton, Sells, & Lucas, 1977; Rie, Rie, & Henderson, 1978; Axelrod & Bailey, 1979). If the prescribed drugs do not change the behavior in question, they should be either discontinued or a different drug or dosage tried. Since body weight and size can affect the influence of a particular dosage, frequent medical checks and continual behavior monitoring by parents and teachers is advisable.

Because doctors who prescribe behavior-control drugs only see the children for a brief time on an infrequent schedule, it has been suggested that teachers assume the responsibility for evaluating the influence of stimulant drugs on classroom behavior. Before this can happen, however, teachers will need inservice training and doctors will have to change their patterns of communication. Weithorn and Ross (1975) found that for only 18 percent of their subjects on medication was there direct contact between doctor and teacher. Okolo, Bartlett, and Shaw (1978) found that 97 percent of teachers felt they should help evaluate the influence of medication, but only 33 percent felt they were adequately informed about drugs. With minor modifications of current operating procedures, doctors and teachers could work closely together to help create the most conducive learning situation for each hyperactive student.

If teachers are involved in the medical management of any of their students, some precautions must be taken. Axelrod and Bailey (1979) point out some important aspects of teachers' potential liability and offer some sound advice to teachers whose pupils are on medication. First, a copy of the doctor's prescription should be kept on file, indicating the name of the doctor, prescription name, dosage of the drug, expiration date, and times of administration. Included in this file should be the reasons for the medication and a release form signed by parents or guardian. Medication should always be sent to school via an appropriate person (not the child). It should be fresh, labeled, and kept in a secure place (preferably not the classroom). Also, precise records of each child's medical management plan and its implementation should be kept.

Behavioral Management

Recently, many professionals have advocated nonmedical management of hyperactivity. Even some doctors (Conners, 1973; Walker, 1974) have stated that drugs merely mask the symptoms, do not cure the underlying problems, and should not be thought of as the sole answer to the treatment of hyperactivity. For these reasons, it was suggested that nonmedical management techniques, such as behavioral management, be tried first (Murray, 1976; Weissenburger & Loney, 1977), or that they be tried in conjunction with medication (Conners, 1973).

Years ago, Patterson (1965) demonstrated that hyperactivity could be brought under control through the use of applied behavior analysis techniques. Later, other studies (Weissenburger & Loney, 1977) found that, through social reinforcement, praise, and a limited number of reprimands, on and off task (hyperactivity) greatly improved. Other studies were designed to compare the influences of medical and behavioral management on hyperactivity. Ayllon, Layman, and Kandel (1975), for example, assessed three children's hyperactive and academic behavior during reading and math. While on medication, the students' hyperactivity decreased, but little improvement in their academic performances was noted. When a consistent and systematic behavioral management program was implemented (as described in Chapters 3, 4, and 5), hyperactivity decreased to the levels noted while these youngsters were on medication. Their academic achievement also improved notably. Other studies (Strong, Sulzbacher, & Kirkpatrick, 1974; Benefield & Hall, 1977) are available to support Ayllon et al.'s research. In fact, these researchers reported even more positive changes in social behavior while the behavioral management procedures were in effect. Shafto and Sulzbacher (1977), also comparing medical with behavioral interventions, found that although increased attention did occur at higher dosage levels, undesirable side effects such as unintelligibility of speech, lack of responsiveness to directions, and insomnia occurred. This concerned the researchers and led them to question the merits of medication.

Some research has been conducted that does not compare behavioral and medical management of hyperactivity, but rather demonstrates the influence of behavioral techniques. For example, Schulman, Suran, Stevens, and Kupst (1979) found that auditory feedback regarding activity levels (from a biomotormeter) and reinforcement for appropriate activity levels reduced a number of children's hyperactivity. Many of the procedures presented in Chapter 5, when directly applied, have reduced hyperactivity levels. Some youngsters obviously benefit from behavioral management of hyperactivity. For them, it should be the preferred treatment strategy.

SOCIAL INTERACTION

A vital part of the school experience is socialization. Youngsters must be able to get along and communicate with each other, play, cooperate, share, and become part of a unit—the class. Social integration is an important aspect of mainstreaming. It does not occur spontaneously and, unfortunately, is often not given enough attention by teachers (Bryan & Bryan, 1978; Strain, Gable, & Hendrickson, 1978). Isolationism often results. This is antithetical to the concept of mainstreaming and to the aim of true integration for the handicapped.

Clearly, the interactive behavior of youngsters can be modified (Bandura, 1977). Careful application of teacher attention alters the frequency and nature of young children's interactions (Buell, Stoddard, Harris, & Baer, 1968; Baer & Wolf, 1970; Strain & Timm, 1974). Peers also are effective interventionists. For example, when peers initiated more social contacts

Social interaction is an important part of the school experience. Because many learning disabled youngsters have difficulties in this area, teachers must allow for, encourage, and oftentimes, guide group interaction.

with their handicapped classmates, less isolation and more interaction occurred (Strain et al., 1978). Evidently, the quality and quantity of social interaction can be altered through systematic application of various intervention procedures. The question is not how to change social behavior but rather what needs to be changed. More research must be conducted to identify how learning disabled students interact with others, how these actions affect social interaction, and what variables can enhance acceptance and integration. In the next sections, social interaction with adults and peers is discussed.

Interaction with Adults

During school, the adults with whom students primarily interact are teachers. The importance of this interaction cannot be underestimated. The manner in which adults interact with specific individuals is directly related to their attitudes toward and impressions of them (Good & Brophy, 1972). According to these researchers, teachers tend to formulate one of four general feelings about each student: attachment, concern, indifference, and rejection. These feelings result in varied interaction patterns. For example, students toward whom the teacher is indifferent are usually passive, avoid contact with the teacher, and are, in turn, avoided by the teacher. Such students are called upon less often to answer questions and to perform classroom duties such as running errands. They receive praise and criticism less often than their peers.

These findings have important implications for learning disabled students. Bryan (1978) determined that they receive different treatment from their teachers. Although they receive about the same number of positive reinforcers from their teachers, they receive twice as many negative contacts and statements. In addition, they are twice as likely to be ignored.

There is evidence that not only supports the above assumptions (that impressions formed relate to the ways students behave and the way others behave towards them), but also indicates that this situation can be altered. Cantor and Gelfand (1977) found that when children acted in an animated, socially responsive manner, they were judged by adults as more attractive and intelligent. Possibly, children who consistently receive negative reactions from adults should be taught to use different interaction patterns.

To demonstrate this point, Cantor and Gelfand did just that. They taught children how to elicit certain behavioral patterns from their teachers. These children controlled the rates of adults' offering and giving help (both verbal and nonverbal). Stokes, Fowler, and Baer (1978) successfully taught children to seek (or cue) teachers' praise. Both normal and deviant children modified their teachers' interactions. This definitely indicates that a new curricular area is in need of development.

Although different from the above research, the implications of the Willner, Braukmann, Kirigin, Fixsen, Phillips, and Wolf (1977) research are probably as great. These researchers were concerned about adolescents' interaction with adults who were responsible for after-school instructional programs. They believe that the way adults interact with adolescents affects the way the youngsters interact with them. They asked the youngsters which kinds of interaction they preferred and which they did not. These youngsters preferred that adults use a calm, pleasant tone of voice, offer and provide help, joke, give positive feedback, be fair, give points, and explain why things must be as they are. On the other hand, they did not like it when adults only described what they did wrong, displayed anger, provided negative feedback, used profanity, showed a lack of understanding, were unfriendly, unpleasant, bossy, or demanding. When the adult workers followed the implied advice about the nature of social interaction provided in these likes and dislikes lists, the adolescents actually were more responsive to them.

Interaction with Peers

Peer popularity and social status is important to youngsters and their social development. The effects of early social integration probably influence how individuals relate to others throughout their lifetimes.

A number of research studies have attempted to identify how learning disabled students relate to their classmates and peers. Once it is clear which actions are deficient or excessive, research may then lead to the development of remediation programs.

The evidence now available indicates that learning disabled students are less popular and have a lower social status than normal children (Bryan, 1974a, 1976, 1978; Bruininks, 1978a, 1978b). Why these youngsters have fewer friends and are generally less popular is not clear. One fruitful line of research follows the assumption that learning disabled students have different social interaction patterns. Bryan and Bryan (1978) found that both the way learning disabled students interact with their peers and the way the peers interact with them is different from normal children interacting with normal children. Learning disabled students are more likely to make nasty and rejecting statements and fail to respond to social initiations from their normal classmates. In turn, they receive many verbal statements indicating rejection and hostility. In other research (Bryan, Wheeler, Felcan, & Henek, 1976), learning disabled students were found to emit fewer considerate and more competitive (even aggressive) statements than normal children.

These youngsters' social abilities tend to be different in other ways, too. They seem to be less able to correctly perceive social situations and are deficient in their abilities to show empathy (Bachara, 1976). They do not interpret nonverbal communications reliably (Bryan, 1977; Minskoff, 1980a; 1980b). Learning disabled girls have been characterized by their peers as unhappy, worried, and not desirable as playmates (Bryan, 1974b). In general, their self-concept tends to be low and they often seem to need to control social situations (Bruininks, 1978b).

Many handicapped youngsters have difficulty sharing, which could affect their relationships with peers. The transition period from nonsharing to sharing normally occurs between the ages of four and six (Fischer, 1963; Larsen & Kellogg, 1974). Many children have difficulties learning about equity. Evidence is abundant, however, that youngsters can be taught to share and that the frequency of sharing can be increased. It seems that modeling is most effective when sharing has to be taught (Harris, 1971; Rice & Grusec, 1975) and that reinforcement contributes to its increased frequency (Rogers-Warren & Baer, 1976; Rogers-Warren, Warren, & Baer, 1977). In one study, where the subjects initially had exceptionally low levels of sharing, positive practice overcorrection (which included instructions, modeling, and practice) caused substantial increases in sharing (Barton & Osborne, 1978).

Social interaction is composed of a number of discrete elements (sharing, verbal and nonverbal communication). Once specifically defined, they should be amenable to behavioral change and result in more positive relationships among youngsters. This was demonstrated in a comprehensive research project in which differential reinforcement procedures were utilized to increase social interaction among children (Walker, Greenwood, Hops, & Todd, 1979). Gable, Strain, and Hendrickson (1979) advise teachers concerned about the social-behavioral status of their learning disabled students to employ peers in remediation programs. They indicate that peer modeling, in particular, has positively altered students' social behavior, but other peer management procedures (see Chapter 5) have been proven beneficial also. A task analysis of nonverbal communication skills is now available (Minskoff, 1980a), as are suggested teaching activities to correlate with this carefully delineated sequence (Minskoff, 1980b). It is apparent that learning disabled children's nonverbal communication skills can be enhanced. For this to occur, however, careful instructional programming by teachers is necessary.

Roedell, Slaby, and Robinson (1976) suggest that teachers restructure their classroom situations. They tell teachers to create a classroom atmosphere conducive to positive social interaction between students. This can be accomplished, for example, by encouraging special group activities involving students considered popular and unpopular, since students seem to increase their liking for group members who have shared in pleasant experiences.

SUMMARY

Learning disabled students frequently have difficulties in the area of social behavior. Some difficulties arise because of the academic and learning problems associated with the handicap. Any individual who is exposed to excessive periods of failure and frustration has a high probability of having adjustment or emotional problems. Some learning disabled students can be considered hyperactive. They exhibit certain characteristics (distractibility, restlessness) that are counterproductive to learning. Teachers have special responsibilities for these youngsters whether they require behavioral or medical management. Certainly, evaluation systems should be even more consistent and sensitive to changes in the performance of the hyperactive youngster.

The development of good social skills can be a goal that is difficult to attain. The complex nature of social interaction and the vast number of independent and interrelated behaviors involved only magnify the problems presented to teachers. Some curriculum guides are now available that should facilitate the presentation of instructional targets in the social skills area. Regardless of the complexity or difficulties this often neglected curricular area presents, it must be given its proper place in the instructional program. Learning disabled students usually are deficient in social interaction skills. The school must assume the responsibility of helping students to master these important social skills as it does in academic areas.

REFERENCES

ADELMAN, H. S., & COMPAS, B. E. Stimulant drugs and learning problems. *The Journal of Special Education,* 1977, *11,* 377–416.

AMAN, M. G. Psychotropic drugs and learning problems—A selective review. *Journal of Learning Disabilities,* 1980, *13,* 87–97.

AXELROD, S., & BAILEY, S. L. Drug treatment for hyperactivity: Controversies, alternatives, and guidelines. *Exceptional Children,* 1979, *45,* 544–550.

AYLLON, T., LAYMAN, D., & KANDEL, H. J. A behavioral-educational alternative to drug control of hyperactive children. *Journal of Applied Behavior Analysis,* 1975, *8,* 137–146.

AYLLON, T., & ROBERTS, M. D. Eliminating discipline problems by strengthening academic performance. *Journal of Applied Behavior Analysis,* 1974, *7,* 71–76.

BACHARA, G. Empathy in learning disabled children. *Perceptual and Motor Skills,* 1976, *43,* 541–542.

BAER, D. M., & WOLF, M. M. Recent examples of behavior modification in preschool settings. In C. Neuringer & J. L. Michael (Eds.), *Behavior modification in clinical psychology.* New York: Appleton-Century-Crofts, 1970.

BANDURA, A. *Social learning theory.* Englewood Cliffs, N.J.: Prentice-Hall, 1977.

BARRISH, H. H., SAUNDERS, M., & WOLF, M. M. Good behavior game: Effects of individual contingencies for group consequences on disruptive behavior in a classroom. *Journal of Applied Behavior Analysis,* 1969, *2,* 119–124.

BARTON, E. J., & OSBORNE, J. G. The development of classroom sharing by a teacher using positive practice. *Behavior Modification,* 1978, *2,* 231–250.

BENEFIELD, B., & HALL, R. Comparative effects of a stimulant drug vs. behavior management techniques in increasing task-related behavior. *School Applications of Learning Theory,* 1977, *9,* 23–37.

BLOCK, G. H. Hyperactivity: A cultural perspective. *Journal of Learning Disabilities,* 1977, *10,* 236–240.

BRADLEY, C. The behavior of children receiving Benzadrine. *Journal of Psychiatry,* 1937, *94,* 577–585.

BRODEN, M., HALL, R. V., DUNLAP, A., & CLARK, R. Effects of teacher attention and a token reinforcement system in a junior high school special education class. *Exceptional Children,* 1970, *36,* 341–349.

BRUININKS, V. L. Actual and perceived peer status of learning-disabled students in mainstream programs. *The Journal of Special Education,* 1978, *12,* 51–58. (a)

BRUININKS, V. L. Peer status and personality characteristics of learning disabled and nondisabled students. *Journal of Learning Disabilities,* 1978, *11,* 484–489. (b)

BRYAN, T. H. Peer popularity of learning disabled children. *Journal of Learning Disabilities,* 1974, *7,* 621–625. (a)

BRYAN, T. H. An observational analysis of classroom behaviors of children with learning disabilities. *Journal of Learning Disabilities,* 1974, *7,* 26–34. (b)

BRYAN, T. H. Peer popularity of learning disabled children: A replication. *Journal of Learning Disabilities,* 1976, *9,* 307–311.

BRYAN, T. H. Learning disabled children's comprehension of non-verbal communication. *Journal of Learning Disabilities,* 1977, *10,* 501–506.

BRYAN, T. H. Social relationships and verbal interactions of learning disabled children. *Journal of Learning Disabilities,* 1978, *11,* 107–115.

BRYAN, T. H., & BRYAN, J. H. *Understanding learning disabilities.* Port Washington, N.Y.: Alfred Publishing Co., 1975.

BRYAN, T. H., & BRYAN, J. H. Social interactions of learning disabled children. *Learning Disability Quarterly,* 1978, *1,* 33–38.

BRYAN, T. H., & WHEELER, R. Perception of learning disabled children: The eye of the observer. *Journal of Learning Disabilities,* 1972, *5,* 484–488.

BRYAN, T., WHEELER, R., FELCAN, J., & HENEK, T. "Come on, dummy": An observational study of children's communications. *Journal of Learning Disabilities,* 1976, *9,* 661–669.

BUELL, J., STODDARD, P., HARRIS, F. R., & BAER, D. M. Collateral social development accompanying reinforcement of outdoor play in a preschool child. *Journal of Applied Behavior Analysis*, 1968, *1*, 167–173.

CANTOR, N. L., & GELFAND, D. M. Effects of responsiveness and sex of children on adults' behavior. *Child Development*, 1977, *48*, 232–238.

CARPENTER, R. L., & SELLS, C. J. Measuring effects of psychoactive medication in a child with a learning disability. *Journal of Learning Disabilities*, 1974, *7*, 545–550.

CARTLEDGE, G., & MILBURN, J. F. The case for teaching social skills in the classroom: A review. *Review of Educational Research*, 1978, *1*, 133–156.

CONNERS, C. K. What parents need to know about stimulant drugs and special education. *Journal of Learning Disabilities*, 1973, *6*, 349–351.

CRUICKSHANK, W. M., BENTZEN, F. A., RATZEBURG, F. A., & TANNHAUSER, M. T. *A teaching method for brain-injured and hyperactive children: A demonstration-pilot study.* Syracuse, N.Y.: Syracuse University Press, 1961.

CSAPO, M. Peer models reverse the "one bad apple spoils the barrel" theory. *Teaching Exceptional Children*, 1972, *5*, 20–24.

CUNNINGHAM, C. E., & BARKLEY, R. A. The role of academic failure in hyperactive behavior. *Journal of Learning Disabilities*, 1978, *11*, 274–280.

DALBY, J. T., KINSBOURNE, M., SWANSON, J. M., & SOBOL, M. P. Hyperactive children's underuse of learning time: Correction by stimulant treatment. *Child Development*, 1977, *48*, 1448–1453.

EATON, M., SELLS, C. J., & LUCAS, B. Psychoactive medication and learning disabilities. *Journal of Learning Disabilities*, 1976, *10*, 403–410.

FISCHER, W. F. Sharing in preschool children as a function of amount and type of reinforcement. *Genetic Psychology Monographs*, 1963, *68*, 215–245.

FLYNN, N. M., & RAPOPORT, J. L. Hyperactivity in open and traditional classroom environments. *The Journal of Special Education*, 1977, *10*, 285–290.

GABLE, R. A., STRAIN, P. S., & HENDRICKSON, J. M. Strategies for improving the status and social behavior of learning disabled children. *Learning Disability Quarterly*, 1979, *2*, 33–39.

GOOD, T. L., & BROPHY, J. E. Behavioral expression of teacher attitudes. *Journal of Educational Psychology*, 1972, *63*, 617–624.

GREENWOLD, W. E., & JONES, P. R. The effect of methylphenidate on behavior of three school children: A pilot investigation. *Exceptional Children*, 1971, *38*, 261–263.

GREENWOOD, C. R., HOPS, H., WALKER, H. M., GUILD, J. J., STOKES, J., YOUNG, K. R., KELEMAN, K. S., & WILLARDSON, M. Standardized classroom management program: Social validation and replication studies in Utah and Oregon. *Journal of Applied Behavior Analysis*, 1979, *12*, 235–253.

HARRIS, M. B. Models, norms, and sharing. *Psychological Reports*, 1971, *29*, 147–153.

HARRIS, V. W., & SHERMAN, J. A. Use and analysis of the "good behavior game" to reduce disruptive classroom behavior. *Journal of Applied Behavior Analysis*, 1973, *6*, 405–417.

KEOGH, B. K. Hyperactivity and learning disorders: Review and speculation. *Exceptional Children*, 1971, *38*, 101–109.

LARSEN, G. Y., & KELLOGG, J. A developmental study of the relation between conservation and sharing behavior. *Child Development*, 1974, *45*, 849–851.

LERER, R. J., ARTNER, J., & LERER, M. P. Handwriting deficits in children with minimal brain dysfunction: Effects of methylphenidate (Ritalin) and placebo. *Journal of Learning Disabilities*, 1979, *12*, 26–31.

MADSEN, C. H., JR., BECKER, W. C., & THOMAS, D. R. Rules, praise, and ignoring: Elements of elementary classroom control. *Journal of Applied Behavior Analysis*, 1968, *1*, 139–150.

MEDLAND, M. B., & STACHNIK, T. J. Good-behavior game: A replication and systematic analysis. *Journal of Applied Behavior Analysis*, 1972, *5*, 45–51.

MINDE, K., LEWIN, D., WEISS, G., LAVIGUEUR, H., DOUGLAS, V., & SYKES, E. The hyperactive child in elementary school: A 5 year, controlled, followup. *Exceptional Children*, 1971, *38*, 215–221.

MINSKOFF, E. H. Teaching approach for developing nonverbal communication skills in students with social perception deficits—Part 1. *Journal of Learning Disabilities*, 1980a, *13*, 118–124.

MINSKOFF, E. H. Teaching approach for developing nonverbal communication skills in students with social perception deficits—Part 2. *Journal of Learning Disabilities*, 1980b, *13*, 203–208.

MULHOLLAND, T. R. It's time to try hardware in the classroom. *Psychology Today*, December 1973, 103–104.

MURRAY, J. N. Is there a role for the teacher in the use of medication for hyperkinetics? *Journal of Learning Disabilities*, 1976, *9*, 30–35.

NEISWORTH, J. T., KURTZ, D., ROSS, A., & MADLE, R. A. Naturalistic assessment of neurological diagnoses and pharmacological intervention. *Journal of Learning Disabilities*, 1976, *9*, 149–152.

OGBURN, K. Interaction with appropriate consequences. *Journal of Learning Disabilities*, 1974, *7*, 204–206.

OKOLO, C., BARTLETT, S. A., & SHAW, S. F. Communication between professionals concerning medication for the hyperactive child. *Journal of Learning Disabilities*, 1978, *11*, 647–650.

O'LEARY, K. D. Pills or skills for hyperactive children. *Journal of Applied Behavior Analysis*, 1980, *13*, 191–204.

O'LEARY, K. D., KAUFMAN, K. F., KASS, R. E., & DRABMAN, R. S. The effects of loud and soft reprimands on the behavior of disruptive students. *Exceptional Children*, 1970, 37, 145–155.

OLSON, W. C. The diagnosis and treatment of behavior disorders of children. In the Thirty-Fourth Yearbook of the National Society of the Study of Education (Eds.), *Educational diagnosis*. Bloomington, Ill.: Public Schools Publishing Co., 1935.

PATTERSON, G. R. An application of conditioning techniques to the control of a hyperactive child. In L. Ullman & L. Krasner (Eds.), *Case studies in behavior modification*. New York: Holt, Rinehart & Winston, 1965.

RAPP, D. J. Does diet affect hyperactivity? *Journal of Learning Disabilities*, 1978, *11*, 383–389.

RICE, M. E., & GRUSEC, J. E. Saying and doing: Effects on observer performance. *Journal of Personality and Social Psychology*, 1975, *32*, 584–593.

RIE, E. D., RIE, H. E., & HENDERSON, D. B. A parent-teacher behavior rating scale for underachieving children. *Journal of Learning Disabilities*, 1978, *11*, 661–663.

ROEDELL, W. C., SLABY, R. G., & ROBINSON, H. B. *Social development in young children: A report for teachers*. Washington, D.C.: National Institute of Education, 1976.

ROGERS-WARREN, A., & BAER, D. M. Correspondence between saying and doing: Teaching children to share and praise. *Journal of Applied Behavior Analysis*, 1976, *9*, 335–354.

ROGERS-WARREN, A., WARREN, S. F., & BAER, D. M. A component analysis: Modeling, self-reporting, and reinforcement of self-reporting in the development of sharing. *Behavior Modification*, 1977, *1*, 307–322.

ROSE, T. L. The functional relationship between artificial food colors and hyperactivity. *Journal of Applied Behavior Analysis*, 1978, *11*, 439–446.

SANDOVAL, J. The measurement of the hyperactive syndrome in children. *Review of Educational Research*, 1977, *47*, 293–318.

SCHULMAN, J. L., SURAN, B. G., STEVENS, T. M., & KUPST, M. J. Instructions, feedback, and reinforcement in reducing activity levels in the classroom. *Journal of Applied Behavior Analysis*, 1979, *12*, 441–447.

SHAFTO, F., & SULZBACHER, S. Comparing treatment tactics with a hyperactive preschool child: Stimulant medication and programmed teacher intervention.

Journal of Applied Behavior Analysis, 1977, *10*, 13–20.

SMITH, M. D. Prediction of self-concept among learning disabled children. *Journal of Learning Disabilities*, 1979, *12*, 30–35.

SPRING, C., BLUNDEN, D., GREENBERG, L. M., & YELLIN, A. M. Validity and norms of a hyperactivity rating scale. *The Journal of Special Education*, 1977, *11*, 313–321.

SROUFE, L. A. Drug treatment of children with behavior problems. *Review of Child Development Research*, 1975, *4*, 347–407.

STEPHENS, T. M. *Social skills in the classroom*. Columbus, Ohio: Cedars Press, 1978.

STEWART, M. A. Hyperactive children. *Scientific American*, April 1970, 94–98.

STOKES, T. F., FOWLER, S. A., & BAER, D. M. Training preschool children to recruit natural communities of reinforcement. *Journal of Applied Behavior Analysis*, 1978, *11*, 285–303.

STRAIN, P. S., GABLE, R. A., & HENDRICKSON, J. M. Peer-mediated social initiations: A procedure for promoting social behavior with mainstreamed children. *Journal of Special Education Technology*, 1978, *2*, 33–38.

STRAIN, P. S., & TIMM, M. A. An experimental analysis of social interaction between a behaviorally disordered preschool child and her classroom peers. *Journal of Applied Behavior Analysis*, 1974, 7, 583–590.

STRAUSS, A. A., & LEHTINEN, L. E. *Psychopathology and education of the brain injured child*. New York: Grune & Stratton, 1951.

STRONG, C., SULZBACHER, S. I., & KIRKPATRICK, M. A. Use of medication versus reinforcement to modify a classroom behavior disorder. *Journal of Learning Disabilities*, 1974, 7, 214–218.

SULZBACHER, S. I. Behavior analysis of drug effects in the classroom. In G. Semb (Ed.), *Behavior analysis and education—1972*. Lawrence, Kans.: The University of Kansas Support and Development Center for Follow Through, 1972.

VAN HASSELT, V. B., HERSEN, M., WHITEHILL, M. B., & BELLACK, A. S. Social skill assessment and training for children: An evaluative review. *Behavior Research and Therapy*, 1979, *17*, 413–437.

WALKER, H. M., GREENWOOD, C. R., HOPS, H., & TODD, N. M. Differential effects of reinforcing topographic components of social interaction: Analysis and direct replication. *Behavior Modification*, 1979, 3, 291–321.

WALKER, S., III. Drugging the American child: We're too cavalier about hyperactivity. *Psychology Today*, December 1974, 43–48.

WARNER, S. P., MILLER, F. D., & COHEN, M. W. Relative effectiveness of teacher attention and the "good behavior game" in modifying disruptive classroom behavior. *Journal of Applied Behavior Analysis,* 1977, *10,* 737.

WEISSENBURGER, F. E., & LONEY, J. Hyperkinesis in the classroom: If cerebral stimulants are the last resort, what is the first resort? *Journal of Learning Disabilities,* 1977, *10,* 339–348.

WEITHORN, C. J., & ROSS, R. Who monitors medication? *Journal of Learning Disabilities,* 1975, *8,* 458–461.

WHALEN, C. K., HENKER, B., COLLINS, B. E., FINCK, D., & DOTEMOTO, S. A social ecology of hyperactive boys: Medication effects in structured classroom environments. *Journal of Applied Behavior Analysis,* 1979, *12,* 65–81.

WILLNER, A. G., BRAUKMANN, C. J., KIRIGIN, K. A., FIXSEN, D. L., PHILLIPS, E. L., & WOLF, M. M. The training and validation of youth-preferred social behaviors of child-care personnel. *Journal of Applied Behavior Analysis,* 1977, *10,* 219–230.

WOLF, M. M., HANLEY, E. L., KING, L. A., LACHOWICZ, J., & GILES, D. K. The timer-game: A variable interval contingency for the management of out-of-seat behavior. *Exceptional Children,* 1970, *37,* 113–117.

WULBERT, M., & DRIES, R. The relative efficacy of methylphenidate (Ritalin) and behavior-modification techniques in the treatment of a hyperactive child. *Journal of Applied Behavior Analysis,* 1977, *10,* 21–31.

ORAL LANGUAGE

VICTORIA RISKO

Peabody College of Vanderbilt University

This chapter deals with language skills that develop during the school years, types of language difficulties prevalent among the learning disabled, and strategies for language assessment and intervention. For our purposes here, language is defined as the receptive and expressive skills of communication. Language skills, related cognitive factors, and their systematic development are discussed as the basis for explaining the language problems of learning disabled students. Because of their problems with communication, many learning disabled students are referred to as language disabled. A close relationship between language and learning disabilities does exist (Johnson & Myklebust, 1967; Lerner, 1976), and many learning disabled students are unable to receive, understand, or use language effectively.

DEFINITIONS OF ORAL LANGUAGE

Language, a total communication process, is a code using sounds, words, and grammatical patterns to explain and organize information and events. Speech, the behavioral manifestation of language (Carroll, 1953), is only part of the language code. Language is a complex process, interpreted in different ways. Many (Myklebust, 1960; Johnson & Myklebust, 1967; Lenneberg, 1962; Spradlin, 1967) define language as being composed of receptive and expressive behavior. Myklebust (1960) suggests that language falls into a developmental hierarchy of five related levels. According to his schema, language develops from students' experiences and becomes associated with meaning through inner language. Inner language provides a basis for understanding spoken words, associating them with past experiences (receptive language). Receptive language then provides a conceptual base for oral language (expressive language). Children must have some knowledge about the input before they can learn the linguistic meaning of the information (Mac-Namara, 1972). Reading and writing skills are acquired by learning visual symbols for previously learned oral language (see Figure 8.1). To help the reader progress through some sections of this chapter more easily, Table 8.1, which includes definitions of many language terms, is included for reference.

Fillion, Smith, and Swain (1976) discuss the interdependence and independence of four language skills (listening, speaking, reading, and writing). Recognizing that there are separate and different skills within each of these four areas, they hypothesized that children's oral language competencies relate to understanding the language used by the author of the spoken or written message. While these areas develop differently, the "lack of skill in one does not necessarily reflect lack of skill in another . . . yet the development of one skill will increase the potential of the individual for development of other skills" (Fillion, et al., 1976, p. 742).

The terms "receptive" and "expressive" provide a general delineation of the language skill areas, but do not specify the nature of the skills that need to be assessed or taught. Wiig and Semel's (1976) set of language processing (receptive) and language production (expressive) skills provides a framework for assessing and teaching specific language skills (see Figure 8.2). While these skills are interrelated, their delineation facilitates under-

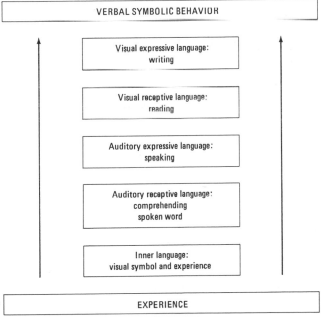

Figure 8.1   The developmental hierarchy of the human language system. (H. R. Myklebust, *The psychology of deafness*. New York: Grune & Stratton, 1960, p. 232. Reprinted by permission.)

Table 8.1 Terms defining the structure of language

Term	Definition/Examples
Phonology	Speech sounds (sounds within words when they are spoken)
Phonologic information	Sounds and sound patterns created through intonation (pitch, stress)
Morphology	Study of and rules for the formation of words
Morpheme	Smallest meaningful unit of word *Unbound morphemes* are root words (classify) *Bound morphemes* are affixes (de-, un-, -ed, -s)
Syntax	Combination of words into sentences according to grammatical rules (noun + verb + object)
Semantics	Meaning expressed by words or by grammatical relationships between words (relationship between the word symbol and the object, event, or idea to which it refers)
Transformations	Alternate ways of presenting information (expanding simple sentences to complex sentences, changing declarative statements to interrogative statements)

standing of the structural aspects of language, which children must learn. According to Wiig and Semel, language processing skills include perception of sensory data, linguistic processing, and cognitive processing. Language is described as having different levels or stages. First, the message is passed through the senses to be recognized at the next level. There, perception of sensory data (including the skills of attending to and locating sounds, identifying different types of sounds, differentiating speech sounds, segmenting sounds, and synthesizing sounds and sound sequences) is achieved. Segmenting skills are used to separate words into their parts or morphemes (see Table 8.1 for definition), and synthesis is combining word parts into whole words ("bl" + "end" to "blend").

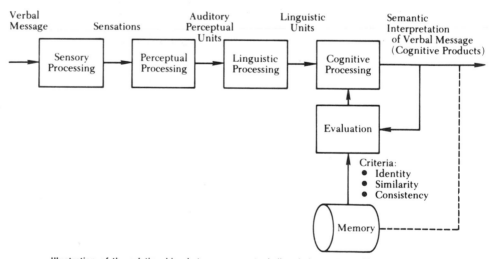

Figure 8.2 Illustration of the relationships between perceptual, linguistic, and cognitive processing in language comprehension (E. H. Wiig & E. M. Semel, *Language disabilities in children and adolescents.* Columbus, Ohio: Charles E. Merrill Publishing Co., 1976, p. 24. Reprinted by permission.)

Linguistic processing skills aid children to understand the structure and meaning of language. At this stage, children combine information learned from the sounds of the words, the meaning and use of words, and structure of words within sentences. Also at this stage, children learn how to combine morphological skills (noun plurals, noun-verb agreement, affixes, adjectives), syntactic skills (use of word sequencing, interrogatives, conjunctions, complex sentences), and semantic skills (word meanings, meanings of words within contexts, meanings of expressions, puns, idioms).

Cognitive processing skills use the mental operations necessary to comprehend the meaning of language. Children rely on the sounds of words (perception of sensory data skills) and the structural features of language and the meanings of words (linguistic processing skills) to form various relationships among the concepts or information presented. Cognitive processing skills include such abilities as solving verbal problems (semantic classes), redefining concepts (semantic transformations), or determining cause and effect relationships (semantic implications).

All language processing skills are interrelated. Understanding language depends upon the recognition of sounds and words, the structure or linguistic aspects of language, and the meanings of words and contexts. These skills also depend on students' abilities to evaluate and remember information presented.

Within Wiig and Semel's conceptual framework, language production is defined as a set of selectional, semantic, linguistic, and verbal encoding skills. The selectional and semantic areas of language relate to the accuracy of producing cognitive processing skills (sounds and sound units, words and concepts, verbal associations, verbal analogies, and verbal problems). Linguistic encoding skills involve the formulation and expression of grammatically acceptable phrases and sentences. Verbal encoding skills include articulatory agility, intonation, sequencing, and verbal fluency. Again, these skills are interrelated and are dependent on memory and evaluative feedback (see Figure 8.3 for a diagram of Wiig and Semel's production schema).

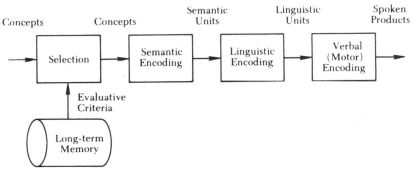

Figure 8.3   Illustration of the relationships between cognitive, linguistic, and expressive aspects in language production. (E. H. Wiig & E. M. Semel, *Language disabilities in children and adolescents.* Columbus, Ohio: Charles E. Merrill Publishing Co., 1976, p. 34. Reprinted by permission.)

As has been noted in many language models, cognitive factors have direct relationships to language processing and production, which should be considered when instructional activities are planned. Gibson and Levin (1975) posit that children must learn to optimize attention, increase the specificity of correspondence between stimulus and information, and increase the economy of information pickup. Considerable detail about cognition is presented in Chapter 6. Information about enhancing attention, processing, and memory—all components of language learning—can also be found in that chapter.

Current language theorists address the relationship between linguistic inputs and learners' current skills, knowledge, and experiences (Bransford, 1979). Language learning occurs in social systems, with students' experiences providing a basis for understanding. The nature and quality of children's early linguistic environment is probably *the* external factor that affects the rate of language development (McCarthy, 1954; Schiefelbusch, 1967). Students' cognitive structures organize and summarize experiences and knowledge (Smith, 1975). Therefore, it is important to present information in a form consistent with the knowledge and experiential level of the students. The availability of relevant knowledge and the opportunity for transfer, practice, and rehearsal may affect the rate at which new information is learned. The context of language forms the frame of reference for subsequent experience, and the redundancy within language allows learners to attend selectively to information, to anticipate meaning, and to identify the key words and phrases that convey meaning (Hittleman, 1978).

LANGUAGE DEVELOPMENT DURING THE SCHOOL YEARS

Educators and linguists distinguish early language acquisition from later language development, expansion and extensions (Fox, 1976). Although a considerable amount of language has been acquired by age six, language learning is not complete. The ability to comprehend and use vocabulary and concepts develops with age (McNeil, 1966; Slobin, 1966). By the end of first grade, children have mastered basic grammatical structures at almost an adult level, yet they lack adults' extensive vocabulary and ability to use alternate sentence structures (Hittleman, 1978). While vocabulary increases significantly during the first six years, complex grammatical structures are mastered later. Chomsky's (1969) research indicates that the ability to understand more complex grammatical structures was not achieved by nine-year-old children.

Students' use and understanding of the semantics and syntax of language occurs developmentally (Brown & Bellugi, 1964; Cazden, 1968; Kolker, 1979; McNeil, 1966, 1970; Slobin, 1966). The use of segmentation, morphology, grammar, and meaning improves with age and may be influenced by the acquisition of literacy (Gibson & Levin, 1975). The ability to make effective use of categories improves with age (classifying animals, body parts) and depends on learners' knowledge of categories (Wortman, 1071). Younger children (preschoolers, first graders) often fail to differentiate vocabulary meanings, which inhibits the formation of meaningful relationships (Gibson & Levin, 1975). Cramer (1972) found that younger children often related words acoustically (fountain-mountain), while older children relied on meaning as a stimulus (hill-mountain). He therefore suggests a developmental progression of semantic generalization. Rice and Di Vesta (1965) found that younger children (third graders) generalized words phonetically, while older students (fifth graders) used semantic similarity. Moreover, conceptual development seems to advance as children segment sentences and make comparisons of the meanings of words rather than of their positions in sentences (Gibson & Levin, 1975).

Children's use of deliberate cognitive strategies for remembering and using language also develops with age. Appel, Cooper, McCarrell, Sims-Knight, Yussen, and Flavell (1972) report that fifth graders employed rehearsal strategies and conceptual organization at a higher level than kindergarten or first grade students. Young children do not rehearse spontaneously, but they seem to rehearse more as they grow older. This may be influenced by prompting provided by teachers or adult models (Bernbach, 1967; Flavell, Beach, & Chinsky, 1966; Haith, 1971; Kingsley & Hagen, 1969; Meacham, 1972) or the use of cognitive modification strategies (refer to Chapter 6).

Learning to expand and extend language during the school years involves learning and applying the rules of language. The systems of language (phonology, syntax, semantics, and morphology) operate in a systematic and orderly manner. Some (Skinner, 1957; Staats, 1968) explain language growth through modeling and reinforcement. These techniques alone, however, do not explain fully how language is acquired (Chomsky, 1959, 1968; Hall, Ribovich, & Ramig, 1979). It seems that children must also "formulate and test hypotheses regarding the rules of language" (Hall, Ribovich, & Ramig, 1979, p. 33). Children and adolescents are involved in a discovery process, trying to learn the various rules of language, starting with the relationship of sounds, meaning, and the structure of language. Children use the discovery process to regulate language after learning to use various rules (the "ed" ending). They go through a period of adding this ending to all words (walked, runned, goed, comed), applying the rules rather than imitating correct forms heard from adults. The set of rules children or adolescents learn expand as memory and experiences with language increase.

Dale (1976) specifies a number of language rules that students learn. He defines linguistic competence as the "set of learned principles that a person must have in order to be a speaker of a language," and states that linguistic performance is the "transition of this knowledge into action" (p. 64). Performance involves unconscious learning and use of the language rules. Youngsters are not asked to state the rules (as they might be asked to state multiplication or subtraction rules), but to understand and use them systematically.

As children and adolescents experience language, they formulate rules for its function and orderly structure. Rules serve as language tools to bring meaning to ideas (Ausubel, 1968). For example, youngsters learn specific rules (the first noun in a sentence is probably the subject of the action) and use them to get meaning from the language they hear. To use syntactic information, Kolker (1979) notes that students must learn the placement and function of connecting words, designative words, inflections indicating tense, number, gender and case, and word order. Berko (1958) found that when children learn a set of morphological rules (see Table 8.1 for definition), they might even be able to comprehend words that are not part of their listening vocabulary. By using semantic cues, students can discover the meanings of words and concepts used in context.

LANGUAGE PROBLEMS OF LEARNING DISABLED STUDENTS[1]

The previous discussion of language learning and language characteristics provides a conceptual base for understanding the language problems of learning disabled youngsters. These students exhibit a wide variety of disabilities in both language processing and production. They also have problems in understanding and using the rules of language. Separate discussions are presented for auditory, linguistic, cognitive, and production problems.

Auditory Processing Problems

As discussed in Chapter 6, difficulty in maintaining attention to meaningful linguistic inputs and in screening out the random or irrelevant is a problem for many learning disabled children. Such problems in the auditory processing area are manifested as deficits in auditory figure-ground, sound localization, phoneme discrimination, and sound blending (Flowers, Costello, & Small, 1970; Lasky & Tabin, 1973; Wiig & Semel, 1976). Therefore, many learning disabled students have difficulty distinguishing sounds on a tape from background noise, locating the source of sounds, noting similar speech sounds, or blending sounds with words.

Auditory memory problems also are prevalent among this population (Chalfant & Scheffelin, 1969). They may have problems recalling certain sequences or semantic units (categories of proper names, adjectives, antonyms, or synonyms). Often they cannot recall semantic relationships to complete verbal analogies (cold is to hot as day is to night) or determine cause and effect relationships (turning off the faucet stops the waterflow). Short-term auditory memory problems affect reproduction of simple sentences, while long-term memory deficits may affect semantic transformations (understanding multiple meanings of words, complex sentences, riddles, or puns).

Linguistic Processing Problems

Delays in the acquisition of morphological and syntactic rules and lack of knowledge about linguistic structure are included in this category of problems (Rosenthal, 1970; Semel & Wiig, 1975; Vogel, 1974; Wiig, Semel, & Crouse, 1973). For example, many learning disabled youngsters have problems making plural words, using the correct sequence of words within a sentence, or understanding the relationship between words, their organiza-

[1] Those who wish more detail should refer to Wiig and Semel s (1976) comprehensive review of the literature, which documents these language problems.

Many learning disabled students do not process information well when it is presented auditorily. For many, practice with tape recorded activities enhances following directions and understanding information presented orally.

tion, and their meaning. They may be able to say the words or identify the noun and verb, but are not able to understand the message of the sentence. They may interpret concepts correctly, but fail to abstract the relationships implied in the sentence structure. "They could understand the concept *girl, boy, hit* but not understand *The girl hit the boy* because the sentence structure was not processed" (Wiig & Semel, 1976, p. 27). Some learning disabled students also may have linguistic processing deficits that result in being unable to interpret ambiguous sentences, idioms, and puns that do not have a one-to-one correspondence between words and their meaning.

Cognitive Processing Problems

Learning disabled students may have varied cognitive processing problems involving concept formation and the understanding of semantic units. They may be able to describe a few attributes of a concept, but be unable to synthesize a comprehensive definition. Following oral directions may be difficult because of an inability to understand the semantic aspects of the directions or the sequence of steps required (Wiig & Semel, 1976). Concept classification (names of fruits) and semantic relations (relationship of flour, dough, bread, and toast; of if-so clause relationships) can be difficult for these students. Difficulties in solving verbal problems or analogies reflect inabilities with classification, seriation, synthesis, or reorganization. Learning disabled youngsters may have problems predicting outcomes, anticipating events, or determining cause and effect because of impaired cognition of semantic implications.

Language
Production
Deficiencies

Problems in naming pictures, producing verbal opposites, redefining words or concepts, and being flexible in forming sentences are prevalent among some learners. These students have reduced ability in producing correct morphology and syntax (Rosenthal, 1970; Semel & Wiig, 1975; Vogel, 1974; Wiig & Semel, 1975; Wiig, Semel, & Crouse, 1973). At times, their vocabulary may seem to be creative or their spontaneous language seems to be grammatically appropriate, yet a study of their oral language indicates morphological and syntactic difficulties. For example, even into adolescence some may continue to say "John comed." Regardless of setting, their oral language lacks complex sentences, descriptive phrases, preciseness, or a range of sentence transformations (Hass & Wepman, 1974).

Different Dialects

Divergent dialects are not indicators of linguistic competence, but are the result of social and geographical factors. The learning disabled student who also has a divergent dialect may present a complex problem to the teacher because that dialect may interfere with learning. It is not the dialect that creates the problem but negative factors within the school, such as teacher attitudes or inappropriate teaching methodology. Rather than try to change dialects, teachers should develop an understanding of the linguistic variations and functions of language (Fillion, Smith, & Swain, 1976). As Cazden (1972) indicates, the differences between black dialect and standard English are minor in linguistic significance. With only a few exceptions (use of "be"), they are related to the surface structure of language use rather than affecting the meaning of communication.

Students using the black English dialect may express any or all ideas in their dialect. If they do not, the reasons might be learning problems, sociological expectations, or instructional mismatches. It is important to know that children can extend their vocabulary while still retaining black English patterns of grammar (Cazden, 1965). Speakers of black English have considerable receptive command of standard English and even though oral language factors may be different, they are capable of using a full range of language functions.

Bilingual students, speaking a native language and English, often are described as having a different dialect. As with black dialect students, their different language patterns, cultural backgrounds, and sociological expectations require adaptations of instructional methodology. These students are often incorrectly labeled as learning disabled. While some of these children may in fact have learning disabilities, the reason for their failure is more often associated with the use of an inappropriate curriculum.

ASSESSMENT

Because language is complex and varies according to its function, listener, and topic, it needs to be assessed by different measures across various settings. While language intervention procedures require precise diagnosis, language assessment tests and procedures have received much criticism. Language assessment instruments do not consider current research and are inconclusive measures of underlying meaning (deep structure) (Irwin, Moore,

& Ramps, 1972; Sitko & Gillespie, 1978; Sitko & Semmel, 1973). They do little to provide suggestions for methodology (Newcomer & Hammill, 1976; Dever, Note 1). These instruments are not valid or reliable measures of adolescents' language (Lee, 1974; McCarthy, Note 2), and do not specify language problems of learning disabled students as compared to normal populations (Sitko & Gillespie, 1978). The tests listed in Table 8.2 are used by many language specialists and can be used by classroom teachers as screening instruments. These tests provide information on the language processing and production skills described earlier in this chapter.

Several procedures also can be used for informal assessment of language. Spontaneous oral language can be analyzed by assessing the number of words, the number of meaningful elements, or the nature of the syntactic structures. The mean length of utterance (MLU) procedure suggested by Brown (1973) presents a method of calculating the number of words and the number of meaningful words. The calculation of the MLU provides an assessment of sentence complexity and sentence differentiation. Because of different definitions of an utterance, the MLU calculations vary according to the person doing the assessment. Brown's (1973) procedure for defining MLU is a useful and consistent method of obtaining this information (for details refer to Table 8.3). Lee and Canter (1971) also present a method of collecting and analyzing spontaneous expressive language samples to determine consistency of language usage. They recommend the procedure of tape recording a conversation between a child and an adult, in which the adult stimulates conversation with materials, pictures, tapes, and verbal prompts such as "Tell me about it." The sample to be analyzed should contain fifty consecutive sentences (which can be selected from a larger sample) so the child has time to relax and be comfortable. The teacher selects and writes fifty sentences from the language sample and examines them for inclusion and consistent usage of articles (a, an, the), possessive forms and contractions, verb endings, appropriate forms of irregular verbs, and prepositions and connectives (with, by, for). If children use all of these elements spontaneously and consistently, their language usually is considered to be well developed. If they omit any of the above, the language usage is missing necessary clues (phonemes or morphemes), and usually is considered in need of remediation.

Lee's (1974) *Developmental Sentence Analysis* provides a formula for analyzing spontaneous language according to eight major categories. A sentence score is derived from this formula, which can be used to compare performance to normal language development. To use this formula, 100 spontaneous utterances are taped and analyzed. The language sample is evaluated for the presence of indefinite pronouns or noun modifiers, personal pronouns, main verbs, secondary verbs, negatives, conjunctions, interrogative reversals, and "wh-" questions. The assumption is that as students increase their length of utterance, they also increase grammatical complexity. Frayer, Frederick and Klausmeier (Note 3) present a concept schema that delineates the stages of concept development. At each stage, activities are suggested that assess students' attainment of that level of understanding.

Table 8.2   Formal test summary

General Assessment	Name of Test	Author and Date	Skills Measured	Normed Population	Comments
Receptive language (language processing) Auditory perception of speech sounds	Auditory Discrimination Test	Wepman (1973)	Discrimination of speech sounds	ages 5–8	Assesses sounds in initial, medial, and final positions in words. Require children to know same-different concepts. Scoring of test is narrow with limited sampling of sounds that students often confuse, such as medial vowels. Does not account for language differences.
	Testing-Teaching Module of Auditory Discrimination	Risko (1975)	Discrimination of speech sounds within various locations of words and auditory blending	grades 1–3	Data-based program. Record sheets and teaching activities are provided.
	Goldman-Fristoe-Woodcock Test of Auditory Discrimination	Goldman, Fristoe, & Woodcock (1970)	Discrimination of speech sounds in one-syllable minimal pair of words with quiet or noise backgrounds	3.8 to 70 + yrs.	Measures figure-ground as well as speech discrimination; uses picture choices.
Auditory figure-ground	Flowers-Costello Tests of Central Auditory Abilities	Flowers, Costello, & Small (1970)	Discrimination of low pass filtered speech and competing messages	K–6th grade	May also measure semantic and linguistic information as words are presented in sentence; syllables of words vary, which may be cues to selection rather than sounds. Therefore, it is somewhat difficult to interpret findings.
Auditory blending	Roswell-Chall Auditory Blending Test	Roswell & Chall (1963)	Auditory blending of sounds into words	grades 1–4	Teacher practice of pronunciation of isolated sounds needed.
Language processing (receptive language)	Peabody Picture Vocabulary Test	Dunn (1981)	Receptive vocabulary comprehension. Child points to picture of the word the examiner pronounces	2 yrs., 3 mos.– 18 yrs., 5 mos.	Test scores can be converted to mental age, I.Q. standard score, and percentile equivalents.

Full-Range Picture Vocabulary Test	Ammons & Ammons (1948)	Receptive vocabulary–child finds cartoon-like picture of word pronounced	2 yrs. to adulthood.	Scores can be converted into mental age or percentile ratings. Dated pictures. Separate nouns are available for Spanish-American children, black children, and white rural children.
Irwin-Hammil Abstraction Test	Hammill & Irwin (1966)	Identifying missing items in a sequence, naming items belonging to a category, matching attributes to concepts	Used with cerebral palsied and mentally retarded children, ages 6–17 (Normative data are not available).	Can be used to determine patterns of strength and weakness across several language areas.
Boehm Test of Basic Concepts	Boehm (1970)	Comprehension of concepts of quantity, number, space, and time	K–2 yrs.	Sampling of basic concepts for most academic areas.
Basic Concept Inventory	Engelman (1967)	Comprehension of basic concepts of conjunction (and), dimension, direction, function, location, negation (not), time, and quantity	No normative data. Recommended for preschool to third grade.	Specific strengths and weaknesses are identified with intervention strategies given in the manual.
Wiig-Semel Test of Linguistic Concepts	Wiig & Semel (1973, 1974a, 1974b)	Comprehension of fifty concepts requiring logic, comparative, passive, temporal-sequential-spatial, and familiar relationships	grades 1–8	Measures a wide variety of ethnic names. Allows for yes/no responses.
Proverbs Test	Gorham (1956)	Interpretation of proverbs, translations of concrete symbols into abstract concepts	grades 5–12	Alternative methods of presenting the proverbs are available.
Test for Auditory Comprehension of Language	Carrow (1973)	Comprehension of variety of language categories. Form classes and function words, morphology, grammar and syntax	3 yrs.–6 yrs., 11 mos.	Age expectations are given for each item; some confusion on the interpretation of errors.

(Continued)

Table 8.2—*Continued*

General Assessment	Name of Test	Author and Date	Skills Measured	Normed Population	Comments
	Northwestern Syntax Screening Test: Receptive Subtest	Lee (1969)	Ability to process, interpret, and recall syntactic structures	3 yrs.–7 yrs., 11 mos.	Can be used to differentiate the nature of language problems. Some ambiguous statements and some confusion with interpretation of errors.
Language production	*McCarthy Scales of Children's Ability:* Verbal Scale	McCarthy (1972)	Ability to produce oral language on the verbal memory, verbal fluency, and opposite analogies subtests	2½–8½ yrs.	Assess language deficits in several areas of language production.
	Detroit Tests of Learning Aptitude Verbal Opposites Subtest Free Association Subtest	Baker & Leland (1959)	Memory and formulation of antonyms Memory and formulation of a series of associated words	5 yrs., 3 mos.–19 yrs. 5 yrs., 3 mos.–19 yrs.	Assesses knowledge of wide vocabulary to formulate antonyms. Allows for analysis of language patterns of spontaneous language.
	Northwestern Syntax Screening Test: Expressive Subtest	Lee (1969)	Ability to listen to and repeat sentence structures with use of grammatical features and prepositions, pronouns, questions, passives		Uses a sentence imitation procedure to determine whether child is capable of producing structures in imitation but not in spontaneous language.
Language processing and production	*Test of Language Development* (TOLD)	Newcomer & Hammill (1977)	Oral and receptive language	4 yrs.–8 yrs., 11 mos.	Assesses total language functioning
	Test of Adolescent Language (TOAL)	Hammill, Brown, Larsen, & Wiederholt (1980)	Oral and receptive language	ages 12–19	Assesses adolescents' language abilities

| Table 8.3 | **Rules for calculating mean length of utterance (MLU)** |

The following rules are reasonable for MLU up to about 4.0; by this time many of the assumptions underlying the rules are no longer valid.

1. Start with the second page of the transcription unless that page involves a recitation of some kind. In this latter case start with the first recitation-free stretch. Count the first 100 utterances satisfying the following rules. (A 50-utterance sample may be used for preliminary estimate.)

2. Only fully transcribed utterances are used. Portions of utterances, entered in parentheses to indicate doubtful transcription, are used.

3. Include all exact utterance repetitions (marked with a plus sign in records). Stuttering is marked as repeated efforts at a single word; count the word once in the most complete form produced. In the few instances in which a word is produced for emphasis or the like ("no, no, no") count each occurrence.

4. Do not count such fillers as "um" and "oh," but do count "no," "yeah," and "hi."

5. All compound words (two or more free morphemes), proper names, and ritualized reduplications count as single morphemes. Examples: "birthday," "rackety-boom," "choo-choo," "quack-quack," "night-night," "pocketbook," "see-saw."

6. Count as one morpheme all irregular pasts of the verb ("got," "did," "want," "saw"). Justification is that there is no evidence that the child relates these to present forms.

7. Count as one morpheme all diminutives ("doggie," "mommy") because these children at least do not seem to use the suffix productively. Diminutives are the standard forms used by the child.

8. Count as separate morphemes all auxiliaries ("is," "have," "will," "can," "must," "would"). Also all catenatives: "gonna," "wanna," "hafta." The latter are counted as single morphemes rather than as "going to" or "want to" because the evidence is that they function so for children. Count as separate morphemes all inflections, for example, possessive "s," plural "s," third person singular "s," regular past tense "d," progressive "ing."

SOURCE: Adapted from R. Brown, *A first language: The early stages.* Cambridge, Mass.: Harvard University Press, 1973, p. 54, Table 7, © 1973 by the President and Fellows of Harvard College. Reprinted by permission.

Direct observation of students' language is a major assessment tool. To obtain a total picture of students' language, observations should be made across settings in activities generating spontaneous (play, sharing periods, learning games) and structured language (teacher interviews of students, asking students to follow directions, teacher reading to students and asking questions). Throughout the assessment process the qualities of language should be monitored (use of simple sentences versus complex sentences, use of sentence transformations, use of elaborative language, use of conversational language.) The chart presented by Bloom and Lahey (1978) (see Table 8.4) illustrates how observational data can be recorded and then correlated with the goals and procedures for intervention. This chart exemplifies the nature of data that can be collected. Wiig and Semel (1976) also provide an outline of questions to be answered during the assessment process (see Table 8.5), which lists processing and production skills and can be used to further define these skill areas.

Table 8.4   **Possible correlations between observational data and instructional goals and procedures**

Information To Be Obtained	Objective of Assessment: To Determine		
	Existence of Language Problem	Goals of Intervention	Procedures for Intervention
Historical			
Age at which language milestones reached	X		
Age at which other developmental milestones reached			X
Changes that have occurred in language behavior in the past, and correlated environmental or physical factors			X
Description of current language behaviors			
General comparison with peers	X		
Amount of verbalizations—how much the child talks	X	X	
Intelligibility of speech—how well the child is understood	X	X	
Comprehension of the language of others—how much the child understands of what others say with accompanying context and without relevant context	X	X	X
Use			
Functions for which language is used (demand, comment, question, tell stories, etc.)	X	X	X
Contexts of referents talked about (here and now, self-actions, etc.)	X	X	X
Form			
Kinds of words used (e.g., nouns, pronouns) and the variety of different words used	X	X	
Typical length of utterances	X	X	
Relative completeness of sentences	X	X	
Variety of sentence structures (e.g., statements, questions)	X	X	
Variety and appropriateness of morphological endings	X	X	
Other forms of communication (e.g., gestures and manual signs)	X	X	X
Content—what the child communicates			
Kinds of objects	X	X	X
Kinds of events	X	X	X
Kinds of states and feelings	X	X	X
Kinds of relationships between objects	X	X	X
Kinds of relationships between people, or people and objects	X	X	X
Kinds of relationships between events	X	X	X
Description of nonlinguistic behaviors			
Social interactions with:			
Children			X
Adults			X
Preferred activities, foods, etc.			X
Medical history			
Current medication, contraindications to activities, possibilities of seizures, etc.			X
Motor skills (coordination for running, catching, drawing, etc.)			X
Attention to sound, both verbal and nonverbal			X
Span of attention to preferred and nonpreferred activities			X
Factors that interfere with attention			X

(*Continued*)

Table 8.4 —*Continued*

	Objective of Assessment: To Determine		
Information To Be Obtained	Existence of Language Problem	Goals of Intervention	Procedures for Intervention
Description of environment			
Availability of others to assist in intervention			X
Factors that may be interfering with language growth (e.g., lack of peers, lack of stimulation, bilingualism)			X
Home setting			X
School setting			X

SOURCE: L. Bloom and M. Lahey, *Language development and language disorders.* New York: John Wiley & Sons, 1978, pp. 344–345. Reprinted by permission.

Table 8.5   **Questions to be asked during assessment**

I. Sensory processing
    A. Are the auditory thresholds for hearing low-frequency and high-frequency pure tones adequate?
    B. Are the auditory thresholds for hearing speech adequate?
II. Auditory-perceptual processing
    A. Attention
        1. Can the child sustain auditory attention over reasonable periods of time? If so, under what conditions?
        2. Is the child's auditory attention distracted by other stimuli (auditory or visual)?
        3. Do novel stimuli (auditory or visual) assist in focusing the child's attention?
    B. Localization
        1. Does the child readily localize environmental sounds (turning his head in the direction of the sound source)?
        2. Does the child readily localize the source of speech sounds in the environment?
    C. Figure-ground
        1. Can the child discern environmental sounds in the presence of competing auditory stimuli?
        2. Can the child distinguish a speaker in the presence of competing messages?
    D. Discrimination of nonverbal stimuli
        1. Can the child discriminate differences in the frequency (pitch), intensity (loudness), rhythm, duration, and timbre (the quality given to a sound by its overtones) of tonal pairs?
    E. Discrimination of verbal stimuli
        1. Can the child discriminate specific phonemes in words differing by only one speech sound, such as *cat* and *sat*?
        2. Does the child have difficulty discriminating between initial consonants, final consonants, medial consonants, vowels, and/or consonant blends?
        3. Can the child identify consonants, vowels, and blends in the initial, final, or medial positions of words?
        4. Can the child discriminate words against a background of noise or competing messages?
    F. Sequencing
        1. Does the child retain the sequence in a series of auditory stimuli consisting of digits, phonemes, words (related and unrelated), phrases and syntactic structures, and sentences?
        2. Can the child recall and repeat series of auditory stimuli consisting of the foregoing elements?
        3. Can the child follow a series of oral directions of increasing length and complexity?

(Continued)

Table 8.5—*Continued*

G. Synthesis: resistance to distortion
   1. Can the child form words out of separated, articulated phonemes?
   2. Can the child predict and formulate words when phonemes or syllables are missing?
H. Segmentation and syllabication
   1. Can the child identify the separate words that are parts of compound words?
   2. Can the child identify the number of syllables in words of increasing length?
   3. Can the child identify the position of a stressed syllable in multi-syllabic words?
   4. Can the child identify the initial and final syllables of multi-syllabic words?
   5. Can the child discriminate between stressed and unstressed syllables?
   6. Can the child identify and discriminate among meaningful prefixes and suffixes in complex words?
   7. Can the child discriminate among and identify inflectional suffixes? (Comparative -er; superlative -est; past tense -d, -t, -id, etc.)
   8. Can the child identify derivational suffixes? (Noun derivation -er, -or, -tion, -ion; adverb derivation -ly, -y, etc.)

III. Cognitive-semantic processing
   A. Semantic units
      1. Does the child comprehend selected vocabulary items such as verbs, adjectives, prepositions, pronouns, etc.?
      2. Does the child comprehend vocabulary items requiring classification such as multiple-meaning words, antonyms, synonyms, homonyms?
      3. Can the child grasp shades of meaning between selected vocabulary items such as laughing, smiling, giggling, etc.?
      4. Can the child comprehend selected vocabulary items in critical word sequences such as *show me the kitten, show me the kitten on the mat, show me the kitten on the mat by the window?*
   B. Semantic classes
      1. Can the child classify selected vocabulary items (concepts) in appropriate semantic categories?
      2. Can the child identify vocabulary items (concepts) that do not belong to a given semantic category?
      3. Can the child comprehend linguistic concepts requiring logical operations such as comparative sentences, if-then constructions, etc.?
   C. Semantic relations
      1. Can the child process and comprehend verbal analogies expressing logical relationships between words and concepts?
      2. Can the child process and comprehend sentences that express logical relationships (comparative, passive, spatial, temporal, or familial) between words or elements?
      3. Can the child process and comprehend sentences containing linguistic concepts of inclusion-exclusion (*some, none, all, any, all except,* etc.) or concepts such as if/then, either/or, because, or when/then?
   D. Semantic systems
      1. Can the child discern the underlying structure of a verbal problem?
      2. Can the child detect errors, inconsistencies, absurdities, and ambiguities in sentences and stories?
   E. Semantic transformations
      1. Can the child grasp and identify similarities and differences between the meanings of selected (words) concepts?
      2. Does the child have difficulty understanding idioms, metaphors, similes, and/or proverbs?

(Continued)

Table 8.5—*Continued*

F. Semantic implications
  1. Can the child predict possible outcomes?
  2. Can the child identify expressed cause-effect relationships?
  3. Can the child identify cause-effect relationships by inference?
  4. Can the child identify fallacies in cause-effect and premise conclusion arguments?

IV. Linguistic processing
  A. Phonology
  B. Morphology
    1. Can the child identify and differentiate morphological structures?
  C. Syntax
    1. Can the child differentiate grammatical phrases, clauses, and sentences from those that are grammatically incorrect or incomplete?
    2. Can the child discriminate among the various sentence transformations (active, declarative, interrogative, passive declarative, negative, etc.)?

SOURCE: E. H. Wiig and E. M. Semel, *Language disabilities in children and adolescents.* Columbus, Ohio: Charles E. Merrill Publishing Co., 1976, pp. 76–79. Reprinted by permission.

Dever (1978) suggests that teachers prepare a task analysis to use as a tool for deciding which skills need to be taught. Dever and Knapczyk (1976) propose a procedure in which teachers begin with a specific language goal and then decide which behaviors are prerequisite to this goal. From this list of prerequisites, teachers can identify which skills students should possess and then match them to instructional objectives and activities. These sequenced activities may change according to daily evaluations, but at the preliminary stage they are suggested as a method that uses the most current information about students' language abilities and language needs.

IMPLICATIONS FOR TEACHERS

A careful study of the characteristics of language and language problems of learning disabled students leads to these implications for teaching:

1. *Teachers should assess carefully the language of children or adolescents to determine its structure and function.*

Various assessment tools and direct observations can be used to supply diagnostic information. Observations should occur across settings with the teacher listening to the child's language output to determine how well the youngster is trying out new rules or using the various language systems. Certain language strengths may be present but this does not mean that all functions are mastered. Record keeping can aid the teacher in noting specific language strengths and weaknesses of each student.

2. *Language should be taught systematically.*

Learning disabled youngsters need systematic language expansion and development to understand and use the various components of language

For students with language problems, a specific time each day should be set aside for group oral language experiences. This teacher has selected the *Peabody Language Development Kit,* and is implementing an activity which encourages discussion through the use of picture cards.

(Johnson & Myklebust, 1967; Wiig & Semel, 1976). An accurate diagnosis can lead to a program that matches materials to the linguistic level of the student.

3. *Improved language understanding and expanded use can be facilitated through numerous activities to "experience" language.*

Children and adolescents need to be immersed in language to understand and use its functions and rules. They should be given many opportunities to learn that language is never independent of function, and that it serves a purpose in solving problems or interpreting information (Moffett, 1968). Youngsters must build competence to comprehend and produce all the possible forms of sentences found in adult language.

4. *Children and adolescents must learn that language has a meaning base.*

Youngsters need to learn the meanings and functions of words they hear and produce, not just the pronunciation of the words. Language cannot be taught without meaning (Fillion, Smith, & Swain, 1976). Children produce language to the extent that it fulfills their own purposes or intentions (Smith, 1979). In the process of encouraging students' language, teachers should use language that is meaningful to the students.

5. *Teachers should provide feedback to help students expand and extend their language.*

Students need adult feedback about their language. Teachers can take advantage of informal discussions within groups of students by providing models and information before eliciting student output. This situation can be used to refine, expand, and enrich students' language (Possien, 1969). Of course, caution must be taken so the adult does not dominate the conversation.

When students are trying out their language, they need two types of information, general and specific. General information keeps them exposed to many adult language models. Specific information is a vehicle for the teacher to provide corrective feedback when (and only when) the students need it. Corrective feedback is nonpunitive, but tells the students whether they are observing and using language rules or systems correctly. Also, students need corrective information as they use the language rules, rather than learning rules according to a curriculum plan.

6. *Teachers should analyze the language they use in the information and directions they give to students.*

Teachers should be certain that they present clear and concise information or directions so as not to confuse the students. Material presented also should be analyzed to determine its conceptual level. Teachers should set a purpose for the listening process and eliminate distracting information or background interference. Ausubel (1960) suggests that teachers provide "advance organizers" to create a "mind set" for listening. When there is a purpose for listening and the information matches the students' linguistic levels, a higher incidence of listening occurs. Lovitt and Smith (1972) demonstrate that instructions specific to the desired outcome can influence language performance.

7. *Children and adolescents need extensive opportunities for spontaneous language production.*

Students need opportunities to "play" with language and experiment with different structures of language to make discoveries about the use of language. Open-ended questions can encourage spontaneous language. Creating dialogue and expressing genuine interest in the students' language can further facilitate expressiveness.

8. *The systems and components of language should be taught in an interrelated manner rather than as a set of discrete skills.*

Cazden (1978) sharply criticizes programs that teach language as a set of discrete skills. Such programs lead students to develop isolated and fragmented pieces of information rather than to assimilate the integrated process of language systems. Activities are needed (problem solving) that incorporate the various processing and production skills. When students make consistent and frequent errors in their language, these errors can be directly remediated, but the program should continually integrate newly learned skills with previously mastered ones.

9. *Students should not be forced to talk.*

For students who are reluctant to talk to the class, opportunities should be provided to talk with the teacher during individual conferences or to share ideas with small groups. Often dramatizations, choral reading, puppet shows, or role-playing activities can be used to facilitate language expression rather than requiring spontaneous language in front of a large group.

10. *Divergent dialects convey the same meanings and serve the same functions.*

Although the syntax of different dialects may vary from standard English, the basic receptive and expressive language convey the same meaning and serve the same function, unless learning problems interfere with processing or production.

INTERVENTION STRATEGIES

Many experts present teaching activities that can be used to teach specific language skills. Using Wiig and Semel's schema for language processing and production, Table 8.6 summarizes some intervention strategies that can be used to develop and expand these skills. Because many instructional progams are available that aim at the remediation of language and its component skills, some of them are summarized in Table 8.7.

The listing of teaching strategies in Table 8.6 and instructional programs in Table 8.7 is not meant to imply that these skills are taught in isolation, or that the activities are meant to teach discrete skills. These procedures can be used to overemphasize particular language areas, but they need to be part of a total language program stressing the interrelatedness of all the components.

Risko and Degler (Note 4) suggest that language learning occurs best when there is a cycling of experiences. A lesson cycle is initiated when the teacher provides a learning opportunity (information, model of language structure, new concepts), and students are encouraged to experience the targeted area, which results in an expression of understanding. Through activities requiring either talking, drama, or some creative expression, students use their language to explain their perceptions. By experimenting with the form and function of language, they come to integrate concepts or information presented. Thus, through successive input experiences, children's understanding of the information progressively expands, while interspersed

Students and teacher are completing a cloze activity by listening to each other and producing possible words which make sense in the passage.

Table 8.6   Language processing skills and intervention suggestions

Skill	Suggested Intervention Strategies
I. Language Processing Skills **A. Auditory-Perception Processing** 1. Recognition of environmental sounds.	1. Use records or audio tapes of environmental sounds to teach recognition (doorbell, telephone, **carpet sweeper**, running water).
2. Recognition of speech sounds	1. Teach differences of sounds according to pitch, frequency, duration, and quality. 2. Teach localization of sounds according to familiar or unfamiliar sounds or the position of sounds according to distance and direction by blindfolding the children and having them locate the sounds. 3. Students who are blindfolded can be asked to walk in the direction of the sound to locate it.
3. Discrimination of speech sounds	1. Students can be asked to tell likenesses and differences of speech sounds in pairs of words. 2. Students tell the position of specific sounds within words. 3. Students pronounce the target sound in a word or a set of words. 4. Students may be able to discriminate sounds within single words rather than pairs of words, which would require listening to sounds within words. 5. See reading chapter.
4. Auditory figure-ground	1. Students listen to and produce messages presented on tapes with varied noise backgrounds.

B. Linguistic Processing
    1. Knowledge of morphology:
        a. Noun plurals and noun-verb agreement
	1. Students name words that mean "one" or "more than one" (Wiig and Semel, 1976, p. 143).
	2. Cloze paragraphs can omit nouns and students name the singular or plural nouns or the nouns or verbs that are omitted.
	3. Students can name singular or plural nouns for specified objects or pictures of objects (one cake, two cakes).

b. Noun derivation	1. Cloze passages can be used to have students supply compound words (firecracker). 2. Students can form meaningful compound words by combining two selected words (milkman).
c. Affixes	1. Cloze passages can be used requiring the students to supply words with the appropriate prefixes or suffixes. 2. Students list root words with prefixes or suffixes. 3. Give directions requiring understanding of root words with and without affixes (lock the door, unlock the door). 4. Students can match list of meanings to list of prefixes or suffixes. 5. Students define words having different affixes (postwar, prewar, prowar, antiwar) (Heilman and Holmes, 1972, p. 35).

(Continued)

Table 8.6—*Continued*

Skill	Suggested Intervention Strategies
d. Adjectives	1. Students complete sentences describing objects by using the correct form of the targeted adjectives: Who is (close) *closer* to the table? 2. Students name the objects that are bigger, smaller, shorter. . . . .
2. Syntactic processing a. Word sequencing	1. Students are given various word formats and asked to arrange the words into sentences or questions. 2. Students complete incomplete sentences by supplying missing words. 3. Change word order to make questions or statements (*Who wants to ride in the boat?* to *John wants to ride in the boat*). 4. Students can be given a set of scrambled sayings and asked to arrange the words correctly (i.e. runs still water deep:still water runs deep) (Heilman & Holmes, 1972, p. 65).
b. Passive sentences	1. Students are given active sentences and asked to say passive forms (I hit the ball. The ball was hit by me). 2. Students rearrange words to form passive sentences.

c. Interrogatives	1. Use activities requiring the student to understand various forms of wh- questions. Wiig and Semel (1976) suggest this developmental hierarchy:
	  1. what
	  2. who—which
	  3. where—when
	  4. why
	  5. how—how many—how much—whose.
	2. Students listen to information and then answer specific wh- questions.
	3. Students form questions from declarative sentences.
	4. Students match names, types of action, places, and times to the *who*, *what*, *when*, and *where* words (Heilman and Holmes, 1972, p. 76).

d. Conjunctions	1. Have students form sentences using various conjunctions. Lee (1974) suggests this sequence for semantic difficulty: and, or, but, besides, also, so, if, when. 2. Give the students two simple sentences and have them combine them by using the appropriate conjunctions (Come out. Play with me. Come out *and* play with me).
e. Complex sentences	1. Give students practice in identifying complete and incomplete sentences. 2. Ask students to name clauses or simple sentences of a complex statement.
3. Cognitive Processing a. Improving verb comprehension	1. Ask students to act out action of verbs, when possible (jumping, running, twisting). 2. Give commands requiring the student to understand the verb (*Bring* me the book). 3. Provide cloze passages in which the students have to supply the verbs.

b. Improving adjective comprehension	1. Students should describe attributes of a concept (frog is green, wet, cold, has webbed feet). 2. Students match adjectives to objects (red and apple) (Wiig & Semel, 1976, p. 165).
c. Improving pronoun comprehension	1. Have students match pronoun to the referent (*Joe* has a dog. *He* has a dog). 2. Students tell whether pronouns are used correctly in sentences.
d. Improving preposition comprehension	1. Have students act out concepts that are prepositions (on, under, between, on top of). 2. Students match concepts of prepositions to pictures (the dog is *under* the table).
e. Improving comprehension of antonyms, synonyms, homonyms, and multiple-meaning words	1. Students can be given sentences and asked to supply antonyms or synonyms for targeted words. 2. Key phrases can be matched to sentences to identify the meanings of words with multiple meanings. 3. Students can be given lists of words and asked to match them by same meanings or opposite meanings. 4. Crossword puzzles can be devised in which students supply words that are antonyms or synonyms for a set of given words (Heilman & Holmes, 1972, p. 39).
f. Improving semantic classification	1. Ask students to classify pictures by their categories (food, clothing, dog supplies). 2. Teach abstracting of semantic classes by asking students to note likenesses or differences of objects, events, ideas (How are cars and trains alike? What is the difference between summer and winter?) (Wiig & Semel, 1976, pp. 178–179).
g. Improving understanding of semantic relations	1. Present verbal analogies and ask students to say whether they are correct or incorrect. 2. Present incomplete analogies that students are asked to explain.
h. Improving processing of linguistic concepts	1. Ask students to compare two or more elements by using such terms as bigger, smaller, shorter than. 2. Present declarative statements and ask students to change the sentences to passive forms. 3. Temporal and familial relationships can be taught by asking students to identify the sequence of days or months and by labeling relationships of family members.
i. Improving understanding of semantic transformation	1. Present cartoons or illustrations and ask students to explain the idiomatic language (His stomach was in knots) (Wiig & Semel, 1976, p. 187). 2. Students can be asked to explain metaphors or proverbs.
j. Improving understanding of semantic implications	1. Ask students to interpret propaganda of ads or T.V. commercials. 2. Ask students to explain the inconsistencies or absurdities in sentences (He hit the baseball with the racquet) (Wiig & Semel, 1976, p. 189).
II. Language Production 1. Improving auditory memory for words, phrases, and sentences	1. Memory can be influenced by several factors, including: a. word frequency—using words within the student's language experiences; b. words that have associative strength—words associated in meaning are more easily remembered (knife-fork-spoon vs. dog-car-apple);

(Continued)

Table 8.6—Continued

Skill	Suggested Intervention Strategies
	c. length of sequences—using length of sentences appropriate for students' level of function (oral commands progress slowly in length);
	d. phrasal cueing with correct syntactic structure—using phrases rather than discrete words to give students meaningful units to recall (Wiig and Semel, 1976).
	2. Ask students to recall and say word sequences, sentences, songs, poems, or jingles.
	3. Ask students to transform sentences to various structures, encouraging them to expand or extend their responses (Fox, 1976). Fox suggests that if the student says "meat hot," the teacher can say "Yes, the meat is hot," which is an *expansion*, or the teacher can say "Yes, it is very hot. Do you think you'd better wait until it cools?" which is an *extension*.
	4. Ask students to imitate sentences or phrases that are said to them.
2. Improving convergent language	
a. Convergent production of semantic units	1. Students can be asked to name groups of objects or a series of related actions.
	2. Students are asked to complete sentences according to meanings (you can fly a _____) or to use synonyms or antonyms of targeted words.
b. Convergent production of semantic relations	1. Students are asked to produce analogies or complete sentences requiring comparative, spatial, temporal, or familial relationships (Wiig & Semel, 1976, p. 279).
	2. Students can be asked to explain cause and effect relationships.
c. Convergent production of semantic systems	1. Oral cloze passages can be used to give students the opportunity to supply targeted words in a meaningful passage.
	2. Specific words (nouns, adjectives) can be deleted in sentences and the student asked to complete them by using language and meaning cues.
3. Improving divergent language production	
a. Divergent production of semantic units	1. Ask students to respond to questions requiring description of objects or pictures.
	2. Present pictures or objects and encourage spontaneous descriptive language (Wiig & Semel, 1976, p. 284).
b. Divergent production of semantic classes, systems, implications	1. Ask students to produce sentences using a set of targeted nouns, verbs, prepositions, or adjectives.
	2. Present incomplete sentences requiring students to tell cause and effect of an action or an event.
4. Improving syntax in language production	1. Present scrambled sentences or phrases and ask students to form sentences using past tense, conjunctions, wh- question forms (Wiig & Semel, 1976, pp. 288–289).
	2. Sentence completion and cloze activities require students to form meaningful sentences.

Table 8.7   Commercial programs to develop language.

Name of Material	Author(s)	Purpose
Language Processing		
Sound-Order-Sense: A Developmental Program in Auditory Perception	Semel (1970)	Activities require discrimination of phonemes, syllables, and word sequences. Teacher comprehension of linguistic concepts such as comparative language, pronouns, and inflections.
Auditory Discrimination in Depth	Lindamood & Lindamood (1969)	Activities teach phoneme discrimination and sequencing and sound-symbol association.
Testing-Teaching Module of Auditory Discrimination	Risko (1975)	Activities teach recognition and discrimination of all speech sounds and their location within words.
Listening Skills Program	Bracken, Hays, & Bridges (1970)	Teaches auditory discrimination, memory, and listening. Also develops awareness of pitch, volume, and sentence patterns.
Auditory Perception Training	Willette, Jackson, & Peckins (1970)	Teaches auditory memory, auditory discrimination, and auditory imagery.
Distar	Engelmann & Bruner (1969)	Teaches sequences of sounds within words, auditory discrimination, rhyming, and sound-symbol association. Very structured format for presentation. Designed for "culturally deprived" and "educably retarded" children.
Wilson Initial Syntax Program	Wilson (1972)	Teaches comprehension of syntactic cues such as personal pronouns.
Goldman-Lynch Sounds and Symbols Development Kit	Goldman & Lynch (1971)	Activities to develop recognition of speech sounds and understanding of concepts.
Language Production		
Peabody Language Development Kits (Revised)	Dunn, Horton & Smith (1981) Dunn, Smith & Dunn (1981) Dunn, Dunn & Smith (1981) Dunn, Smith & Smith (1981)	Activities to develop oral expression. A four-year sequential program, from preschool through third grade, which was field-tested extensively and has a strong research base.
Interactive Language Development Teaching	Lee, Koenigsknecht, & Mulhern (1975)	Teaches production of various forms of syntax in exercises of scrambled sentences, sentence completion, and cloze paragraphs. Develops dialogue between teacher and student.
The World of Language Books A Student-Centered Language Arts Curriculum (Grades K–13)	Crosby & Bennett (1973) Moffett (1973) Moffett & Wagner (1976)	Activities to develop production of a variety of language structures. Numerous activities to elicit oral language.

output opportunities expand their receptive and expressive language abilities and provide the teacher with feedback. Within such a process, certain areas can be overemphasized through specific skill activities, but they must be related to the total language process, as in the two examples that follow.

THE WANTED CHEESE

Students are asked to describe the characteristics of foxes. To elicit language, the children may be encouraged to think about fox characters they have heard of in stories or on television. When the children suggest such words as strong, wise, agile, or tricky, they are asked to list synonyms for each of the words. Then they are asked to complete this cloze passage using the synonyms. This particular cloze activity provides practice with synonyms and adjectives.

> *Jane the _____ fox watched Sam the _____ crow fly away with a _____ piece of yellow cheese in his _____ beak. _____ Jane wanted the cheese and decided to outsmart the _____ crow by tricking him into dropping the cheese. First, _____ Jane challenged _____ Sam to a singing contest.*
>
> *_____ Sam looked disinterested and continued to hold the cheese in his _____ beak.*
>
> *_____ Jane then whizzed by with her tap shoes and asked _____ Sam to dance with her.*
>
> *_____ Sam spread his _____ wings but looked bored and continued to hold the cheese in his _____ beak.*
>
> *_____ Jane brought a long pole and dared _____ Sam to enter a pole-vaulting race. _____ Jane swung over the _____ pole several times but _____ Sam continued to hold the cheese in his _____ beak.*
>
> *Jane asked her friend Tommie the _____ kangaroo to look eye-to-eye with the _____ crow in the tree and scare him into dropping the cheese.*
>
> *_____ Sam seemed excited to see _____ Tommie but continued to hold the cheese in his _____ beak.*
>
> *All of a sudden a _____ noise was heard in the forest. It was _____ Might Mouse on his annual walk through the forest. Mighty Mouse said, "If I can't have a piece of _____ cheese, I'll take a singing fox, a dancing fox, or a pole-vaulting fox."*
>
> *_____ Sam waved his _____ wings and dropped the cheese for _____ Mighty Mouse. He exclaimed, "Oh please, take the cheese, as I would dearly miss the wonderful antics of my friend the fox."*
>
> *_____ Mighty Mouse ate the cheese as the _____ fox sang and danced and pole-vaulted through the trees.*

THE SAGA OF THE WANTED CHEESE

Students are asked to name rhyming words for the words *go, cheese, mouse, away,* and *vault.* They then complete this poem, using the correct poetic rhythm and the rhyming words.

The fox did a-hunting go.
She looked _____
She found a crow with some appealing cheese,
But was _____
Instead of the squeeze by Mighty Mouse,
Who happened _____
The mouse took the cheese and sauntered away.
The fox _____
The fox happily began to pole-vault
And offered _____

Conceptual learning is an important aspect of language development and expansion. It is necessary to provide students with a conceptual base so they can understand (process) the information and reproduce it accurately. When students learn the meaning of a new word, they learn a matrix of semantic features that define the word through a set of relevant and non-relevant attributes (Clark, 1973; Frayer, Frederick, & Klausmeier, Note 3). During concept development, students learn the general feature first, then the specific attributes of the concept. Students also need to learn the meaning of concepts within the context of language systems to understand communication: to determine the meaning of the word "promise," students need to analyze the syntactic, semantic, and social functions of the word in a selected context.

Student and teacher are developing the relevant attributes of the concept of "mystery".

Various language systems can be interrelated continuously in language activities and in activities occurring throughout the school day. This chapter provided only two examples of language activities that integrate several language-processing and production skills in "The Wanted Cheese" activities. Other activities to extend and expand language are provided in texts by Heilman and Holmes (1972) and Smith (1972). Students of all ages need to become aware of the language around them and talk about what they are hearing or doing. Asking students to talk about stories they have heard, to talk about films or books without words (Degler, 1979), or to discuss propaganda techniques are activities requiring several interrelated language areas. Secondary students also need to be encouraged to use language skills in various content-related activities, such as those requiring them to solve problems, explain procedures, interview community members, or develop classroom news programs. Direct experience in using language is helpful in providing models (preparing students for job interviews can be facilitated by practicing the language skills that may be necessary for successful interviewing).

SUMMARY

Language is a complex system of receiving and expressing information. Learning disabled students exhibit receptive and expressive language problems. While the definition of the various language skills facilitates assessment and intervention, the teaching strategies must provide for integration of all the skills, since they are interrelated and dependent upon each other in their development.

REFERENCE NOTES

1. DEVER, R. A. *A comment on the testing of language development in retarded children* (Technical Report 1.22). Bloomington, Ind.: Indiana University, Center for Innovation in Teaching the Handicapped, 1971.

2. McCARTHY, J. *Report of leadership training institutes.* Paper presented at the National Conference for the Association for Children with Learning Disabilities, New York, February, 1975.

3. FRAYER, D. A., FREDERICK, W. C., & KLAUSMEIER, H. J. *A schema for testing the level of concept mastery* (Working Paper #16). Madison, Wis.: The University of Wisconsin Research and Development Center for Cognitive Learning, 1969.

4. RISKO, V. J., & DEGLER, L. S. *Concept development for the mainstreamed sensory impaired children* (Manuscript for TEMPO, Dean's Project Grant). Nashville, Tenn.: George Peabody College for Teachers, 1979.

REFERENCES

AMMONS, R. B., & AMMONS, H. S. *Full-range picture vocabulary test.* Missoula, Mont.: Psychological Test Specialists, 1948.

APPEL, L. F., COOPER, R. G., McCARRELL, N., SIMS-KNIGHT, J., YUSSEN, S. R. & FLAVELL, J. H. The development of the distinction between perceiving and memorizing. *Child Development*, 1972, *43*, 1365–1381.

AUSUBEL, D. P. The use of advance organizers in the learning and retention of meaningful verbal material. *Journal of Educational Psychology*, 1960, *51*, 267–272.

AUSUBEL, D. P. *Educational psychology: A cognitive view.* New York: Holt, Rinehart & Winston, 1968.

BAKER, H. J., & LELAND, B. *Detroit tests of learning aptitude.* Indianapolis: Bobbs-Merrill Co., 1959.

BERKO, J. The child's learning of English morphology. *Word,* 1958, *14,* 150–177.

BERNBACH, H. A. The effect of labels on short-term memory for colors with nursery school children. *Psychonomic Science,* 1967, 7, 149–150.

BLOOM, L., & LAHEY, M. *Language development and language disorders.* New York: John Wiley & Sons, 1978.

BOEHM, A. E. *Boehm test of basic concepts.* New York: Psychological Corp., 1971.

BRACKEN, D. K., HAYS, J. D., & BRIDGES, C. J. *Listening skills program.* Chicago: Science Research Associates, 1970.

BRANSFORD, J. D. *Human cognititon: Learning, understanding, and remembering.* Belmont, Calif.: Wadsworth Publishing Co., 1979.

BROWN, R. *A first language: The early stages.* Cambridge, Mass.: Howard University Press, 1973.

BROWN, R., & BELLUGI, U. Three processes in the child's acquisition of syntax. *Harvard Educational Review,* 1964, *34,* 133–151.

CARROLL, J. B. *The study of language: A survey of linguistic and related disciplines in America.* Cambridge, Mass.: Harvard University Press, 1953.

CARROW, E. *Tests for auditory comprehension of language.* Austin, Tex.: Learning Concepts, 1973.

CAZDEN, C. B. Environmental assistance to the child's acquisition of grammar (Doctoral dissertation, Harvard University, 1965). *Dissertation Abstracts,* 1969, *29,* 2144A-2145A. (University Microfilms No. 68-1118)

CAZDEN, C. B. The acquisition of noun and verb inflections. *Child Development,* 1968, *38,* 433–448.

CAZDEN, C. B. *Child language and education.* New York: Holt, Rinehart & Winston, 1972.

CAZDEN, C. B. Commentary: Environments for language learning. *Language Arts* 1978, *55,* 681–682.

CHALFANT, J. C., & SCHEFFELIN, M. *Central processing dysfunctions in children and a review of research* (NINDS Monograph No. 9). Washington, D.C.: U.S. Government Printing Office, 1969.

CHOMSKY, C. *The acquisition of syntax in children from 5 to 10.* Cambridge, Mass.: M.I.T. Press, 1969.

CHOMSKY, N. A review of B. F. Skinner's "Verbal behavior." *Language,* 1959, *35,* 26–28.

CHOMSKY, N. *Language and mind.* New York: Harcourt Bruce Jovanovich, 1968.

CLARK, E. V. How children describe time and order. In C. A. Ferguson & D. I. Slobin (Eds.), *Studies of child language development.* New York: Holt, Rinehart & Winston, 1973.

CRAMER, P. A. A developmental study of errors in memory. *Developmental Psychology,* 1972, 7, 204–209.

CROSBY, M., & BENNETT, R. A. (Eds.) *The world of language books: Grades K-8.* Chicago: Follett Publishing Co., 1973.

DALE, P. S. *Language development: Structure and function* (2nd ed.). New York: Holt, Rinehart & Winston, 1976.

DEGLER, L. S. Putting words into wordless books. *The Reading Teacher,* 1979, *32,* 399–402.

DEVER, R. B. Language assessment through specification of goals and objectives. *Exceptional Children,* 1978, *45,* 124–129.

DEVER, R., & KNAPCZYK, D. The Indiana University preservice undergraduate program for training teachers of the moderately, severely, and profoundly handicapped. *Teacher Education Forum,* 1976, *5,* 2.

DUNN, L. *Peabody picture vocabulary test* (rev. ed.). Circle Pines, Minn.: American Guidance Service, 1981.

DUNN, L. M., DUNN, L. M., & SMITH, J. O. *Peabody language development kit: Level #2-Revised.* Circle Pines, Minn.: American Guidance Service, 1981.

DUNN, L. M., HORTON, K. B., & SMITH, J. O. *Peabody language development kit: Level #P-Revised.* Circle Pines, Minn.: American Guidance Service, 1981.

DUNN, L. M., SMITH, J. O., & DUNN, L. M. *Peabody language development kit: Level #1-Revised.* Circle Pines, Minn.: American Guidance Service, 1981.

DUNN, L. M., SMITH, J. O., & SMITH, D. D. *Peabody language development kit: Level #3-Revised.* Circle Pines, Minn.: American Guidance Service, 1981.

ENGELMANN, S. E. *The basic concept inventory.* Chicago: Follett Publishing Co., 1967.

ENGELMANN, S., & BRUNER, E. C. *Distar language: An instructional system.* Chicago: Science Research Associates, 1969.

FILLION, B., SMITH, F., & SWAIN, M. Language "basics" for language teachers: Towards a set of universal considerations. *Language Arts,* 1976, *53,* 740–745.

FLAVELL, J. H., BEACH, D. R., & CHINKSY, J. M. Spontaneous verbal rehearsal in a memory task as a function of age. *Child Development,* 1966, *37,* 283–299.

FLOWERS, A., COSTELLO, M. R., & SMALL, A. *Flowers-Costello tests of central auditory abilities.*

Dearborn, Mich.: Perceptual Learning Systems, 1970.

Fox, S. Assisting children's language development. *The Reading Teacher*, 1976, *29*, 666–670.

Gibson, E. J., & Levin, H. *The psychology of reading*. Cambridge, Mass.: M.I.T. Press, 1975.

Goldman, R., Fristoe, M., & Woodcock, R. W. *Goldman-Fristoe-Woodcock test of auditory discrimination*. Circle Pines, Minn.: American Guidance Service, 1970.

Goldman, R. & Lynch, M. E. *Goldman-Lynch sounds and symbols development kit*. Circle Pines, Minn.: American Guidance Service, 1971.

Gorham, D. R. *Proverbs test*. Missoula, Mont.: Psychological Test Specialists, 1956.

Haith, M. M. Developmental changes in visual information processing and short term visual memory. *Human Development*, 1971, *14*, 249–261.

Hall, M. A., Ribovich, J. K., & Ramig, C. J. *Reading and the elementary school child* (2nd ed.). New York: D. Van Nostrand Co., 1979.

Hammill, D. D., Brown, V., Larsen, S. D., & Wiederholt, J. L. *Test of adolescent language* (TOAL). Austin, Tex.: Pro-Ed Co., 1980.

Hammill, D. D., & Irwin, O. C. An abstraction test adapted for use with mentally retarded children. *American Journal of Mental Deficiency*, 1966, *70*, 807–812.

Hass, W. A., & Wepman, J. M. Dimensions of individual difference in the spoken syntax of school children. *Journal of Speech and Hearing Research*, 1974, *17*, 455–459.

Heilman, A. W., & Holmes, E. A. *Smuggling language into the teaching of reading*. Columbus, Ohio: Charles E. Merrill Publishing Co., 1972.

Hittleman, D. R. *Developmental reading: A psycholinguistic perspective*. Chicago: Rand McNally College Publishing Co., 1978.

Irwin, J. V., Moore, J. M., & Ramps, D. L. Nonmedical diagnosis and evaluation. In J. V. Irwin & M. Marge (Eds.), *Principles of childhood language disabilities*. New York: Appleton-Century-Crofts, 1972.

Johnson, D. J., & Myklebust, H. R. *Learning disabilities: Educational principles and practices*. New York: Grune & Stratton, 1967.

Kingsley, P. R., & Hagen, J. W. Induced versus spontaneous rehearsal in short-term memory in nursery school children. *Developmental Psychology*, 1969, *1*, 40–46.

Kolker, B. Processing print. In J. E. Alexander (Ed.), *Teaching reading*. Boston: Little, Brown & Co., 1979.

Lasky, E. Z., & Tabin, H. Linguistic and nonlinguistic competing message effects. *Journal of Learning Disabilities*, 1973, *6*, 243–250.

Lee, L. L. *Northwestern syntax screening test*. Evanston, Ill.: Northwestern University Press, 1969.

Lee, L. L. *Developmental sentence analysis: A grammatical assessment procedure for speech and language clinicians*. Evanston, Ill.: Northwestern University Press, 1974.

Lee, L. L., & Canter, S. M. Developmental sentence scoring: A clinical procedure for estimating syntactic development in children's spontaneous speech. *Journal of Speech and Hearing Disorders*, 1971, *36*, 315–340.

Lee, L. L., Koenigsknecht, R. A., & Mulhern, S. *Interactive language development teaching: The clinical presentation of grammatical structure*. Evanston, Ill.: Northwestern University Press, 1975.

Lenneberg, E. H. Understanding language without ability to speak: A case report. *Journal of Abnormal and Social Psychology*, 1962, *65*, 419–425.

Lerner, J. W. *Children with learning disabilities* (2nd ed.). Boston: Houghton Mifflin Co., 1976.

Lindamood, C., & Lindamood, P. *Auditory discrimination in depth*. Boston: Teaching Resources, 1969.

Lovitt, T. C., & Smith, J. O. Effects of instructions on an individual's verbal behavior. *Exceptional Children*, 1972, *38*, 685–693.

MacNamara, J. Cognitive basis of language learning in infants. *Psychological Review*, 1972, *79*, 1–13.

McCarthy, D. Language disorders and parent-child relationships. *Journal of Speech and Hearing Disorders*, 1954, *19*, 514–523.

McCarthy, D. *McCarthy scales of children's abilities*. New York: Psychological Corp., 1972.

McNeil, D. Developmental psycholinguistics. In F. Smith & G. A. Miller (Eds.), *The genesis of language: A psycholinguistic approach*. Cambridge, Mass.: M.I.T. Press, 1966.

McNeil, D. The development of language. In P. H. Mussen (Ed.), *Carmichael's manual of child psychology* (3rd ed.). New York: John Wiley & Sons, 1970.

Meacham, J. A. The development of memory abilities in the individual and society. *Human Development*, 1972, *15*, 205–228.

Moffett, J. *A student-centered language arts curriculum, grades K-13: A handbook for teachers*. Boston: Houghton Mifflin Co., 1968.

Moffett, J. *A student-centered language arts curriculum, grades K-13: A handbook for teachers*. Boston: Houghton Mifflin Co., 1970.

Moffett, J., & Wagner, B. J. *A student-centered language arts curriculum, grades K-13: A handbook for teachers (2nd ed.). Boston: Houghton Mifflin Co., 1976.

MYKLEBUST, H. R. *The psychology of deafness: Sensory deprivation, learning, and adjustment.* New York: Grune & Stratton, 1960.

NEWCOMER, P. L., & HAMMILL, D. D. *Psycholinguistics in the schools.* Columbus, Ohio: Charles E. Merrill Publishing Co., 1976.

NEWCOMER, P. L., & HAMMILL, D. D. *The test of language development* (TOLD). Austin, Tex.: Empiric Press, 1977.

POSSIEN, W. M. *They all need to talk: Oral communication in the language arts program.* New York: Appleton-Century-Crofts, 1969.

RICE, U. M., & DI VESTA, F. J. A developmental study of semantic and phonetic generalization in paired-associate learning. *Child Development*, 1965, *36*, 721–730.

RISKO, V. J. *Teaching-testing module of auditory discrimination.* San Rafael, Calif.: Academic Therapy Publications, 1975.

ROSENTHAL, J. H. A preliminary psycholinguistic study of children with learning disabilities. *Journal of Learning Disabilities*, 1970, *3*, 391–395.

ROSWELL, F. G., & CHALL, J. S. *Roswell-Chall auditory blending test.* New York: Essay Press, 1963.

SCHIEFELBUSCH, R. L. The development of communication skills. In R. L. Schiefelbusch, R. H. Copeland, & J. O. Smith (Eds.), *Language and mental retardation: Empirical and conceptual considerations.* New York: Holt, Rinehart & Winston, 1967.

SEMEL, E. M. *Sound-order-sense: A developmental program in auditory perception.* Chicago: Follett Educational Corp., 1970.

SEMEL, E. M., & WIIG, E. H. Comprehension of syntactic structures and critical verbal elements by children with learning disabilities. *Journal of Learning Disabilities*, 1975, *8*, 46–51.

SITKO, M. C., & GILLESPIE, P. H. Language and speech difficulties. In L. Mann, L. Goodman, & J. L. Wiederholt (Eds.), *Teaching the learning-disabled adolescent.* Boston: Houghton Mifflin Co., 1978.

SITKO, M. C., & SEMMEL, M. I. Language and language behavior of the mentally retarded. In L. Mann & D. A. Sabatino (Eds.), *The first review of special education* (Vol. 1). Philadelphia: The JSE Press, 1973.

SKINNER, B. F. *Verbal behavior.* New York: Appleton-Century-Crofts, 1957.

SLOBIN, D. I. Grammatical transformations and sentence comprehension in childhood and adulthood. *Journal of Verbal Learning and Verbal Behavior*, 1966, *5*, 219–227.

SMITH, F. *Comprehension and learning: A conceptual framework for teachers.* New York: Holt, Rinehart & Winston, 1975.

SMITH, F. The language arts and the learner's mind. *Language Arts*, 1979, *56*, 118–125; 145.

SMITH, J. A. *Adventures in communication.* Boston: Allyn & Bacon, 1972.

SPRADLIN, J. E. Procedures for evaluating processes associated with receptive and expressive language. In R. L. Schiefelbusch, R. H. Copeland, & J. O. Smith (Eds.), *Language and mental retardation: Empirical and conceptual considerations.* New York: Holt, Rinehart & Winston, 1967.

STAATS, A. W. *Learning, language, and cognition: Theory, research, and method for the study of human behavior and its development.* New York: Holt, Rinehart & Winston, 1968.

VOGEL, S. A. Syntactic abilities in normal and dyslexic children. *Journal of Learning Disabilities*, 1974, *7*, 103–109.

WEPMAN, J. *Auditory discrimination test* (revised ed.). Chicago: Language Research Associates, 1973.

WESTMAN, A. S. *A developmental study of the ability to perceive and utilize categorical structure.* Unpublished doctoral dissertation, Cornell University, 1971.

WIIG, E. H., & SEMEL, E. M. Comprehension of linguistic concepts requiring logical operations. *Journal of Speech and Hearing Research*, 1973, *16*, 627–636.

WIIG, E. H., & SEMEL, E. M. Development of comprehension of logico-grammatical sentences by grade school children. *Perceptual and Motor Skills*, 1974, *38*, 171–176. (a)

WIIG, E. H., & SEMEL, E. M. Logico-grammatical sentence comprehension by learning disabled adolescents. *Perceptual and Motor Skills*, 1974, *38*, 1331–1334. (b)

WIIG, E. H., & SEMEL, E. M. Productive language abilities in learning disabled adolescents. *Journal of Learning Disabilities*, 1975, *8*, 578–586.

WIIG, E. H., & SEMEL, E. M. *Language disabilities in children and adolescents.* Columbus, Ohio: Charles E. Merrill Publishing Co., 1976.

WIIG, E. H., SEMEL, E. M., & CROUSE, M. A. The use of English morphology by high-risk and learning disabled children. *Journal of Learning Disabilities*, 1973, *6*, 457–465.

WILLETTE, R., JACKSON, B., & PECKINS, L. *Auditory perception training.* Chicago: Developmental Learning Materials, 1970.

WILSON, M. S. *The Wilson initial syntax program.* Cambridge, Mass.: Educators Publishing Service, 1972.

READING

VICTORIA J. RISKO

**George Peabody College for Teachers
of Vanderbilt University**

By identifying learning disabled students' capabilities and learning problems and by recognizing what they bring to the reading situation, teachers can determine what kind of reading instruction is required. A vast number of reading approaches, programs, and activities are available. This diversity allows for a match of teaching style and methodology with students' learning characteristics. An immense base of knowledge is required to make appropriate decisions about which reading programs and strategies should best help individual students master reading. This chapter includes discussions of several specific assessment and instructional procedures that can facilitate the achievement of proficiency in reading.

DEFINITIONS OF READING

Because educators define reading in so many ways, confusion often results about which procedures are most appropriate for specific students. Reading is defined as: a perceptual process; a skills or decoding process; a cognitive activity; and a meaning-oriented, language-centered process. As a perceptual process, reading is described as the meaningful memory and interpretation of visual (graphic) and auditory stimuli (Dechant, 1964; Kirk, Kliebhan, & Lerner, 1978). When defined as a skills process, decoding strategies of "sounding out" letters to pronounce words correctly often are overemphasized (Flesch, 1955; Fries, 1963). Other models of reading as a skills process place equal emphasis on the various word recognition, word analysis, and comprehension skills (Ekwall, 1976). These skills are described as being interrelated and part of a complex process also influenced by such factors as motivation, background experiences, and language development (Kennedy, 1974). Many applied behavior analysts define reading as sets of independent skills and behaviors that are "learned and used separately" (Lahey & McNees, 1975, p. 198). Influenced by cognitive psychologists, some reading authorities relate reading to the developmental processes of learning, thinking, and information processing. They describe the reader as one who uses a set of linguistic rules to extract meaning from the text (Bloom, 1971; Gibson, 1970; Samuels, 1971).

Psycholinguists view reading as a process of reconstructing meaning from language represented by graphic symbols. To them, reading is the interaction of the content to be read and the knowledge and experiences of the reader (Bond, Tinker, & Wasson, 1979; Goodman, 1965, 1978; Gephart, Note 1). At present, the "schema theory" gives support to instruction that capitalizes on students' experiences and language to facilitate interpretation of the author's message (Johnson, Note 2).

In this chapter, reading is viewed as a meaning-oriented process developed when a synergy exists among various decoding and comprehension strategies, students' language and experiences, and students' learning characteristics, motivation, and self-concept. Synergetic reading programs not only show children how to use decoding, thinking, and language cues, but also illustrate why they are used within a positive reinforcing environment.

ASSESSMENT

The first part of this chapter discusses how to decide where to begin reading instruction; the following section provides information about various instructional strategies.

Plans and Procedures for Reading Assessment

The differing viewpoints of the reading process lead to a variety of procedures for assessing students' reading abilities (classroom assessment, individualized testing, use of standardized and informal tests, ecological evaluations).

Regardless of the procedure selected, reading assessment should:

1. be efficient yet complete.

2. appraise more than skills and abilities.

3. lead to precise program planning.

4. be continuous.

5. accurately interpret assessment data.

6. occur in a situation analogous to actual reading.

7. cross-reference various sources of data (Bond, Tinker, & Wasson, 1979; Ekwall, 1976; Gilliland, 1974; Hittleman, 1978; Kennedy, 1971).

Hierarchical plan.   Bond and Tinker (1967) present the successive levels of diagnosis for reading assessment within a regular classroom. The three levels of assessment are: general, analytical, and case study. They should facilitate efficient test selection, yielding more useful results. These levels, each with increasing complexity and specificity, reveal different kinds of information about students' reading performances.

Achievement test results often are used to collect initial general diagnostic level data. By studying these scores and profile sheets, the teacher can determine a student's range of abilities across several skill areas (word knowledge, word analysis, comprehension), as well as general areas of strengths and weaknesses. This should help the teacher decide what kind of testing still is required. For example, if Pam received a high score in word knowledge but a low score in word analysis and reading comprehension, the next tests that the teacher selects should help determine the specific nature of Pam's reading problems.

Further assessment can be accomplished with diagnostic tests administered on a one-to-one or small group basis at the analytical diagnostic level. Pam took tests that assessed her use of contextual cues, phonetic or structural cues, oral contextual reading, and comprehension strategies. In most cases, with these data formal diagnosis can be concluded and plans for an appropriate instructional program developed.

At the third level, case study diagnosis, a detailed study of the student is made. This is recommended only if the previous levels did not lead to educational solutions. Some (Clements, 1966; Johnson & Myklebust, 1967; Kennedy, 1971) recommend that the case study or comprehensive assessment format be used for all students who have serious reading and learning problems. Severe reading difficulties should be studied in depth (several oral and silent reading tests, and direct and daily measurements). Diagnostic data are combined with information obtained about the child's environment, physical and behavioral development, intellectual capabilities, and emotional adjustment. In addition, vision, hearing, and academic history should be evaluated.

The plan for successive levels of diagnosis offers several advantages. It is valuable for the classroom teacher who must make diagnostic decisions for a large group of children. Teachers can take advantage of data collected from group and individual standardized tests, teacher-made tests, criterion referenced tests, and direct and daily measurements. Theoretically, use of this system prevents children from being overtested because precise decision-making occurs at each level to determine the appropriateness of further testing.

There are disadvantages to this plan, too. A major argument against this approach is the use of often unreliable group tests that can be used only as gross screening instruments rather than "the" placement test. Also, at the first two levels, diagnostic procedures tend to be skill oriented. The resulting data should be supplemented with data collected from observations, interest inventories, interviews, and class records.

Diagnostic-prescriptive assessment.   An alternative plan for assessment is the diagnostic-prescriptive procedure, which provides a plan for identifying those skills students do and do not possess and developing corresponding activities to remediate deficiencies. The assumption is that reading is composed of a set of skills that can be defined, task analyzed, and measured.

While there are various uses of this plan, the one most frequently used (and misused) is illustrated in Figure 9.1. Max's skills were assessed after a series of tests: his performance was recorded and a prescription was written. On the prescription, the teacher listed the learning objectives and the corresponding activities Max was supposed to complete. Posttesting determined attainment of the objectives, and the next stage of programming was initiated.

This version of the diagnostic-prescriptive plan is commonly adhered to in *systems* or *management reading programs* and approaches reading as a set of independent skills (Lahey & McNees, 1975). Unfortunately, this view of reading isolates reading skills and sometimes makes no provision for application to the act of reading. Those who view reading as an integrated whole argue that the sum of isolated skills does not equal reading (Giordano, 1978; Tucker, 1979). For example, Max may learn to name short vowels, read inflectional endings, and name literal details, but may not understand how to use these skills to decode the author's message. This occurs when there is no provision for integration and application within the prescribed activities.

While this system does contribute to exact measurement and follow through in educational programming, the lack of integration and application that can occur is a serious disadvantage. The problem of teaching isolated

Skill Assessment			Prescription
	Has skill	*Does not have skill*	*Objectives:* Max will be able to:
Use of context clues	X		1. Name short vowels when he names picture words;
Use of phonic clues			2. Read inflectional endings (-s, -ed, -ing) when he reads
consonant blends	X		a set of selected words;
consonant digraphs	X		3. Name literal details when he recalls from the stories
long vowels	X		that he reads.
short vowels		X	
vowel diphthongs		X	*Activities:*
vowel digraphs		X	1. Complete worksheets, such as: name the vowel of the
Read inflectional endings		X	words presented on the tape and encircle the target
Comprehension			word. Self-check answers.
name literal details		X	2. Complete task cards by adding *s, ed, ing* to words;
name sequence	X		read the complete word on the language master. Self-check answers.
			3. Read five sentences. Write the answers to the literal detail questions. Self-check answers.
			4. Read a story and use knowledge of short vowels and inflectional endings in combination with context cues to decode "unknown."
			5. Find and discuss the literal details of the story with the teacher or peers.

Figure 9.1   A sample of an assessment of reading skills with a correlated instructional plan for Max, a student. Objectives 4 and 5 illustrate a method to integrate and apply the skills learned.

skills can be overcome by teachers who provide activities that illustrate the use of the learned skills in "real" reading situations. Students need to do things that look like and are reading (Hammill, Note 3). In Max's prescription (see Figure 9.1), Objectives 4 and 5 facilitate integration of the skills with story content and illustrate to Max how he can use his "new" skills when he is reading.

Within this assessment plan, the criterion for attainment of each objective must be stated and evaluation procedures be designed; see suggestions provided in Chapter 3.

Analytical teaching assessment. Analytical, precision, and direct teaching methods provide continuous assessment of student performance, while evaluating how students learn and how the teaching strategies are scheduled (Gaasholt, 1970; Hittleman, 1978). Although Hittleman's steps for analytical teaching and Gaasholt's precision teaching model parallel each other, Gaasholt's plan includes a vehicle for more "precise" record keeping. For example, if a teacher wanted to encourage a student's voluntary reading, he would observe and record the number of times she voluntarily read within specific time intervals. He would change teacher behaviors (modeling reading, reading to students), record them, and then determine which intervention plan contributed to that student's voluntary reading behavior.

Kennedy's (1971) direct teaching method represents a modified version of this approach. Problem areas are identified, direct practice is provided, and progress is evaluated. For example, Mrs. Jones learned that Sam could not distinguish the likenesses and differences between pairs of similar words. She implemented several intervention procedures (Sam was asked to discuss the characteristics of the word shapes, read the words in different sentence contexts). Sam's performance with each intervention strategy was recorded at various time intervals. The teacher chose activities that facilitated learning to teach Sam the next set of words.

Standardized Reading Tests

Some general achievement tests can be used as screening instruments. A brief summary of them is found in Chapter 2. Some diagnostic tests were designed specifically to test reading. Most are administered individually and often are included in a battery of standardized tests. A few commonly used special reading tests are summarized here.

The *Diagnostic Reading Scales* (Spache, 1972) measure word recognition (pronouncing words presented in lists), oral and silent contextual reading, oral and silent reading comprehension, listening comprehension, and phonics. The teacher listens to the student's oral reading, observes silent reading, reads paragraphs to the pupil, and asks comprehension questions. Student behavior and reading habits are recorded for each subtest. The oral reading errors recorded and analyzed are omissions, additions, substitutions, reversals, and aided words. Spache identifies three levels of reading: independent (silent reading), instructional (oral reading), and potential (listening). The definitions of them are confusing because they do not correspond to the three levels identified on most other reading inventories. Teachers should be aware of these differences. The Spache passages vary in levels of difficulty and are normed for students in grades one through six.

The *Durrell Analysis of Reading Difficulty* (Durrell, 1955) measures oral and silent contextual reading and comprehension, listening comprehension, word recognition, alphabet knowledge, visual memory, phonics, phonetic spelling, spelling, handwriting, and learning rate. The test is designed for nonreaders and students in grades one through six. The format for oral and silent reading, listening comprehension, letter and word recognition, phonics, spelling, and handwriting follows traditional testing procedures. One variation is found in the silent reading subtest, in which the student is required to retell the story before being asked comprehension questions. Although the manual does not suggest this, the order of the student's responses can be numbered to analyze correct sequencing of facts. Oral reading errors noted are substitutions, mispronunciations, words added, punctuation errors, hesitations, word-by-word reading, omissions, additions, and repetitions. In the primary section, visual memory is measured by asking the student to circle a letter or word flashed for two to three seconds. The visual memory subtest of the intermediate section requires the student to write words after a flashed exposure. A "visual memory grade level score" can be obtained but this is not a reliable indicator for placement into reading materials. However, the diagnostic information obtained on these two subtests can be valuable. The evaluator can analyze these data to determine sequencing of letters, left-right analysis, memory of total words, and reversals or rotations. The two spelling subtests provide the teacher with data to compare the student's use of phonic cues (phonic spelling subtest) and use of combined visual and phonic cues (regular spelling subtest).

The *Gates-McKillop Reading Diagnostic Tests* (Gates & McKillop, 1962) provide a measure of oral contextual reading, word recognition, phrase reading, letter and sound recognition, word analysis, oral spelling, oral vocabulary, auditory discrimination, auditory blending, and syllabication. Comprehension is not evaluated. This test is appropriate for students in grades one through seven and adults. Several subtests not found in other diagnostic instruments provide useful diagnostic data. For example, comparisons can be made of a student's ability to read words in isolation, in short phrases, and in longer contexts. The record of oral spelling gives clues to how the student is processing the word units (letter by letter, syllable units). The work attack subtest can help the teacher determine the student's ability to pronounce nonsense word parts (blend and word family) and blend them to pronounce the total word.

Reading comprehension, vocabulary meanings, auditory discrimination, syllabication, beginning and ending sounds, blending, and sound discrimination are measured in the *Stanford Diagnostic Reading Test* (Karlson, Madden, & Gardner, 1976). This screening instrument can be used for students in grades 2.5 through 8.5. Students read silently and their performances are analyzed on protocols, which is less preferable to hearing them read aloud and recording reading behavior.

The *Gilmore Oral Reading Test* (Gilmore & Gilmore, 1968) assesses oral contextual reading, literal comprehension, and rate of reading. The following errors are noted: substitutions, mispronunciations, disregard of punctuation, insertions, hesitations, repetitions, and omissions. Separate

Table 9.1

Summary of subtests and information provided*

Skills	Subtests/Tests
Oral reading and comprehension	Oral reading section of *Durrell, Spache,* or *Gilmore*
Silent reading and comprehension	Silent reading section of *Durrell, Spache,* or *Test of Reading Comprehension*
Silent reading and retelling	Silent reading section of *Durrell*
Listening comprehension	Listening section of *Spache* or *Durrell*
Visual memory of letters, words	Visual memory section of *Durrell*
Word recognition	Word lists of *Spache, Durrell, Gates-McKillop,* or *W.R.A.T.*
Phrase reading	Words in phrases subtest of *Gates-McKillop*
Word attack	Word attack subtest of *Gates-McKillop* or *Stanford-Diagnostic*
Letter, sound recognition	Letters, sounds section of *Spache, Durrell,* or *Gates-McKillop*
Auditory blending	Auditory blending section of *Gates-McKillop*
Phonic spelling	Phonic spelling section of *Durrell*
Spelling	Spelling section of *Durrell, W.R.A.T.,* or *Gates-McKillop* (oral spelling)

* *References for these subtests are found at the end of this chapter.*

scores are obtained for each skill area rather than a composite score, which is recorded on most oral reading tests.

The *Test of Reading Comprehension* (Brown, Hammill, & Wiederholt, 1978) measures vocabulary meanings and reading comprehension. Normative data are provided for students from six years six months to fourteen years six months. Knowledge of general vocabulary and content vocabulary (mathematics vocabulary, social studies vocabulary, and science vocabulary) is measured. The subtest Syntactic Similarities evaluates understanding of meaningfully similar but syntactically different sentences. The abilities to answer questions on paragraphs, follow written directions, and form relationships among sentences are measured in the subtests Paragraph Reading, Sentence Sequencing, and Reading the Directions of Schoolwork

Teachers should study the strengths and weaknesses of many diagnostic instruments and choose tests or subtests that measure important skills within the reading process. Testing batteries should change for each student. Table 9.1 presents a set of skills and possible subtests to be used when answers to specific questions about students' reading abilities are sought. After administering a set of these instruments, the data are cross-referenced to determine skill performances in word recognition, word analysis, contextual reading, and comprehension.

Informal Reading Assessment

Informal assessment procedures often are more reliable estimators of reading levels than standardized tests (Betts, 1946; Ekwall, 1976; Guszak, 1970; Jones & Pikulski, 1974) because standardized reading achievement tests tend to overestimate actual placement in reading materials. Therefore, a number of nonstandardized, informal ways of assessing reading performances are discussed in this section.

The informal reading inventory (IRI). The IRI is a commercially available or teacher-constructed diagnostic instrument that evaluates word recognition, oral and silent contextual reading, oral and silent reading comprehension, and listening comprehension (McCracken, 1966; Silvaroli, 1973). The passages generally are taken from graded basal readers. Student performance indicates an estimated placement level into basal readers or other reading materials.

Some reading levels are identified in the IRI (Betts, 1946; Ekwall, 1976; Johnson & Kress, 1965). These reading levels estimate a "fit" between student abilities and level of materials.

1. *Independent reading level* is judged as an oral accuracy correct percentage score between 98 percent and 100 percent. This level of material is where pupils can read with few or no errors.

2. *Instructional reading level* is achieved when the oral accuracy correct percentage score is between 95 percent and 97 percent, or comprehension is between 70 percent and 89 percent. Teacher introduction of new concepts or experiences is required to aid pupil reading and understanding of the material at this level.

3. *Frustration reading level* is said to be an oral accuracy correct percentage score of 94 percent or lower, or comprehension below 70 percent. Material is too difficult for continued reading and should be avoided.

After reading levels are recorded, student performance is analyzed to determine strengths and problem areas. The examiner records oral reading errors of substitutions, mispronunciations, unknown words, additions, omissions, and repetitions.

Direct oral reading assessment. Many teachers have found that direct measurement of children's oral reading performance offers both a means of initial assessment leading immediately to remediation and also a method for continuous evaluation throughout the school year. This system utilizes the evaluation procedures detailed in Chapter 3.

The measurement system in this plan is collecting rate scores when the students read contextual material. To get an indication of both quality and quantity of a student's reading abilities, both correct rate and incorrect rate scores are needed. Therefore, three pieces of information are required: number of correctly read words, number of incorrectly read words, and the total time the student took to read the passage. For example, if the teacher had a student read orally for two minutes, the teacher would count the number of words read correctly and the number of words read incorrectly during that time period. The correct rate score is calculated by dividing the number of correctly read words by two (the amount of time spent reading). The error rate score is obtained by dividing the number of words read incorrectly by two.

Several suggestions can be offered to simplify the data collection process. First, if possible, collect the data on the student's oral reading by using a constant time. This makes the division required easier. For example, if the

This teacher is determining a youngster's correct and error rates for oral reading. The student reads for two minutes. As he reads, she uses a double counter to keep a record of the number of words read correctly and incorrectly.

student is requested to read an entire passage orally, data are collected only during a set time period (two minutes, three minutes, five minutes). It might have taken the student six minutes and twenty-two seconds to read the entire passage. If correct rate scores were obtained from reading the entire passage, the divisor (the amount of time spent reading) used to obtain the rate scores would be 6.37. This adds unnecessary difficulty to the data collection process. Also, experience indicates that data collected from a two- or three-minute time sample are as reliable as data collected from a longer period of time. Using a shorter time sample reduces the number of correct and incorrect notations, which also simplifies the evaluation process.

One caution must be stated. Do not obtain the number of incorrectly read words by subtracting the number of correctly read words from the number of words printed in the passage. This distorts the data because it does not allow for errors from the addition or deletion (omissions) categories. If a student adds five words to the passage, they are not accounted for by the above mentioned subtraction system. It is best to use either a handheld counter, which keeps two running tallies (one for correct number of words read and one for incorrect number of words read), or to mark a copy of the passage as the student reads orally.

An error analysis of a student's oral reading skills can be easily accomplished through the direct measurement system by marking the kinds of errors the student made while reading the passage orally. A simple coding system can be used (see Table 9.2) to indicate the kinds of errors students frequently make (additions, substitutions, omissions, repetitions). This coding system follows the traditional procedure of standardized and informal oral reading tests.

During the assessment period, usually two or three sessions in which an error analysis is conducted are sufficient. Usually, students consistently

Table 9.2 Error definitions and code system

Symbol	Error Type
(omit)	Omissions—one or more words deleted from the text.
~~actual~~	Substitutions—actual words that took the place of words from the reading material.
mean	Mispronunciations—vocalizations made for a word in the text that had no meaning of their own.
^words	Additions—words added to the text.
right ✓	Hesitations—not scored as errors but recorded when child did not pronounce a word within five seconds.
ⓒ correct	Self-correction—incidences when the child erred and subsequently pronounced the word correctly. These are not scored as errors.

make specific kinds of errors while they read. Some students have a propensity for substitution errors; others tend to make many addition errors. Once an indication of typical error patterns is determined, error analyses need only to be conducted intermittently (once a week, several times a month).

Error analyses are useful and should be conducted with each student who has difficulties in reading. This procedure provides the teacher with useful information for determining which intervention strategies to use with individual students by allowing a match of types of errors made with specific remedial procedures.

There are some definite advantages of using the direct and daily measurement approach for assessment and evaluation of reading performance. First, these assessment techniques involve the use of materials that become part of the daily instructional situation. Second, the data collection technique can be one of several evaluation procedures recommended for daily use in the classroom. Because of this continuity, assessment leads to direct instruction without the need for time-consuming intermediate assessment procedures, for it provides teachers with information about the student's oral reading abilities.

Since reading is more than oral accuracy skills, critics argue that this assessment technique can lead to a narrowly defined assessment and intervention plan (Hammill, Note 3; Wiederholt, Note 4). However, this technique can be used in combination with other sources of information and presents a systematic procedure for collecting these data.

Miscue analysis. Miscue analysis provides an alternate method of analyzing oral reading performance and comprehension in a testing procedure that differs in terminology and focus from traditional oral reading tests or direct measurement procedures. Miscues, rather than oral reading errors, are recorded when a student's "actual response doesn't correspond to the actual passage" (Hittleman, 1978, p. 113). Instead of counting oral and reading errors, miscues are analyzed qualitatively (Goodman, 1972) to determine which strategies the student is using to obtain meaning from the written discourse. Rather than focusing on the correction of an "error," this analysis allows for an interpretation of how the student is processing the information (Pearson, 1976). For example, repetitions are not counted as errors but regarded as possible indicators of the student's ability to read and use cues to determine the unknown word or words (Quandt, 1977). Miscues are analyzed differentially; those that change the meaning of the passage (house-horse) are more important than those that do not interfere with comprehension (substitution of a-the). The cues that present information and enable meaningful guesses while reading are: language (syntax, semantics, grammar), graphophonics (word configurations, letter-sound relationships), and reader expectations or previous experiences and information. This analysis views reading as a system of many interrelated factors rather than a series of separate skills.

The *Goodman-Burke Reading Miscue Inventory* (RMI) (Goodman & Burke, 1972) and its shortened version (Burke, 1976) present an assessment method requiring students to read an unfamiliar passage orally and retell the content. Goodman and Burke suggest that the examiner choose from materials approximately one level above the student's instructional level so that at least twenty-five miscues can be recorded and analyzed. Kibby (1979) also recommends that the teacher assess the student's reading with less difficult material. His research found different performances on difficult passages (weakness, no pattern of errors) than on less difficult passages (use of syntactic and contextual cues).

> *The child who demonstrates adequate use of syntactic and contextual strategies (which would have been overlooked on a single administration of a difficult passage) on less difficult material does not need to be taught to use these strategies on more difficult material, but rather needs to learn the specific skills, sight words, or content that will decrease the number of difficult words in the passage and will allow the reader to apply syntactic and contextual skills.* (Kibby, 1979, p. 396)

In his study, "adequate use" of these skills (syntactic and contextual) was overlooked on a single administration of a difficult passage. Although Kibby's conclusion requires validation, it seems reasonable to collect pupil performance on at least two passages (less difficult and difficult) and cross-analyze the reading behaviors.

Examples of the coding system and seven miscues are shown in Table 9.3. Once recorded, miscues are evaluated by a set of questions that help the teacher analyze the cues each student is using to read the context (Table 9.4). First, how effective are the student's strategies for recognizing words in context? Second, how effective are the student's strategies for using knowledge of language? And third, how do the miscues change the intended meaning of the written passage? Word recognition questions are asked only when the student substitutes one word for another during oral reading. The answers to the word recognition questions (see Table 9.4) indicate the extent of the pupil's use of graphophonological cues and knowledge of grammatical functions. When determining the difference between "high" similarity and

Table 9.3   **Tabulating miscues**

Type of Miscue	Recording Method	Example
Substitution of a word	The substituted word is written above the word in the text. Nonsense words should be spelled phonetically. If a partial word is produced, the miscue should be followed by a dash.	He didn't when to walk to the corner. want She wore cord— slacks. corduroy
Omission	The word, words, or word parts are circled.	The weeds are killing (the) flowers. They exercised (by playing basketball) at the center.
Insertion	The inserted word is written in, with a caret to indicate where the insertion occurs.	after She was playing basketball at ∧ school.
Reversal	A transposition symbol is used to show which word, words, or parts of words have been reversed in order.	They talked about the noisy basketball game. Who was at the game?
Repetition	The repeated word or words are underlined. A symbol within a circle indicates the type of repetition: C indicates correcting a miscue; AC indicates changing or abandoning a correct response; UC indicates unsuccessfully attempting to correct a miscue; A indicates anticipating difficulty; R indicates repeating to maintain continuity.	They were walking as they ate their breakfast. talking The football players were unhappy with the rest results. AC tracked UC She took piano lessons. The volunteers were not helpful to the team. C The paper route covered two blocks.
Intonation	Accent marks are used when incorrect syllables are stressed, and plus signs are used to show an artificial pronunciation.	They were listening to records. The teacher records the grades. The boys went together. to + get + her
Dialect difference	If the miscue is a sound, vocabulary, or grammatical variation caused by a different dialect, it is marked with a circled d.	(d) goed We went for the ice cream.

SOURCE: Adapted from Goodman and Burke (1972). Readers should refer to that source for more detailed information on miscue tabulation.

Table 9.4   Analyzing miscues

Area		Question		Acceptability
1. Word recognition a. graphic similarity	a.	Does the miscue look like the word in the text?	High: Some: None:	There is a high degree of similarity. There is some degree of similarity. There is no similarity in any part of the word.
b. sound similarity	b.	Does the miscue sound like the word in the text?	High: Some: None:	There is a high degree of similarity. There is some degree of similarity. There is no similarity in any part of the word.
c. grammatical function	c.	Does the miscue retain the same grammatical function as the word in the text?	Same: Questionable: Different:	The miscue is an identical part of speech. It is difficult to determine whether there is a change in the part of speech. There is a change in the part of speech, as the grammatical functions differ.
2. Knowledge of language	a.	Is the sentence as finally produced an acceptable and grammatical sentence?	Yes: No:	The sentence as finally read by the pupil is an acceptable sentence that could stand by itself as grammatically correct. The sentence as finally read by the pupil is not acceptable and could not stand by itself as grammatically correct.
	b.	Does the sentence as finally produced have an acceptable meaning?	Yes: No:	The sentence as finally read by the pupil can stand by itself as a meaningful sentence. The sentence as finally read by the pupil cannot stand by itself as a meaningful sentence.
3. Comprehension	a.	Does the sentence as finally produced change the meaning or the story in relation to its plot and theme?	No: Minimal: Yes:	The sentence as finally read by the pupil does not change the intended meaning of the author. The sentence as finally read by the pupil moderately changes the minor incidents, characters, or sequences in the story. The sentence as finally read by the pupil importantly changes the major incidents, characters, sequences, or theme in the story.

SOURCE: Adapted from Burke (1975) and Hittleman (1978).

"some" similarity for word recognition, one looks at the appearance of the word. For example, when two of three parts of the word are similar to the incorrectly said word, high similarity is indicated. If only one part is similar, some similarity exists. Teacher judgment often is needed to make these decisions.

     Knowledge of language is the next area considered. This is done for every sentence in which a miscue is observed. Answers to the questions found in Table 9.4 indicate whether the student is concerned with accepta-

			Graphic (Q-1)			Sound (Q-2)			Grammatical Function (Q-3)		
No.	Reader	Text	High	Some	None	High	Some	None	Same	Questionable	Different
Column total											
Question total											
Column percentage											

Miscue Evaluation, Part I

Figure 9.2   Miscue profile chart.

blc language during oral reading. The sentence (even with miscues) is considered acceptable if the speech and language used match the student's typical oral language patterns (Burke, 1975). For each sentence containing a miscue, a comprehension question is asked to determine whether the student understood the intended meaning of the passage.

A profile chart (Figure 9.2) can be used to present data visually to help determine patterns of strengths and problems in the student's cueing abilities (a student can use sound and graphic cues consistently but change

				Meaning Change (Q-6)		
Sentence or Line Number	*Numbers of Miscues*	*Syntactic Acceptability (Q-4)*	*Semantic Acceptability (Q-5)*	*No*	*Minimal*	*Yes*
Total miscues		Total y	Total y			
		%	%	%	%	%

Miscue Evaluation, Part II

the meaning of the passage by overlooking the grammatical and syntatical information) (Hittleman, 1978).

Page (1976) cautions that miscues are complicated and may have to be analyzed extensively before categorization. D'Angelo and Wilson (1979) suggest that some miscues are less important and require little study. Finding that omissions and insertions are infrequent and seldom change the semantics or syntax of passages, they conclude that teachers should be most concerned with substitution miscues. Tortelli (1976) simplifies miscue analysis by asking only two questions: do the miscues reflect knowledge of language information and do they have meaning in the passage?

An analysis of comprehension is assessed by asking the student to retell the story. Retellings are recorded on an outline of the story content (Goodman & Burke, 1972), and indicate whether the reader has integrated, synthesized, and related the information to previous experiences (Hansen, 1978).

After students complete the reading assignments, they retell the story without the aid or interruption of the teacher. To elicit additional information and interpretation, the teacher can ask questions that:

1.   Do not provide any information from the story that the pupil has not already said;

2.   Are general rather than specific so the pupil is not guided to make conclusions that are not formed from the reading of the story;

3.   Are consistent with the information or substitutions the pupil has already reported.

To provide the encouragement some pupils need to retell a story, some general questions can be prepared beforehand (Goodman & Burke, 1972). For example, Hittleman (1978, p. 117) suggests the following questions to stimulate student responses:

Tell me more about . . . (Use information already offered by the pupil).

Who was in the story? or Who else was in the story?

What did (he, she, they) do?

What kind of person was . . . (Use characters pupil offers)?

What else happened in the story?

Where did the story take place?

What was the whole story about? or What kind of problem was the story about?

Why do you think the story was written? or What did the author want you to know when he (she) wrote the story?

Retellings are analyzed on the RMI by establishing a retelling score and examining the content. (Were the retellings in sequential order? Did the student note cause and effect relationships?) Kintsch's Proposition Analysis (Kintsch, 1974) presents a method of quantifying the retellings and analyzing student ability to detect main ideas and supporting details (Fillmore, 1968).

Cloze passage test. The cloze passage test measures how well the student is using language and comprehension strategies and can be used to place students in reading or content materials. Students are required to supply words deleted from a written discourse.

A procedure for developing a cloze test was suggested by Bormuth (1975):

1. Select a 250-word passage (for placement purposes, select the passage from the materials you want to determine whether the student can read).

2. Beginning with any one of the first five words of the second sentence of the passage, delete every fifth word until fifty words are deleted. The first and last sentence are always left intact. Punctuation and hyphens are never deleted, and numerals, such as 1975, are deleted as if they are whole words. Apostrophes and the words they appear in are deleted.

3. Type the passage on a master, double spacing between lines. For each deleted word, type a line fifteen spaces long. The spaces should be uniform in length regardless of the length of the original word.

4. Provide the pupils with instructions and a sample test before giving them the actual cloze test.

The passage that follows illustrates a cloze test that could be utilized for an adult reader. When the cloze is used as a test, the student is required to insert the exact words deleted from the original selection. The percentage scores are determined by the number correct divided by the number possible (total number of blank spaces). The correct percentage scores are interpreted as follows: 40 percent to 60 percent accuracy indicates instructional level for material; above 60 percent accuracy, independent level material; below 40 percent accuracy, material may be too difficult (Bormuth, 1968; Jones & Pikulski, 1974). This procedure is fairly reliable in placing students into appropriate content materials. Passages in the reading or content material are selected randomly. Students' facility with context, semantic, grammatical, and syntactic cues can be studied in this way.

When developing a cloze passage, teachers should verify that the deleted words have context clues within the sentences and that the students understand the directions (Pace & Winsch, Note 5). The cloze test should be used with students who have some contextual reading ability (second grade through adult). Younger children may need to have a practice cloze exercise before completing a cloze passage for placement to be certain that they understand the directions.

Table 9.5 **Analytical reading diagnosis**

Name _Melinda_ School _Hawthorne_

Grade _6_ Age _10½_

Name of Parent _John Jones_ Address _913 Grand_

Telephone _626-1942_

Date of Report _Sept. 10_ Compiled by _Mrs. Risko_

General Information		Vocabulary					Comprehension								Phonics			
Grade	Mental (Formula) Grade	(Durrell) Visual Memory	Sight Words (Durrell)	Word Analysis (Durrell)	Words in Phrases (Gates-McKillop)	Words in Context (Oral Rdg./Durrell)	Word Meanings	Literal	Inferential	Evaluative	Imaginative (Durrell)	Listening (Durrell)	Silent Rdg. (Durrell)	Oral Rdg. (Durrell)	Phonic Spelling (Durrell)	Sound in words (Durrell)	Visual Match (Gates-McKillop)	Oral Reading Placement

Chart (grade-level scale from .0 to 8.0):

- Grade: 4.5
- Mental (Formula) Grade: 4.0
- (Durrell) Visual Memory: 3.5
- Sight Words (Durrell): 3.5
- Word Analysis (Durrell): 2.5
- Words in Phrases (Gates-McKillop): 3.0
- Words in Context (Oral Rdg./Durrell): 3.0
- Word Meanings: 3.0
- Literal: 3.0
- Inferential: 2.5
- Evaluative: 1.5
- Imaginative (Durrell): 3.0
- Listening (Durrell): 2.0
- Silent Rdg. (Durrell): 2.0
- Oral Rdg. (Durrell): 2.0
- Phonic Spelling (Durrell): 2.0
- Sound in words (Durrell): 3.0
- Visual Match (Gates-McKillop): 3.0
- Oral Reading Placement: 3.0

Skill	*Below Aver.*	*Aver.*	*Above Aver.*
Decoding:			
configuration		✓	
context		✓	
structural		✓	
root words		✓	
word beginnings	✓		
syllabication		✓	
morphological cues		✓	
semantic cues		✓	
syntactic cues		✓	
Use of Phonic Cues:			
letter sounds	✓		
initial sounds	✓		
medial sounds	✓		
ending sounds	✓		
single consonants	✓		
consonant blends	✓		
vowels	✓		
vowel diphthongs	✓		
Comprehension			
meaningful substitution of words in context		✓	
Understanding of concepts in instructional materials	✓		
retelling of story content	✓		
Answering various types of questions			
literal	✓		
sequential	✓		
inferential	✓		

A CLOZE PASSAGE COMPREHENSION TEST FOR ADULTS[1]

Running may well turn out to be one of the most significant experiences of your life. Yet it ___*does*___ *not always seem fun* ___*when*___ *you first try it.* ___*For*___ *one thing, chances are* ___*you're*___ *out of shape. Not* ___*irreparably*___ *but, if you're beyond* ___*your*___ *teens, you're probably not* ___*in*___ *the best condition. Your* ___*muscles*___ *are soft. Your joints* ___*are*___ *stiff. Your heart and* ___*lungs*___ *aren't used to working* ___*hard*___*. As a result, you'll* ___*feel*___ *slow and awkward when* ___*you*___ *run and will ache* ___*a*___ *bit afterward. But even* ___*if*___ _____ *you're severely out of* ___*condition*___ *it only means it* ___*will*___ *take a bit longer* ___*to*___ *get back into shape.* ___*I*___ *ask you to trust* ___*me*___*. The goal, I promise,* ___*is*___ *worth the struggle. Within* ___*a*___ *few weeks you'll be* ___*covering*___ *a mile or two* ___*at*___ *a time. After a* ___*run*___ *you'll feel refreshed. You'll* ___*have*___ *more energy, more zest.* ___*You'll*___ *take more pleasure in* ___*both*___ *work and play. You'll* ___*sleep*___ *more soundly, lose weight* ___*if*___ *you need to, and* ___*feel*___ *better than you have* ___*in*___ *years.*

You won't get ___*these*___ *results from your very* ___*first*___ *day, but there's no hurry.* ___*Running*___ *isn't something you do* ___*only*___ *in the spring in* ___*order*___ *to look good in* ___*a*___ *bathing suit. It's best when it's worked into the fabric of your life, as an indispensable part of each day.*

Ecological Assessment. Diagnostic information can be collected from a variety of sources other than those already discussed. Daily observations of the student's reading habits can be recorded on teacher-made checklists (Ekwall, 1976; Kennedy, 1971). Samples of written work, tapes of oral reading, recorded interviews, descriptions of oral conversations, and student

[1]Paragraphs taken from J. F. Fixx, *The Complete Book of Running* (New York: Random House, 1977, pp. (57–58). Reprinted by permission of the publisher.

progress charts can be collected and analyzed (Goodman, 1978). Wiederholt (Note 4) suggests that much diagnostic information can be obtained without submitting the student to formal testing. Teachers can be interviewed to determine what they know about the child, what materials and teaching methods have been used, what is expected within the reading program, and what is the language of the instruction. The analysis should include information about the student's self-concept, use of language, understanding of concepts, and behavior in the class. Wiederholt further suggests that if students are going to be directly tested, the evaluation should occur in a natural setting (classroom) and should evaluate the act of reading and what the student is thinking while reading (miscue analysis, retelling). Daily observations can be recorded on the teacher-made checklists, and samples of students' written work, tapes of their reading, and other information may be used.

Reading Assessment Summary

Children who have difficulties in reading often are submitted to a variety of diagnostic instruments and procedures, which can be administered by a number of different people. Many times this information is not summarized in a way useful for planning instruction, thus wasting student and teacher time.

Test and observational data can be summarized as illustrated in the Analytical Reading Diagnosis Form (Table 9.5). This chart graphically illustrates Melinda's strengths and weaknesses and compiles all diagnostic data in one form to be used as a reference source when a comparison is needed to assess daily probes or posttest information. When planning a program, the teacher must cross-analyze the data and decide how the student is using or not using pertinent skills (cue systems) to read and interpret the content.

INSTRUCTION

Precise assessment should lead to accurate decisions about specific educational programs designed for individual learning disabled students with reading problems. Traditional programs (basal readers, reading kits) often are not appropriate to help students overcome specific learning difficulties. Numerous approaches and methods are available to meet the needs of these students, some of which are discussed here.

This part of the chapter presents strategies and programs designed for specific reading problems of learning disabled students (inability to use language or meaning cues, confusion of graphophonic cues, letter or sound difficulties). Since reading was earlier defined as a process for obtaining meaning from print, the discussions of the instructional methods proceed from meaning-oriented programs (meaning-oriented, language-centered approaches, contextual reading, comprehension) to skill-building strategies (graphophonic cues, word recognition, letter and sound recognition). The skill-teaching strategies are presented in a way that illustrates the skill as it relates to obtaining meaning in reading, rather than learning it as a discrete entity.

Meaning-Oriented In language-centered programs, the student learns to apply language and
Language-Centered meaning cues as a reading strategy (Kibby, 1979). Language-centered pro-
Programs grams are particularly appropriate for learning disabled students who may be
weak in concept development and word meanings, listening comprehension,
and oral expression. These students' oral language production often lacks
preciseness, variety, clarity, and vividness (Bannatyne, 1971; Johnson &
Myklebust, 1967; Lerner, 1976; Vogel, 1975, 1977; Wiig & Semel, 1975).
The authors of the language-centered programs are not implying that receptive and expressive language skills be built as prerequisites to reading instruction. For the language-disabled reader, language-centered programs
build and extend language and concepts in a manner parallel to the development of reading. The reading strategies would teach language-disabled
as well as normal readers how to use language skills as cues for interpreting
the printed message.

Developing an experiential and language base to facilitate reading development is supported by psycholinguists (Goodman, 1976; Smith, 1971)
and learning disabilities specialists (Johnson & Myklebust, 1967). While
language and reading develop independently (see Chapter 8), an interdependent relationship exists. Reading is a linguistic performance using the
same linguistic information that underlies listening and speaking. For example, the strategies of hypothesizing and predicting the meaning of the spoken
message have to be transferred to interpreting written language (Gibson,
1970).

Numerous listening and oral language activities develop meaning-
oriented strategies that students use when reading. Specific activities, for
example, may encourage students to predict the author's message, model
oral language, use concepts correctly, confirm predictions by using thinking
strategies, and extend oral expression (see Table 9.6). The activities in this
approach would encourage students to use language as a medium for relating
new information with previous understanding (Athey, Note 6).

Several procedures can be used to further develop oral language as it
relates to the reading process. Structured language models, for example,
encourage some students to develop complete thoughts and express responses that are expanded (This is a hammer.) and extended (This is a red
hammer that I use to hit the shiny nail.) (Fox, 1976, p. 669). Concept development activities—which ask students to name, describe, discriminate
and generalize concepts—provide information and require language to explain perceptions (Risko & Degler, 1980). *The Peabody Language Development Kits*-Revised (Dunn, Dunn, & Smith, 1981; Dunn, Horton, & Smith,
1981; Dunn, Smith & Dunn, 1981; Dunn, Smith & Smith, 1981), the
Sound-Order-Sense Program (Semel, 1970) and the *Semel Auditory Processing Program* (Semel, in press) provide additional activities for developing
receptive and expressive language.

The importance of language and conceptual abilities as they relate to
reading acquisition cannot be overstressed. Without these abilities, reading
has little meaning. Children impaired in these areas have great difficulty
comprehending and explaining the meaning of written material.

Table 9.6	Suggested activities for the improvement of language reading skills

1. Listen to predictable materials (nursery rhymes, songs, folk tales) and say these with the reader (Gillespie-Silver, 1979).
2. Listen to others and appropriately contribute to discussions, first with one-, two-, and three-word responses; then responding in complete sentences; and finally using a variety of sentence patterns.
3. Listen to new words and their meanings, and use these words correctly in describing events or following directions.
4. Listen to narrated stories and poems, and dramatize the main ideas and the sequence of events.
5. Listen to stories, poems, and directions; name the main ideas, specific details, and the sequence of events.
6. Verbally express thoughts, feelings, and experiences using appropriate sentence structure in a series of sentences.
7. Ask and answer questions related to personal experiences or stories heard.
8. Retell stories heard.
9. Tell episodes to complete an unfinished story.
10. Orally categorize information (animals, foods, places).
11. Orally describe sensory impression using an appropriate vocabulary.
12. Describe the characters of people in stories by reporting on their appearance, their feelings, and what others in the stories think of the characters.

Relating oral language and the printed message. As students develop receptive and expressive linguistic abilities, visual counterparts of language should be illustrated during classroom and school activities. The teacher can display language collected from numerous sources (quotes from television, radio, and books; directions to complete tasks; phrases, sentences, song lyrics, poems, or riddles) and encourage students to relate their oral language to words in print. Instead of displaying words in isolation (single word labels on charts, tables, an aquarium, the clock), the teacher should use sentences or short contexts (It is Mary's turn to clean the aquarium. What is the name of this book on the table? John thinks the door is brown, but Mary says that it is orange!). This should help illustrate that words can be presented in different forms of language (statements, questions, exclamations) (Mackay, Thompson, & Schaub, 1970). Discussing these messages with students can help them transfer their use of oral cues (semantics, grammar, syntax) to written language, demonstrating how reading is a meaningful activity.

Language experience approach. The language experience approach to teaching reading (Hall, 1970) is a procedure that illustrates the relationship between language and reading. When using this approach with learning disabled students, the teacher must structure the activities to provide review and repetition of the concepts, vocabulary words, or targeted skills. *The Breakthrough to Literacy Program* (Mackay et al., 1970) presents a language experience approach appropriate for many learning disabled students. Although not specifically designed for this population of learners, the stress on language development and the practice and review elements provided in the lessons are appropriate for them. This program provides an example of a

This student is constructing sentences using his vocabulary words in the Breakthrough to Literacy Program.

structured method aimed at the development of language and reading skills in an integrated, experience-oriented approach.

In the initial stages, students participate in numerous activities that provide information and models of language. As students engage in activities, they learn to develop and use language strategies that encourage them to make predictions about what they are doing, confirm their predictions by discussing or problem solving, and explain the process they use to comprehend (Goodman, Burke, & Sherman, Note 7). The activities might require the students to:

1. Clean the aquarium, draw pictures of the fish, confirm the pictures by comparing them with illustrations from science books, and write short descriptions of the fish.

2. Listen to stories being read by peers or the teacher, predict story happenings, and discuss the story by using story vocabulary and concepts.

3. Complete math problems using geometric or concrete objects, predict mathematical relationships, and discuss the reasons for selecting answers.

4. Read language displayed in the room by making guesses about unknown words and deciding the accuracy of the guesses by determining whether they make sense.

At the second stage, formal reading begins. When the teacher determines that a student or small group can read approximately twelve words, he or she presents some of these words in a sentence written on a stand. The teacher and students read the sentence and then compose different sentences using all twelve words. A written record of every sentence is kept. As the students learn additional words, they are given personal stands and sentence makers (words to build sentences from). Every day they are encouraged to compose sentences and short stories about information they learn in classroom activities, field trips, or personal experiences. Sentence frames (I came _____ the car. I had a _____, _____ orange for lunch.) can be provided by the teacher to help students write complete sentences. Every student has a personal notebook to record the sentences or stories. Some students learn quickly using this program, demonstrated in a story written and read by a six-year-old boy.

THE LION[2]

The lion is a member of the cat family. As a cat they can see much better than us and other animals. Lions camouflage in the sun. In brushes they can camouflage very well. Lions can jump very far. The male lion is most of the time hunting for the female lion. They do it in the night. It is much better in the dark so they can creep up on other animals. Lions aren't very good at climbing trees. The male lion has a mane. He is the king of the beasts.

Lions do not hunt on their own. They hunt together. The mother stays with the cubs. The male lion hunts with another lion. Lions climb up trees in danger.

At the third stage, students read other materials (books, magazines, poems, riddles). They are shown that they can read many words, and are asked to read for meaning and discuss story happenings. New vocabulary words are introduced and experiences are developed to extend understanding of the stories. As stated earlier, many skills are developed through this process. Students continue to use the language strategies to predict, confirm, and comprehend written materials. They repeatedly use a set of words, and gradually add new vocabulary words as they are learned in different but related activities. Through this method, they also learn other specific language and reading skills (use of capital letters, paragraphs, forms of sentence structure, left-right analysis, word recognition, vocabulary meaning, comprehension). Children's language differences also are accounted for in this program, because reading begins and extends from each student's personal language. Similar procedures can be used with language experience stories by providing practice and repetition of vocabulary and a transfer to other reading materials. These activities are an application of Smith's (1971) rec-

[2]A sample story written and read by a six-year-old boy who was taught through *The Breakthrough to Literacy Program* (Mackay et al., 1970).

ommendations that teachers stress the concepts that: reading is meaningful activity, personalized to the reader; and print is different from speech in form and style.

Contextual
Reading

Various procedures and materials can be used to develop reading and understanding of context. Steps followed in the *Directed Reading Activity* (DRA) (Kennedy, 1971) are one means of guiding children through contextual reading. The steps used in this traditional method are presented in basal manuals; and, therefore, often are overlooked because many teachers feel that they are boring. Yet, if the procedure is used correctly, it can motivate student interest while providing an integration of many factors related to the reading process. The DRA can be used as a developmental lesson format to emphasize all of the skill areas or as a remedial lesson format to overemphasize particular aspects (vocabulary development, comprehension, oral fluency). It is one way to provide application and integration of the three language systems (graphophonics, syntax, and semantics) to contextual reading. The activities in the procedure develop meaning by focusing on the interaction of the printed message with the reader's previous knowledge (Athey, Note 6; Goodman, Burke, & Sherman, Note 7). Stauffer (1975) modified the DRA procedures in his *Directed Thinking Reading Activity* (DTRA) to place stress on thinking strategies skills. The DRA and DTRA activities are appropriate for students at all levels who can read contexts of any length. They are applicable to various content materials (social studies, science). Table 9.7 lists DRA steps and corresponding teaching suggestions. These suggestions can be used for any contextual reading activity, even if the teacher is not using the DRA or DTRA format.

Numerous materials can be used for contextual reading, including high-interest, low-vocabulary books, magazines, newspapers, T.V. guides, sheet music, transcripts of television commercials (Hirst & O'Such, 1979), folktales (Crook, 1979), or nursery rhymes.

The cloze and SQ3R procedures also are helpful aids in developing contextual reading. The cloze can be used as a teaching strategy as well as for

The teacher is developing background information and concepts prior to reading the selected story. Students are encouraged to discuss key concepts and read these words in various contexts to predict and confirm their meanings. The language charts provide contextual meaning for vocabulary words.

Table 9.7   **Applying the directed reading activity method**

DRA Steps	Teaching Suggestions
Motivation	Personalize the reading content and excite student interest by providing experiences relevant to the student. For example, Berger (1978) found a significant relationship between acquisition of new information and prior knowledge and recommends that teachers expand the experience and background of the reader. It is helpful to elicit what the students know about the content and extend their knowledge to facilitate comprehension when they are reading.
Vocabulary development	Concepts critical to the understanding of the content should be taught (Risko & Degler, 1980, model described earlier). It is important to choose only those few concepts necessary for comprehension. For example, a teacher who introduced the words animal, mane, photograph, Africa, customs, hunting, habitat, and life styles, found that she introduced too much new information and did not adequately develop understanding of any of the words. A discussion about the concepts should help students confirm and extend their understanding of new words.

Decoding skills	Key or new vocabulary words should be presented in sentences to encourage children to use syntactical, semantic, morphological, grammatical, and decoding cues to predict and confirm word meaning and pronunciation (Van Etten, 1978; Vogel, 1975, 1977).
	 Children can learn to use key words as signals to convey meaning of words (look for a verb to correspond with a noun) (Berger, 1978).
	 The following procedure illustrates a way to help a child use various decoding skills to understand and pronounce the word "oneirocritic."
	 Teacher presents this sentence: "The *oneirocritic* told me that my dream meant a surprise." The student is encouraged to "read around" the unknown word and predict the meaning of the word, predict that the word is a person (noun), and read to make sense and confirm the meaning.
	 Second, the teacher shows the structural and phonic elements of the word.
	       o nei ro crit' ic
	             oneirocritic
	 Finally, the student rereads the sentence to comprehend the meaning of the sentence.
	     The *oneirocritic* told me that my dream meant a surprise.

Stating the purpose	Stauffer (1975) suggests that the teacher guide pupils to predict and state a reason for reading. If the students are unable to set the purpose, the teacher can help the students focus on the content by presenting a few questions or leading statements.
Reading	Students can orally or silently read the selection. For the student who is reluctant to read, the teacher can alternate with him or her by taking turns reading sentences or paragraphs. Bliss (Note 8) found that older students' performance increased when they read along with tapes of content materials. Other suggestions are discussed in the next section on reading fluency.
Comprehension	Comprehension taxonomies (Clymer & Barrett, 1968) often are used as a guide for levels of questions teachers ask during and after student reading. Other authorities who prefer to define comprehension as multidimensional and without a sharp delineation of skills (Hittleman, 1978) direct teachers to ask students to retell the story content and analyze retellings (Goodman & Burke, 1972; Kintsch, 1974; Athey, Note 6). Students can be taught to rehearse for retelling by looking for information such as imagery, main ideas, and supporting details. Using Kintsch's procedure, Haviland and Clark (1974) found that children remember main ideas better and old information is processed more rapidly than new information. Roberts and Smith (1980) found that when instruction was targeted on increased comprehension ability, correct reading rates were enhanced and error rates were decreased.
Extension or enrichment	Activities can be provided to practice (contextual cues, structural analysis) and extend (application of concepts) the knowledge, attitudes, or skills developed in the prior steps.

assessment. Students at all levels can be given incomplete short sentences or longer cloze passages and asked to predict and confirm the selection of meaningful vocabulary. The cloze procedure can be adapted to meet instructional needs (students can rewrite the paragraphs and expand sentences, change the mood of the author, or provide another ending). The SQ3R is a procedure designed for aiding students' comprehension of content materials. It requires the student to skim the material (S), predict or identify questions from headings (Q), read the text (R), review to answer questions and identify information (R), and recite or explain what was learned (R) (Tinker & McCullough, 1975).

Comprehension

In addition to the practical reasons for using methods such as those described above to develop comprehension, research supports the effectiveness of these strategies. In a study of kinds of comprehension questions (literal, inferential, evaluative) teachers ask, Guszak (1967) found that teachers usually rely on those requiring simple recall of literal details and often limit students' critical thinking and interpretation by implying that all questions have single, right answers. Whenever comprehension questions are asked about a reading passage, several different kinds of questions should be asked.

Research indicates that comprehension, when directly remediated, can improve (Carroll & Chall, 1975; Jenkins, Barksdale, & Clinton, 1978; Klann, 1972; Proe & Wade, 1973; Waechter, 1972). Hansen and Lovitt (1976) report that recall questions were more easily answered and that performance on recall, sequencing, and interpretation questions improved with direct instruction on these skills during oral and silent reading. An effective strategy used in their study was to require students to correct their answers to comprehension questions. Orienting students to the structure and organizational patterns of paragraphs is another method of assisting them to understand the ideas presented (Johnson & Myklebust, 1967; Guthrie, 1979). The Request Procedure (Manzo, 1969) requires students to ask questions about each sentence of the first few paragraphs of the text as another method for providing direct instruction in comprehension.

In a study specifically designed to determine the relationship between correct and error oral reading rates and comprehension, Roberts and Smith (1980) made some interesting findings. Eight learning disabled boys participated in their study, all of whom were seriously deficient in their reading abilities. When correct rates were targeted for improvement, the students' correct rate scores dramatically improved, but comprehension did not. When reductions in error rate scores were the aim, they improved, but comprehension did not. When improved comprehension was the target, comprehension scores as well as oral reading rate scores improved substantially. They concluded that since one of the major purposes of teaching is for students to understand the printed message, teachers should focus on that goal early in the remedial process.

Fluency

The tactics outlined in Chapter 4, particularly the reinforcement procedures, have been very successful when students' oral reading fluency (speed of correct reading) needs to be increased. As a guide, some suggest that elementary-age students' correct reading rate should be approximately 100 words per minute (Mercer, 1979; Starlin, Note 9).

Several nonreinforcement procedures have proven to be effective in aiding the disabled readers who read word by word or lack contextual reading skills. For example, Smith (1979) demonstrated that modeling can influence increases in students' oral reading correct rates. The teacher read aloud a passage from the child's basal reader before the youngster read aloud the remaining passages in the story. This caused substantial improvements in both correct and error rate scores. An "immersed" or "assisted" reading approach is described by Hoskisson (1975, 1977, 1979). The teacher reads a phrase or sentence first, and the student rereads the phrase or sentence. The teacher reads out loud again but omits words he or she thinks the student knows, and the student rereads the sentence in its entirety. Finally, the student reads the sentence independently with teacher assistance when necessary. Other modeling or imitative tactics have been recommended. For example, some (Chomsky, 1976; Huey, 1968) suggest that students listen to prerecorded, taped sections of their books. The students listen as they read silently until they can read the story without the aid of the tape. The neurological impress method proceeds with the student and teacher reading the material aloud for several trials, until the teacher's reading is faded out and the pupil is reading independently (Heckelman, 1969). The repeated readings procedure requires student rereading of short passages (50–200 words) until satisfactory fluency is recorded (Samuels, 1979; Dahl, Note 10, Dahl & Samuels, Note 11)

Placement of
Students

Teachers are often concerned about the placement of remedial readers in curricula materials (basal readers, programmed materials, content textbooks). Often they are overconcerned with having the children read all materials on lower levels even when they have gained the skills to be reading on higher levels. Also, diagnostic measures do not always clearly identify the child's instructional levels. One way to more accurately place students is the use of the Informal Reading Inventory (discussed previously), if it is constructed from the material in which the student is to be placed. The cloze procedure also is a technique used to place students into content materials.

Another procedure, developed by Lovitt and Hansen (1976a), was used by them in their Skip and Drill method (Lovitt and Hansen, 1976b). The purpose of Skip and Drill is to move students through readers more quickly so they can achieve substantial grade level improvements within a reasonable amount of time. To use the Skip and Drill method, youngsters are placed in readers where their correct rate scores are between 45 and 65 (of course, higher correct rate scores could be used also); their error rate scores between 4 and 8; and their comprehension correct percentage scores between 50 and 75. The assigned reader is divided into four equal parts by counting the number of stories in the book and dividing by four. A baseline mean on all three measures (correct rate, error rate, and comprehension) is obtained by having the student read from the beginning of the book over a seven-day period. Criterion for desired improvement is 25 percent on each measure. If, for example, a student's baseline correct rate mean was 60, the error rate mean was 6, and the correct comprehension percentage was 70, the improvement criterion scores were 75, 4.5, and 87.5 percent for the three measures. Once baseline means are obtained, the student can select which stories he or she wants to read first in the first section of the book. Once the criterion for improvement is met, the rest of that section of the book is skipped. The student then prioritizes the stories in the next section, and reads them until criterion for improvement is noted. If a student does not meet the skipping criterion within seven days, drilling procedures are initiated for the deficient areas. Once a section is skipped, drilling is not reinstituted until the student has a seven-day opportunity to skip the newly assigned section.

Methods to Develop Graphophonic and Other Decoding Skills

In addition to language and experiential cues, students need to learn graphophonic strategies to decode words. Reading authorities do not agree on the amount of stress that should be placed upon the various cues during reading instruction. Pearson (1976) indicates that good readers rely more heavily on syntactic and semantic information in their search for meaning and rely less on phonic cues. He further describes poor or novice readers as being overanalytical phonetically; therefore, they lose their attention to meaning. Other reading authorities recommend equal stress on sight words and graphophonic instruction and criticize "whole-word" programs because they overstress visual memory cues (Cawley, Goodstein, & Burrow, 1972; Durkin, 1972; Groff, 1979; Spache, 1976).

The need for phonic skills may be determined by the age of the students and the purpose of instruction. Spache (1976) reports that phonics instruction makes a significant contribution to word recognition and comprehension for second and third graders, but it seems to be less helpful for older readers who rely on other strategies (meaning cues or syllable units) for word pronunciation. If the reading program stresses reading words in isolation, phonics instruction may be preferred over visual memory drills (Gillespie-Silver, 1979). However, if contextual reading is the goal of the program, phonic skills should be taught in combination with the other strategies.

The goal of phonics instruction is to teach students to sound out letters or letter combinations that represent sounds within words. In general, students are taught to pronounce sounds for single consonants, consonant blends, consonant digraphs, long and short vowels, vowel digraphs, vowel diphthongs, and phonograms. Wylie and Durrell (1970) found that first graders learned whole phonograms (all, ain, ell) more easily than short vowel sounds. Glass and Burton (1973), Spache (1976), and Groff (Note 12) indicate that students tend to deal with letter clusters rather than analyzing individual sounds. Rozin, Poritsky, and Sotsky (1971) and Harrigan (1976) found that letters and individual phonemes were too abstract to be used as an aid to remember long words. They taught syllables as building blocks to words, as in the example *o pen,* and then blending these to *open,* rather than the individual letters of *o, p, e, n,* to then be blended into the word. Little or no conclusive research supports a hierarchy of skills or a list of prerequisite skills other than some common sense practices, such as teaching single consonants before consonant blends (White, 1973). The value of rules is debatable (Spache, 1976). Some seem to be applicable and helpful, but the goal is to have students generalize and use them meaningfully rather than just repeat them verbatim.

It is important to remember that teaching activities should relate phonic skill practice to actual reading. Rather than ask students to write letters for sounds heard, teachers should require them to name letter cluster sounds and blend them into words. For example, the Word Attack sections in the *Gates-McKillop* (1962) and the *Ekwall Phonics Inventory* (1976) assess whether students can pronounce initial blends and word families and then blend them:

$$sp + ack = spack$$
or
$$p + ate = pate$$

These activities are similar to the procedure a reader uses when sounding out unknown words and, therefore, present relevant diagnostic information. Oral reading tests and miscue analysis measure students' flexibility in using phonic cues in contextual reading.

Students should learn phonic strategies because they help them make predictions about words they encounter in context. Students can make predictions and confirm their hunches by using questions such as these presented by Spache (1976, p. 221):

1. *What is the sound of the first letter (or letters)?*

2. *What word beginning with this sound would make sense here?*

3. *How many vowels are there? Where are they?*

   a. *If there is one vowel in the beginning or middle, try the short sound of the vowel.*

   b. *If there is one vowel and an e at the end, try the long sound of the vowel.*

   c. *If there is one vowel at the end, try the long sound.*

   d. *If there are two vowels next to each other or at the end, try the long sound of the first vowel (except in oi, oy, ou, ew, oo, au, aw).*

4. *Now say the word. Do you know it? If not, try the other vowel sound.*

5. *Does the word seem to make sense? If not, write it down, and get help later from your teacher or your dictionary. Go on with your reading.*

A sixth question could be: Does this word make sense in this sentence and the context of the paragraph?

The common goal in teaching students decoding strategies is for them to combine sources of information and use all cues effectively. Students often learn to use phonic, semantic, and syntactic cues in isolation, then integrate them as they read long contexts. For example, Pearson (1976) suggests that

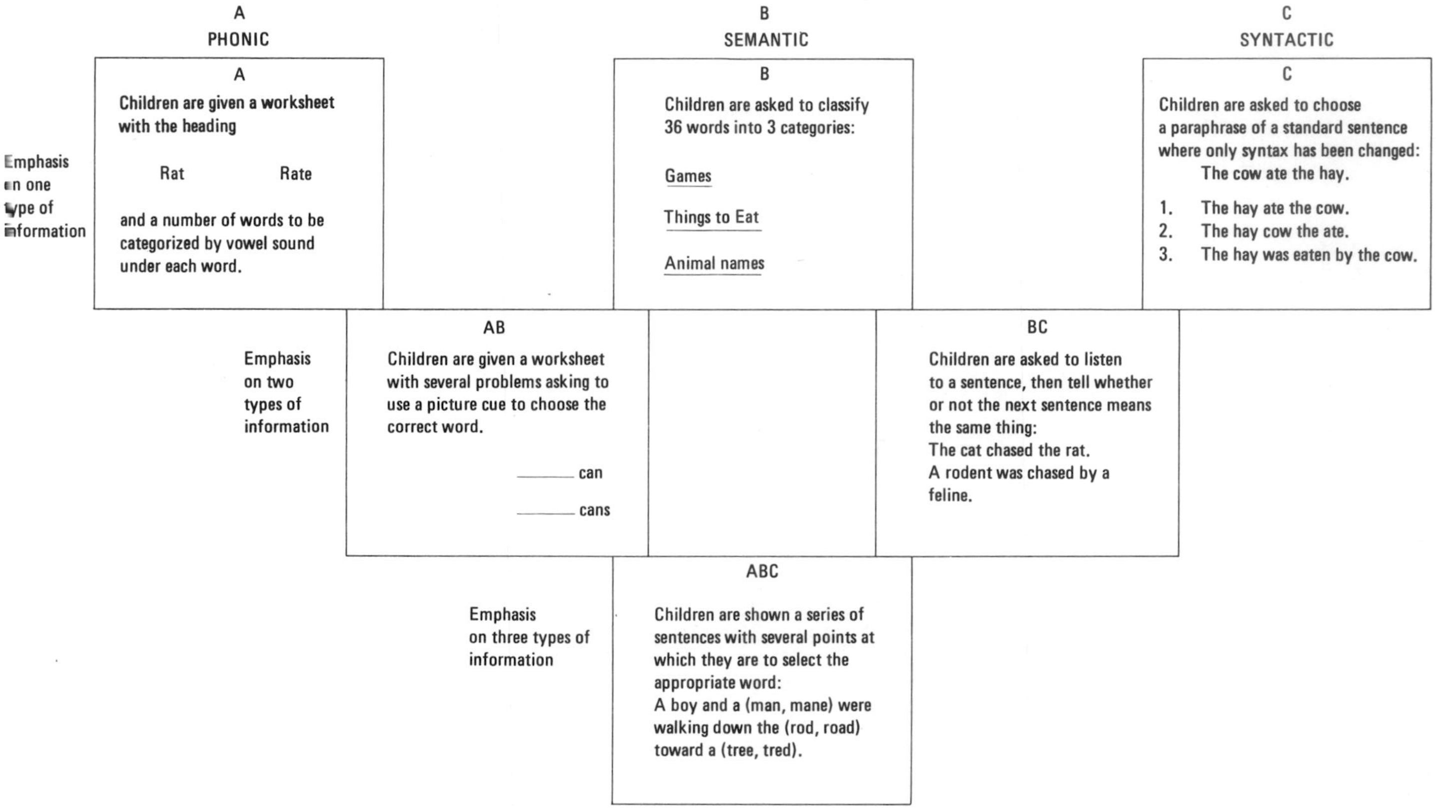

A
PHONIC

A

Children are given a worksheet with the heading

Rat   Rate

and a number of words to be categorized by vowel sound under each word.

B
SEMANTIC

B

Children are asked to classify 36 words into 3 categories:

Games

Things to Eat

Animal names

C
SYNTACTIC

C

Children are asked to choose a paraphrase of a standard sentence where only syntax has been changed:

The cow ate the hay.

1. The hay ate the cow.
2. The hay cow the ate.
3. The hay was eaten by the cow.

AB

Children are given a worksheet with several problems asking to use a picture cue to choose the correct word.

_____ can

_____ cans

BC

Children are asked to listen to a sentence, then tell whether or not the next sentence means the same thing:

The cat chased the rat.
A rodent was chased by a feline.

ABC

Children are shown a series of sentences with several points at which they are to select the appropriate word:

A boy and a (man, mane) were walking down the (rod, road) toward a (tree, tred).

Emphasis on one type of information

Emphasis on two types of information

Emphasis on three types of information

Figure 9.3   Suggested activities to integrate three strategies for phonics practice in context.

the three strategies be integrated by providing activities to practice phonics in context. As shown in Figure 9.3, the activities of A, B, and C teach the skills separately, and the activities A B and B C integrate two of the three cues. The activity ABC is valuable because it provides integration and application of the cues in short contexts before requiring application to longer contexts.

This activity is another illustration of an integrated activity that develops phonics in short contexts (Bond & Tinker, 1967, p. 323).

1. *Exercises to teach initial blend sounds.*
   Write in the blank the word that begins with the same blend as the word underlined.

   (1) *The* branch *soon* _____
   bring fell broke

   (2) *The* block *was painted* _____
   brown blue green

   (3) *There was* plenty *to do at the* _____
   playground school park

   (4) *The brown* string *was* _____
   street strong splashed

Cloze paragraphs can be adapted to allow students to practice context and phonic skills (single consonants are given for the deleted words and students complete the word, or vowels are omitted in the words and students complete the word). The DRA or DTRA procedure can be used to overstress phonetic elements when practicing the decoding of unknown words if students have difficulty using these skills in combination with the others.

A wide range of phonic programs and materials are available for teachers to choose or adapt. For example, *Distar* (Engelmann & Bruner, 1969), although developed for culturally different and slow-learning children, may be useful for learning disabled students, because in the beginning they are taught sequencing, left-right analysis, and sound-symbol associations. They then produce and blend sounds of words before reading these words in story books.

Word Recognition Strategies A three-pronged debate exists among reading authorities: Should words be practiced in context, in isolation, or in combination? Various formats are used to provide students with practice reading words in context (reading multiple new contexts containing the same words, rereading the same text until accuracy improves, using language experience stories containing the review words) (Fleisher & Jenkins, 1978). Word games, word lists, and visual memory exercises provide practice of words in isolation.

Several authors report that the practice of words in isolation (decontextualized practice) facilitates fluent contextual reading (Dolch, 1942; Hartley, 1970; Otto, McMenemy, & Smith, 1973; Perfetti & Hogaboam, 1975;

Samuels, 1970; Shankweiler & Liberman, 1972). Samuels (1970) indicates that decontextualized instruction requires students to attend more closely to the graphic features of the words, since they cannot rely on semantic and syntactic cues. Fleisher and Jenkins (1978) found that practicing words in isolation and in context contributed to improvement on isolated words, but did not contribute to fluency in contextual reading. Jenkins and Larson (1979) found that recognition of words in context improved when students were drilled on these specific words out of context.

Psycholinguists argue that reading instruction should always provide students with opportunities to develop strategies to decode the author's message. Contextual reading fluency is developed by presenting words in context and requiring readers to search for the meaning by using a combination of the decoding cues, semantics, syntax, and graphophonics (Pearson, 1976).

Both procedures may have a place in reading instruction. Some severely disabled or unmotivated students never become fluent readers, yet must learn survival reading skills. It is important for them to develop word recognition skills so they can read maps, signs, menus, directories, and application forms. Many "real world" reading situations do not require reading of written discourse. Students also need to acquire word recognition skills to succeed in reading programs that emphasize reading words in isolation (some readers require mastery performance on word lists to move to the next higher level reader).

Numerous procedures and activities have facilitated improvement of recognition abilities. Hendrickson, Roberts, and Shores (1978), for example, found that antecedent modeling and reinforcement facilitated mastery with fewer failures on word recognition. This technique proved to be superior to subsequent or contingent modeling procedures. They also noted motivational side effects when using this method, because success and positive interactions with teachers were incorporated into the teaching procedure.

Vaughan, Crawley, and Mountain (1979) devised a "vocabulary scavenger hunt," which requires students to define, illustrate, and categorize a set of unknown words as a method of encouraging them to develop mental images of words. Word banks can be used as a way to record words being studied so that students can review them independently or in word recognition activities (Garton, Schoenfelder, & Skriba, 1979).

Several commercially available instructional programs might prove helpful to teachers confronted with youngsters who need to improve their word recognition skills. The *Edmark Reading Program* (Bijou, 1972) presents a series of word recognition activities for a 150-word vocabulary. The program, designed for retarded children or nonreaders, guides the students through activities that provide self-review, repetition, positive reinforcement, and self-pacing. Pictures or symbols for words such as those presented in the *Peabody Rebus Reading Program* (Woodcock & Clark, 1969) may be necessary to help low-functioning students associate meanings to word recognition. Also, instructional programs often rely on various published word lists as sources of high frequency words students encounter in various contexts (Dolch, 1942; Walker, 1979).

Visually Oriented Remedial Techniques

Many learning disabled students have problems with recognition, discrimination, and memory of letters, words, word parts, or a series of words. For example, Max reversed the letters of his name (wrote his name backwards) and confused many of the letters of the alphabet. Max can learn the letters through activities that develop recognition (This is letter *b*), gross discrimination (Find letter *b*—m b s), fine discrimination (Find letter *b*—b h d p), and memory (Write letter *b* from memory). During this process Max is encouraged to use his language to describe the distinctive features of the letters or words (Gibson, 1970). Using concrete representations (wooden letters) to provide sensory information (feeling the parts) may aid in Max's recognition of the parts so that he may visualize them later when he is shown only the symbolic representations (written letters). Assigning a name to the letters (as one distinctive feature) and discussing the likenesses and differences of the letters should help Max develop the necessary language to use when asked to distinguish the letters.

Alexander and Money (1967), Gibson (1970), Money (1967), and Moyer and Newcomer (1977) suggest that children often reverse letters because they are unfamiliar with direction as it relates to letter discrimination. To emphasize direction, Moyer and Newcomer recommend that teachers use direct and delayed matching tasks:

1. Show the letters together and discuss with the children the directional differences (b/d). Have children directly match the letters:

2. Build visualization by having the children recall from memory and encircle the letter that was flashed for two to three seconds.

3. Use the same letter for several consecutive trials to facilitate learning.

Overlearning is provided at the third stage to encourage retention, but it should occur at each stage since short-term memory capacity is limited, and information is not retained if it is introduced too quickly (Smith, 1971; Hargis & Gickling, 1977). Throughout this process, tasks must have ecological validity (Montgomery, 1977). For example, if a student confuses certain letters and words, the remedial activities should facilitate practice of *those* letters and words. It is not realistic to expect practice with geometric designs, pictures, or objects to improve recognition of confused letters or words.

Memory can be further enhanced by visual and linguistic mediation. Often, children copy letters and words using visual information, but are unable to name them correctly. However, if the words and letter names become part of the children's language, the integration of the verbal and visual components should facilitate memory (Vellutino, Smith, Steger, & Kaman, 1975). Hargis and Gickling (1977) found that high imagery words are learned more easily. This suggests that meaningful words relay linguistic cues (in addition to visual cues). They further hypothesized that abstract or isolated words (the *Dolch Word List*) are learned primarily through visual cues and require memory training because only one cueing system is used. For words that are easily confused (was-saw, on-no), Allington and Fleming (1978) found that poor readers confused these words in isolation but could distinguish them in context. This is probably because these students used the linguistic cues of semantics and syntax. Although pictorial cues— and —and color cues (blue b's, white w's) often confuse students, Goodman (1976) found that color cueing aided visual memory of letter orientation when it was faded gradually while other cues were progressively added.

Auditory Training Techniques

Even though reading is sometimes described as a visual task, many (Dechant & Smith, 1977; Dykstra, 1966; Harrington & Durrell, 1955; Johnson & Myklebust, 1967; Risko, 1972; Robinson, 1946; Smith, 1963; Wepman, 1960) stress the importance of auditory training. The rationale and procedures for teaching auditory recognition, discrimination, memory, and blending of speech sounds emphasize the need for parallel development of auditory and visual skills. To provide ecological validity for reading, speech sounds rather than environmental sounds should be taught. Students must learn the distinctive characteristics of speech sounds as they are presented in words and natural language contexts. Practicing discrimination of sounds within minimal pairs of words (man-men) is not a natural language context and the results of such assessments and drill are irrelevant to the task of listening for specific sounds as they occur at various locations within words (Durrell, 1956; Johnson & Myklebust, 1967; Blank, 1968; Hare, 1977). Monroe and Rogers (1964) emphasize that poor discrimination of the beginning, medial, and ending sounds is an important factor related to reading disability.

Children should learn to hear a sound selectively and determine its placement in a word, then compare it with corresponding sounds within other words (Harris, 1970). Auditory blending—synthesizing sounds into words—has been shown to relate to learning the graphophonic cues necessary for reading achievement (Hare, 1977; Harris, 1970; Risko, 1972). A set of activities that teach children to differentiate sounds, locate sounds in specific positions within words, and blend sounds into total words is presented in a data-based program, *Testing/Teaching Module of Auditory Discrimination* (Risko, 1975).

Multisensory Strategies

Multisensory strategies are used to build visual memory cues for word recognition (Fernald, 1943) or alphabetic phonetic cues (Gillingham & Stillman, 1960). The procedures require students to process the stimuli through the visual, auditory, kinesthetic, and tactile channels (VAKT).

The Fernald approach stresses visual memory of sign words and capitalizes on the student's language. The procedure has four stages. During Stage One, children learn by tracing words. After a word is selected, it is written for the children with crayon on paper in blackboard-size script, or in print. They trace the word with their index finger or a combination of index and middle fingers, and say each part as it is traced. They repeat this process as many times as necessary until they can write the word without looking at the copy. They write the word once on scrap paper and then in their "story." Once the story is finished it is typed, and the students read it in print. New words are then filed in their word file, thereby giving them the opportunity to learn the alphabet without rote learning, and giving them training for later dictionary use.

There are several important points about Stage One. Finger contact is essential to tracing. The student must always write the word from memory. The word should always be written as a unit. If, when writing the word, the child makes a mistake, the incorrect form is covered or crossed out. Words must always be used in context.

Stage Two is similar to the first, except that tracing is no longer necessary. Eventually, the child is able to learn any new word by simply looking at the copy made by the teacher. The pupil says the entire word over and over while looking at it; then writes the word from memory. The child continues to incorporate the words learned into stories, which are still typed, and reads the printed copy. During this stage the child's stories should become longer and more complicated than those in Stage One.

There are some important points regarding Stage Two. First, the child must say each part of the word either silently or aloud while tracing and writing it. If the word is monosyllabic, the child says the entire word. If the word has more than one syllable, each syllable is pronounced as it is written. For example, with the word "important," the child would say im-por-tant while tracing or writing each particular syllable. Second, whatever the student writes must be typed and read before too long an interval passes. Third, the length of the tracing period varies from child to child. The student should continue tracing until able to write the word independently. At first, a few words are learned without tracing, and on the same day some words still may be traced. Eventually, the tracing is dropped out completely. The average tracing period is two months, with a one- to eight-month range. When tracing is discontinued, a small word file is substituted for the larger one used up to this point. Fourth, from the beginning of the remedial work with children of normal or superior intelligence, the material they write or read should not be simplified. Children are more interested in fairly difficult material that is on their level of understanding.

In Stage Three, the child is able to learn from the printed word by merely looking at it and saying it silently before writing it. In this stage, the teacher no longer has to write the word. Children usually begin to want to read books, and should be allowed to read as much and whatever they wish. They are told unfamiliar words. Once again, the new words are reviewed and practiced in the format described above.

In Stage Four, the ability to recognize new words from their similarity to words or parts of words already learned is stressed. The student is encouraged to look at new words and try to identify known word parts and apply them to the unfamiliar words. Students are allowed to read as much as they want and about anything that interests them.

During this last stage students usually are excited about sounding out words phonetically, but are encouraged to develop the habit of looking for familiar parts of words. They are never read to during remedial sessions.

The Gillingham and Stillman (1960) method teaches letter and sound recognition through a highly structured procedure. While the program is recommended as a two-year program and requires exclusiveness from the use of other materials, several authors have reported successful modifications (Otto, McMenemy, & Smith, 1973; Kirk, Kliebhan, & Lerner, 1978). The procedures used during this method are broken into three association phases. Association Phase I consists of two parts: association of the visual symbol with the name of the letter and association of the visual symbol with the sound of the letter (the association of the feel of the child's speech organs in producing the name or sound of the letter also is stressed). Associations between auditory and auditory, and auditory and kinesthetic channels are encouraged initially. Once a letter name is mastered, the sound is made by the teacher and repeated by the pupil. During the second association phase, the teacher makes the sound represented by the letter (or phonogram) and tells the student the name of the letter. During the third association phase, target letters are made carefully by the teacher; their forms and orientations are explained to the student. The pupil traces over the teacher's lines, then copies, writes from memory, and finally writes again with eyes averted while the teacher stresses letter formation.

SUMMARY

Reading is a meaning-oriented process in which students develop and learn to use experience and previously learned information, thinking strategies (inferences, evaluations, literal recall), language cues (semantics, syntax), and graphophonic cues (sounds within words) to understand the written message. Various plans of assessment can provide a comprehensive study of what students are doing as they read and what is happening in their environment to influence reading. Understanding of students' abilities and problems in interpreting the code leads to precise program planning in which various methods can be used. Many learning disabled students have specific reading problems and, therefore, need appropriate adjustments in their programs (teacher overstresses the use of language, comprehension, fluency, graphophonics, word recognition, letter orientation, or sound discrimination skills). The ultimate goal of instruction is that the students understand why reading is important to them and how they can use the various strategies and cues in an integrated way to obtain meaning from print.

REFERENCE NOTES

1. GEPHART, W. J. *Application of the convergence technique to basic studies of the reading process* (Project No. 8-0737, Grant No. 0E6-0-8-080737-4335). Washington, D.C.: U.S. Office of Education, 1970.

2. JOHNSON, D. D. *Children's prose comprehension. Research and practice.* Paper presented at International Reading Association Convention, Atlanta, Ga., 1979.

3. HAMMILL, D. D. *The field of learning disabilities: A futuristic perspective.* Paper presented at the National Conference on Learning Disabilities, Louisville, Ky., October 1979.

4. WIEDERHOLT, J. L. *Assessing reading behavior.* Paper presented at the National Conference on Learning Disabilities, Louisville, Ky., October 1979.

5. PACE, J., & WINSCH, J. L. *The effectiveness of the cloze procedure as an indicator of comprehension ability.* Unpublished manuscript, Queens College of the City University of New York, 1975.

6. ATHEY, I. *Language skills of pre-readers and beginning readers.* Presentation at the International Reading Association Convention, Houston, Tex., 1978.

7. GOODMAN, Y., BURKE, C., & SHERMAN, B. *Strategies in reading.* In preparation.

8. BLISS, B. A. *Audio-assisted reading: A necessity for educating teen-aged non-readers.* Unpublished paper, Madison, Wis.: Barneveld High School, 1977.

9. STARLIN, C. *Screening for grade and instructional levels (elementary): Examiner's manual.* Kansas City, Mo.: International Management Systems, Inc., 1977.

10. DAHL, P. R. *An experimental program for teaching high speed word recognition and comprehension skills* (Project Report No. 3-1154). Washington, D.C.: U.S. Department of Health, Education and Welfare, 1974.

11. DAHL, P. R., & SAMUELS, S. J. *Teaching high speed word recognition and comprehension skills.* Unpublished manuscript, 1973.

12. GROFF, P. *The syllable: Its nature and pedagogical usefulness.* Portland, Ore.: Northwest Regional Educational Laboratory, 1971.

REFERENCES

ALEXANDER, D., & MONEY, J. Reading disability and the problem of direction sense. *The Reading Teacher*, 1967, *20*, 404–409.

ALLINGTON, R. L., & FLEMING, J. T. The misreading of high-frequency words. *The Journal of Special Education*, 1978, *12*, 417–421.

BANNATYNE, A. *Language, reading and learning disabilities: Psychology, neuropsychology, diagnosis and remediation.* Springfield, Ill.: Charles C. Thomas, 1971.

BERGER, N. S. Why can't John read? Perhaps he's not a good listener. *Journal of Learning Disabilities*, 1978, *11*, 633–638.

BETTS, E. A. *Foundations of reading instruction, with emphasis on differentiated guidance.* New York: American Book Co., 1946.

BIJOU, S. W. *The Edmark reading program.* Seattle, Wash.: Edmark Associates, 1972.

BLANK, M. Cognitive processes in auditory discrimination in normal and retarded readers. *Child Development*, 1968, *39*, 1091–1101.

BLOOM, R. D. Learning to read: An operant perspective. In F. B. Davis (Ed.), *The literature of research in reading with emphasis on models.* New Brunswick, N.J.: Graduate School of Education, Rutgers State University, 1971.

BOND, G. L., & TINKER, M. A. *Reading difficulties: Their diagnosis and correction* (2nd ed.). New York: Appleton-Century-Crofts, 1967.

BOND, G. L., TINKER, M. A., & WASSON, B. B. *Reading difficulties: Their diagnosis and correction* (4th ed.). Englewood Cliffs, N.J.: Prentice-Hall, 1979.

BORMUTH, J. R. The cloze readability procedure. In J. R. Bormuth (Ed.), *Readability in 1968: A research bulletin.* Champaign, Ill.: National Council of Teachers of English, 1968.

BORMUTH, J. R. The cloze procedure. In W. D. Page (Ed.), *Help for the reading teacher: New directions in research.* Urbana, Ill.: National Conference on Research in English, 1975.

BROWN, V. L., HAMMILL, D. D., & WIEDERHOLT, J. L. *The test of reading comprehension: A method for assessing the understanding of written language.* Austin, Tex.: Pro-Ed Publishers, 1978.

BURKE, C. L. Oral reading analysis: A view of the reading process. In W. D. Page (Ed.), *Help for the reading teacher: New directions in research.* Urbana, Ill.: National Conference on Research in English, 1975.

BURKE, C. *Reading miscue inventory—Short form.* Bloomington, Ind.: Indiana University, 1976.

CARROLL, J., & CHALL, J. S. (Eds.). *Toward a literate society: The report of the Committee on Reading of the National Academy of Education with a series of papers commissioned by the committee.* New York: McGraw-Hill, 1975.

CAWLEY, J. F., GOODSTEIN, H. A., & BURROW, W. H. *The slow learner and the reading problem.* Springfield, Ill.: Charles C. Thomas, 1972.

CHOMSKY, C. After decoding: What? *Language Arts*, 1976, *53*, 288–296; 314.

CLEMENTS, S. D. *Minimal brain dysfunction in children.* (NINDS Monograph No. 3, U.S. Public Health Service Publication No. 1415). Washington, D.C.: U.S. Government Printing Office, 1966.

CLYMER, T., & BARRETT, T. The Barrett taxonomy— Cognitive and affective dimensions of reading comprehension. In H. M. Robinson (Ed.), *Innovation and change in reading instruction: Sixty-seventh yearbook of the National Society for the Study of Education* (Part 11). Chicago: University of Chicago Press, 1968.

CROOK, P. R. Folktales teach appreciation for human predicaments. *The Reading Teacher*, 1979, *32*, 449–452.

D'ANGELO, K., & WILSON, R. M. How helpful is insertion and omission miscue analysis? *The Reading Teacher*, 1979, *32*, 519–520.

DECHANT, E. V. *Improving the teaching of reading.* Englewood Cliffs, N.J.: Prentice-Hall, 1964.

DECHANT, E. V., & SMITH, H. P. *Psychology in teaching reading* (2nd ed.). Englewood Cliffs, N.J.: Prentice-Hall, 1977.

DOLCH, E. W. *Basic sight word test.* Champaign, Ill.: Garrard Publishing Co., 1942.

DUNN, L. M., DUNN, L. M., & SMITH, J. O. *Peabody language development kit: Level #2-Revised.* Circle Pines, Minn.: American Guidance Service, 1981.

DUNN, L. M., HORTON, K. B., & SMITH, J. O. *Peabody language development kit: Level #P-Revised.* Circle Pines, Minn.: American Guidance Service, 1981.

DUNN, L. M., SMITH, J. O., & DUNN, L. M. *Peabody language development kit: Level #1-Revised.* Circle Pines, Minn.: American Guidance Service, 1981.

DUNN, L. M., SMITH, J. O., & SMITH, D. D. *Peabody language development kit: Level #3-Revised.* Circle Pines, Minn.: American Guidance Service, 1981.

DURKIN, D. *Teaching young children to read.* Boston: Allyn & Bacon, 1972.

DURRELL, D. *Durrell analysis of reading difficulty* (2nd ed.). New York: Harcourt Brace & World, 1955.

DURRELL, D. *Improving reading instruction.* New York: Harcourt, Brace & World, 1956.

DYKSTRA, R. Auditory discrimination abilities and beginning reading achievement. *Reading Research Quarterly*, 1966, *1*, 5–34.

EKWALL, E. E. *Diagnosis and remediation of the disabled reader.* Boston: Allyn & Bacon, 1976.

ENGLEMANN, S., & BRUNER, E. C. *Distar reading series: An instructional system* Chicago, Ill.: Science Research Associates, 1969.

FERNALD, G. M. *Remedial techniques in basic school subjects.* New York: McGraw-Hill, 1943.

FILLMORE, C. J. The case for case. In E. Bach & R. T. Harms (Eds.), *Universals in linguistic theory.* New York: Holt, Rinehart & Winston, 1968.

FIXX, J. F. *The complete book of running.* New York: Random House, 1977.

FLEISHER, L. S., & JENKINS, J. R. Effects of contextualized and decontextualized practice conditions on word recognition. *Learning Disabilities Quarterly*, 1978, *1*, 39–47.

FLESCH, R. *Why Johnny can't read—And what you can do about it.* New York: Harper & Row, 1955.

FOX, S. E. Assisting children's language development. *The Reading Teacher*, 1976, *29*, 666–670.

FRIES, C. C. *Linguistics and reading.* New York: Holt, Rinehart & Winston, 1963.

GAASHOLT, M. Precision techniques in the management of teacher and child behaviors. *Exceptional Children*, 1970, *37*, 129–135.

GARTON, S., SCHOENFELDER, P., & SKRIBA, P. Activities for young word bankers. *The Reading Teacher*, 1979, *32*, 453–457.

GATES, A. I., & McKILLOP, A. S. *Gates-McKillop reading diagnostic tests.* New York: Teacher College Press, 1962.

GIBSON, E. J. The ontogeny of reading. *American Psychologist*, 1970, *25*, 136–143.

GILLESPIE-SILVER, P. *Teaching reading to children with special needs.* Columbus, Ohio: Charles E. Merrill, 1979.

GILLILAND, H. *A practical guide to remedial reading.* Columbus, Ohio: Charles E. Merrill Publishing Co., 1974.

GILLINGHAM, A., & STILLMAN, B. *Remedial training for children with specific disability in reading, spelling, and penmanship* (7th ed.). Cambridge, Mass.: Education Publishing Service, 1960.

GILMORE, J. V., & GILMORE, E. C. *Gilmore oral reading test.* New York: Harcourt Brace Jovanovich, 1968.

GLASS, G. G., & BURTON, E. H. How do they decode? Verbalizations and observed behaviors of successful decoders. *Education*, 1973, *94*, 58–65.

GIORDANO, G. Convergent research on language and teaching reading. *Exceptional Children*, 1978, *44*, 604–611.

GOODMAN, K. A linguistic study of cues and miscues in reading. *Elementary English*, 1965, *42*, 639–643.

GOODMAN, K. Behind the eye: What happens in reading. In H. Singer & R. B. Ruddell (Eds.), *Theoretical models and processes of reading* (2nd ed.). Newark, Del.: International Reading Association, 1976.

GOODMAN, Y. M. Reading diagnosis: Qualitative or quantitative? *The Reading Teacher*, 1972, *26*, 32–37.

GOODMAN, Y. M. Kid watching: An alternative to testing. *The National Elementary Principal*, 1978, *57*, 41–45.

GOODMAN, Y., & DURKE, C. L. *Reading miscue inventory manual: Procedure for diagnosis and evaluation.* New York: Macmillan Co., 1972.

GROFF, P. A critique of teaching reading as a whole-task venture. *The Reading Teacher,* 1979, *32,* 647–652.

GUSZAK, F. Teacher questioning and reading. *The Reading Teacher,* 1967, *21,* 227–234.

GUSZAK, F. Dilemmas in informal reading assessments. *Elementary English,* 1970, *47,* 666–670.

GUTHRIE, J. Paragraph structure. *The Reading Teacher,* 1979, *32,* 880–881.

HALL, M. A. *Teaching reading as a language experience.* Columbus, Ohio: Charles E. Merrill Publishing Co., 1970.

HANSEN, C. L. Story retelling used with average and learning disabled readers as a measure of reading comprehension. *Learning Disability Quarterly,* 1978, *1,* 62–69.

HANSEN, C. L., & LOVITT, T. C. The relationship between question type and mode of reading on the ability to comprehend. *The Journal of Special Education,* 1976, *10,* 53–60.

HARE, B. A. Perceptual deficits are not a cue to reading problems in second grade. *The Reading Teacher,* 1977, *30,* 624–628.

HARGIS, C. H., & GICKLING, E. E. The function of imagery in word recognition development. *The Reading Teacher,* 1977, *31,* 870–874.

HARRIGAN, J. E. Initial reading instruction. Phonemes, syllables or ideographs? *Journal of Learning Disabilities,* 1976, *9,* 74–80.

HARRINGTON, M. J., & DURRELL, D. D. Mental maturity versus perception abilities in primary reading. *The Journal of Educational Psychology,* 1955, *46,* 375–380.

HARRIS, A. J. *How to increase reading ability: A guide to developmental and remedial methods* (5th ed.). New York: David McKay Co., 1970.

HARTLEY, R. N. Effects of list types and cues on the learning of word lists. *Reading Research Quarterly,* 1970, *6,* 97–121.

HAVILAND, S. E., & CLARK, H. H. What's new? Acquiring new information as a process in comprehension. *Journal of Verbal Learning and Verbal Behavior,* 1974, *13,* 515–521.

HECKELMAN, R. G. A neurological-impress method of remedial-reading instruction. *Academic Therapy Quarterly,* 1969, *4,* 277–282.

HENDRICKSON, J., ROBERTS, M., & SHORES, R. E. Antecedent and contingent modeling to teach basic sight vocabulary to learning disabled children. *Journal of Learning Disabilities,* 1978, *11,* 524–528.

HIRST, L. T., & O'SUCH, T. Using musical television commercials to teach reading. *Teaching Exceptional Children,* 1979, *11,* 80–81.

HITTLEMAN, D. R. *Developmental reading: A psycholinguistic perspective.* Chicago: Rand McNally College Publishing Co., 1978.

HOSKISSON, K. The many facets of assisted reading. *Elementary English,* 1975, *52,* 312–315.

HOSKISSON, K. Reading readiness: Three viewpoints. *The Elementary School Journal,* 1977, *78,* 44–52.

HOSKISSON, K. A response to "A critique of teaching reading as a whole-task venture." *The Reading Teacher,* 1979, *32,* 653–659.

HUEY, E. B. *The psychology and pedagogy of reading: With a review of the history of reading and writing and of methods, texts, and hygiene in reading.* Cambridge, Mass.: The M.I.T. Press, 1968.

JASTAK, J. F., & JASTAK, S. R. *(WRAT) The wide range achievement test* (revised ed.). Los Angeles: Western Psychological Services, 1978.

JENKINS, J. R., BARKSDALE, A., & CLINTON, L. Improving reading comprehension and oral reading: Generalization across behaviors, settings, and time. *Journal of Learning Disabilities,* 1978, *11,* 607–617.

JENKINS, J. R., & LARSON, K. Evaluating error-correction procedures for oral reading. *The Journal of Special Education,* 1979, *13,* 145–156.

JOHNSON, M. S., & KRESS, R. *Informal reading inventories.* Newark, Del.: International Reading Association, 1965.

JOHNSON, D. J., & MYKLEBUST, H. R. *Learning disabilities: Educational principles and practices.* New York: Grune & Stratton, 1967.

JONES, M. B., & PIKULSKI, E. C. Cloze for the classroom. *Journal of Reading,* 1974, *17,* 432–438.

KARLSON, B., MADDEN, R., & GARDNER, E. F. *Stanford diagnostic reading test.* New York: Psychological Corporation, 1976.

KENNEDY, E. C. *Classroom approaches to remedial reading.* Itasca, Ill.: F. E. Peacock Publishers, 1971.

KENNEDY, E. C. *Methods in teaching developmental reading.* Itasca, Ill.: F. E. Peacock Publishers, 1974.

KIBBY, M. W. Passage readability affects the oral reading strategies of disabled readers. *The Reading Teacher,* 1979, *32,* 390–396.

KINTSCH, W. *The representation of meaning in memory.* Hillsdale, N.J.: Laurence Erlbaum Associates, 1974.

KIRK, S. A., KLIEBHAN, J. M., & LERNER, J. W. *Teaching reading to slow and disabled learners.* Boston: Houghton Mifflin Co., 1978.

KLANN, H. *The effects of utilizing team tutors in a fourth and fifth grade individualized reading program.* (ERIC Document Reproduction Service No. ED 102 729) 1972.

LAHEY, B. B., & McNEES, M. P. Letter discrimination errors in kindergarten through third grade: Assessment and operant training. *The Journal of Special Education*, 1975, 9, 191–199.

LERNER, J. *Children with learning disabilities: Theories, diagnosis and teaching strategies* (2nd ed.). Boston: Houghton Mifflin Co., 1976.

LOVITT, T. C., & HANSEN, C. L. Round one—Placing the child in the right reader. *Journal of Learning Disabilities*, 1976, 9, 347–353. (a)

LOVITT, T. C., & HANSEN, C. L. The use of contingent skipping and drilling to improve oral reading and comprehension. *Journal of Learning Disabilities*, 1976, 9, 481–487. (b)

McCRACKEN, R. A. *Standard reading inventory*. Klamath Falls, Ore.: Klamath Printing Co., 1966.

MACKAY, D., THOMPSON, B., & SCHAUB, P. *Breakthrough to literacy*. London: Schools Council Publications, 1970.

MANZO, A. V. The request procedure. *Journal of Reading*, 1969, 13, 123–126.

MERCER, C. D. *Children and adolescents with learning disabilities*. Columbus, Ohio: Charles E. Merrill Publishing Co., 1979.

MONEY, J. Dyslexia: A postconference review. In J. Money (Ed.), *Reading disability*. Baltimore: The John Hopkins Press, 1967.

MONROE, M., & ROGERS, B. *Foundations for reading: Informal pre-reading procedures*. Chicago: Scott, Foresman & Co., 1964.

MONTGOMERY, D. Teaching prereading skills through training in pattern recognition. *The Reading Teacher*, 1977, 30, 616–623.

MOYER, S. B., & NEWCOMER, P. L. Reversals in reading: Diagnosis and remediation. *Exceptional Children*, 1977, 43, 424–429.

OTTO, W., McMENEMY, R. A., & SMITH, R. J. *Corrective and remedial teaching* (2nd ed.). Boston: Houghton Mifflin Co., 1973.

PAGE, W. D. Semantic acceptability and semantic change. In P. D. Allen & D. J. Watson (Eds.), *Findings of research in miscue analysis: Classroom implications*. Urbana, Ill.: National Council of Teachers of English, 1976.

PEARSON, P. D. A psycholinguistic model of reading. *Language Arts*, 1976, 53, 309–314.

PERFETTI, C. A., & HOGABOAM, T. Relationship between single word decoding and reading comprehension skill. *Journal of Educational Psychology*, 1975, 67, 461–469.

PROE, S., & WADE, D. *The effects of contingent praise upon the achievement of a junior high school student in oral reading accuracy in probes above functional grade level*. 1973. (ERIC Document)

QUANDT, I. J. *Teaching reading: A human process*. Chicago: Rand McNally College Publishing Co., 1977.

RISKO, V. J. Differential auditory discrimination skills as related to reading achievement (Doctoral dissertation, West Virginia University, 1972). *Dissertation Abstracts International*, 1972, 32, 3571A-3572A. (Xerox University Microfilms No. 72-5144)

RISKO, V. J. *Teaching-testing module of auditory discrimination*. San Rafael, Calif.: Academic Therapy Publications, 1975.

RISKO, V. J., & DEGLER, L. S. *Concept development for the mainstreamed sensory impairment children*. Nashville, Tenn.: George Peabody College for Teachers, 1979. (ERIC Document)

ROBERTS, M., & SMITH, D. D. The relationship among correct and error oral reading rates and comprehension. *Learning Disability Quarterly*, 1980, 3, 54–64.

ROBINSON, H. M. *Why pupils fail in reading*. Chicago: The University of Chicago Press, 1946.

ROZIN, P., PORITSKY, T., & SOTSKY, R. American children with reading problems can easily learn to read English represented by Chinese characters. *Science*, 1971, 171, 1264–1267.

SAMUELS, S. J. Recognition of flashed words by children. *Child Development*, 1970, 41, 1089–1094.

SAMUELS, S. J. Success and failure in learning to read: A critique of the research. In F. B. Davis (Ed.), *The literature of research with emphasis on models*. New Brunswick, N.J.: Graduate School of Education, Rutgers State University, 1971.

SAMUELS, S. J. The method of repeated readings. *The Reading Teacher*, 1979, 32, 403–408.

SEMEL, E. M. *Sound-order-sense: A developmental program in auditory perception*. Chicago: Follett Educational Corporation, 1970.

SEMEL, E. M. *Semel auditory processing program*. Chicago: Follett Educational Corporation, in press.

SHANKWEILER, D., & LIBERMAN, I. Misreading: A search for cues. In J. F. Kavanagh & I. C. Mattingly (Eds.), *Language by ear and eye: The relationship between speech and reading*. Cambridge, Mass.: The M.I.T. Press, 1972.

SILVAROLI, N. J. *Classroom reading inventory* (2nd ed.). Dubuque, Iowa: William C. Brown Co., 1973.

SMITH, D. D. The improvement of children's oral reading through the use of teacher modeling. *Journal of Learning Disabilities*, 1979, 12, 172–175.

SMITH, F. *Understanding reading: A psycholinguistic analysis of reading and learning to read*. New York. Holt, Rinehart & Winston, 1971.

Smith, N. B. *Reading instruction for today's children.* Englewood Cliffs, N.J.: Prentice-Hall, 1963.

Spache, G. D. *Diagnostic reading scales* (revised ed.). Monterey, Calif.: California Test Bureau, 1972.

Spache, G. D. *Diagnosing and correcting reading disabilities.* Boston: Allyn & Bacon, 1976.

Stauffer, R. G. *Directing the reading-thinking process.* New York: Harper & Row, 1975.

Tinker, M. A., & McCullough, C. M. *Teaching elementary reading* (4th ed.). Englewood Cliffs, N.J.: Prentice-Hall, 1975.

Tortelli, J. P. Simplified psycholinguistic diagnosis. *The Reading Teacher*, 1976, *29*, 637–639.

Tucker, D. L. Improving classroom reading instruction. *Practical Applications of Research*, 1979, *1*, 4–5.

VanEtten, G. A look at reading comprehension. *Journal of Learning Disabilities*, 1978, *11*, 30–39.

Vaughan, S., Crawley, S., & Mountain, L. A multiple-modality approach to word study: Vocabulary scavenger hunts. *The Reading Teacher*, 1979, *32*, 434–437.

Vellutino, F. R., Smith, H., Steger, J. A., & Kaman, M. Reading disability: Age differences and the perceptual-deficit hypothesis. *Child Development*, 1975, *46*, 487–493.

Vogel, S. A. *Syntactic abilities in normal and dyslexic children.* Baltimore: University Park Press, 1975.

Vogel, S. A. Morphological ability in normal and dyslexic children. *Journal of Learning Disabilities*, 1977, *10*, 35–43.

Waechter, M. A methodology for a functional analysis of the relationship between oral reading and comprehension in beginning readers (Doctoral dissertation, University of Oregon, 1972). *Dissertation Abstracts International*, 1973, *33*, 4992A. (Xerox University Microfilms No. 73-7973)

Walker, C. M. High frequency word list for grades 3 through 9. *The Reading Teacher*, 1979, *32*, 803–812.

Wepman, J. M. Auditory discrimination, speech and reading. *The Elementary School Journal*, 1960, *60*, 325–333.

White, R. T. Research into learning hierarchies. *Review of Educational Research*, 1973, *43*, 361–375.

Wiig, E. H., & Semel, E. M. Productive language abilities in learning disabled adolescents. *Journal of Learning Disabilities*, 1975, *8*, 578–586.

Woodcock, R. W., & Clark, C. L. *Peabody rebus reading program.* Circle Pines, Minn.: American Guidance Service, 1969.

Wylie, R. E., & Durrell, D. D. Teaching vowels through phonograms. *Elementary English*, 1970, *47*, 787–791.

10 WRITTEN COMMUNICATION

Writing—transmitting thoughts onto paper—is a very important skill, particularly during school years. As a youngster progresses through school, writing changes from an academic target for instruction to a skill that teachers assume students possess. In later school years, students are required to write in ever-increasing amounts. Proof of their learning advanced academic subjects often rests upon their ability to communicate in writing. Once young adults leave school, however, the necessity for proficient written communication greatly decreases. Even simple forms of written communication (letter writing) have almost been replaced by the telephone. Although one could debate the actual importance of written communication and the emphasis schools place on it, writing remains an important component of school success. Until such time as the entire educational curriculum is altered substantially, teachers must continue to concern themselves with the acquisition, proficiency, and maintenance of their students' writing abilities.

Many learning disabled youngsters are deficient in writing. They have the skills necessary to communicate to others in a satisfactory way, but they have difficulty transmitting their thoughts in a logical, orderly, or presentable fashion when required to write. These students can learn to use this form of communication, but direct and concentrated instruction must be given if they are to become proficient. In this chapter, various means of communication (handwriting and typing), mechanics of writing (spelling, capitalization, grammar), composition (functional and creative writing), and survival writing (dictation, business and life related writing) are discussed.

MEANS OF WRITTEN COMMUNICATION

This section is devoted to the foundation skill of written communication: the formation of letters and symbols. There are various means of putting information into the written mode. In school, handwriting is the most commonly used form, but typing is gaining in popularity and use in adult life and in school. Since some learning disabled persons are not able to gain proficiency in letter formation, and because their handicap often becomes more apparent when handwriting is required, some information about typing instruction is included.

Prewriting Skills   Before children learn to write letters and symbols, they must possess some prerequisite skills. Information about attention, motor, visual, and perceptual skills was provided in Chapter 6. In addition, other skills should be mastered before (or taught concurrently with) handwriting. Many children come to school already possessing these skills; others do not.

Miller and Schneider (1970) identified a number of skills they believe to be prerequisite to freehand printing. They believe that a child must be able to hold a pencil correctly, draw straight lines at different angles, draw curved lines at different angles, draw freehand lines, and draw a variety of shapes in which lines are joined and crossed at specific points. LeBrun and Van de Craen (1975) add spatial orientation and directional sense to the above list. It is important, for example, for students to understand the concepts of left to right sequencing, up and down, and around. It is possible to teach these concepts concurrently with letter formation, but instruction proceeds most efficiently if they are already mastered. Table 10.1 lists many prewriting skills and offers suggested activities that might facilitate their acquisition.

Before handwriting instruction is actually initiated, the teacher must determine the handedness of each student. Although only 11 percent of the population is left-handed, accommodations must be made for those who are. For example, when writing at a blackboard, the right-handed student stands to the left and the left-handed student to the right of the letters or symbols being written. The left-handed student should place the top of the paper in a clockwise position (to the right), while the right-handed child should place the paper square to the body or turned slightly to the left. Since the writing motion for left-handed persons requires them to push rather than pull their pens, care must be taken to find a pen with a point that moves easily across paper. Left-handed youngsters should not be allowed to cup their hands over the letters being formed; first because this is not a comfortable position and second because it impairs later speed and proficiency. Enstrom (1968) even suggests that during the initial period of handwriting instruction, left-handed students be separated from right-handed students to avoid unnecessary confusion. Regardless of the precautions taken, it is important for teachers to be aware of the handedness of their students and plan instruction accordingly.

Some students have difficulty holding a pencil correctly; their hands

Table 10.1

Prehandwriting skills and related activities

Targets	Activities
Gross writing movements	Fingerpainting Painting with a brush Coloring Practicing writing movements in sand or on sand- paper with finger
Hold a stylus	Painting Coloring Scribbling with a pencil Writing on a magic slate
Draw straight and curved lines at different angles	Use geometric templates Tracing Copying
Draw freehand lines	Joining two preprinted places on paper (travel from the house to the school) Dot-to-dot exercises
Left to right sequence	Drawing lines from go sign to stop sign Block designs

slip too far down. Turnbull and Schulz (1979) suggest that a grip be placed on a pencil for students with poor motor abilities. A ball of clay or piece of sponge molded around the pencil approximately three-quarters of an inch from the pencil point might help students with this problem. Other students with minor motor problems find that writing with larger pencils is easier than writing with standard sized pencils. Teachers should allow students to find and use the size most comfortable for them until later, when their fine motor skills are better developed.

Once a child possesses the skills listed in Table 10.1 and can manipulate a crayon, pencil, or pen with purpose and control, he or she is ready to begin handwriting instruction.

Manuscript

As with many areas in education, a long debate has raged about the necessity of teaching manuscript writing. Although it is relatively easy to teach to young children and does more closely match the print that appears in basal readers, it is a skill that is taught and used for only a few years and then dropped from the curriculum. Long ago, Strauss and Lehtinen (1951) suggested that learning disabled students not be taught manuscript writing but instead learn only the cursive.

> *We have found it advantageous for several reasons to make an early start in teaching connected writing to the brain-injured child and to omit specific instruction in the manuscript form. The perceptual disturbances of the brain-injured child act as a definite handicap in ac-*

*ceptably spacing letters and words. Perception of a word form as a
unified whole is aided when the letters of the word are actually joined
to form a whole. Connected or cursive writing also seems to lend itself
more effectively to developing a kinesthetic perception of word forms.*
(p. 187)

Another reason for not teaching disabled students to write using manuscript is some students' propensity to reverse letters. Because of the way
letters are formed and joined in cursive writing, the opportunity for making
reversals is reduced. The frequency of writing a letter *b* backwards in the
cursive form is substantially lower than printing a *b* in reverse. The confusion between *b* and *d*, and *p* and *q* is not as common when using the cursive
means of writing because the letters have more definitive characteristics.

One other reason for not teaching manuscript printing to academically
deficient youngsters is efficiency of learning and instruction. Why spend
time teaching a skill that soon is discontinued from the school curriculum?
For students who have a difficult time mastering academic tasks, might it not
be more beneficial to spend classroom instructional time on the skill expected in the later school years? Unfortunately, special education teachers
do not control the curriculum, and many (particulary those assigned to resource rooms) have no choice about whether manuscript is taught. It is part
of the regular curriculum and is a skill regular education teachers expect of
their students. In these cases, the special education teacher must help learning disabled students learn to write using the manuscript mode.

Manuscript instruction. When manuscript must be taught, some general
guidelines should be followed. Fauke, Burnett, Powers, and Sulzer-Azaroff
(1973) suggest that students first be able to identify letters orally by using
letter names, then be able to trace over letters using their index finder, then
a magic marker, and then a pencil. After they are able to trace over letters,
they should copy letters from a model made by the teacher. Finally, they are
required to print letters without a model. Once letters in isolation are
formed correctly, instruction on letter spacing to form words is initiated.
Salzberg, Wheeler, Devar, and Hopkins (1971) suggest a similar instructional sequence, but feel that letters should be grouped by form (straight line
letters are taught concurrently, curved letters are clustered). They found
that adding corrective feedback (including a teacher demonstration) and
reinforcement for correct letters served to quickly reduce the number of
errors made and facilitated maintenance.

Once letter formation is acquired, students should become proficient
in writing. Hopkins, Schutte, and Garton (1971) found that free-time reinforcement enhanced first graders' printing proficiency. In their study, a
fifty-minute printing period was scheduled. As soon as a child finished the
assignment and it was scored and corrected, the remainder of the time was
free. Gradually, the writing period was shortened. To receive free time the
students had to write faster. At the conclusion of the study, their mean
correct rate improved to 11.5 letters per minute.

Manuscript evaluation.   Evaluation of handwriting can be laborious, often subjective, and therefore not very reliable. The teacher should establish rules for evaluating students' printing and consistently apply them. For instance, if slant or writing within the lines is important to readers of the students' written work, that should be included in the evaluation. Certainly correct letter formation is a central issue and must be given proper consideration. Some teachers grade each letter written and give a point for each salient feature. Stowitschek (1978) suggests that the following dimensions of letter formation be included in the evaluation process: width, height, position, shape, alignment with baseline, line correction, and slant. To facilitate

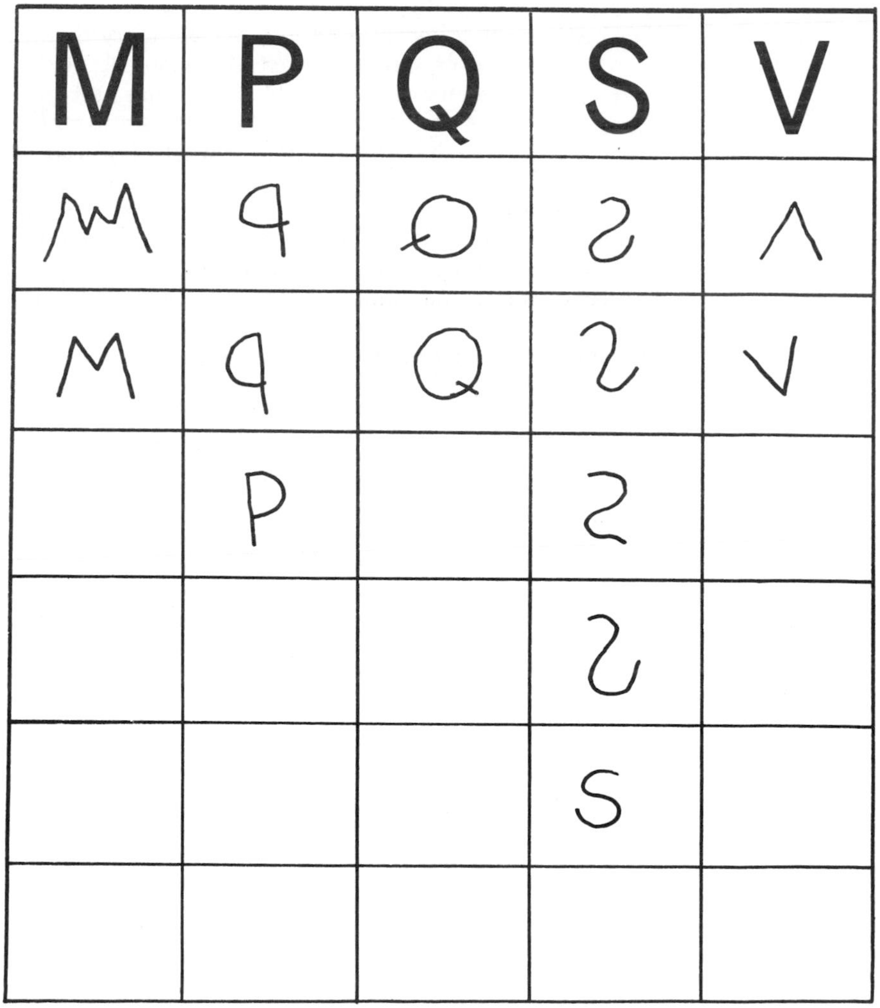

Figure 10.1   A sample of a worksheet suggested by Stowitschek and Stowitschek (1979) that incorporates practice and self-evaluation.

in the evaluation of manuscript letters, Helwig, Johns, Norman, and Cooper (1976) developed a set of overlays that silhouette the correct letter. If a student's letter falls within the space outlined on the overlay, it is counted as correct. Overlays can be made rather easily by using clear transparency acetate. Using such a system facilitates the evaluation process and guarantees consistency.

Several authors suggest that students be taught to evaluate their own and classmates' writing. Jones, Trap, and Cooper (1977) taught young children to use overlays to evaluate each other's writing. Stowitschek and Stowitschek (1979) developed a system that combines writing practice and self-evaluation, using preprinted worksheets. In the first row, model letters are provided for the student to copy. In the second row, the student prints the appropriate letter. In the next row, the student only prints letters incorrectly formed above. A sample worksheet is shown in Figure 10.1. The Stowitschek and Stowitschek system has several advantages. The student works independently and self-monitors work produced. Teacher time is saved because a final check is necessary only at the completion of a worksheet, rather than continual monitoring of a student's work.

It is advisable to establish a criterion for manuscript writing, both for accuracy and proficiency. According to the information provided by Hopkins, Schutte, and Garton (1971) and Mercer (1979), a desired rate of eleven to twenty letters per minute should serve as an indication of acceptable proficiency for the early elementary grades. Because of the enormous amount of teacher time that can be spent evaluating students' handwriting performances, teachers should follow the suggestions of Stowitschek and Stowitschek, and Jones et al. to teach youngsters to evaluate their own and others' writing.

Reversals.   Because written reversals are most predominant when students print, discussion about the remediation of reversals was placed in this section. It is important for teachers to remember that most young children make reversals when first learning to write. This is part of the normal developmental process and should not be viewed as unacceptable. Several early studies of young children's academic performance clearly indicate that reversals correlate with age (the younger the student, the higher the probability of reversals in written work). Davidson (1934, 1935) and Hildreth (1934) demonstrated that with increasing maturity and experience, children's frequency of reversing letters and symbols decreased. In those studies, practically all kindergarten children confused *b* and *d,* and *q* and *p.* This tendency was still prevalent among first graders, but to a lesser degree. Whether these data suggest that no direct remediation efforts should be initiated until second grade has not been answered through research. Logically, it seems that teachers should not adopt a laissez-faire attitude about reversals in young children, and should at least provide corrective feedback when they occur. On the other hand, referral to a class for learning disabled students merely because a kindergartener reverses letters does not seem reasonable either.

A substantial amount of literature is available indicating that reversal problems in students' written work can be remediated through direct instructional techniques. Through modeling and corrective feedback, Stromer (1975, 1977) remediated several students' number and letter reversal tendencies. Hasazi and Hasazi (1972) remediated a student's digit reversals (writing 21 for 12) through an ignoring and praising procedure. Smith and Lovitt (1973) remediated a boy's b/d reversal problem by showing him an error (written by the teacher on an index card) and instructing the boy not to write a *b* for a *d*. One interesting feature of this study is the finding that, at least for this child, the frequency of reversals related to the position the letter had in the word (initial, medial, or final). During instruction, they targeted for remediation the letter (d) and the position (initial) most frequently in error. As that letter in that position was corrected, the student's pervasive b/d reversal problem was eliminated.

More recently, Deno and Chiang (1979) demonstrated that letter reversals can be ameliorated through the use of reinforcement contingencies. They believe that "reversal errors can be explained in educational rather than neurological terms" (p. 45). Certainly the data available indicate that teachers should try direct remediation efforts with students who have a tendency to reverse letters or numbers.

Cursive Writing   Whether students begin learning to write using the manuscript or cursive mode seems to be more of an administrative decision than one based on empirical findings. In some school districts, children first learn to print. In others, manuscript is not presented and students begin their writing experiences with the cursive form. There is not a definite instructional sequence that begins with manuscript writing and terminates with mastery of the cursive system. When manuscript is taught first, usually instruction on cursive begins in the middle of the second grade. Regardless, there is no evidence that mastery of manuscript writing is a prerequisite to success in learning the cursive form.

As with all other academic areas, there are at least three stages of learning that teachers must address when teaching students to write: acquisition, proficiency, and maintenance. A substantial amount of time is spent in schools teaching students how to write using the cursive system. Children spend hours practicing correct letter formation. Once the skill is acquired, however, teachers must help students become proficient. Youngsters must be able to write fast enough to be able to complete assignments in other academic areas (history, social studies, literature). If a student is not proficient in writing skills, other subject areas will suffer. For example, if a student is too slow in forming letters, dictation is an impossible task. Spelling assignments are unfinished, possibly not because of a spelling deficiency, but due to a writing deficiency. Therefore, information included in the next section is divided by tactics facilitating acquisition of handwriting skills and those aiming at increased proficiency.

Cursive instruction.   A number of tactics have been used historically to help students learn to write. Although not intrinsically motivating, tracing, copying, and practice seem to be the most commonly used traditional methods. Because tracing and copying tend not to hold the interest of young children, Birnbrauer, Bijou, Wolf, and Kidder (1965) used a token reinforcement system to enhance motivation. When drill and practice are used, the addition of a reinforcement system can certainly prove beneficial.

Trap, Milner-Davis, Joseph, and Cooper (1978) suggest that writing instruction incorporate the following components: modeling, copying, feedback, rewriting of errors, and rewards. In their study, the teacher modeled the correct letter formation (through demonstration and leaving a permanent model for the students). The students were then required to write the letter(s). The teacher again provided corrective feedback, including a redemonstration of error letters, and the students rewrote those letters formed incorrectly the first time. Rewards or reinforcement were given for correct letter production.

Towle (1978) offers a ten-part instructional sequence for handwriting instruction:

1. Copy straight lines.

2. Copy curved lines.

3. Copy letters from a model in close proximity to the student.

4. Write letters from memory (after just seeing the correct formation).

5. Copy letters from a model placed at some distance from the student (on the blackboard).

6. Write letters from memory.

7. Copy letters sequenced in words from a model in close proximity to the student.

8. Copy letters sequenced in words from a model placed at some distance from the student.

9. Copy sentences in close proximity to the student.

10. Copy sentences from a model placed at some distance from the student.

Some researchers (Towle, 1978) suggest that letters be taught in clusters; letters with common characteristics (swing up, swing over) are taught as units. Hansen and her colleagues (Hansen, 1978), however, could not give validity to this system of letter presentation through their research, which found no pattern of how children acquired correct letter formation. There were no consistently troublesome letters, and no definite pattern of specific letters acquired first. All of her students learned to write, but each mastered letters in a different order.

Hansen describes a five-level cursive writing program developed at the Experimental Education Unit of the University of Washington:

1. Say letter names (and print them if the child knows how).

2. Write lowercase letters.

3.   Connect letters.

4.   Write capital letters.

5.   Write in context.

Each day while the program was in effect, the student wrote the alphabet. A maximum of five letters drawn from a pool of letters the student could not form legibly was taught and drilled daily. Once a letter was mastered (written legibly two out of three days), it was dropped from the daily list and another one added. If a student mastered a letter without direct instruction, it was no longer included in the pool of letters from which the daily lists were drawn. Connecting letters and writing sentences were taught in a similar fashion.

There are other, less comprehensive tactics teachers have used to help children acquire legible handwriting. For example, students who do not use the correct slant often are given writing paper with slant indicators pre-printed on the page. Students who have a tendency to write too large are given paper on which the top lines are some distance apart; as the child works down the page the distance between the lines decreases, forcing the student to write smaller. Space gauges can be placed on a writing worksheet to help students judge the appropriate width of letters and the proper space to be left between words.

When specific letters are in error, teachers often resort to the "copy-cover-write" technique as a form of error drill. Other times an index card with problem letters correctly formed is taped to the student's desk so the student can have a referent as writing assignments are produced. For students who have a direction problem, arrows and starting indicators can be added to the index card.

The techniques just described are appropriate when students need to learn how to correctly form letters and symbols. As mentioned earlier, this is not sufficient. Students must be able to write quickly enough to keep up with class assignments and take dictation. Therefore, once legibility is no longer of concern, quality and quantity (proficiency) must become the target. In addition to the proficiency tactics described in Chapter 4, several other procedures are available. Hansen suggests a "Beat Your Rate" game, which incorporates feedback and self-charting of student progress. Carter and Synolds (1974) feel that one reason why learning disabled students' handwriting is neither legible nor proficient is tension; some students try too hard. By helping these students to relax, both legibility and speed of writing improved.

Towle concurs; fluency (or proficiency) is important. Through repeated practice she helped students achieve proficient rates of performance. She suggests setting fifty letters per minute as the desired rate, and had her students practice "The quick brown fox jumps over the lazy dog."

Cursive evaluation.   When acquisition is the target, correct percentage scores give an indication of accuracy. Also, letters can be scored independently—each worth a set number of points—to obtain a frequency count per letter. Once mastery is achieved, evaluation of that letter is discontinued and another letter chosen as the target. Letters can be evaluated on a number of dimensions: slant, formation, ending, connectives, and spacing. The teacher should decide what dimensions and what criteria should be established. Once they are set, however, consistency must reign. To facilitate reliable and consistent evaluation, Trap et al. used plastic overlays to judge letter formation. This not only produced consistent measurement, but also allowed others to grade the students' work (aides, outside observers, other students).

When proficient handwriting is of concern, rate is the appropriate measurement system to apply. Words, rather than each letter, can be evaluated. Unfortunately, there are no guidelines on the number of words per minute children should be able to write legibly if they are to be considered proficient writers. Towle suggests fifty letters per minute as an aim. Mercer (1979) states that twenty-five letters per minute for first graders, forty letters for third graders, and eighty-eight letters for sixth graders might be used as desired scores. If the words average five letters in length, a rate of eight words per minute could be expected of third grade students.

Typing

So far, researchers have not carefully studied typing instruction and the learning disabled youngster. It does seem sensible that typing instruction be offered to normal learners. At what point typing instruction should be initiated is not known. Many learning disabled persons avoid tasks requiring them to write because they find handwriting laborious, difficult, and the product unpleasing. As stated earlier, some learning disabled persons' handicap is not apparent until their handwriting is observed. Some individuals select careers that do not require them to write, not because their interests direct them to those occupations, but because they seek to avoid writing. Typing is a good alternative, particularly for those students whose motor skills are deficient. Some (Davis, 1971; Davis & Brownlee, 1977) even suggest that spelling skills improve if typing is used as the means of written communication.

Some typing programs are available for use by late elementary and middle school students. At least one was specially developed for middle school and includes evaluation procedures (rate and accuracy) in the program (Wanous & Haggblade, 1971). The selection of typing programs that include evaluation (both accuracy and rate) criteria could prove useful for learning disabled students.

MECHANICS OF WRITTEN COMMUNICATION

Possessing manuscript, cursive, or typing skills certainly does not guarantee proficiency in written communication. They are only the means by which information is put onto paper. When at least one has been mastered, instruction can be initiated on the mechanics of written communication: the way words are put together to communicate with others.

Unfortunately, mastery of oral communication does not ensure mastery of written communication. Although the basic rules used to communicate orally are the same as those for writing, tolerance for incorrect usage is

Some students' handwriting will never be legible or proficient. For these youngsters, teachers should consider including typing in their instructional programs.

greater in oral communication. When words are put on paper, correct spelling, grammar, and punctuation, variation in sentence construction, and some consistency in style are expected. The youngster's writing shown in Figure 10.2 shows phonetic spelling and grammar correlated to his oral language. This youngster grew up in the Ozark region of Missouri, and his written communication abilities reflect his regional upbringing. Regardless of where individuals are from, they are expected to use standard English in their written communication. The mechanics of written communication are fairly precise, and the demands on the learner are considerable.

Spelling

Spelling is a difficult subject area for most youngsters because standard English does not follow consistent rules. There seem to be as many exceptions as there are rules. In fact, through a comprehensive research project, the frequency of specific grapheme-phoneme relationships was studied and data are now available on which spelling patterns are most common (Hanna, Hodges, & Hanna, 1971). Suggestions have even been considered about revamping the spelling curriculum to correspond with these data. Regardless, there is a tradition in spelling instruction that has been followed for a number of years. A critical part of that tradition is the spelling workbook. Although a number of different publishers have their own versions, they are remarkably similar. A list, usually twenty to twenty-five words, is generally presented on Monday. Every day a different type of exercise is followed (one day a paragraph with the new words is read and dissected, dictionary and phonetic spellings are practiced another day). The weekly culminating experience usually is a Friday test. Such has been the practice for years, and probably will remain so. There are several reasons for retaining the *status quo*. First, for many youngsters the procedure works and they become better spellers. Second, at least thirty minutes of the school day is planned for the teacher; the lesson plan and student materials are provided.

Many youngsters, particularly learning disabled students, do not seem

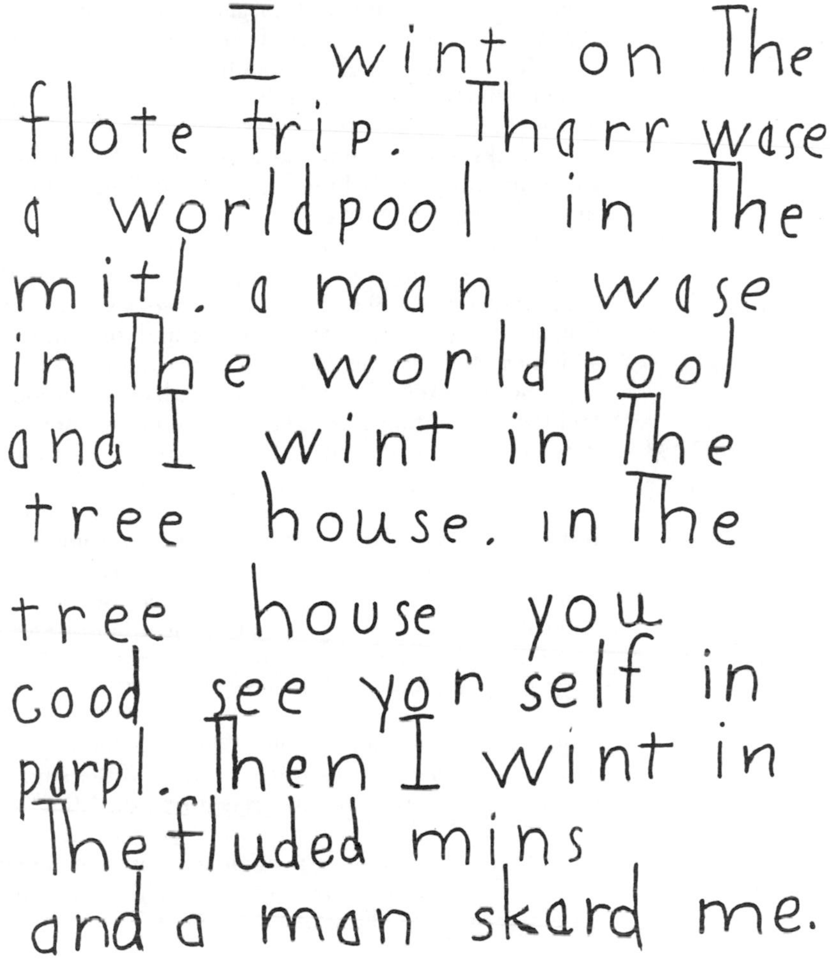

I wint on The
flote trip. Tharr wase
a worldpool in The
mitl. a man wase
in The worldpool
and I wint in The
tree house. in The
tree house you
cood see yor self in
parpl. Then I wint in
The fluded mins
and a man skard me.

Figure 10.2   A sample of a youngster's writing that reflects his oral language dialect.

to learn through this traditional group method. There are some interesting
facts about how learning disabled students spell. Holmes and Peper (1977)
hypothesized that learning disabled students (retarded readers) make different kinds of spelling errors (confusing letter orders, reversals) than normal
readers. In their study, however, although the poor readers made more
spelling errors, the types of errors made were not different. This might
indicate that a different approach to spelling instruction is not necessary, but
that more concentrated efforts are warranted.

Spelling instruction.   There are two general categories for spelling remediation. One involves an adaptation of the traditional approach; the other
requires the teacher to develop specialized instructional sequences for his or
her particular students. The first option is certainly more desirable and for

many spellers is sufficient to gain the desired results. Those procedures involving modifying the standard curriculum are presented first.

In several studies, researchers used standard spelling workbooks and added reinforcement procedures to encourage students to study harder and get higher Friday test scores. Sidman (1979), for example, used group and individual reinforcement contingencies with middle school students. When free time was provided for improved spelling test scores, accuracy increased (more during the group contingency conditions). In a now well-known study, Lovitt, Guppy, and Blattner (1969) modified traditional spelling procedures by giving a spelling test four days a week (Tuesday through Friday). Once a student received 100 percent on that week's word list, he or she was excused from spelling the rest of the week and that time could be spent in free activities. A substantial increase in the number of perfect papers was noted.

Reith, Axelrod, Anderson, Hathaway, Wood, and Fitzgerald (1974) feel that presenting students with twenty or more words at one time is too difficult for some students. They modified the traditional approach by presenting five to six words each day. Scores on the overall Friday tests dramatically improved when this distributed practice procedure was in effect. Axelrod and Paluska (1975) also presented only a small number of words daily. A test of six different words was given daily. When a behavior game procedure was implemented (see group contingency section of Chapter 5 for details), and half the room competed against the other half for reinforcement, spelling improved remarkably.

Foxx and Jones (1978) demonstrated the effectiveness of an overcorrection procedure in reducing the number of errors made during spelling. During the experimental conditions, Wednesday and Friday spelling tests were given. Those words missed required the student to go through a positive practice overcorrection procedure consisting of five parts: provide the correct spelling of the error word; provide its correct phonetic spelling; indicate its part of speech; provide its complete dictionary definition; and use that word correctly in five sentences. This was done with each word missed on either of the spelling tests. Needless to say, spelling errors were drastically reduced.

Broden, Beasley, and Hall (1978) utilized a different tactic, one which did not require the teacher to alter any of his or her routines. In this study, the boys' mother served as a tutor. Each day, the boys were drilled on the weeks' spelling word list, using both oral and written drill. The mother used systematic praise and feedback, which resulted in improved weekly spelling test scores (mean of baseline was 41 percent; mean of intervention condition was 94 percent) and better retention on a follow-up test.

Other researchers found that for some students a modification of the traditional spelling approach is not sufficient and more drastic means are necessary. All of the procedures discussed next require that new and special word lists be developed. Many of these procedures, however, can be modified to fit into the standard spelling format if a teacher so desires. Kauffman and his colleagues believe that for children over the mental age of five, imitation functions as a decoloration tactic. In one study (Kauffman, Hallahan, Haas, Brame, & Boren, 1978), they demonstrated that modeling combined with imitation of the student's error serves to decrease errors. Each week the students in their study were given ten words they did not know how to spell. During the imitation conditions, the teacher told the children which words were spelled incorrectly, showed them the correct spelling (on an index card written by the teacher), and then demonstrated how to spell the words correctly. This tactic, reminiscent of the one used by Smith and Lovitt (1973) to remediate a boy's b/d reversals, caused a substantial increase in spelling accuracy.

Stowitschek and Jobes (1977) helped deficient spellers acquire and retain new words through a modeling, drill, and praise procedure. For each word on the abbreviated spelling list, the teacher followed certain steps. First, she told the student the name of the word and then used it in a sentence. She spelled the word out loud for the child, then showed the child a card with the word written on it. Pointing to each letter, the teacher spelled the word again. The child then spelled the word out loud, and wrote it on the blackboard. Acquisition and retention were excellent.

Hansen (1978) describes a procedure involving the use of flow (rather than fixed) word lists. In other words, once a student masters a specific word, that word is dropped from the daily word list and a new word replaces it. One advantage of using this system is that it ensures that students truly master each word rather than moving on to a new set of words each week regardless of performance. During the first phase of the teaching system she describes, a cover-copy-compare procedure was used that effectively produced accuracy about two-thirds of the time. When that procedure did not produce mastery of specific words, a contingency for errors (write the word ten times) and a language master technique were implemented.

Rosendal (1968) offers a creative solution to some students' specific spelling problems. Often, only specific words present consistent difficulties. He suggests that rebuses or pictures could serve as mnemonic aids to facilitate retention of specific words. One such example is shown in Figure 10.3. The diverse number of possibilities for spelling pictures might well add some fun and creativity to an otherwise often laborious subject area.

Although not a spelling tactic per se, one auxiliary skill students should master can help them find correct word spellings. Children should learn how to alphabetize and use the dictionary. This allows them to look up words they do not know how to spell or use correctly. Convenient spellers are also available that allow students to find correct spellings of words quickly.

Figure 10.3   A rebus of *cup* designed to help students spell this specific word.

Spelling evaluation. Spelling performances usually are evaluated by correct percentage scores. Because the teacher normally controls the rate of dictation and therefore the student's rate of production, rate is not an appropriate measure of student's spelling performance.

Spelling, capitalization, grammar, punctuation, and word division are all mechanical components of written communication. Only the first, however, has received systematic attention from researchers interested in the remediation of learning disabled children's academic deficiencies. Although teachers must meet their students' needs in these other areas as well, few guidelines are available from the research literature. Therefore, some guidelines are provided in the remaining segments of this section on the mechanics of written communication. The reader should refer back to the two chapters on generic intervention strategies (Chapters 4 and 5) for information about procedures that might facilitate improvement of students' writing mechanics.

Capitalization

The purpose of using capital letters is to distinguish proper nouns and adjectives from common nouns and adjectives, and to indicate the beginning of new sentences, salutations, and direct quotations. The rules for capitalizing the first letter in specific words are straightforward and should be the simplest mechanical form for disabled students to learn. Unfortunately, these youngsters are deficient in this skill area because the rules are not taught to them. If systematically taught, this skill should be mastered by most learning disabled youngsters.

Grammar

This is probably the most difficult component of the mechanics of written communication. Although the rules of grammar are generally followed, the number of exceptions and variations is enormous. Even bright, academically talented youngsters often do not truly master these skills until early adulthood. Regardless, if learning disabled students are to compete in regular education classes (particularly at the high school level), grammar instruction must be included in their curriculum.

A number of different subskills must be mastered in grammar. Learning the parts of speech (identification and use of nouns, pronouns, verbs, adjectives, adverbs, conjunctions, prepositions, and interjections) is usually the first topic of instruction. Instruction on sentence construction, phrases, and clauses can then be initiated. Students must master the rules of verb/noun agreement and become proficient in the use of simple, compound, and complex sentence construction.

Some learning disabled students will never completely master the complicated variations of grammar. To expect it is unrealistic and not even advisable. Some students, however, who are capable of learning advanced writing skills are not afforded the opportunity because the curriculum for most learning disabled students does not include the mechanics of writing. For those students who are capable, instruction should be provided (possibly a regular education English teacher could help modify the standard material available). For most learning disabled students, the teacher should include elementary grammar in the instructional program. The development of simple and compound sentences and questions using fairly standard formats could be taught so that these youngsters have some means of written communication.

Punctuation
In line with the above discussion, some simple rules of punctuation should be taught. Certainly the use of periods, question marks, and commas could become part of the instructional sequence without much difficulty. Whether all learning disabled students can master the use of the colon and semicolon is doubtful. But, again, if instruction is never provided, these skills will not be learned.

Word Division
To divide words at the end of a line correctly, a dictionary or speller must be used frequently. This requires the ability to alphabetize (certainly an important survival skill and one that must be taught). Students who do not or cannot use a dictionary should be taught not to break words at the end of a line but to always begin a new line of writing with a complete word.

COMPOSITION

Students do not master written communication if they are not required to write. Although writing is not as important in today's society as it once was, it is still a vital process used in daily life. Writing essays is not the typical leisure pastime of most Americans. In some professions, however, it is a requirement, and for success in school it is a necessity. To write in composition format, a means of written communication must be selected and the mechanics of writing employed. In Figure 10.4 a high school senior's handicap is particularly apparent because of faulty mechanical elements in his written communication.

A norm-referenced test of written language is available (Hammill & Larsen, 1978) that directly measures students' writing abilities by utilizing both contrived and spontaneous writing samples to assess students' performance levels in the following areas: vocabulary, thematic maturity, thought units, handwriting, spelling, word usage, and style. The test areas could easily be transformed into instructional areas for those who wish to develop their own instructional sequence in the area of written communication.

Two general areas of composition are discussed here: functional composition and creative writing. As with the areas described above, little research is available on these topics. A few studies have been conducted indicating that mildly handicapped students can learn to compose.

Functional Composition
In some cases, functional composition is assessed and evaluated by the student's ability to combine the skills acquired during means and mechanics instruction. Belch (1975) studied junior and senior high school students' abilities in essay writing by measuring grammatical errors, misspelled words, and errors in punctuation. The students were required to write about

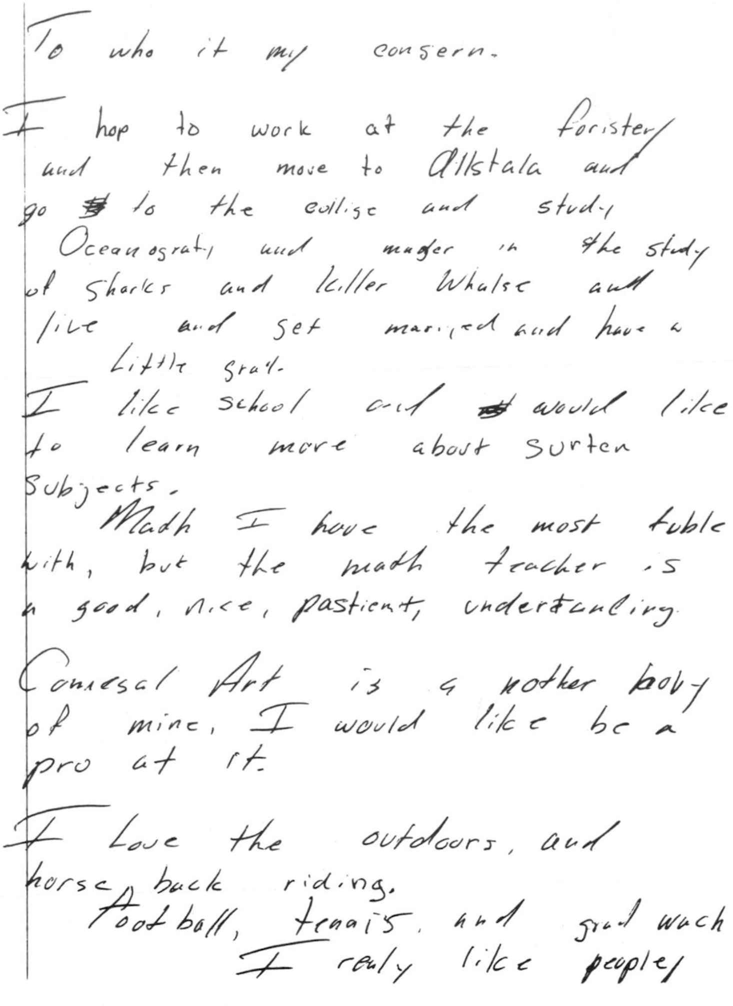

To who it my consern.

I hop to work at the foristery
and then move to Allstala and
go to the collise and study
Oceanograty and maner in the study
of sharks and killer Whalse and
live and get married and have a
little grall.
I like school and would like
to learn more about Surten
subjects.
Madh I have the most tuble
with, but the math teacher is
a good, nice, pastient, understanding.

Comiesal Art is a nother boby
of mine, I would like be a
pro at it.

I love the outdoors, and
horse, back riding.
football, tennis, and grul waching.
I realy like peoples

Figure 10.4   A sample of a high school senior's plans for after graduation.

the information covered in their reading assignment during a twenty-minute period each day. Instructions combined with point losses (response cost) caused improvement in their compositions.

Mortinger (1979) used letter legibility, sentence beginnings, and sentence length as his targets for improvement. He found that through systematic instruction the student's stories improved in content, creativity, and style. Ballard and Glynn (1975) used self-management techniques (self-assessment and self-scoring) as the primary intervention to cause improvement in third graders' story writing. The number of sentences, number of different action words, and number of different describing words were the targets. When free-time reinforcement was given for each target, story writing improved. The students graded their own writing performances (which saved substantial teacher time). Even for those students who were not reliable checkers, story-writing performance improved, as evaluated qualitatively by outside observers.

Fifth graders in a remedial class participated in a study aimed at enhancing the quality of student writing (Van Houten, Morrison, Jarvis, & McDonald, 1974). The students were given a topic to write about and were given points for improvement in three areas: number of words written, number of different words, and number of new words. Those variables improved during the reinforcement conditions. Although the students were not reinforced directly for quality, that improved also. Five dimensions were used to judge the quality of the students' stories: mechanical aspects (length, spelling, grammar, and punctuation); vocabulary (variety and word usage); number of ideas; development of ideas; and internal consistency of the story. On all dimensions, the students' story writing improved when the frequency in the three target areas increased.

Van Houten and his colleagues have spent some time researching the variables that serve to improve children's writing performances (Van Houten, Hill, & Parsons, 1975; Van Houten et al., 1974). Second, fourth, and fifth graders participated in their studies. Instead of using points or tokens as the intervention strategy, they utilized precise academic feedback and public posting of the children's scores. The children were told to beat their own writing rate (repetitious and nonsense sentences were not counted). In both studies, increased rate of writing correlated with improved quality of the children's stories. Through this research, some information about desired rate for story writing can be gleaned. During intervention, the second graders' mean writing rate was twelve words per minute; the fourth graders' averaged nine words per minute (one class achieved thirteen and the other five); and the fifth graders' mean was fourteen. Although no normed data are available, these mean scores might give some indication of acceptable limits.

Alley and Deshler (1979) refer to a carefully sequenced instructional program designed to teach junior and senior high school learning disabled students composition skills (*Writing to the point: Six basic steps,* by W. J. Kerrigan, 1974). Through this carefully structured program, students are taught to develop themes, topic sentences, well-developed paragraphs, and transitional sentences. The program begins at very elementary levels (starting with simple sentences) and systematically teaches students to write compositions. Using developed instructional programs or modifying existing ones might prove beneficial for teachers attempting to help their students gain proficiency in writing skills.

Creative Writing   The problems of defining creativity are not of concern here. Probably a better topic heading would be "Interesting Writing." In the pertinent, new studies available, remedial efforts do seem to be aimed at increasing novelty and interest. Difference and variation rather than creativity seem to be the key. In the Maloney and Hopkins study (1973), fourth, fifth, and sixth graders were given a topic noun and instructed to write a ten-sentence story.

Each student's story was rated and points were given for each of the following: each adjective, adverb, action verb, different sentence beginning, different adjective, different adverb, prepositional phrase, compound sentence, and sentences over eight words in length. The classes were divided into two teams, and a modified version of the good behavior game (see Chapter 5) was employed. The students competed against each other, and whichever team received the most points on a given day could leave for recess five minutes early. Interestingly, raters judged the students' writing subjectively to be more creative when the above variables were increased.

Glover and Sautter (1977) took a slightly different tack to improve the creative writing of junior and senior high school students. They define creativity as being composed of four different components: fluency (number of different responses, points, or illustrations); elaboration (number of words per response, point, or illustration); originality (responses different from classmates); and flexibility (number of different response forms: analogies, syntheses, comparisons). Reinforcement, practice, and instructions were given for each of the four components. Although all of the variables did change, elaboration was the most responsive and originality the least subject to improvement.

Some learning disabled students cannot reach this level of written communication. For them, mastery of simple, consistent, and rule-based writing is the aim. For a few, writing skills can be substantially enhanced, and interesting (possibly even creative) writing can be the goal of writing instruction.

SURVIVAL WRITING SKILLS

There are a number of writing skills all persons should possess if they are to cope successfully in everyday life. For many adults, the use of written communication markedly decreases once the school years are over. Some basic writing abilities, however, are required by society. If learning disabled students are to be independent adults, these skills must be mastered. Unfortunately, many of these writing skills are not taught in most school settings. Only a slight modification of the educational curriculum, however, is required for them to be included.

One writing skill that is very important in modern society is a signature. Not only must students learn to write their names, but they should also understand the implications of placing their signatures at the bottom of documents. Another commonly needed skill is check writing. This requires not only a signature, but also the ability to write dates and money amounts using both symbols and number names. Correct spelling of numbers often is not included in our educational curriculum, but it is a common requirement of daily life. The spelling of some numbers causes students particular difficulty. There is no reason why they could not be written down somewhere in the checkbook for reference. Some junior and senior high school learning disabilities teachers who use various token or reinforcement

This youngster is learning how to fill out a job application form. Continued instruction is necessary to teach the student how to fill out the form correctly and to remediate basic spelling and handwriting deficiencies.

systems have their students write checks to purchase free time and other privileges.

People must fill out various forms periodically (job applications, loan and credit applications). Most such forms require that the individual print (or type) his or her name, address, phone number, social security number, and employer's name and address. Job applications ask the individual to list former employers, personal references, and schools attended. Classroom instruction on how to fill out forms and applications is advisable, and certainly a worthwhile expenditure of instructional time. There are even commercially available workbooks for students to use to gain accuracy and some proficiency in these tasks (Kahn, Jew, & Tong, 1975). For many learning disabled youngsters, a prepared sheet listing all of their previous employers' names and addresses and other required information is helpful for completing various forms.

Being able to write simple letters and notes is very useful. Many learning disabled people have relatives and friends who live in other parts of the country and find that long-distance phone calls are too expensive. Being able to write simple notes and knowing the proper form to address envelopes are valuable skills.

Note taking is another related writing skill that is both useful and necessary. Being able to write down the time and place of various appointments is useful for success in daily life, as is taking down information over the phone, including directions to places of business or friends' homes. In school, being able to take notes during classes is essential for receiving passing grades.

SUMMARY

A number of components make up the overall skill of written communication. One must be able to use a means of writing proficiently. Whether the means chosen is printing (manuscript), cursive writing, or typing is not important. The critical issue is that at least one of these is mastered.

There are a number of mechanical components of written communication. Knowing the correct spelling of many words is important, as is the ability to find the correct spelling of difficult words, which requires recognizing when a word is not written correctly. Although many remedial programs spend a great deal of time on handwriting and spelling, mastery of those two skills does not guarantee proficiency in written communication. An individual must also be able to use the rules of capitalization, punctuation, grammar, and word division.

Written communication requires that people have something to write about and can translate thoughts and feelings into the written mode. For many learning disabled youngsters, desire and skills are not sufficient; as adults, they do not select this mode. In many cases, this is acceptable, for there are other even more efficient means of communicating. A number of survival skills, however, require writing (filling out job and other application forms, check writing). The mastery of survival writing skills is a necessity and must become a target of the educational system.

REFERENCES

ALLEY, G., & DESHLER, D. *Teaching the learning disabled adolescent: Strategies and methods.* Denver, Colo.: Love Publishing Co., 1979.

AXELROD, S., & PALUSKA, J. A component analysis of the effects of a classroom game on spelling performance. In E. Ramp & G. Semb (Eds.), *Behavior analysis: Areas of research and application.* Englewood Cliffs, N.J.: Prentice-Hall, 1975.

BALLARD, K. D., & GLYNN, T. Behavioral self-management in story writing with elementary school children. *Journal of Applied Behavior Analysis,* 1975, 8, 387–398.

BELCH, P. The effect of verbal instructions and instructions combined with point loss on the writing behavior of students. *School Applications of Learning Theory,* 1975, 8, 27–33.

BRODEN, M., BEASLEY, A., & HALL, R. V. In-class spelling performance: Effects of home tutoring by a parent. *Behavior Modification,* 1978, 2, 511–530.

BIRNBRAUER, J. S., BIJOU, S. W., WOLF, M. M., & KIDDER, J. D. Programmed instruction in the classroom. In L. Ullmann & L. Krasner (Eds.), *Case studies in behavior modification.* New York: Holt, Rinehart & Winston, 1965.

CARTER, J. L., & SYNOLDS, D. Effects of relaxation training upon handwriting quality. *Journal of Learning Disabilities,* 1974, 7, 236–238.

DAVIDSON, H. P. A study of reversals in young children. *Journal of Genetic Psychology,* 1934, 45, 452–465.

DAVIDSON, H. P. A study of the confusing letters b, d, p, and q. *Journal of Genetic Psychology,* 1935, 47, 458–468.

DAVIS, M. *Typing keys for remediation of reading and spelling: A developmental approach for children with perceptual handicaps.* San Rafael, Calif.: Academic Therapy Publications, 1971.

DAVIS, M., & BROWNLEE, M. I. *Encounter words useful for everyday living.* San Rafael, Calif.: Academic Therapy Publications, 1977.

DENO, S. L., & CHIANG, B. An experimental analysis of the nature of reversal errors in children with severe learning disabilities. *Learning Disability Quarterly,* 1979, 2, 40–45.

ENSTROM, E. A. Left-handedness: A cause for disability in writing. *Journal of Learning Disabilities,* 1968, 1, 410–414.

FAUKE, J., BURNETT, J., POWERS, M. A., & SULZER-AZAROFF, B. Improvement of handwriting and letter recognition skills: A behavior modification procedure. *Journal of Learning Disabilities,* . 1973, *6,* 296–300.

FOXX, R. M., & JONES, J. R. A remediation program for increasing the spelling achievement of elementary and junior high school students. *Behavior Modification,* 1978, *2,* 211–230.

GLOVER, J. A., & SAUTTER, F. Procedures for increasing four behaviorally defined components of creativity within formal written assignments among high school students. *School Applications of Learning Theory,* 1977, *9,* 3–22.

HAMMILL, D. D., & LARSEN, S. C. *The test of written language* (TOWL). Austin, Tex.: Pro-Ed, 1978.

HANNA, P. R., HODGES, R. E., & HANNA, J. S. *Spelling: Structure and strategies.* Boston: Houghton Mifflin Co., 1971.

HANSEN, C. L. Writing skills. In N. G. Haring, T. C. Lovitt, M. D. Eaton, & C. L. Hansen, *The fourth R: Research in the classroom.* Columbus, Ohio: Charles E. Merrill Publishing Co., 1978.

HASAZI, J. E., & HASAZI, S. E. Effects of teacher attention on digit-reversal behavior in an elementary school child. *Journal of Applied Behavior Analysis,* 1972, *5,* 157–162.

HELWIG, J. J., JOHNS, J. C., NORMAN, J. E., & COOPER, J. O. The measurement of manuscript letter strokes. *Journal of Applied Behavior Analysis,* 1976, *9,* 231–236.

HILDRETH, G. Reversals in reading and writing. *Journal of Educational Psychology,* 1934, *25,* 1–20.

HOLMES, D. L., & PEPER, R. J. An evaluation of the use of spelling error analysis in the diagnosis of reading disabilities. *Child Development,* 1977, *48,* 1708–1711.

HOPKINS, B. L., SCHUTTE, R. C., & GARTON, K. L. The effects of access to a playroom on the rate and quality of printing and writing of first and second grade students. *Journal of Applied Behavior Analysis,* 1971, *4,* 77–87.

JONES, J. C., TRAP, J., & COOPER, J. O. Technical report: Students' self-recording of manuscript letter strokes. *Journal of Applied Behavior Analysis,* 1977, *10,* 509–514.

KAHN, C., JEW, W., & TONG, R. *My job application file* (2nd ed.). Hayward, Calif.: Janus, 1975.

KAUFFMAN, J. M., HALLAHAN, D. P., HAAS, K., BRAME, T., & BOREN, R. Imitating children's errors to improve their spelling performance. *Journal of Learning Disabilities,* 1978, *11,* 217–222.

LEBRUN, Y., & VAN DE CRAEN, P. Developmental writing disorders and their prevention. *The Journal of Special Education,* 1975, *9,* 201–207.

LOVITT, T. C., GUPPY, T. E., & BLATTNER, J. E. The use of a free-time contingency with fourth graders to increase spelling accuracy. *Behaviour Research and Therapy,* 1969, *7,* 151–156.

MALONEY, K. B., & HOPKINS, B. L. The modification of sentence structure and its relationship to subjective judgments of creativity in writing. *Journal of Applied Behavior Analysis,* 1973, *6,* 425–433.

MERCER, C. D. *Children and adolescents with learning disabilities.* Columbus, Ohio: Charles E. Merrill Publishing Co., 1979.

MILLER, L. K., & SCHNEIDER, R. The use of a token system in project head start. *Journal of Applied Behavior Analysis,* 1970, *3,* 191–197.

MORTINGER, G. J. Use of specific instructions to modify several aspects of creative writing. *The Directive Teacher,* 1979, *1,* pp. 7; 23.

RIETH, H., AXELROD, S., ANDERSON, R., HATHAWAY, R., WOOD, K., & FITZGERALD, C. Influence of distributed practice and daily testing on weekly spelling tests. *Journal of Educational Research,* 1974, *68,* 73–77.

ROSENDAL, A. The difficult art of spelling: An historical review of orthography. *Journal of Learning Disabilities,* 1968, *1,* 192–195.

SALZBERG, B. H., WHEELER, A. J., DEVAR, L. T., & HOPKINS, B. L. The effect of intermittent feedback and intermittent contingent access to play on printing of kindergarten children. *Journal of Applied Behavior Analysis,* 1971, *4,* 163–171.

SIDMAN, M. T. The effects of group free time and contingency and individual free time contingency on spelling performance. *The Directive Teacher,* 1979, *1,* 4–5.

SMITH, D. D., & LOVITT, T. C. The educational diagnosis and remediation of written b and d reversal problems. A case study. *Journal of Learning Disabilities,* 1973, *6,* 356–363.

STOWITSCHEK, C. E., & JOBES, N. K. Getting the bugs out of spelling—Or an alternative to the spelling bee. *Teaching Exceptional Children,* 1977, *9,* 74–76.

STOWITSCHEK, C. E., & STOWITSCHEK, J. J. Evaluating handwriting performance: The student helps the teacher. *Journal of Learning Disabilities,* 1979, *12,* 203–206.

STOWITSCHEK, J. J. Applying programming principles to remedial handwriting practice. *Journal of Special Education Technology,* 1978, *1,* 21–26.

STRAUSS, A. A., & LEHTINEN, L. E. *Psychopathology and education of the brain injured child.* New York: Grune & Stratton, 1951.

STROMER, R. Modifying letter and number reversals in elementary school children. *Journal of Applied Behavior Analysis,* 1975, *8,* 211.

STROMER, R. Remediating academic deficiencies in learning disabled children. *Exceptional Children*, 1977, *43*, 432–440.

TOWLE, M. Assessment and remediation of handwriting deficits for children with learning disabilities. *Journal of Learning Disabilities*, 1978, *11*, 370–377.

TRAP, J. J., MILNER-DAVIS, P., JOSEPH, S., & COOPER, J. O. The effects of feedback and consequences on transitional cursive letter formation. *Journal of Applied Behavior Analysis*, 1978, *11*, 381–393.

TURNBULL, A. P., & SCHULZ, J. B. *Mainstreaming handicapped students: A guide for the classroom teacher*. Boston: Allyn & Bacon, 1979.

VAN HOUTEN, R., HILL, S., & PARSONS, M. An analysis of a performance feedback system: The effects of timing and feedback, public posting, and praise upon academic performance and peer interaction. *Journal of Applied Behavior Analysis*, 1975, *8*, 449–457.

VAN HOUTEN, R., MORRISON, E., JARVIS, R., & McDONALD, M. The effects of explicit timing and feedback on compositional response rate in elementary school children. *Journal of Applied Behavior Analysis*, 1974, *7*, 547–555.

WANOUS, S. J., & HAGGBLADE, B. *Personal typewriting for junior high schools* (3rd ed.). Cincinnati: South-Western Publishing Co., 1971.

11 MATHEMATICS

Although an often underrated and undervalued curriculum area, mathematics provides learners with many of the basic skills needed for successful independence in adult life. Managing a personal budget, shopping, making simple repairs at home, and many business and vocational skills require mastery of curriculum targets that fall within the mathematics area. Surprisingly, many programs for learning disabled students do not emphasize this important area, and efforts are concentrated almost exclusively on reading. Teachers of mildly handicapped students should plan for mastery of subskills that make up the mathematics curriculum. Possibly more direct instructional time should be assigned to these critical life skills for all students, but certainly it is easily justified for the learning disabled.

Experts in the area of mathematics are questioning the content and sequence of the standard curriculum for normal as well as for handicapped students. Chandler (1978), for example, stresses the importance of handicapped people possessing basic arithmetic skills. He points out, however, that only fourth grade skill levels (numeration, computation, measurement, and simple problem solving) are truly vital to maintain oneself in typical employment situations. If this achievement level were the minimum goal for mildly handicapped youngsters, where instructional emphasis should be placed might be more apparent. With the advent of the hand-held calculator, there is no reason why the majority of learning disabled students cannot achieve basic mathematical competencies.

In an attempt to document the effectiveness of the contemporary mathematics curriculum, mathematics assessments were first conducted in 1972–1973, and a second assessment was just completed. The interesting and important information collected during these national assessments provides an indication of what skills students possess and what areas are in need of further concentration. Despite the common notion that the modern mathematics approach to instruction lowered achievement levels in computational arithmetic, students were able to compute problems from the basic arithmetic processes (addition, subtraction). In both assessments problem solving (word problems) was not a strength (Carpenter, Coburn, Reys, & Wilson, 1975a; Carpenter, Kepner, Corbitt, Lindquist & Reys, 1980). What good is proficiency in computational arithmetic if those skills are not functional outside of the traditional arithmetic worksheet paradigm? Aware of this problem, these authors later concluded, "The development of problem-solving skills is extremely important; teachers should make problem solving a regular part of mathematics instruction." (Carpenter, Coburn, Reys, & Wilson, 1978, p. 45). This renewed emphasis on problem-solving abilities and mathematics is important for both handicapped and nonhandicapped learners. In revised mathematics curricula more emphasis probably will be given to the development of problem-solving abilities.

What should constitute the mathematics curriculum for learning disabled students? Should there be one curriculum for regular education and another for special education? Should there be one curriculum with the special education students leaving the sequence at an earlier point than others who have a proclivity for mathematics? If there are two distinct curricula, at what point are students tracked into one sequence or the other? Definitive answers to these questions are not available. Nevertheless, conscious decisions must be made if appropriate educational goals are to be developed for individual students.

Vast numbers of instructional topics fall within the mathematics category. Different professional organizations and individual researchers have identified various lists including those skills they think should make up the mathematics curriculum. Intertwined with discussions about the modification of this curriculum area is a concern about basic competencies for each academic area. For example, both the National Council for Teachers of Mathematics (NCTM) and the National Institute of Education (NIE) have attempted to identify the basic skills that constitute mathematics. This has great implications for how mathematics instructional time is spent.

Curriculum topics often are revealed through the testing of children. Assessment instruments have a great impact upon classroom instruction. One excellent example of this occurred within the area of special education. Since the publication of the *Key Math Diagnostic Arithmetic Test* (Connolly, Nachtman, & Pritchett, 1971), the mathematics curriculum for many mildly handicapped youngsters has included noncomputational topics. For example, questions such as "How much do you think this man weighs?" "What is a good room temperature?" "What is the temperature of a healthy person?" and children's subsequent answers have changed the emphasis of instruction in many special education classes.

There are many ways to organize mathematics curricula. Many different areas or topics can be emphasized. The content matrix used in the first national mathematics assessment of NCTM (Carpenter et al., 1978) the ten basic skill areas arrived upon at the NIE Basic Skills Group meeting (Smith,

Table 11.1 Organizational schemes for mathematics curricula

NCTM Content Matrix	NIE 10 Basic Skills	Key Math Organizational Areas
Numbers and numeration concepts	Problem solving	Content
Properties of numbers and operations	Apply math to everyday situations	numeration
Arithmetic computations	Alertness to reasonableness of results	fractions
Sets	Estimations and approximations	geometry and symbols
Estimation and measurement	Appropriate computational skills	Operations
Exponents and logarithms	Geometry	addition
Algebraic expressions	Measurement	subtraction
Equations and inequalities	Reading, interpreting, and construct-	multiplication
Functions	ing tables, charts, and graphs	division
Probability and statistics	Using mathematics to predict	mental computation
Geometry	Computer literacy	numerical reasoning
Trigonometry		Applications
Mathematical proofs		word problems
Logic		missing elements
Miscellaneous topics		money
Business and consumer mathematics		measurement
Attitude and interest		time

1978), and the Key Math organizational areas are displayed in Table 11.1. Other organizational schemes also have been proposed. NCTM, for example, suggests that categories be organized according to three general uses: social, technical, and academic. Social mathematics includes personal living skills, technical math focuses on those skills necessary for various skilled jobs and professions, and academic math is the basis for understanding various mathematical processes. The types and variations of such organizational schemes are almost infinite. No optimal, unanimously agreed upon system is available. The teacher, therefore, is left to use his or her training, skills, and common sense in planning appropriate instructional sequences for each student.

This chapter is organized by those skills necessary for learning disabled students. For those students whose learning disabilities are not manifested in the mathematics area, the assumption is that they move through the regular mathematics curriculum (algebra, geometry, trigonometry). For the others, mastery of these advanced skills is not attainable and spending instructional time on these topics is not appropriate. Instead, valuable classroom time should be spent on mastery of those skills needed in adult life. Therefore, the following topics are included in this chapter: numeration, computation, measurement, problem solving, and survival mathematics.

NUMERATION

There are a number of skills children should master before they begin to use numbers to calculate or solve problems. For example, they must understand that objects and things in their environment are related to each other. Many children master numerical concepts before they come to school. Others, however, need direct instruction on one-to-one correspondence, counting, quantitative relationships, and other topics. Because these concepts are not well-established in many learning disabled youngsters, some discussion is provided about them and possible remediation strategies. Following that discussion, information is provided about number usage (a precursory skill to computation).

Number Concepts Very young children seem interested in number concepts (how many, how old) almost naturally. Because the concept of numbers, however, is based on an abstraction related to quantity, some learning disabled students have difficulty from the outset. Classification and the grouping of objects is an early requisite skill. The notion of sets or clusters should come early in the instructional sequence (Johnson, 1979). To be able to group things together, one must be able to discriminate objects. Because shapes are relatively easy to discriminate, usually they are taught during this initial period. For children who have difficulty with discrimination tasks, the priming tactics described in Chapter 4 might be useful. Circles, for example, can become a set separate from triangles and squares. Size is another common discriminating feature used in instruction about sets. Once children have learned to discriminate objects on several variables, relationships between sets can be established and instruction about one-to-one correspondence initiated.

Other number concepts are important in students' early contact with mathematics. Peterson (1973), for example, believes that pupils must develop a numerical vocabulary early. Words like most, few, many, big, little, heavy, long, short, top, and bottom must become part of young children's usable vocabulary. Such word knowledge and usage facilitates the development of more difficult numerical concepts. When one-to-one correspondence is taught, for instance, the phrase "one too many" is important to learn, for later concepts are related to that notion (greater than). Once these foundation skills are mastered, students should move on easily to the use of numbers in their environment.

Number Usage As with many numerical concepts, a large number of students come to school already possessing an ability to use simple numbers. A standard instructional sequence is often used to teach number usage. It usually starts with rote counting by ones (to ten or twenty), number recognition of simple (one-digit) numbers, and number writing (if the students possess the necessary prerequisite writing skills—see Chapter 10, Written Communication). Whether the student matches, says, or writes numbers, indicating how many objects are within a set usually is the next skill in the sequence.

Once counting objects is mastered, students are taught to count and compare. Relationships between sets (greater than, less than, and equal to) become the topic of instruction. Many teachers have found that for students who have difficulty with this skill when the task is presented on worksheets, concrete representation of sets and their composition is helpful.

Other general number usage skills must be mastered before computational instruction is initiated. Whether these miscellaneous skills are taught concurrent with or subsequent to the skills listed above is up to the teacher and the performance of the student. Regardless, at some time early in the mathematics curriculum, students should be able to count by ones, twos, fives, and tens, and should also master ordinal numbers (first, second, third).

The exact and precise sequence of these precomputational skills is not definite. Clearly, however, these skills should be mastered before computation is presented in any concentrated way. Many learning disabled youngsters possess "spotty" skills. Teachers of students having difficulty with computation and other mathematical skills should assess their students' abilities in numeration, to be certain that these prerequisite skills are definitely part of their repertoires.

Numeration Evaluation

The first subtest on the *Key Math Diagnostic Arithmetic Test* (Connolly et al., 1971) can help teachers ascertain that their students have mastered numeration skills. Certainly, teacher-made skill sequence lists provide a good criterion check of number concept and number usage. Many teachers find that for most skills in this area, accuracy (percentage correct or frequency scores) is sufficient. For number writing, however, proficiency is eventually an important issue. How early number writing proficiency should be demanded is not clear, but guidelines on desired rates are available. Mercer (1979) indicates that from kindergarten to second grade, students' correct rate of writing numerals per minute should be approximately twenty-five; anywhere from forty to sixty numerals per minute should be expected from older students.

COMPUTATION

Computational arithmetic has received considerable attention from teachers and researchers. Possibly too much attention has been paid to this mechanical area within mathematics. Almost the first instruction many learning disabled students receive in mathematics is computation. Unfortunately, often it is their last. The overemphasis on computation can be observed through the following example. John was a high school student who received help from the special education teacher. Thirty minutes each day was devoted to mathematics. He spent ten minutes putting cards with multiplication facts written on them through a Language Master machine, and twenty minutes computing problems on a worksheet. Sometimes these problems were only multiplication, but other days the processes were mixed. Day in and day out, for the eleven years he spent in school, mathematics instruction was composed of similar activities. This is a travesty for all parties involved: The youngster is still not proficient in computational skills and the teacher is not providing an appropriate educational program. This overemphasis on the importance of computational arithmetic leaves a student with no usable mathematics skills.

NCTM (1979) estimates that students devote at least 1,000 classroom hours during elementary school to the study of mathematics. They stress that too much time has been spent on computational drill and not enough on developing an ability to use mathematics to solve problems. Many authorities in this area (Suydam, 1979) feel that a reprioritization is needed, in which computation is given less emphasis and problem solving is stressed. Particularly with the advent of the inexpensive, portable, and convenient calculator, at least a reevaluation of curriculum topics and emphasis is warranted.

In this section, suggestions are offered regarding the acquisition, proficiency, and maintenance of computational skills (arithmetic processes and fractions). In addition, the use of calculators as supplemental aids and compensating devices is discussed.

Computational Processes

There are four computational areas: addition, subtraction, multiplication, and division. Each can be further divided into two general types of problems: facts and process problems. The facts (7×8, $5 + 2$, $7 - 4$) are those problems to be committed to memory. The process problems ($74 - 27$, 68×84) are solved by utilizing the facts and following specific operational rules. Generally, the instructional tactics scheduled to teach basic facts for each area are different from those used to teach the rules for solving the process problems. Also, the evidence seems rather clear that the different stages of learning (as described in Chapter 4) are particularly evident for arithmetic (Lovitt, 1978; Smith & Lovitt, 1976). When a student is first learning how to solve a specific type of arithmetic problem (acquisition stage), one kind of tactic has a higher probability of being successful. When developing proficiency or fluency, another set of tactics is more likely to be influential.

Usually, the first computational area taught is addition. Once addition is mastered, subtraction is taught, then multiplication, followed by division. For each area, the facts are taught first and the larger, process problems later.

A number of specific tactics have been used to help students learn the basic facts for each computational area. It is particulary important that students master facts in both the acquisition and proficiency stages of learning. They should know all of the facts for each computational area. If several facts ($8 + 4$, $7 + 3$) are not mastered, performance on the process ($243 + 587$) will be erratic. The percentage correct scores from worksheets that include problems requiring carrying might indicate to the teacher that the student has not mastered the carrying process. The reason for low accuracy, however, might be due to poor performance on basic facts. Therefore, the acquisition stage for each fact must be completed. Proficiency in solving facts is also vital. If a student answers fact problems too slowly, process problems worksheets will not be completed in the allotted time. Many students have difficulty in computational arithmetic not because they do not know how to solve complicated problems, but because they are neither accurate nor proficient in answering fact problems.

A number of traditional techniques have been used to help students learn basic facts. Drill, practice, flashcards, and various counting activities are the commonly applied procedures. Recently, more novel aids have found their way into classrooms. Various programmed instructional machines complete with lighted answer displays have proven to motivate students to learn arithmetic facts more quickly. Even calculators used during practice sessions have been helpful. Lovitt (Note 1) facilitated mastery of learning disabled students' acquisition of basic facts by reorganizing the task analysis. The facts for each process were divided into two parts (in addition, the facts yielding a single-digit answer were grouped into one set and the facts producing two-digit answers into another). The single-digit answer problems were mastered first. The students were then taught to solve process (larger) problems not requiring carrying. Once mastery was achieved for them, the two-digit facts were mastered, followed by the problem types requiring carrying. The same logic system was used for the task analysis of the problems in the other computation areas.

It is very important for students not only to know how to solve various types of arithmetic problems, but to become proficient at arriving at their solutions. If students are not proficient (requiring accuracy and speed) in solving the basic facts, they will not be able to solve the large process problems within a reasonable amount of time.

A number of different tactics have been used to encourage fluency or proficiency in answering fact problems. Spinner and dice-throwing games (Bright, Harvey, & Wheeler, 1979), self-recording, contingent free time, verbalizing each problem during practice and use of a number wheel (Romeo, 1978), multiple ratio reinforcement (Lovitt & Esveldt, 1970), instructions plus reinforcement (Smith & Lovitt, 1976; Vasta & Stirpe, 1979), and praise and corrective feedback (Kirby & Shields, 1972) have all facilitated students' fact proficiency. In an interesting study, Van Houten, Morrison, Barrow, & Wenaus (1974) improved children's correct rate scores through daily practice, self-correction, praise, and public posting of each student's highest correct rate score.

Experience has shown that students who have demonstrated proficiency in facts tend not to have a difficult time demonstrating proficiency in the larger process problems. Once they know how to correctly solve a type of problem (carrying, borrowing), proficiency is automatically achieved. Smith and Lovitt (1975) used a demonstration plus permanent model technique to teach individual students how to solve specific problem types. Before a child solved problems on a worksheet, the teacher came to the child's desk and solved the first problem on the page. That remained as a referent as the student worked on his or her own. Accuracy dramatically improved. In a later study (Smith & Fleming, Note 2), a group application of this modeling technique was investigated and comparable results were achieved.

Other researchers have found that homework (Harris & Sherman, 1974; Maertens & Johnston, 1972), if carefully monitored, can influence positive increases in mathematics performance. Others (Hamrick, 1979; Lovitt & Curtiss, 1968) found that accuracy increased when students verbalized the problems as they computed their assignments. When students make careless errors (clearly not because of lack of knowledge of the facts or rules to solve process problems), withdrawal of positive reinforcement (response cost, loss of recess time, fines, or loss of privileges) has influenced increases in accuracy (Lovitt & Smith, 1974).

In many instances, however, student error is consistent; standard but

These students are learning how to solve problems which require borrowing with zeroes. The teacher is using the demonstration technique used by Smith and Lovitt and Smith and Fleming.

1. 47 + 62 = 118

2. 249
    −192
    ───
    157

3.   429
    +179
    ────
    5918

4.   420
    −179
    ────
     359

5.   52   64   72   89
    −16   −17   −22   −46
    ───   ───   ───   ───
     12   34   56   78

1. In Problem 1, the child added 4 and 7, then 6 and 2.

2. In Problem 2, the child subtracted the smaller number from the larger number in each column.

3. In Problem 3, the child added without carrying.

4. In Problem 4, the child subtracted the larger number in each column from the smaller one.

5. In the series in Problem 5, the child simply wrote as answers the numbers 1 to 8 in sequence.

Figure 11.1　　　Common error patterns in computation.

incorrect rules arc followed. Systematic error patterns are very common. Several common error patterns are shown in Figure 11.1. Cox (1975), Blankenship (1978), and Killian, Cahill, Ryan, Sutherland, and Taccetta (1980) have studied this phenomenon specifically. Systematic errors tend to be persistent and continue for long periods of time if direct instruction is not initiated to correct the error pattern. Blankenship found that a demonstration plus corrective feedback tactic was a most effective remediation strategy.

Table 11.2 summarizes various strategies and their influence during the acquisition stages of learning. Table 11.3 summarizes the proficiency stage. The implementation of these procedures might be helpful for improving students' computational performance.

Fractions

Fractions often present a problem to both students and teachers. Many youngsters have great difficulty understanding and using fractions. Most seem to be able to develop a firm concept of simple fractions and are able to divide circles and other geometric figures into halves, thirds, fourths, and even eighths. Using fractions in computations, however, can become an insurmountable task for many, particularly learning disabled students. Adding and subtracting fractions with uncommon denominators, for example, is laborious and seemingly incomprehensible to many youngsters.

Fraction instruction presents two problems to teachers. First, a substantial amount of instructional time often is spent on this pursuit without much success or mastery from students. Second, the usefulness of this curriculum area is open to question. Whether instructional time spent beyond simple fractions is justified is certainly an issue for debate. With the national move toward the metric system (which does not utilize fractions) and the advent of the calculator, the place of fractions in the traditional elementary curriculum can be questioned (Firl, 1977). Some suggest that decimals be introduced much earlier; that students be taught to round off to the 100th place (which correlates to our currency system); that common, everyday fractions (halves, quarters, and thirds) be mastered; and that more complicated fractions be eliminated from the standard elementary curriculum.

If such discussion is being held regarding the regular curriculum, what is the justification for spending undue instructional time on fractions for learning disabled students? Certainly the value of being able to solve equations using complicated fractions ($3/34 + 67/83$, $6/15 + 9/20$) could be questioned. For those, however, who believe that fractions must be taught to all students or those who must adhere to the regular education curriculum, which gives substantial weight to fractions, the following advice might be helpful. First, the learning of fractions, as in other computational areas, tends to follow the stage of learning theory presented previously (for a review refer to Chapter 4). The students must first acquire basic knowledge of fractions. By using a task analysis of fractions and teaching the component skills one at a time, students can soon be requested to solve fractions at a proficient rate of performance (a set desired rate is not available). By using instructions, modeling, demonstrations, and corrective feedback (redemonstrations for error problems), students should acquire the basic skills. Rein-

Table 11.2   Possible interventions for acquisition of computational skills

Tactic	Classroom Application
I. Before the child performs A. Teacher provides a *model* or example. 1. Demonstrates appropriate process	a) Sample problem worked on a chalkboard b) Sample problem worked on the child's paper
2. Solves problem printed on page before it is given to the child	a) Sample problems worked in programmed text or math textbook
B. Teacher gives *verbal directions* on the appropriate procedures for the type of problem.	a) General directions given to entire class b) Directions given to the individual child
C. *Rules* for correct computation are *written* down.	a) Written directions and text in math books
D. *Drill* and practice are encouraged.	a) Practice sheets b) Flashcard drill c) Homework
II. While the child performs A. *Mnemonic* aids are suggested. 1. Cue sheets with the correct answers	a) Problems and answers kept in view of the class (chalkboard or chart) b) Cues written on the top of the child's page
2. Manipulating devices	a) Devices such as cuisinare rods or abacuses given to the child
3. Counting devices	a) Use of fingers, hatch marks, or number lines explained and encouraged
II. After the child performs A. The math page is *corrected.* 1. Correct problems noted	a) After each problem is computed b) Immediately after entire page or timed session is concluded c) Later when paper is returned to child
2. Incorrect problems noted	Same as a, b, c above

B. *Correct answers are provided.*
1. Teacher provides correct answers

    a) To entire class verbally
    b) To individual child verbally
    c) Correct answers written on the child's page

2. Child corrects page

    a) Answer sheets provided (back of textbook, or as in programmed texts, or by the teacher)
    b) Child rechecks answers by using a calculator or adding machine
    c) Child corrects peer's paper

C. The correct process is *demonstrated* and incorrect problems are reworked.

    a) Immediately after the child performs
    b) Later with the child
    c) Corrected later and correct answer and process noted on child's page

D. Teacher *rewards* correct computation of problems.
1. Special activities or recognition

    a) Special parties, field trips, free time
    b) Special recognition or privilege

2. Tokens or prizes

    a) Money, candy, toys, games, or other tangible rewards

3. Praise

    a) For each correct answer
    b) For a percentage score

E. The child is *punished* or positive reinforcement is withdrawn for errors.

    a) Child must stay after school or during lunch or recess until problems are performed correctly
    b) Loss of earned activities

F. *Remediation* tactics are arranged.
1. Study groups

    a) Teacher works with small groups of children

2. Peer teaching

    a) Student tutoring—best student or older student from another class

G. *Competition* is arranged.
1. Gamelike team activities

    a) Team with best score wins a prize

2. Child competes against himself or herself

    a) Improve on yesterday's score

3. Child competes against whole class

    a) Best in the class is recognized
    b) A 100% club

Table 11.3   Possible interventions for proficiency in computational skills

I. Before the child performs A. Teacher *demonstrates* how fast the arithmetic problems should be computed.	a) Quickly computes problems orally b) Does so on a chalkboard
B. Teacher gives a *verbal* direction or requests child to increase speed.	a) "Please do these problems as fast as you can."
C. *Directions* to work quickly are *written* on the top of each child's page.	a) "Time is important. Work as quickly as possible."
D. *Drill* and practice are encouraged.	a) Flashcards b) Games in which teacher verbally gives additional problems
II. While the child performs A. Child is *reminded* to work fast.	a) Teacher prompts dawdling child to keep working b) Teacher reminds whole class to work fast c) Teacher tells individual child to work fast
B. Child is *informed* how much *time* is *left* in the session.	a) General announcement made to class b) Individual children prompted
III. After the child performs A. The math page is *corrected*. 1. Speed noted for correct problems	a) Child is told his or her correct rate b) Child is told how many problems he or she computed correctly c) Child is told how long it took him or her to compute problems correctly
2. Speed noted for both correct and incorrect problems	a) Child is told his or her correct and incorrect error rates b) Child is told how many problems he or she computed, both correct and incorrect

3. Speed noted for total problems computed

   a) Child is told the total rate for both correct and incorrect problems
   b) Child is told the time it took him or her to compute problems

B. Teacher *rewards speed* of computing problems.
  1. Special activities or recognition

   a) Special parties, free time, activities
   b) Special recognition for those who worked quickly or above a certain rate

  2. Tokens or prizes

   a) Money, candy, toys, games, or other tangible rewards

  3. Praise for increased proficiency

   a) Directed toward the entire class
   b) Directed toward those who did "better than most" of their classmates
   c) Directed toward those who "bettered their speed"

  4. Various schedules arranged by teacher

   a) DRH
   b) Multiple ratios

C. The child is *punished* for slow computation.

   a) Child must stay after school until he or she can compute problems at a faster rate
   b) Loss of earned activities

D. *Competition* is arranged.
  1. Gamelike activities

   a) Team with the fastest speed wins a prize

  2. Child competes against himself or herself

   a) Work faster than yesterday

  3. Child competes against whole class

   a) Fastest in the class is recognized
   b) A club is set up for those exceeding a certain speed rate

forcement procedures aimed at increased speed of production should help students reach proficiency in completing the task.

Computational Evaluation

While students are acquiring the skills necessary to correctly solve arithmetic problems, accuracy is of utmost importance, and percentage scores are the appropriate measure for evaluating it. Experience indicates that students should be able to solve every fact $(8 + 7, 15 - 6, 9 \times 3, 6 \div 2)$ correctly. Correct solutions to these problems should be arrived at without the use of aids such as fingers, counting sticks, or crib sheets. Once the knowledge of facts is acquired, proficiency must become the instructional target. Table 11.4 provides data from various sources regarding suggested desired rate scores for various types of fact problems. Unfortunately, detailed average rate scores are not available across grade levels for each specific type of arithmetic fact. Table 11.4 summarizes the data available from the following sources: Van Houten, Morrison, Barrow, and Wenaus (1974); Lovitt (Note 3); and Kidder, Blankenship, and Lovitt (Note 4). Recent evidence, however, indicates that these rates may be too low (Wood, Burke, Kunzelmann, & Koenig, 1978); therefore, adult rates from their study are included in Table 11.4.

Once the facts are solved at proficient rates of performance, proficiency on the larger process problems is not a necessary target. Accuracy seems to

Table 11.4   **Average rate scores for arithmetic facts***

| | Elementary Grades | | | | | | | |
	1	2	3	4	5	6	Grade Unspecified	Adults
Write numbers 0–9	46	54	62	72	76	83		155
Add sums 0–9	18	30	30	37	45	49		
Add sums 10–18	8	24	36	42	53	48		
Combine addition facts		63		52				125
Subtract one digit from one digit							30–35	
Subtract one digit from two digits							10	
Combine subtraction facts		70		64				68
Multiplication facts through 9	0	0	13	44	53	63		
Other multiplication facts							10–20	
Combine multiplication facts		49		48				80
Divide one digit into one digit							50	
Other division facts							10–35	
Combine division facts		39		34				47

*   *The average rate scores shown in this table can be used as guides in developing aim scores for students working on specific types of problems. For some problem types, information is available by grade level; for others the grade level is not specified; for several problem types, adult rates are available.*

be a sufficient concern for the process problems and correct percentage scores are an appropriate evaluation measure.

Calculators

For some, this section could negate all of the previous discussions about computational arithmetic instruction. For others, it might change computational arithmetic's traditional emphasis. It is important to remember that computation is merely the mechanical tool of mathematics, and is only one component of a large curricular area. Because computation is complicated, the tendency has been for practically all of the instructional time allotted to mathematics in many elementary and middle school classes to be devoted to it. For students who are academically delayed, computational arithmetic has even taken the place of all mathematics instruction in high school.

A number of experts in the area of mathematics instruction suggest that more emphasis be placed on the development of problem-solving skills and less time be spent on computation (Teitelbaum, 1978; Capps & Hatfield, 1977). These experts believe that with the onset of the hand-held calculator, curriculum priorities for all elementary and middle school students must shift. In a report endorsed by the NCTM, Caravella (1977) stresses the value of the calculator in the classroom. No longer must students spend untold amounts of time engaged in complicated and laborious computations. Real-life problems, in which the computations are often difficult and time-consuming, can now be included in the academic activities even for young children (comparisons of unit pricing, verification of bills and cash register tapes, figuring discounts, balancing checkbooks, determining family budgets, computing gasoline mileage, figuring tips and shared costs of a dinner).

This youngster is learning how to use calculators to solve complex problems which relate to daily living situations.

Students who have difficulty in computation often lose interest in all of mathematics (Gawronski & Coblentz, 1976). When the tediousness of the computations is removed and real-life problems are presented, students come to understand the importance of mathematics to themselves personally, resulting in more interest and motivation. At a meeting in 1975, the Board of Directors of NCTM endorsed the use of calculators in the classroom and listed nine ways these devices could initially be used (Caravella 1977, pp. 17–18).

1. To encourage students to be inquisitive and creative as they experiment with mathematical ideas

2. To assist the individual to become a wiser consumer

3. To reinforce the learning of basic number facts and properties in addition, subtraction, multiplication, and division

4. To develop the understanding of computational algorithms by repeated operations

5. To serve as a flexible "answer key" to verify the results of computation

6. To promote student independence in problem solving

7. To solve problems that previously have been too time consuming or impractical to be solved with paper and pencil

8. To formulate generalizations from patterns of numbers that are displayed

9. To decrease the time needed to solve difficult computations.

A number of other benefits are cited by many who support the use of calculators in schools. For example, Bell (1976) indicates that as long as students are given interesting things to do with their calculators, high interest in using the machine persists across time. Shult (1978) adds that they are easy to learn how to use, reliable, durable, and portable. It has even been suggested that students learn and improve in basic computational skills through the use of calculators (Beardslee, 1978; Creswell & Vaughn, 1979; Wheatley, Shumway, Coburn, Reys, Schoen, Wheatley, & White, 1979).

A number of regular mathematics curriculum experts have addressed the problems of learning disabled and behaviorally disordered students in computation and support the notion of introducing calculators into classroom experiences for these youngsters. Shult, for example, strongly advises that exceptional students be taught to use calculators, because they increase motivation, facilitate drill and practice of mathematical concepts, and are an aid to computation. Capps and Hatfield (1977) feel that it is much wiser to teach mildly handicapped students to use calculators in conjunction with solving everyday problems than to teach computational arithmetic. Caravella (1977) believes these youngsters should be freed from laborious writing and computations and be allowed to move on to more difficult yet practical elements of mathematics, which calculator usage allows. In a bold statement, Gawronski and Coblentz (1976) even suggest that the calculator replace computational arithmetic for those who have difficulty in this area. They reason that mathematics must be usable for the individual and basic competencies achieved regardless of the means.

> *For a small percentage of the population this minimal skill level might be low enough for nearly all arithmetic operations. Whenever these individuals are identified, usually in the upper elementary grades, they should be provided with a calculator to help them with all arithmetic computations.* (p. 511)

Whether calculator usage should replace computational arithmetic instruction in classrooms for the mildly handicapped or not is an extreme view of a potential curricular debate. Clearly, there are advantages in teaching young children how to use calculators. That stressing mastery of computational arithmetic is no longer viable for learning disabled students not capable of memorizing all of the facts and rules for solving process problems is not debatable. Teachers and parents of learning disabled students must come to a decision regarding when (not if) calculators should be introduced into the curriculum.

The introduction of calculators into classroom situations causes some important curriculum changes. Gallery and Rickert (1978) caution that mildly handicapped youngsters must be taught systematically to use calculators correctly. For example, decimals must be introduced earlier. Since most calculators do not conclude an answer with only two decimal numbers, students must be taught to round off numbers earlier in the mathematics instructional sequence. Students also must be taught to estimate what answers should be. Estimation is important because calculators do not give an indication of the reasonableness of answers. Therefore, students must be exposed to more mathematical situations requiring problem solving, so that they can gain the necessary experience with specific types of problems to judge whether solutions indicated on the answer display of a calculator are reasonable. Problem solving and analysis certainly will play a more integral role in the mathematics curriculum in the near future, and can be taught in conjunction with calculator instruction (Fisher, 1979; Meyer, 1980; Reys, Bestgen, Rybolt, & Wyett, 1980).

MEASUREMENT

With the move to a more practical mathematics curriculum, measurement becomes a vital component of the instructional sequence. Rather than being relegated to the back of mathematics textbooks, linear and liquid measurement, time, and money concepts and their use should become integral parts of the instructional sequence. How long such a shift in curriculum priorities takes for the regular mathematics sequence is impossible to estimate, but certainly such a shift is critical for most learning disabled students because of the importance of measurement knowledge in vocational and life skills functions for adults. The *Key Math Diagnostic Arithmetic Test* certainly brought to the attention of many special educators the great deficiencies that many of their students have in these crucial life skills areas. Teachers of learning disabled students clearly must include these topics in their instructional programs.

Continuous measurement (variables represented on an uninterrupted scale) includes time, height, weight, temperature, volume, and distance. Although things can be measured differently (hands, fathoms), standard units of measurement are used for uniform communication. Rulers, clocks, and thermometers are some instruments used to obtain standard measurements. In addition to instrument use, students need to develop a sense or concept of measurement. In the following sections, both concept and use development are discussed for linear and liquid measurement, time, and money.

Linear and Liquid Measurement   Carpenter, Coburn, Reys, and Wilson (1978) claim that the measurement curriculum should include: (1) converting and comparing units of measure; (2) estimating and measuring length; (3) determining perimeter, area, and volume; (4) using maps, scales, and drawings; and (5) using measurement instruments. Students certainly should learn how to use various linear and liquid measurement devices such as rulers, thermometers, and measuring cups. According to some researchers (Carpenter et al., 1975b), measuring length is the easiest skill for students to learn. Determining volume and area is more difficult, and they suggest that concrete manipulations be used in the instructional process.

For many learning disabled students, developing measurement concepts is very difficult. Some (Copeland, 1970) suggest that Piagetian theory be employed. Students first visually compare the size of objects, estimating length and height. For example, students can build block towers, compare heights, learn to make them equivalent, and use primitive measurements (three blocks high, two blocks high). A sense of height and length can be developed gradually using these types of teaching procedures. Others might seek to develop these concepts through continued practice in games and other independent and group activities. Regardless of the philosophy employed, exposure, contact, and instruction in measurement are vital.

During the past decade, increased discussion has focused on the use of the metric system of measurement. The NCTM has endorsed the inclusion of metric measurement in school and has encouraged a national conversion to this system. If metrics are adopted, more efficient instruction will occur, since many of the difficult elements of measurement will be eliminated (conversion to inches, feet, yards; use of fractions; cups, pints, quarts). Some school district officials have even suggested that only metric measurement be taught. Unfortunately, conversion to the metric system has not been speedy. Students who possess only knowledge of metrics will be as handicapped as those who only possess knowledge of our current standard measurement systems. Therefore, although confusing to many, it is advisable to teach both systems (at least for the present).

Time

Many teachers of learning disabled students find that their students do not tell or understand time as well as their normal counterparts. Forer and Keogh (1971) verified this observation through their research. Apparently learning disabled students perform, on the average, three grade levels below normal children in time perception and time-understanding activities.

Before students can understand time (beyond the gross distinctions of morning, afternoon, night, lunch time, and dinner time), they must be able to tell time. A number of time-telling instructional programs are commercially available. VanEtten and Watson (1978) recommend one particular program developed by special educators under the auspices of the Bureau for the Education of the Handicapped (Tringo & Roit, 1977). Many teachers have had success in teaching this skill through the use of teacher-made aids and modified clock faces. A task analyzed sequence of time-telling objectives is available that identifies small and specific skills needed to lead the learner to mastery of time telling (Reisman, 1972). Jeffers (1979) found that using a color coded, digital clock matched to a standard clock face facilitated mastery. For those who seem not to be able to readily master the use of standard clock faces, digital clocks are now commonly available in a variety of forms (wall and desk clocks as well as wristwatches). To facilitate the development of time concepts, students must learn to use time. If this is only possible through the use of a digital clock, then students should be allowed to use it.

Once the student is able to tell time accurately, concentrated instruction can be initiated on time concepts. The continuation of the instructional sequence into the area of time concepts is particularly important. Unfortu-

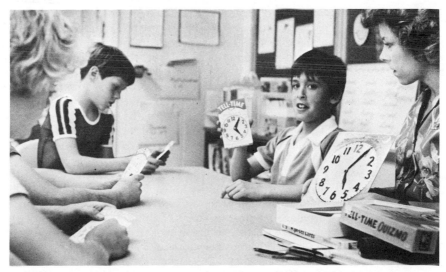

Many learning disabled youngsters need specific instruction to master time telling. These students and their teacher are using a game-like situation for practice with this skill.

nately, instruction often ceases once time telling is mastered. In a fascinating study, Lovitt and Fantasia (Note 5) dramatically demonstrated the deficiency many learning disabled students have in the time concept area. Students were asked simple questions such as "How long does it take you to brush your teeth?" "How long does it take to send a letter from one town to another?" and "How long does it take for a broken bone to mend?" The answers to these and other questions are both remarkable and shocking. For example, students said that it takes anywhere from twenty seconds to an hour to brush their teeth, from five minutes to nine hours to ski downhill, and from ten minutes to a year to get a letter from one town to the next.

Teachers who have used the *Key Math* time subtest with learning disabled students probably have noticed comparable deficient skills in this very important prevocational and life-skill area. Teachers who observe such deficiencies in their students' conceptual abilities must implement instructional procedures. Using time concepts throughout the school day possibly is sufficient for some students. For others, more direct remedial procedures are necessary. Regardless, parents and teachers must help students gain an accurate perception of time.

Money

As with time telling and other measurement skills, making change and money management are often neglected yet vital areas that should be topics of instruction for learning disabled students. As Connolly, Nachtman, and Pritchett (1971) pointed out, a number of different skills are required for proficiency in the use of money. They suggest that at least the following skills be incorporated into the mathematics curriculum: coin value and identification, counting money, making change, using money to make purchases, interpreting a budget, and having knowledge and understanding of checks and checking accounts. Also, in today's society it is important for students to understand the use of credit cards and develop a concept of credit.

At present, no comprehensive money management program is available for teachers to use with learning disabled students. Splinter skills usually are taught in isolated units. Making change, for example, is commonly presented in arithmetic texts. Interestingly, that skill often is taught through subtraction (the amount given to the clerk minus the price of the item). In real-life situations, however, change is obtained through a counting process (counting up from the price of the item to the amount given the clerk). Therefore, students do not need to know how to subtract to make change, and change making and other simple money usage activities can be introduced early in the student's educational career.

Teachers who include a token economy facet in their classrooms have an excellent opportunity to teach such money related skills as comparing the amount of money (or points) one possesses with the cost of an item (or privilege). Some teachers of middle and secondary school students even capitalize on this situation by setting up banking procedures, in which students make deposits into their accounts and write checks to purchase items or privileges they have earned through good work.

Dahlquist (1977) described a learning experience for fifth graders that taught money management as well as economics. These students were taught to run the school store (which sold school supplies and other sundries). Every customer filled out preprinted order forms for desired purchases and the students had to keep an inventory, price the items, and deliver purchase orders. This provided a unique and productive opportunity for these students to practice money management skills.

Money management should include information about such topics as budgeting, consumer awareness, and comparison shopping. Before students can learn about these advanced topics, they must be able to identify money (coins and bills), make change, and make value judgments about purchases in relation to their own financial situation. Although these topics normally are not part of the elementary or middle school curriculum, teachers should at least be aware of their importance and begin to include related topics in their instructional day. By the high school years, money management should become an emphasized topic of instruction.

PROBLEM SOLVING

Only limited efforts have been directed toward learning disabled students' abilities to solve problems having a mathematical base. A few studies have been conducted using story problems as the dependent variable, but few conclusive recommendations can be made to teachers. If the mathematics curriculum is to be reorganized with a greater emphasis placed on problem-solving skills, researchers also will have to readjust their interests and begin systematic study of this area of concern.

Many students have difficulty with story problems (one version of mathematical problem solving) because of the syntax complexity and the wording used to present the problems (Larsen, Parker, & Trenholme, 1978). In an analysis of story problems as they appear in basic arithmetic texts, Blankenship and Lovitt (1976) found that there is little consistency in the way word problems are organized or presented to children. They developed twelve classes of word problems and controlled for word difficulty, sentence complexity, extraneous information, and other variables (Lovitt, 1978; Blankenship, Note 6). Through systematic instruction and careful organization of the material presented, students' correct percentage scores improved on all of the classes of word problems, indicating improved problem-solving abilities.

As mentioned earlier in this chapter, many experts in the area of mathematics instruction (Cawley, Fitzmaurice, Shaw, Kahn, & Bates, 1979) and the NCTM advocate the introduction of more problem-solving activities into the mathematics curriculum. Until more research efforts provide guidelines about what types of problem-solving activities lead students most effectively to the basic competencies these experts recommend, teachers are left to use what scant materials they have at their disposal. Because many learning disabled students also have difficulty reading, a creative approach to instruction must be used. Such problems are particularly apparent for learning disabled youngsters who participate in regular education mathematics activities. When presented with students who have reading difficulties and are ready for problem-solving exercises, teachers might find the instructional program titled *Project MATH* (Cawley, Fitzmaurice, Goodstein, Lepore, Sedlak, & Althaus, 1976a, 1976b) helpful.

SURVIVAL MATHEMATICS

In the next chapter, the use of survival mathematics and other daily living skills is discussed. Many skills that adults need and use in daily life have a basis in mathematics, and teachers should consider the utility of the mathematics skills they teach. Most of the efforts in identifying the important targets in functional mathematics were conducted for the mentally retarded. That, however, should not limit the usefulness or hinder the adaptation of that work to the curriculum for the learning disabled. Peterson (1973) identified a number of objectives important for students to master if they are to have a functional use of mathematical skills. For example, they must develop a functional business and money based vocabulary, be able to use number symbols, be able to use all common measurement instruments (time schedules, clocks, calendars, thermometers), use dry and liquid measures (for cooking, sewing, and vocational skills), read maps, and understand financial concepts that enable them to use banks and credit services.

SUMMARY

The topics discussed in this chapter—numeration, computation, measurement, and problem solving—should bring the learner to a functional use of mathematics. The use of calculators should allow learning disabled students to break free from the tediousness of basic computation. If the thrust of mathematics instruction is changed from an overemphasis on addition, subtraction, multiplication, and division to learning how and why those processes are applied, functional, survival mathematics and the basic competency level needed in adult life can be achieved.

REFERENCE NOTES

1. LOVITT, T. C. Curriculum research. In N. G. Haring (Project Director), *A program project for the investigation and application of procedures of analysis and modification of behavior in handicapped children* (NIE Grant No. OEG-0-70-3916-607). Seattle, Wash.: University of Washington, Experimental Education Unit, Child Development and Mental Retardation Center, 1974.

2. SMITH, D. D., & FLEMING, E. C. *A comparison of individual and group modeling techniques aimed at altering children's computational abilities.* Unpublished manuscript, George Peabody College for Teachers, 1976.

3. LOVITT, T. C. *Curriculum research for learning disabled youngsters.* Paper presented at the meeting of the New Mexico State Council for Exceptional Children, Albuquerque, October 1977.

4. KIDDER, J., BLANKENSHIP, C., & LOVITT, T. C. *Math rates.* (Working paper). Seattle, Wash.: University of Washington, Experimental Education Unit, 1978.

5. LOVITT, T. C., & FANTASIA, K. *How much time?* (Working paper). Seattle, Wash.: University of Washington, Experimental Education Unit, 1978.

6. BLANKENSHIP, C, *Story problems.* Seattle, Wash.: University of Washington, Experimental Education Unit, 1975.

REFERENCES

BEARDSLEE, E. C. Teaching computational skills with a calculator. In M. Suydam & R. Reys (Eds.), *Developing computational skills: 1978 yearbook*. Reston, Va.: National Council of Teachers of Mathematics, 1978.

BELL, M. S. Calculators in elementary schools? Some tentative guidelines and questions based on classroom experience. *The Arithmetic Teacher*, 1976, 23, 502-508.

BLANKENSHIP, C. S. Remediating systematic inversion errors in subtraction through the use of demonstration and feedback. *Learning Disability Quarterly*, 1978, 1, 12-22.

BLANKENSHIP, C. S., & LOVITT, T. C. Story problems: Merely confusing or downright befuddling. *Journal for Research in Mathematics Education*, 1976, 7, 290-298.

BRIGHT, G. W., HARVEY, J. G., & WHEELER, M. M. Using games to retrain skills with basic multiplication facts. *Journal for Research in Mathematics Education*, 1979, 10, 103-110.

CAPPS, L. R., & HATFIELD, M. M. Mathematical concepts and skills: Diagnosis, prescription, and correction of deficiencies. *Focus on Exceptional Children*, 1977, 8, 1-8.

CARAVELLA, J. R. *Minicalculators in the classroom*. Washington, D.C.: National Education Association, 1977.

CARPENTER, T. P., COBURN, T. G., REYS, R. E., & WILSON, J. W. Results and implications of the NAEP mathematics assessment: Elementary school. *The Arithmetic Teacher*, 1975a, 22, 438-450.

CARPENTER, T. P., COBURN, T. G., REYS, R. E., & WILSON, J. W. Notes from national assessment: Basic concepts of area and volume. *The Arithmetic Teacher*, 1975b, 22, 501-507.

CARPENTER, T. P., COBURN, T. G., REYS, R. E., & WILSON, J. W. *Results from the first mathematics assessment of the National Assessment of Educational Progress*. Reston, Va.: National Council of Teachers of Mathematics, 1978.

CARPENTER, T. P., KEPNER, H., CORBITT, M. K., LINDQUIST, M. M., & REYS, R. E. Results and implications of the second NAEP mathematics assessment: Elementary school. *Arithmetic Teacher*, 1980, 27, 10-12; 44-47.

CAWLEY, J. F., FITZMAURICE, A. M., GOODSTEIN, H. A., LEPORE, A. V., SEDLAK, R., & ALTHAUS, V. *Project math* (level 1). Tulsa, Okla.: Educational Development Corp., 1976a.

CAWLEY, J. F., FITZMAURICE, A. M., GOODSTEIN, H. A., LEPORE, A. V., SEDLAK, R., & ALTHAUS, V. *Project math* (level 2). Tulsa, Okla.: Educational Development Corp., 1976b.

CAWLEY, J. F., FITZMAURICE, A. M., SHAW, R., KAHN, H., & BATES, H. LD youth and mathematics: A review of characteristics. *Learning Disability Quarterly*, 1979, 2, 29-44.

CHANDLER, H. N. Confusion compounded: A teacher tries to use research results to teach math. *Journal of Learning Disabilities*, 1978, 11, 361-369.

CONNOLLY, A. J., NACHTMAN, W., & PRITCHETT, E. M. *Key math diagnostic arithmetic test* (manual). Circle Pines, Minn.: American Guidance Service, 1971.

COPELAND, R. W. *How children learn mathematics: Teaching implications of Piaget's research*. New York: Macmillan Co., 1970.

COX, L. S. Diagnosing and remediating systematic errors in addition and subtraction computations. *The Arithmetic Teacher*, 1975, 22, 151-157.

CRESWELL, J. L., & VAUGHN, L. R. Hand-held calculator curriculum and mathematical achievement and retention. *Journal for Research in Mathematics Education*, 1979, 10, 364-367.

DAHLQUIST, J. Playing store for real. *The Arithmetic Teacher*, 1977, 24, 208-210.

FIRL, D. H. Fractions, decimals, and their futures. *The Arithmetic Teacher*, 1077, 24, 238-240.

FISHER, B. Calculator games: Combining skills and problem solving. *Arithmetic Teacher*, 1979, 27, 40-41.

FORER, R. K., & KEOGH, B. K. Time understanding of learning disabled boys. *Exceptional Children*, 1971, 37, 741-743.

GALLERY, M. E., & RICKERT, D. C. It figures: A program to teach calculator skills to the mildly handicapped. *Journal of Special Education Technology*, 1978, 2, 15-21.

GAWRONSKI, J. D., & COBLENTZ, D. Calculators and the mathematics curriculum. *Arithmetic Teacher*, 1976, 23, 510-512.

HAMRICK, K. B. Oral language and readiness for the written symbolization of addition and subtraction. *Journal for Research in Mathematics Education*, 1979, 10, 188-194.

HARRIS, V. W., & SHERMAN, J. A. Homework assignments, consequences, and classroom performance in social studies and mathematics. *Journal of Applied Behavior Analysis*, 1974, 7, 505-519.

JEFFERS, V. Using the digital clock to teach the telling of time. *Arithmetic Teacher*, 1979, 26, 53.

JOHNSON, S. W. *Arithmetic and learning disabilities: Guidelines for identification and remediation*. Boston: Allyn & Bacon, 1979.

KILLIAN, L., CAHILL, E., RYAN, C., SUTHERLAND, D.,

& TACCETTA, D. Errors that are common in multiplication. *Arithmetic Teacher*, 1980, *27*, 22–25.

KIRBY, F. D., & SHIELDS, F. Modification of arithmetic response rate and attending behavior in a seventh-grade student. *Journal of Applied Behavior Analysis*, 1972, *5*, 79–84.

LARSEN, S. C., PARKER, R. M., & TRENHOLME, B. The effects of syntactic complexity upon arithmetic performance. *Learning Disability Quarterly*, 1978, *1*, 80–85.

LOVITT, T. C. *Managing inappropriate behaviors in the classroom*. Reston, Va.: The Council for Exceptional Children, 1978.

LOVITT, T. C., & CURTISS, K. A. Effects of manipulating an antecedent event on mathematics response rate. *Journal of Applied Behavior Analysis*, 1968, *1*, 329–333.

LOVITT, T. C., & ESVELDT, K. A. The relative effects on math performance of single- versus multiple-ratio schedules: A case study. *Journal of Applied Behavior Analysis*, 1970, *3*, 261–270.

LOVITT, T. C., & SMITH, D. D. Using withdrawal of positive reinforcement to alter subtraction performance. *Exceptional Children*, 1974, *40*, 357–358.

MAERTENS, N., & JOHNSTON, J. Effects of arithmetic homework upon the attitudes and achievement of fourth, fifth, and sixth grade pupils. *School Science and Mathematics*, 1972, *72*, 117–126.

MERCER, C. D. *Children and adolescents with learning disabilities*. Columbus, Ohio: Charles E. Merrill Publishing Co., 1979.

MEYER, P. I. When you use a calculator you have to think! *Arithmetic Teacher*, 1980, *27*, 18–21.

NATIONAL COUNCIL OF TEACHERS OF MATHEMATICS. Toward a better balanced curriculum. *Arithmetic Teacher*, 1979, *26*, 2;59.

PETERSON, D. L. *Functional mathematics for the mentally retarded*. Columbus, Ohio: Charles E. Merrill Publishing Co., 1973.

REISMAN, F. K. *A guide to the diagnostic teaching of arithmetic*. Columbus, Ohio: Charles E. Merrill Publishing Co., 1972.

REYS, R. E., BESTGEN, B. J., RYBOLT, J. F., & WYATT, J. W. Hand calculators: What's happening in schools today? *Arithmetic Teacher*, 1980, *27*, 38–43.

ROMEO, C. L. Increasing correct responses on math test. *The Directive Teacher*, 1978, *1*, 8–9.

SHULT, D. L. Calculators, computers, and exceptional children. *Journal of Special Education Technology*, 1978, *2*, 59–65.

SMITH, D. D., & LOVITT, T. C. The use of modeling techniques to influence the acquisition of computational arithmetic skills in learning-disabled children. In E. Ramp & G. Semb (Eds.), *Behavior analysis: Areas of research and application*. Englewood Cliffs, N.J.: Prentice-Hall, 1975.

SMITH, D. D., & LOVITT, T. C. The differential effects of reinforcement contingencies on arithmetic performance. *Journal of Learning Disabilities*, 1976, *9*, 32–40.

SMITH, W. D. Minimal competencies: A position paper. *Arithmetic Teacher*, 1978, *26*, 25–26.

SUYDAM, M. N. The case for a comprehensive mathematics curriculum. *Arithmetic Teacher*, 1979, *26*, 10–11.

TEITELBAUM, E. Calculators for classroom use? *Arithmetic Teacher*, 1978, *26*, 18–20.

TRINGO, J. L., & ROIT, M. L. *Telling time—time instruction by modular elements*. Northbrook, Ill.: Hubbard, 1977.

VANETTEN, C., & WATSON, B. Arithmetic skills: Assessment and instruction. *Journal of Learning Disabilities*, 1978, *11*, 155–162.

VAN HOUTEN, R., MORRISON, E., BARROW, B., & WENAUS, J. The effects of daily practice and feedback on the acquisition of elementary math skills. *School Applications of Learning Theory*, 1974, *7*, 1–16.

VASTA, R., & STIRPE, L. A. Reinforcement effects on three measures of children's interest in math. *Behavior Modification*, 1979, *3*, 223–244.

WHEATLEY, G. H., SHUMWAY, R. J., COBURN, T. G., REYS, R. E., SCHOEN, H. L., WHEATLEY, C. L., & WHITE, A. L. Calculators in elementary schools. *Arithmetic Teacher*, 1979, *27*, 18–21.

WOOD, S., BURKE, L., KUNZELMANN, H., & KOENIG, C. Functional criteria in basic math skill proficiency. *Journal of Special Education Technology*, 1978, *2*, 29–36.

# LIFE-CENTERED CAREER EDUCATION

Specialized educational programming for secondary learning disabled students is a relatively new concern, one fraught with confusion, indecisiveness, and lack of coordination. Concentrated efforts to establish specialized school services for learning disabled adolescents began during the late 1970s. Because these programs are evolving and because their initiators are from differing backgrounds, little consensus exists about what should constitute secondary programs. Individual school districts have been forced to take the responsibility for deciding what is best for their students. Therefore, the range of program offerings varies greatly across the nation. Some school districts provide their learning disabled students with tutorial assistance aimed at maintaining them in the traditional, regular curriculum. Others track youngsters into vocational education, where job skills are taught. Some have adopted the work-study plan that was developed initially for mentally retarded students. A few include instruction in functional life skills needed for successful independent living. Unfortunately, in most instances only one option is available.

According to Deshler, Lowrey, and Alley (1979), five major service options usually are available to learning disabled youngsters. In their national survey of secondary schools to determine what options were being used, they found that programs attempting to remediate basic skills that should have been mastered in elementary school were the most common (45 percent of those surveyed). They determined that 24 percent functioned in a tutorial fashion, attempting to help students keep up in content subjects. Three other areas of emphasis were also operational: functional and life skills (17 percent); work-study (5 percent); and learning strategies, where emphasis is placed on teaching students how to learn and study (4 percent).

None of these approaches has been validated, and, to date, it has not been determined which of these is the best. Probably no one plan is the most appropriate for all learning disabled high school students.

Concern about the nature of high school programs for learning disabled students has been voiced recently. Some (Laurie, Buchwach, Silverman, & Zigmond, 1978) feel that resource or tutorial approaches might not be appropriate. Until regular secondary teachers modify the instructional methods used and significant changes in secondary schools occur, many learning disabled students will have great difficulty in school, regardless of the amount of supplementary assistance provided, and they and their teachers will face insurmountable obstacles. For example, if accommodations for handicapped learners are to be arranged, communication and cooperation between regular and special education is necessary. Many disabled learners cannot survive in typical high school content classes unless instructional methods, grouping arrangements, modes for presentation of material, and testing practices are adapted. This places considerable demands on regular educators already overburdened with the responsibilities of instilling content information into their average learners. Public concern and demand for the mastery of minimum, basic competencies for all general education students has placed more responsibilities on the shoulders of secondary teachers. If the structure and format remain the same, expecting regular educators to accommodate to handicapped learners' needs might be too much to expect.

Partially because of the above considerations, Malouf and Halpern (1976) question the appropriateness of mainstreaming learning disabled students in secondary school settings. They criticize secondary mainstreaming efforts on the basis that secondary personnel and their environments are inflexible and unreceptive to individual differences. They also cite the inappropriateness of instructional methods used, the irrelevance of the curricular content, and the lack of efficacy research to justify mainstreaming, as reasons for considering alternatives. Malouf and Halpern question the relevance of the content taught in most high school courses. Such questioning is a worthwhile pursuit, particularly for learning disabled adolescents. What is it worth to Jose, his parents, and his teachers for him to remain in English literature? In some cases, the emotional and academic costs are too great. In these instances, options must be available.

What, then, should the goals of secondary programs for learning disabled adolescents involve? Again, few definitive guidelines are available to teachers, but some consensus can be gleaned from the literature. For example, Touzel (1978) indicates that individualization of student goals, survival skills, career knowledge and vocational skills, and a healthy self-concept are important. Swart (1979) suggests that secondary-age students should develop independence from parents, be assured of social and economic independence, select and prepare for an occupation, prepare for marriage and family life, assume responsibility, have a sense of ethics, and cope with changing bodies. Although these are developmental tasks for most adolescents, they can become major problem areas for those who have other significant difficulties at school. Effective secondary learning disabilities teachers must be aware of these potential crisis areas and be prepared to deal with them within the school program. Most position statements about the content of secondary curriculum for learning disabled students include preparation for adult life (home, career, and society) as a vital area for instruction.

The educational and social needs of learning disabled adolescents are diverse. Their demands on the educational system are great, and the necessity for numerous educational alternatives is obvious. "Perhaps more than any others, these students exemplify the need for a *continuum* of services from the elementary through secondary school" (Goodman, 1978, p. 237). Wiederholt (1978) suggests that six types of service delivery options are necessary for learning disabled adolescents: "noneducational services (medical, welfare), residential schools, full-time special classes, part-time special classes, resource programs, and consultation to teachers of handicapped students in regular education programs" (p. 20). In addition to the availability of diverse service delivery options, the instructional content presented must be flexible. For some, only one tutorial period per day is necessary. This is sufficient for them to make continued progress in the regular program. For others, special accommodations are necessary (special textbooks, modified course objectives). For a substantial few, continuing failure in the regular setting is the best that mainstreaming can provide. For these students, alternatives to standard content classes should be provided. Possibly separate and unique curricula are the most appropriate educational options public schools can provide. Mori (1980) suggests a plan for a comprehensive career education program that is flexible and provides sufficient alternatives to meet the diverse needs of learning disabled students. Mori's comprehensive plan (Figure 12.1) might be useful to those who must provide a variety of experiences for such students.

Although a case could be made that the traditional curricula are not appropriate for most students, the point of this discussion is not to seek modification of general education for all students, although it does seem that all students could be better prepared for adult life. In a plea for life skills to be included in minimum competency expectations, Guerriero (1978) stresses the importance of life-role competencies being mastered by high school students. If concern regarding the content of the general education program is being raised, certainly the curricula for learning disabled youth should be reexamined.

Because American society is increasing in complexity, the mastery of survival or independent living skills is vital. Rarely is this an integral part of either regular or learning disabilities programs. A change in emphasis and content for most learning disabilities secondary programs is necessary. Some reasons for change in thrust and orientation are apparent in the following true vignette. A class of learning disabled students about to graduate from high school was asked what they intended to do after graduation. The unanimous agreement was that each was going to buy a car, rent an apartment, and get a job (in that order). These students had academic achievement levels below fourth grade; none of them could explain how to qualify for a car loan, what steps are involved in renting an apartment and making it functional, and so on. Although some would argue that these students' nor-

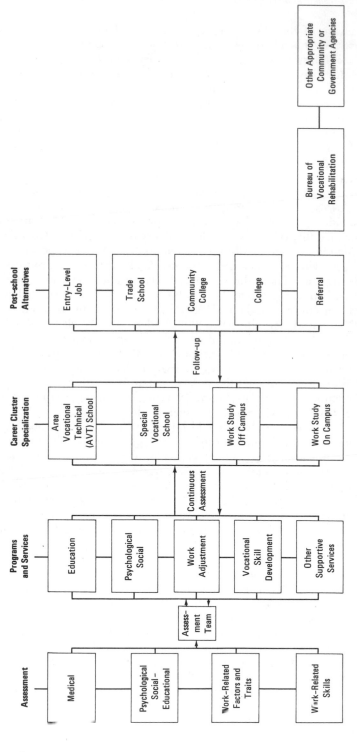

A Model for Comprehensive Career Education for the Learning Disabled. (A. A. Mori, Career education for the learning disabled—Where are we now? *Learning Disability Quarterly*, 1980, 3, 92–101. Reprinted by permission.)

Figure 12.1

mal peers could not correctly answer comparable questions either, it does seem imperative that the handicapped be even better prepared to enter adulthood. Therefore, in this chapter a case is made for life-centered career education to be a part of every learning disabled adolescent's educational program. The degree of emphasis should vary; for some students career education might make up the bulk of their programs; for others it might be one course taken for only one academic year. Preparation for participation in society cannot be overemphasized and should become an important aspect of school curricula.

In this chapter, information is provided about the development of job skills, providing students with the necessary information to make career decisions, to be able to seek, find, and hold a job, and to be able to function as independent adults in modern society. Although none of the above are mutually exclusive, several educational alternatives used in public school settings result in isolated and separate instructional units. Unfortunately, this can result in preparation programs that are neither integrated nor comprehensive. Fortunately, the trend is for more integration of instructional topics. The chapter is divided into four major sections: vocational training, job-centered career education, life-centered career education, and implications for instruction. The emphasis of each varies in scope, vocational training being the most exclusive, and life-centered career education the most inclusive.

VOCATIONAL TRAINING

Vocational training has been part of the school curriculum for some handicapped students since the early 1940s. As moderately handicapped students were placed in public schools, it became apparent to special educators that traditional academic programs were not appropriate and could not meet their educational and social needs. Therefore, work-study programs were developed to teach job skills, and included field-based extensions of that training through on-the-job experience. During a student's senior year as many as fifteen hours per week could be spent working in community or sheltered situations. This internship is considered part of the academic program. This model, considered by many to be narrow in scope, still is commonly used for handicapped students, including the learning disabled.

Hoyt (1977) clarifies the differences in terminology and meaning between career education and vocational training. Vocational training provides students with the vocational skills necessary to enter the world of work. In many cases, vocational programs prepare students for only one type of work (auto mechanics, food service). Career education's main thrust is broader. It aims at providing students with the skills necessary to adapt as the needs of our technical society change. In other words, more general skills are emphasized. Students are taught work-related skills such as decision making, job seeking, job getting, job holding, and good work habits. Most career educational programs include vocational training, but are more inclusive in scope and content.

A common work-study/vocational training program is auto repair and body work.

Many school districts operate two separate vocational training programs, one conducted under the auspices of special education and one under the auspices of vocational education. One serves handicapped students (including the learning disabled), and the other serves students enrolled in the general education program. Basically, their goals are the same: to train students to enter the world of work with specific job skills.

Vocational education (conducted by regular educators) is a viable part of many public school programs. Its applicability and appropriateness for some learning disabled students should be investigated. Razeghi and Davis (1979) assert that vocational education must be made available to handicapped students (as mandated by P.L. 94–142). These authors point out that although states are required to spend 10 percent of their vocational education allotment for handicapped students and their training needs, few handicapped students are served. Brolin and D'Alonzo (1979) estimate that only 2 percent of the estimated 10 percent of the school population considered handicapped actually receive services from vocational education. These specialized services are available and can be found in most comprehensive high schools. Those who advocate for the handicapped must ensure that these services are rendered. Razeghi and Davis also point out that many times handicapped learners are tracked into lower skill occupations and do not receive the opportunities to learn more advanced job skills. Those who monitor students' Individual Education Programs (IEPs) must ensure that handicapped students receive appropriate and advanced training commensurate with their potential and capabilities.

As handicapped students move into vocational education, several precautions must be taken to ensure that they advance as much as possible.

Because many vocational educators are not experienced or trained in working with handicapped students, they might have preconceived notions about handicapped students' potentials. These students could be tracked into inappropriate sequences. Folman and Budoff (1971) and Bingham (1978) indicate that handicapped students mature more slowly, and their vocational interests reflect this immaturity. They caution about making life or career choices too early. If career decisions are made concurrent with those of their age-mates, learning disabled students might be subjected to faulty plans, based on inaccurate information.

Special educators also must monitor other aspects of vocational training programs that include handicapped students. Past research with the mildly handicapped has revealed important information about preparing them for work. Chaffin (1969), for example, determined that workers with higher production rates are more successful on the job than those with lower production rates. He demonstrated that handicapped students' production rates are modifiable through direct intervention procedures. Instruction and evaluation of students' rates of completing job tasks, therefore, should be an important aspect of vocational training programs for handicapped youngsters.

Several studies have investigated variables that determine the success or failure of vocational training efforts aimed at handicapped persons. Many teachers have found that work experience is a vital part of vocational training, for it bridges the gap between school and work. Work experiences, however, must be monitored carefully, so that instruction time at school can be spent remediating deficiencies seen on the job. Phelps (1978) stresses the need for continuous evaluation of learners' progress as they proceed through vocational training, so that instruction can be sensitive to students' weaknesses and direct remedial efforts initiated as needs arise.

Phelps also points out the importance of continued communication and cooperation between special educators and all others who work with handicapped students. Weisenstein (1977), advancing this point, suggests that vocational training be a multidisciplinary effort, including all those who work with the handicapped student (special educators, regular educators, counselors, vocational trainers, parents). Unless a collaborative model is implemented, the goal of giving handicapped students marketable occupational skills cannot be achieved. This important point must be underscored, for it requires a major shift in current procedures. Many special education teachers feel separated from the vocational training aspects of their students' programs. Cooperation and communication among all those involved in the education of learning disabled students are essential to the effectiveness of any vocational education program.

JOB-CENTERED CAREER EDUCATION

Career education encompasses vocational training, but is more inclusive. Vocational training is limited in scope and prepares people to work in only one job area (Phelps, 1978). Most vocational programs are segregated in separate facilities or in one centralized high school (Cegelka, 1977), and usually are initiated during the later years of high school. Some suggest that career education should be part of the school curriculum beginning in the early school years (Hoyt, 1977). The State Department of Education in Kentucky (Note 1) and D'Alonzo (1977), for example, outline a total school program that includes four phases: career motivation or awareness (grades K through 6); career orientation (grades 7 and 8); career exploration (grades 9 and 10); and career preparation (grades 11 and 12). D'Alonzo states that instruction in career education should lead individuals to competence and attainment of basic academic skills necessary to adapt continually to modern society; good work habits; a good and meaningful set of work values; career decision-making skills; job hunting and getting skills; vocational skills; knowing how to get reeducated when necessary; and being able to choose a desirable and attainable life style. Clearly, the attainment of these competencies cannot be achieved in one or two school years. Efforts must begin early.

Career Motivation and Orientation   The discussions of career motivation or awareness (suggested for grades K through 6) and career orientation (suggested for grades 7 and 8) are combined because most of the instructional topics appropriate for each overlap. The goal of career awareness is to gain familiarity with the plentiful and diverse jobs available to adults in modern society. As students get older, the types and depth of information provided increase. Younger students usually learn about community helpers (police, fire, postal workers); as students become more sophisticated, so too should the information presented. Not only should students learn about different occupations, but also about the

These students are learning about different careers in a unit on career awareness.

demands of those occupations. For example, students should be aware of the training required for various types of work, degrees of responsibility involved, the physical demands required, and other aspects.

Most students are not aware of the vast number of career opportunities available to them. One purpose of the career awareness phase is to broaden their views of the job world. Activities in which students review Sunday newspapers, Department of Employment job listings, or the *Dictionary of Occupational Titles* (U.S. Department of Labor, Employment and Training Administration, 1977) can be beneficial to both students and teachers. Phelps and Lutz (1977) suggest that teachers use the U.S. Office of Education's fifteen occupational clusters for the organization of career awareness programs. Included within these clusters are: agribusiness and natural resources, business and office, communication and media, consumer and homemaking education, construction, environment, fine arts and humanities, health, hospitality and recreation, manufacturing, marine science, marketing and distribution, personal services, public services, and transportation occupations. A number of interesting activities both at and away from school can be arranged to broaden students' career horizons.

In addition to career awareness activities, teachers of young special education students should address other aspects of career education, aspects that could have impact on later vocational success. Many career education experts (D'Alonzo, 1977; Schwartz & Westling, 1976) stress the importance of developing good work habits and interpersonal skills. Clark (1979) firmly believes these skills are best instilled during the elementary years. Teachers should reexamine their classroom procedures to determine whether independent work habits are fostered. Some questions teachers should ask are: Are my students required to complete their assignments? Are they required to meet deadlines? Is punctuality required? Are they allowed to work independently? If the answers to many of these questions are "no," modifications in the instructional program and classroom organization are justified. In most instances, only minor alterations are required to teach academic and career education skills concurrently.

The development of good interpersonal relationships should receive the direct attention of learning disabilities teachers. As indicated in previous chapters, many learning disabled students have difficulty relating to and interacting with others. Interpersonal skills are related to job success (Clark, 1979). Because of its importance in later life, teachers must include social interaction as part of their instructional programs (refer to Chapter 7 for more details).

Career Exploration

During this phase of job-centered career education, students begin to explore the skills and competencies needed in their career interests. Career exploration can occur in many places and through a variety of experiences. For example, discussion groups with people representing various occupational clusters can broaden students' interests and knowledge about career opportunities. Through such discussions, information can be gained about what certain jobs involve, what kind and how much training is required, and whether these initial choices are feasible for them as individuals. Parents can be vital resources for students and teachers in this capacity by leading class discussion groups and arranging for field trips.

Career exploration also can be arranged through job stations at school or in the community. Through structured classroom activities such as guided reading (Janus Book Publishers' *People Working Today Series*, 1977) or the use of modularized programs (Guidance Associates' *Career Discovery Series*, 1978; *Job Attitudes Series*, 1978), the career exploration phase can be enriched.

Simulated work experiences and part-time jobs also can help students become aware of the general expectations of work. Students usually find that punctuality, dependability, responsibility, and completion of tasks are crucial to a successful experience.

Many youth organizations provide excellent career exploration opportunities. Organizations like Junior Achievement, Scouting, and community youth groups can help youngsters develop many qualities and skills desirable to future employers. Special education teachers should facilitate their students' entry into these organizations and guide them through participation. Teachers can expand upon and enhance these experiences at school.

Career Preparation

This phase of career education includes vocational training as well as education in other important job-related skills. Students begin to prepare for entry into the world of work by starting to learn how to make career decisions. In addition to learning specific job skills, students master general job finding and getting skills. A number of modularized programs might be helpful to teachers. Workbooks and modularized instructional units are available for many important skills: completing job application forms (Kahn, Jew, & Tong, 1980); job interviewing (Jew & Tong, 1976; Livingstone, 1977); using the want ads (Jew & Tandy, 1977); career decision making (Weagraff & Lynn, 1977); and on-the-job skills (Wilson, 1977). In addition, some comprehensive instructional packages (McVey & Associates, 1977) include a number of topics (finding job openings, applying for a job, interviewing, safety). *Entering the World of Work* (Kimbrell & Vineyard, 1978), a program developed specifically for handicapped learners, is comprehensive in content and scope and could be useful to teachers who are not certain of what or how to teach career related skills.

LIFE-CENTERED CAREER EDUCATION

Brolin (1978) and Brolin and Kokaska (1979) define life-centered career education as the process by which individuals learn to become consumers, citizens, workers, family members, and sociopolitical members of society. Brolin's comprehensive, life-centered curriculum is composed of three primary categories: daily living, personal-social, and occupational guidance and preparation. Developed for educable mentally retarded students, the curriculum is relevant for learning disabled students as well. Although the means for mastering curricular targets might vary, the twenty-two student competencies specified could become the goals and objectives for meaningful high school programs. Because the competencies Brolin outlines are succinct, his competency matrix is shown in Figure 12.2.

While reviewing the life-centered competency statements provided by Brolin, the reader should note that these are suggested topics for instruction. Teachers must select means of instruction and instructional materials that most closely match students' needs, interests, and abilities. Nevertheless, Brolin's matrix should be helpful for teachers seeking to obtain an overview to insure comprehensiveness of content.

Brolin is not alone in adhering to the view that career education should become a curricular area inclusive of vocational and adult life preparation. Others (Cegelka, 1977; Clark, 1979; Hansen, 1977; Jacks & Keller, 1978) express concern that students must be prepared for more than just obtaining and holding a job. Justification for expanding the traditional curriculum can be found in the data obtained during a national assessment (National Assessment of Educational Progress, Note 2). In that study, it became apparent that most students and many adults do not possess the necessary skills to survive with ease in society. For example, 36 percent of the seventeen-year-olds and 42 percent of the adults tested could not write a job application letter that included all of the required information. Only 50 percent of the seventeen-year-olds and 66 percent of the adults could calculate finance charges correctly. These are only a few examples of the deficiencies found in those about to enter, or those coping with, adult society. A case could be made that school curricula should be altered to include instruction in skills necessary and expected in daily life.

A number of basic skills are not now taught to most learning disabled students that should be considered for inclusion. For example, conversions (minutes to seconds, pounds to ounces) and geometric measurements and computation (calculation of area and square footage) are commonly used in adult life, but rarely are these topics of instruction during the school years. Many graphic and reference material skills are critical to many adults. Although important, the following are often omitted from instructional sequences: reading graphs and tables, reading maps, using reference books, using materials arranged in alphabetical order (dictionary, telephone book), and reading demarcations on measurement instruments (thermometers, measuring cups, clocks, calendars, rulers). Writing skills are taught in school, but practice activities are often irrelevant. People have to be able to fill out mail-order forms, respond to ads, write job application letters (including a means of contacting the potential applicant), and write business letters. Possibly during high school, learning disabilities teachers should discontinue units on creative story writing and shift the emphasis to survival writing skills. Certain manual and perceptual skills should be developed for use in adult life. For example, the ability to use common tools, construct things, make simple repairs, and use a ruler are practical and frequently used, but often are not taught to learning disabled students.

A reexamination of the instructional sequence for learning disabled students is warranted. In some cases, simply changing the types of assignments given to practice those basic skills taught in the class is sufficient.

Curriculum Area	Competency		
	1. Managing Family Finances	1. Identify money and make correct change	2. Make wise expenditures
	2. Selecting, Managing, and Maintaining a Home	6. Select adequate housing	7. Maintain a home
	3. Caring for Personal Needs	10. Dress appropriately	11. Exhibit proper grooming and hygiene
Daily Living Skills	4. Raising Children, Enriching Family Living	14. Prepare for adjustment to marriage	15. Prepare for raising children (physical care)
	5. Buying and Preparing Food	18. Demonstrate appropriate eating skills	19. Plan balanced meals
	6. Buying and Caring for Clothing	24. Wash clothing	25. Iron and store clothing
	7. Engaging in Civic Activities	28. Generally understand local laws & government	29. Generally understand Federal Government
	8. Utilizing Recreation and Leisure	34. Participate actively in group activities	35. Know activities and available community resources
	9. Getting around the Community (Mobility)	40. Demonstrate knowledge of traffic rules & safety practices	41. Demonstrate knowledge & use of various means of transportation
	10. Achieving Self Awareness	43. Attain a sense of body	44. Identify interests and abilities
	11. Acquiring Self Confidence	48. Express feelings of worth	49. Tell how others see him/her
	12. Achieving Socially Responsible Behavior	53. Know character traits needed for acceptance	54. Know proper behavior in public places
Personal-Social Skills	13. Maintaining Good Interpersonal Skills	58. Know how to listen and respond	59. Know how to make & maintain friendships
	14. Achieving Independence	62. Understand impact of behaviors upon others	63. Understand self organization
	15. Achieving Problem Solving Skills	66. Differentiate bipolar concepts	67. Understand the need for goals
	16. Communicating Adequately with Others	71. Recognize emergency situations	72. Read at level needed for future goals
	17. Knowing & Exploring Occupational Possibilities	76. Identify the personal values met through work	77. Identify the societal values met through work
	18. Selecting & Planning Occupational Choices	82. Identify major occupational needs	83. Identify major occupational interests
Occupational Guidance & Preparation	19. Exhibiting Appropriate Work Habits & Behaviors	87. Follow directions	88. Work with others
	20. Exhibiting Sufficient Physical-Manual Skills	94. Demonstrate satisfactory balance and coordination	95. Demonstrate satisfactory manual dexterity
	21. Obtaining a Specific Occupational Skill		
	22. Seeking, Securing, & Maintaining Employment	98. Search for a job	99. Apply for a job

Figure 12.2 Brolin's life-centered career education matrix. (D. E. Brolin (Ed.), Life centered education: A competency based approach. Reston, Va.: The Council for Exceptional Children, 1978, pp. 10, 11. Reprinted by permission.)

3. Obtain and use bank and credit facilities	4. Keep basic financial records	5. Calculate and pay takes		
8. Use basic appliances and tools	9. Maintain home exterior			
12. Demonstrate knowledge of physical fitness, nutrition, & weight control	13 Demonstrate knowledge of common illness prevention and treatment			
16. Prepare for raising children (psychological care)	17. Practice family safety in the home			
20. Purchase food	21. Prepare meals	22. Clean food preparation areas	23. Store food	
26. Perform simple mending	27. Purchase clothing			
30. Understand citizenship rights and responsibilities	31. Understand registration and voting procedures	32. Understand Selective Service procedures	33. Understand civil rights & responsibilities when questioned by the law	
36. Understand recreational values	37. Use recreational facilities in the community	38. Plan and choose activities wisely	39. Plan vacations	
42. Drive a car				
45. Identify emotions	46. Identify needs	47. Understand the physical self		
50. Accept praise	51. Accept criticism	52. Develop confidence in self		
55. Develop respect for the rights and properties of others	56. Recognize authority and follow instructions	57. Recognize personal roles		
60. Establish appropriate heterosexual relationships	61. Know how to establish close relationships			
64. Develop goal seeking behavior	65. Strive toward self actualization			
68. Look at alternatives	69. Anticipate consequences	70. Know where to find good advice		
73. Write at the level needed for future goals	74. Speak adequately for understanding	75. Understand the subtleties of communication		
78. Identify the remunerative aspects of work	79. Understand classification of jobs into different occupational systems	80. Identify occupational opportunities available locally	81. Identify sources of occupational information	
84. Identify occupational aptitudes	85. Identify requirements of appropriate and available jobs	86. Make realistic occupational choices.		
89. Work at a satisfactory rate	90. Accept supervision	91. Recognize the importance of attendance and punctuality	92. Meet demands for quality work	93. Demonstrate occupational safety
96. Demonstrate satisfactory stamina and endurance	97. Demonstrate satisfactory sensory discrimination			
100. Interview for a job	101. Adjust to competitive standards	102. Maintain postschool occupational adjustment		

Many daily living activities require alphabetizing skills: library, filing, and telephone directory use.

Instead of practicing basic computational skills on traditional worksheets, problems could be arranged for students to practice calculating the square footage of a proposed playroom as an addition to their home, dividing a recipe in half, or calculating miles per gallon.

Several other areas might be added to secondary learning disabled students' instructional programs. For example, modules covering transportation (see Table 12.1 for suggested topics), domiciles (renting an apartment,

Students need to be taught how to perform basic household activities.

Table 12.1   **Suggested topics for a module on transportation**

Basic Transportation
1. Locating addresses
   a. telephone directory
   b. newspaper advertisements
   c. phone calls
2. Following oral directions
   a. taken over the phone without a map
   b. taken by marking a map
3. Using a local map
   a. using street guides
   b. marking a map from place of origin to destination
4. Reading bus schedules
   a. direct line
   b. connections

Public Transportation
1. Using buses and means of rapid transit
   a. kinds of tickets available
   b. fares (exact change and tokens)
   c. schedules
2. Using taxis
   a. fares
   b. tips

The Personal Vehicle
1. Purchase of the vehicle
   a. comparison shopping
   b. season of purchase and its effect upon price
   c. bargaining
   d. depreciation
   e. used versus new vehicles
2. Financing
   a. finance charges
   b. monthly payments
3. Fixed expenses
   a. monthly payments
   b. insurance
   c. state registration and licenses
   d. driver's license
4. Variable expenses
   a. gas and oil
   b. repair
   c. maintenance (tires, tune-ups, oil changes)

Long-distance Travel
1. Knowledge about various modes of transportation
   a. airplanes
   b. buses
   c. trains
2. How to make reservations
   a. travel agents
   b. with carrier
3. Comparison of fares and discounts
   a. advance reservations
   b. off-hour flights
   c. time of travel (need to purchase meals)
   d. amount of time off from work

buying a home), family budgeting, emergency preparedness, banking and credit systems, consumer awareness, common household and auto repairs, and taxation could be included. These would provide youngsters with information required in adult life, and might stimulate a renewed interest in school.

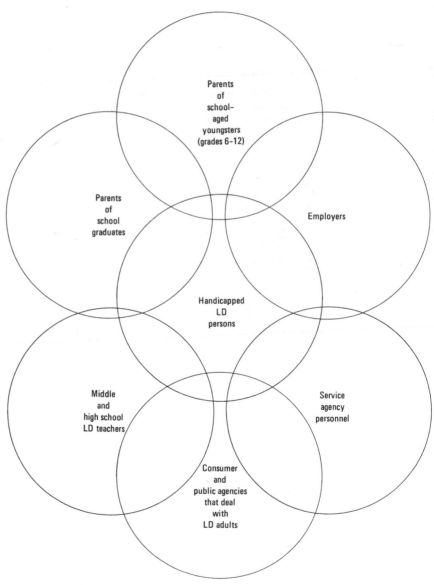

Figure 12.3   Important sources for perspectives on curricula for learning disabled students.

IMPLICATIONS FOR INSTRUCTION

The implications of altering the traditional elementary and secondary curricula for learning disabled students are great. In some cases, only minor adjustments to the traditional instructional sequence are necessary (inclusion of units on career awareness, altering practice assignments to be more survival skills oriented), but in most instances the necessary changes are dramatic. If life-centered career education becomes a priority for a segment of the learning disabled population, instructional materials must be developed, personnel retrained, and the concept of mainstreaming reconsidered.

Gillet (1978) conducted a survey of institutions of higher education and found that very few offered specific course work in career education. Many (Brolin, 1973; Brolin & D'Alonzo, 1979; Cegelka, 1977; Razeghi & Davis, 1979) believe that special education personnel should be trained to provide career education learning experiences for their students. Razeghi and Davis (1979) state that career education should be a joint venture between vocational and special educators. Vocational training activities should be conducted by those specifically prepared for that role, and special educators should be responsible for life-centered career education goals and objectives. This is an awesome responsibility, and until personnel are trained, special education teachers are left with one more set of goals and objectives that are their new responsibility to implement.

Until a standardized, commercially produced curriculum is available, teachers must use their search-and-patch-together skills to develop a sensible career education program. Often, the question arises: "If I don't have time for a comprehensive unit, what should I teach?" One way to establish priorities for goals and objectives is to survey, even informally, the consumer. It is enlightening to talk with parents and graduates of learning disabilities programs to determine what should be part of the instructional program. Valuable information also can be gained through discussions with people who work with handicapped adults. These people often are keenly aware of programming deficiencies and omissions in the education of the handicapped. Figure 12.3 indicates some of the people who can provide valuable information about handicapped students and the implications for their education.

SUMMARY

This chapter described the preparation of learning disabled students to enter modern society, including vocational training, job-centered career education, and life-centered career education. Figure 12.4 illustrates the relationship of these areas as being inclusive of one another.

Merely teaching learning disabled persons how to perform a particular job is not sufficient. "Career planning for a learning disabled student soon to be looking for a job should concern itself with marketable skills that apply to many occupations" (Irvine, Goodman, & Mann, 1978, p. 268). The training these students receive should be general enough to apply to a variety of

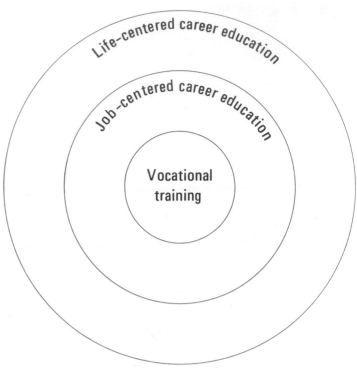

Figure 12.4   The relationship of vocational education, job-centered career education, and life-centered career education.

specific jobs; the skills that transcend all jobs must be taught. For real success to occur, however, students must also know how to cope in an increasingly complex society. They must know what society demands of its members, and they must understand their individual responsibilities and obligations to that society. Because learning disabled students must be completely prepared to enter adult life, life-centered career education is recommended as a necessary and vital part of every learning disabled students' educational program.

REFERENCE NOTES

1. BUREAU OF VOCATIONAL EDUCATION. *Philosophy of vocational education in Kentucky.* Frankfort, Ky.: Kentucky Department of Education, 1977.

2. NATIONAL ASSESSMENT OF EDUCATIONAL PROGRESS. *Adult work skills and knowledge: Selected results from the first national assessment of career and occupational development* (Contract agency is the National Center for Educational Statistics, Contract No. OEC-0-74-0506) Denver, Colo.: National Assessment of Educational Progress, 1976.

REFERENCES

BINGHAM, G. Career attitudes among boys with and without specific learning disabilities. *Exceptional Children*, 1978, *44*, 341–342.

BROLIN, D. E. Career education needs of secondary educable students. *Exceptional Children*, 1973, 39, 619–624.

BROLIN, D. E. (Ed.). *Life centered career education: A competency based approach*. Reston, Va.: The Council for Exceptional Children, 1978.

BROLIN, D. E., & D'ALONZO, B. J. Critical issues in career education for handicapped students. *Exceptional Children*, 1979, 45, 246–253.

BROLIN, D. E., & KOKASKA, C. J. *Career education for handicapped children and youth*. Columbus, Ohio: Charles E. Merrill Publishing Co., 1979.

CEGELKA, P. T. Exemplary projects and programs for the career development of retarded individuals. *Education and Training of the Mentally Retarded*, 1977, *12*, 161–163.

CHAFFIN, J. D. Production rate as a variable in the job success or failure of educable mentally retarded adolescents. *Exceptional Children*, 1969, *35*, 533–538.

CLARK, G. M. *Career education for the handicapped child in the elementary classroom*. Denver, Colo.: Love Publishing Co., 1979.

D'ALONZO, B. J. Trends and issues in career education for the mentally retarded. *Education and Training of the Mentally Retarded*, 1977, *12*, 156–158.

DESHLER, D. D., LOWREY, N., & ALLEY, G. R. Programming alternatives for LD adolescents: A nationwide survey. *Academic Therapy*, 1979, *14*, 389–397.

FOLMAN, R., & BUDOFF, M. Learning potential and vocational aspirations of retarded adolescents. *Exceptional Children*, 1971, 34, 121–130.

GILLET, P. Career education: A survey of teacher preparation institutions. *Exceptional Children*, 1978, *44*, 516–518.

GOODMAN, L. Educational programming: A survey of current practice. In L. Mann, L. Goodman, & J. L. Wiederholt (Eds.), *Teaching the learning-disabled adolescent*. Boston: Houghton Mifflin Co., 1978.

GUERRIERO, C. A. Educational quality assessment in Pennsylvania. *Mathematics Teacher*, 1978, *71*, 620–623.

GUIDANCE ASSOCIATES. *Career discoveries series*. New York: Guidance Associates, 1978.

GUIDANCE ASSOCIATES. *Job attitude series*. New York: Guidance Associates, 1978.

HANSEN, L. S. *An examination of the definitions and concepts of career education*. Washington, D.C.: U.S. Government Printing Office, 1977.

HOYT, K. B. *A primer for career education*. Washington, D.C.: U.S. Government Printing Office, 1977.

IRVINE, P., GOODMAN, L., & MANN, L. Occupational education. In L. Mann, L. Goodman, & J. L. Wiederholt (Eds.), *Teaching the learning-disabled adolescent*. Boston: Houghton Mifflin Co., 1978.

JACKS, K. B., & KELLER, M. E. A humanistic approach to the adolescent with learning disabilities: An educational, psychological and vocational model. *Adolescence*, 1978, *13*, 59–68.

JEW, W., & TANDY, C. *Using the want ads*. Hayward, Calif.: Janus Book Publishers, 1977.

JEW, W., & TONG, R. *Janus job interview kit*. Hayward, Calif.: Janus Book Publishers, 1976.

KAHN, C., JEW, W., & TONG, R. *My job application file*. Hayward, Calif.: Janus Book Publishers, 1980.

KIMBRELL, G., & VINEYARD, B. S. *Entering the world of work*. Bloomington, Ill.: McKnight Publishing Co., 1978.

LAURIE, T. E., BUCHWACH, L., SILVERMAN, R., & ZIGMOND, N. Teaching secondary learning disabled students in the mainstream. *Learning Disability Quarterly*, 1978, *1*, 62–72.

LIVINGSTONE, A. *Janus job interview guide*. Hayward, Calif.: Janus Book Publishers, 1977.

McVEY & ASSOCIATES. *Follett coping skills series*. Chicago: Follett Publishing Co., 1977.

MALOUF, D. M., & HALPERN, A. A review of secondary level special education. *Thresholds in Secondary Education*, 1976, 2, 6–7; 25–29.

MORI, A. A. Career education for the learning disabled—Where are we now? *Learning Disability Quarterly*, 1980, *3*, 91–101.

People working today: 10 books about teenage workers. Hayward, Calif.: Janus Book Publishers, 1977.

PHELPS, L. A. Vocational education for special needs learners: Past, present, and future. *School Psychology Digest*, 1978, *7*, 18–34.

PHELPS, L. A., & LUTZ, R. J. *Career exploration and preparation for the special needs learner*. Boston: Allyn & Bacon, 1977.

RAZEGHI, J. A., & DAVIS, S. Federal mandates for the handicapped: Vocational education opportunity and employment. *Exceptional Children*, 1979, 45, 353–359.

SCHWARTZ, S. E., & WESTLING, D. L. Academics for vocational competence: A secondary special education issue. *Thresholds in Secondary Education*, 1976, 2, 8–9; 21.

SWART, R. A secondary school resource room makes mainstreaming work. *Teaching Exceptional Children*, 1979, *11*, 77-79.

TOUZEL, S. W. Secondary ld curricula—A proposed framework. *Learning Disability Quarterly*, 1978, *1*, 53-61.

U.S. DEPARTMENT OF LABOR, EMPLOYMENT, AND TRAINING ADMINISTRATION. *Dictionary of occupational titles* (4th ed.). Washington, D.C.: U.S. Government Printing Office, 1977.

WEAGRAFF, P. J., & LYNN, J. J. *Making decisions work.* New York: McGraw-Hill, 1977.

WEISENSTEIN, G. R. Vocational education's contribution in the career development of retarded individuals. *Education and Training of the Mentally Retarded*, 1977, *12*, 158-160.

WIEDERHOLT, J. L. Adolescents with learning disabilities: The problem in perspective. In L. Mann, L. Goodman, & J. L. Wiederholt (Eds.), *Teaching the learning-disabled adolescent.* Boston: Houghton Mifflin Co., 1978.

WILSON, M. E. *Growing on the job.* New York: McGraw-Hill, 1977.

COMMUNICATING WITH OTHERS:

PARENTS AND PROFESSIONALS

In the not so distant past, many teachers believed that their only responsibility was to teach the established curriculum. This responsibility began at 8:30 in the morning and ended at 3:00 in the afternoon. A corollary of this parochial logic was adhered to by many special education teachers: handicapped students were their sole obligations. These youngsters were their responsibilities; no other teacher in the building was or should have been truly concerned about the welfare or education of "their children." Such beliefs and educational practices are now relegated to history. No longer can teachers live and work in isolation and no longer can youngsters be thought of as "belonging" to one person.

The education of America's younger citizens, particularly those receiving services from special education, is a team effort. *All* those who live and work with a handicapped youngster must be active participants in the educational process. Parents,[1] diagnosticians, regular and special educators, and those who deliver supplemental services (physical education, music, art, speech, and language) must now become partners to ensure an appropriate education for each student. This sound premise, though often tumultuous, is not advocated just by educational leaders but is mandated by federal law (refer to Chapter 2 for review). Whether the special education teacher is ready for broadened horizons, ready for public scrutiny, or ready to work with many diverse people does not matter. This is the new reality of life in the special education classroom.

[1]The term *parents* is used in this chapter to refer to the adult or adults who serve in the role of primary caretaker(s) of the child. That may be both parents, a single parent, grandparent, foster parent, or guardian.

Teachers must know what and how to teach. Most of this text is devoted to those issues. Teaching skills alone, however, are no longer sufficient. Teachers must possess other important competencies. Some of the most critical of these are communicating and working with others. Communication and cooperation are two-way systems. Teachers must be able to understand the needs and concerns of others, and must also be able to convey their concerns and transmit information to other people. Normally, teachers must communicate with two different groups of people: parents and other professionals. Many teachers view their roles in these two communication situations as different. Therefore, this chapter is divided into two parts. The first focuses on communicating and cooperating with parents; the second on other educators and professionals from other disciplines.

COMMUNICATING WITH PARENTS

Many educators hold a peculiar view of parents, particularly those of handicapped youngsters. These parents are often approached as though they are ignorant, hostile, and sometimes even as though they are stupid. These same people could be the doctors, lawyers, merchants, and clerks from whom these educators, when not functioning in the role of teacher, seek advice. Somehow many teachers seem to feel that once the role of parent is assumed, all intelligence is lost. Some parents do need counseling and training to live and work better with their handicapped child, but many do not. It is fallacious to assume that once an individual takes on the role of parent all competence disappears. If a teacher conveys this attitude to a parent, communication and cooperation are difficult. The teacher must enter into a new, open relationship with another adult who shares a common concern—the handicapped student. Decisions about how cooperative the parent will be and whether the parent needs counseling or specific training to deal effectively with the child should be made not *a priori*, but after a number of contacts have been made.

The teacher should remember that the needs and concerns of each parent are different. McDowell (1976) describes two general groups of parents of handicapped youngsters. One has long been aware that their children have learning problems, and the often experienced feelings of hostility, anger, denial, guilt, and helplessness have long since been coped with and resolved. Parents who have recently discovered that their children have educational difficulties have a much different perspective of school from those who work in the educational system. If teachers know how long a parent has known about a child's handicap, communication can prevent rather than create crises.

According to McLoughlin, Edge, and Strenecky (1978), when parents are involved in their child's education, three positive outcomes should become apparent: exchange of information, growth in their parental role, and a productive relationship between teacher and parents. The onset of parental involvement should come early in the child's educational career. Certainly, if special education placement is being considered by school personnel, the parents should at least be informed, if not active, participants in the decision-making process. McLoughlin et al. believe there are five stages in which parents play a major role: identification, assessment, programming, implementation, and evaluation. Because in the past parents were excluded at these decision points, mutual trust and cooperation were not fostered between school and home. The resulting situation detracts from the total educational environment for the individual child.

The first step in developing a feeling of mutual trust with parents is to talk with them about their child. This is usually done at a parent conference where major issues about the child's educational plan (placement, goals and objectives, and educational strategies) are discussed.

Parent Conferences

The initial parent conference is very important, for during this meeting parents and teacher begin to come to a common understanding of each other's perspective of the general purpose of the goals and objectives of the educational program for the child. In addition, the teacher must become aware of the parents' needs and concerns as well as their expectations from the school and the educational program designed for their child. This initial meeting should come early in the school year or, if possible, even before school begins. Because initial and often lasting impressions are made at this meeting and because emotions can run particularly high, the teacher must be prepared. An ineffective initial contact could jeopardize a cooperative working relationship that must last the entire school year. Kroth (1975) suggests a useful outline to follow in this initial meeting, which can help the teacher gather useful information about the child and his or her family in an organized and efficient manner (see Table 13.1).

Many experts in the area of parent education provide suggestions about the way teachers should communicate with parents. For example,

It is important for parents and teachers to feel comfortable with each other. Some meetings should be casual to encourage free communication.

Table 13.1

Getting a picture of the child: Initial interview guide

A. Present status
   1. Age
   2. Sex
   3. Grade/Class/Last year's teacher's name
B. Physical appearance and history
   1. General impression made by child
   2. Obvious physical strengths and limitations
   3. General mannerisms, appearance, etc.
C. Educational status
   1. Present school achievement/Kind of work/Samples of work
   2. Promotions, accelerations, retardations/Causes
   3. Relations with individual teachers, present and past
   4. Books, etc., used in last educational setting
   5. Tests, individual or group/Types of measures used
D. Personal traits
   1. Personality, general statement
   2. Attitudes toward home, friends, self, family, other students, school
   3. Hobbies, play life, leisure time activities
   4. Educational and vocational goals
   5. Marked likes and dislikes—foods, toys, TV programs, etc.
E. Home and family
   1. Individuals in the home
   2. Socioeconomic level
   3. Relations with the home—favorite brothers/sisters, parent/other relative
   4. Regular chores, pets, etc.
   5. Home cooperation
   6. Record at social agencies
F. Work experience
   1. Part-time jobs (summer, after school)
   2. Attitude toward work, etc.
G. Additional information needed
   1. Sending school
   2. Outside agencies
   3. Private sources, doctor, mental health center, etc. (need release forms)
   4. Health information

SOURCE: R. L. Kroth, *Communicating with parents of exceptional children: Improving parent-teacher relationships.* Denver, Colo.: Love Publishing Co., 1975, p. 20. Reprinted by permission.

Rutherford and Edgar (1979) caution that use of educational jargon can only lead to confusion and misunderstanding. They feel that jargon is a serious barrier to effective communication and should be avoided. Losen and Diament (1978, p. 40) suggest that teachers adopt the following behavioral attitudes:

1. Behave as nonauthoritatively as possible.

2. Be truly emphathetic and listen without judging.

3. Ask questions that open the range of further discussion rather than delimit a line of inquiry.

4. Be considerate of the parent's potential vulnerability regarding the child's problems.

5. Be willing to accord to all parents the same rights and respect regarding knowledge of their child that we would accord to parents whom we respect as professional colleagues.

After the initial conference, communication and dialogue must continue. Rutherford and Edgar point out that teacher-parent conferences reduce the possiblity of faulty communication because they allow for face-to-face encounters in which exchange of information can occur through questioning and verbal clarification. Parent conferences should be held periodically. For some parents, formal meetings need only be conducted at the beginning, midpoint, and end of the school year. Other parents request and require formal meetings more often to understand clearly the goals and objectives for their child, solve problems, gain feedback about the progress they and their child are making, and evaluate the outcomes of the educational program.

Information about the child's progress should not, however, be provided only three times a year. For an effective, cooperative relationship to exist, communication should be ongoing. This can be accomplished without the necessity of formal meetings. There are a number of different ways through which parents can be informed about their child's school performance. The most traditional of these, and probably the least effective, is the report card. This means of communication is not very effective because it is ambiguous, infrequent, and impersonal. Report cards could, however, be adapted and modified to reflect more specifically a student's academic and social behavioral growth. For example, when a student meets the criterion for mastery of an objective, a report that includes the evaluation data (see Chapter 3) could be sent home. A daily report card procedure is suggested and a sample form provided (see Figure 13.3) later in this chapter.

Informal notes could also be used to communicate with parents about their child's school performance, an efficient way to involve parents in the educational situation. Rutherford and Edgar (1979) offer excellent guidelines for using this format. They suggest that a ratio be developed regarding the number of positive and negative notes sent home. They suggest that four positive notes be written for every negative one. Another alternative is to write a note or make a phone call that includes both positive and negative information. Again, caution should be used regarding the amount and type of negative information presented. Too often in the past, parents were only contacted when their children were misbehaving or failing in school. This inhibits the development of an open and trusting relationship.

There are other ways of opening channels of communication between parents and teachers. An open house, where all parents of students in a class are invited, allows the parents to meet others in their situation and share their concerns and interests. It also provides a mechanism for parents to gain an overview of the total program for the entire class. This can be advantageous, for many parents have a microscopic view of a special education program, since only details of their child's plan and its implementation have been presented to them. Another means of accomplishing the same goal is to invite parents to visit the class during the day to observe the typical classroom routine. Direct observation in the classroom situation often allows parents to see a different picture of the children's functioning levels.

Kroth and Simpson (1977) suggest that data be kept on the number and types of parent conferences or meetings held. There are many reasons for keeping a record of parent contacts (legal protection, recommendation for types of services required for the students and their families). A sample summary sheet is provided in Figure 13.1 that facilitates record keeping on the frequency and nature of parent contacts. A sample form is provided in Figure 13.2 for anecdotal records on the content of each parent contact.

Of course, there are many other means of enhancing and facilitating communication. Kroth (1975) suggests that a handbook be prepared for parents that provides them with vital information about the school and the school year, including school calendar, names and phone numbers of school personnel whom they may need to contact, classroom procedures including daily time schedules, materials and supplies used in the class, transportation information, conference and reporting system, and miscellaneous information (supplemental services and local parent organizations).

Occasionally, a problem-solving meeting should be held, either because previous communications were ineffective or incomplete, or because the student presents a new or different problem to school personnel. Experts tend to agree that first the parties involved must define the problem, determine who should deal with the problem directly, find a mutually agreeable solution, identify the procedures to be adopted, develop an evaluation plan,

Occasionally, problems at school necessitate a parent–teacher meeting to solve difficulties. Here, the regular and special education teachers are sharing data about a social problem with the student's parents. Hopefully, a joint home and school program will result from this meeting.

Paul — Student's name   **Sue and Tom Jones** — Parents' name   **Becky Smith** — Teacher's name   Academic year

Type of Contact	Sept.	Oct.	Nov.	Dec.	Jan.	Feb.	Mar.	Apr.	May	June
Formal parent-teacher conference	9/7			12/5						
Phone call	9/6 9/20		11/16							
Note sent home	9/22 9/28	10/2 10/7 10/14 10/21	11/1 11/8 11/15 11/22 11/29							
Chat after school										
Miscellaneous										

Figure 13.1   Record keeping sample for frequency and type of parent contact.

_____

_____
Student's Name

_____   _____   _____
Parent's Name   Date of Contact   Type of Contact

Content of the contact:

Tone of the contact:

_____

Figure 13.2   Sample anecdotal record for parent-teacher contacts.

and agree upon an implementation schedule (Kroth, 1975; Rutherford &
Edgar, 1979).

   If the teacher handles the problem-solving conference with sensitivity
and without defensiveness, an even stronger partnership can result. If, however, maturity does not prevail, problem-solving conferences can result in ill
will, withdrawal, and a closing of communication channels—certainly a situation worth avoiding. One of the strongest allies a teacher has is parents.

Parent Counseling Some parents do require specific training to better manage and educate their
and Education children. In some schools, the school counselor conducts parent counseling
and parent training sessions. Unfortunately, this resource is not available in
all school systems to all teachers, and specially trained teachers must fill this
void. In these instances, the teacher serves in the roles of counselor, parent
educator, and educator of children.

   Brown, Wyne, Blackburn, and Powell (1979) make a clear distinction
between parent counseling and parent education. Frequently, parent counseling groups are designed to help parents understand their feelings, beliefs,
and attitudes about their handicapped children. It is not advisable for un-
trained or inexperienced persons to lead parent counseling groups. If no

counselor is available and school district administrators firmly believe that parent counseling should be offered in the community, persons interested in becoming group leaders should seek training before becoming involved in this line of intervention.

Parent groups are also established to help parents deal more effectively with their children. These groups have as their central mission the training of parents in the use of specific intervention procedures. They are more directive in nature and could be offered by less extensively trained personnel. For example, teachers proficient in the use of specific intervention strategies and evaluation procedures could hold classes aimed at helping parents master knowledge and skills in the area of applied behavior analysis. By following the general outline of the chapters on evaluation of instruction and generic intervention strategies included in this text, a mini-course could be developed that might be helpful to parents.

Some professionals have devoted a substantial portion of their careers to the issue of parent training. From that work, some guidelines are available that should be helpful to instructors of parent training groups. For example, attendance is a frequent problem (McWhirter, 1976; Cooper & Edge, 1978). McWhirter suggests that an incentive for attendance be provided. Parent attendance was encouraged for his group through a fee payment system that offered a refund for perfect attendance.

Others have studied the effectiveness of different methods of instructing parents. Some (O'Dell, Mahoney, Horton, & Turner, 1970) found that incorporating films in the instructional period was very beneficial; others (Flanagan, Adams, & Forehand, 1979) found roleplaying to be an effective means of teaching parents new skills. Regardless of the method used, there is consensus that parents who receive training in instructional techniques to use with their children generally become more effective in dealing with their children than parents who receive no training (Flanagan et al., 1979; Lindsley, 1966; Mira, 1970; O'Dell et al., 1979).

Cooper and Edge (1978) offer some useful guidelines on the implementation of parent training programs. They suggest that before the first meeting, the scope and sequence of the training program be clearly delineated, the content task analyzed, handouts carefully prepared, and the content thoroughly reviewed by the group's instructor. They also suggest that groups be limited in size (no more than five couples or six individual parents). They feel that the meetings should be held at school during a convenient time in the evening when both parents can participate. In addition to attendance at the training sessions, they insist that parents participating in their groups plan and conduct a small modification project for their own child.

A number of texts and other materials are available for use in parent training groups. Many are available to aid in teaching behavior modification techniques to parents. One of the oldest parent manuals is still in common use (Patterson & Gullion, 1968), though many others are quite popular (Becker, 1971; Buckley & Walker, 1978). A packaged instructional program for use with parents (McDowell, 1978) and a set of behavioral goals, objectives, and lesson plans (Cooper & Edge, 1978) are also available.

Parent and
Teacher Together

For truly effective behavioral management and learning to occur, all those who are with the child must be consistent with and supportive of each other. If concepts taught at school are reinforced and practiced at home, maintenance and generalization of learning are more likely to occur. Moreover, if the school is to help in remediation of problems that occur primarily at home, teachers must be aware of those problems and the strategies parents have elected to employ. Not all parents want to be actively involved in matters originating at school. Many parents, however, do desire active participation in their children's education, but have been thwarted in their efforts to assume an active role.

A considerable amount of evidence exists demonstrating that parents can be effective interventionists with their own children. Probably the first reported case of home treatment by parents using behavioral modification procedures was supervised by Williams (1959). In that study, bedtime tantrums disappeared because the parents consistently used an ignoring procedure. Some inappropriate behaviors have been modified through parents serving as direct change agents: withdrawn, isolated, and bizarre behavior (Patterson, McNeal, Hawkins, & Phelps, 1967); self-mutilation (Allen & Harris, 1966); reading (Ryback & Staats, 1970); music practice (Hall, Cristler, Cranston, & Tucker, 1970); compliance with parents' requests (Bucher & Reaume, 1979; Green, Forehand, & McMahon, 1979; Zeilberger, Sampen, & Sloane, 1968); tantrums (Patterson, 1965); and completing household tasks, whining, and bickering (Christophersen, Arnold, Hill, & Quilitch, 1972; Hall, Axelrod, Tyler, Grief, Jones, & Robertson, 1972).

Although parents have served as the primary interventionists in many research studies, in practice the parents' role is to follow through with intervention programs and procedures initiated in the clinic or classroom. Parents help to program for generalization rather than serve as initial change agents. As pointed out earlier in this text, generalization (exhibiting a new behavior in different settings and expanding on specific learning) is vital to the instructional process. Unfortunately, in many cases generalization does not occur automatically and procedures must be implemented to stimulate it. In a study specifically designed to investigate generalization of treatment effects, Forehand, Sturgis, McMahon, Aguar, Green, Wells, and Breiner (1979) found that when parents were involved in the treatment program in the clinic, behavior changes (by both parents and child) were noted in the home. When treatment programs were initiated in the home, generalization did not occur automatically at school. This indicates that school and home must actively work together.

Parents have facilitated generalization and have proven to be excellent workers with their own children. In addition, they are invaluable resources whose support of school activities can enhance the entire educational program. Some researchers have investigated a cooperative relationship between teacher and parent in the implementation of instructional strategies, in which the teacher evaluated the social behavior or academic performance of the student and the parent dispensed the reward. In the first of these studies (McKenzie, Clark, Wolf, Kothera, & Benson, 1968), ten learning disabled students and their parents participated. The students received weekly grades from their teachers, and the parents determined their weekly allowances on the basis of the grades received. Since this initial study, a number of researchers and teachers have implemented variations of this technique and achieved substantial success. Ayllon, Garber, and Pisor (1975), for example, reduced classroom disruption (which was initially at 90 percent) to an exceptionally low level (10 percent) by using daily good behavior letters. If a student went home with a good behavior letter, it indicated that he or she had met the criterion for acceptable classroom behavior. This signalled the parent to deliver reinforcement. In two studies (Hickey, Imber, & Ruggiero, 1979; Imber, Imber, & Rothstein, 1979), researchers found that the percentage of completed reading seatwork assignments increased and general academic performance improved when frequent notes were sent home praising the student.

In another study (Schumaker, Hovell, & Sherman, 1977), a daily report card system was implemented for three middle school students. Each student had six teachers, and each teacher used a preprinted form (see Figure 13.3) to evaluate the student's behavior. Points were given at home and privileges were earned through the points each student accrued. Specific behavior as well as semester grades improved. Lahey, Gendrich, Gendrich, Schnelle, Gant and McNees (1977) also found the daily report system useful. The disruptive behavior of fifty kindergarten children improved substantially when this technique was added to the classroom routine. The researchers offer an important caution, however; they warn of the possible danger that some parents may misunderstand information presented in daily report cards and be too harsh with their children. They suggest that the tone of daily report cards be generally positive and that personal communication between parents and teacher be frequent. As clearly evidenced in Barth's (1979) comprehensive review, daily or weekly reports have proven to be most popular with parents, pupils, and teachers, as they foster communication and a cooperative working relationship between school and home. This easy-to-manage system is a good initial vehicle to the development of a total partnership between these two very important factors in a child's educational career.

It is important to remember that parents need to receive reinforcement for their performance and involvement. They need to know whether their efforts are fruitful and whether they are serving in the role intended. Periodic parent conferences or short phone calls are usually sufficient to retain the interest of the parents and insure program continuity. So great a return is possible at so little a cost to teachers.

COMMUNICATING WITH OTHER PROFESSIONALS

Teachers of exceptional children must work with many people to achieve the fulfillment of a total, appropriate educational program for each handicapped child. Ultimately, it is not just parents and special educators who must work

NAME: _____

DATE: _____

TEACHER: _____

Did the student . . .

	YES	NO	
Come on time?			
Bring supplies?			
Stay in seat?			
Not talk inappropriately?			
Follow directions?			Rules Section
Raise his hand?			
Not physically disturb others?			
Clean up?			
Pay attention?			
Speak courteously?			
Were you pleased with his performance today?			Teacher Satisfaction Section
Points on today's classwork			Classwork Section
Grade on test assignment			Grades Section

Figure 13.3   Sample daily report card form. (J. B. Schumaker, M. F. Hovell, & J. A. Sherman. An analysis of daily report cards and parent-managed privileges in the improvement of adolescents' classroom performance. *Journal of Applied Behavior Analysis*, 1977, *10*, p. 452. Copyright 1977 by the Society for the Experimental Analysis of Behavior, Inc. Reprinted by permission.)

together, but a myriad of diverse persons, often from many disciplines, who must coordinate their efforts. Who should orchestrate the services of specially trained personnel such as speech clinicians, recreational therapists, private tutors, counselors, doctors, regular educators, and other specialists? In many instances, the special education teacher is the person who must coordinate services so that they complement each other. This requires very special interpersonal and organizational skills, which are certainly necessary for all teachers of learning disabled students. Unfortunately, a list of these specific skills and an educational curriculum does not now exist. Until such time, teachers must at least be cognizant of these critical responsibilities.

Regular Educators

As mainstreaming comes closer to its full realization, the role of the teacher of learning disabled students becomes more complex. Whether the teacher is a resource or self-contained classroom teacher, coordination of efforts between the special and regular education program must be carefully planned. The regular classroom teacher and all those who provide supplemental services (librarian, music teacher, art teacher, and physical education teacher) must be actively involved in the development and attainment of specific goals and objectives for each learning disabled student for whom they share responsibility (Wiederholt, Hammill, & Brown, 1978).

The recognition of different goals and objectives for individual students is a departure from regular educators' usual operating procedures. The inclusion of the learning disabled student in their programs requires a change of attitude and methodology. They must individualize instruction, allow for

Regular education and special education teachers should share information and form a partnership to develop cohesive and comprehensive programs for learning disabled students participating in both classes.

greater individual differences, and incorporate evaluation procedures into their instructional plans. Special education teachers can help regular educators modify their instructional programs. They can offer assistance in the development of specific instructional goals and objectives that include criterion statements. They can suggest classroom management techniques and aid in the selection of instructional materials that will ease mainstreaming efforts.

This assistance will only be accepted, however, if the special educator understands regular educators' new dilemma (Hawisher & Calhoun, 1978). Suggestions must be offered in such a way that the regular educators are not offended or insulted. Suggestions must be realistic and possible to implement when there are thirty youngsters, all with different needs, in the class. Brown, Wyne, Blackburn, and Powell (1979) point out that mutual trust, open communication, genuineness, and a positive regard must exist between the regular and special educator if a truly cooperative working relationship is to be fostered.

Medical Personnel The relationship between teachers of the learning disabled and medical personnel was discussed in Chapter 7. Because learning disabled students are so frequently placed on psychotropic drugs to control academic and social behavior, doctors, nurses, and teachers must communicate and share information. Unfortunately, the medical and educational professions frequently do not coordinate efforts. Whether blame for this lack of communication rests with teachers or doctors does not matter. What does matter is that teachers of learning disabled students have open dialogue with their students' doctors.

Because teachers work closely with students many hours each day, they are in the unique position of having the opportunity to systematically and consistently observe and evaluate behavior changes. The data teachers can provide doctors about influences of various medications (types and dosages) could be invaluable. Unfortunately, this resource often goes unused. Volunteering, through the parent or directly (with the parent's permission), to work with the medical profession could possibly lead to quicker resolutions of health or management problems.

SUMMARY

In this chapter, the need for parent and family involvement in the educational program for learning disabled children was stressed. The new and expanded role of the special education teacher was presented. The importance of opening channels of communication not only with parents but also with regular educators, those from supplemental services, and members of other disciplines was emphasized. Clearly, the education of learning disabled students has become a team effort that must be coordinated by the special educator who takes full advantage of all the expertise available in the school and community.

REFERENCES

ALLEN, K. E., & HARRIS, F. R. Elimination of a child's excessive scratching by training the mother in reinforcement procedures. *Behaviour Research and Therapy*, 1966, *4*, 79–84.

AYLLON, T., GARBER, S., & PISOR, K. The elimination of discipline problems through a combined school-home motivational system. *Behavior Therapy*, 1975, *6*, 616–626.

BARTH, R. Home-based reinforcement of school behavior: A review and analysis. *Review of Educational Research*, 1979, *49*, 436–458.

BECKER, W. C. *Parents are teachers: A child management program.* Champaign, Ill.: Research Press Co., 1971.

BROWN, D., WYNE, M. D., BLACKBURN, J. E., & POWELL, W. C. *Consultation: Strategy for improving education.* Boston: Allyn & Bacon, 1979.

BUCHER, B., & REAUME, J. Generalization of reinforcement effects in a token program in the home. *Behavior Modification*, 1979, *3*, 63–72.

BUCKLEY, N. K., & WALKER, H. M. *Modifying classroom behavior: A manual of procedure for classroom teachers.* Champaign, Ill.: Research Press Co., 1978.

CHRISTOPHERSEN, E. R., ARNOLD, C. M., HILL, D. W., & QUILITCH, H. R. The home point system: Token reinforcement procedures for application by parents of children with behavior problems. *Journal of Applied Behavior Analysis*, 1972, *5*, 485–497.

COOPER, J. O., & EDGE, D. *Parenting: Strategies and educational methods.* Columbus, Ohio: Charles E. Merrill Publishing Co., 1978.

FLANAGAN, S., ADAMS, H. E., & FOREHAND, R. A comparison of four instructional techniques for teaching parents to use time-out. *Behavior Therapy*, 1979, *10*, 94–102.

FOREHAND, R., STURGIS, E. T., McMAHON, R. J., AGUAR, D., GREEN, K., WELLS, K. C., & BREINER, J. Parent behavioral training to modify child noncompliance: Treatment generalization across time and from home to school. *Behavior Modification*, 1979, *3*, 3–25.

GREEN, K. D., FOREHAND, R., & McMAHON, R. J. Parental manipulation of compliance and noncompliance in normal and deviant children. *Behavior Modification*, 1979, *3*, 245–266.

HALL, R. V., AXELROD, S., TYLER, L. GRIEF, E., JONES, F. C., & ROBERTSON, R. Modification of behavior problems in the home with a parent as observer and experimenter. *Journal of Applied Behavior Analysis*, 1972, *5*, 53–64.

HALL, R. V., CRISTLER, C., CRANSTON, S. S., & TUCKER, B. Teachers and parents as researchers using multiple baseline designs. *Journal of Applied Behavior Analysis*, 1970, *3*, 247–255.

HAWISHER, M. F., & CALHOUN, M. L. *The resource room: An educational asset for children with special needs.* Columbus, Ohio: Charles E. Merrill Publishing Co., 1978.

HICKEY, K. A., IMBER, S. C., & RUGGIERO, E. A. Modifying reading behavior of elementary school special needs children: A cooperative resource-parent program. *Journal of Learning Disabilities*, 1979, *12*, 444–449.

IMBER, S. C., IMBER, R. B., & ROTHSTEIN, C. Modifying independent work habits: An effective teacher-parent communication program. *Exceptional Children*, 1979, *46*, 218–221.

KROTH, R. L. *Communicating with parents of exceptional children: Improving parent-teacher relationships.* Denver, Colo.: Love Publishing Co., 1975.

KROTH, R. L., & SIMPSON, R. L. *Parent conferences as a teaching strategy.* Denver, Colo.: Love Publishing Co., 1977.

LAHEY, B. B., GENDRICH, J. G., GENDRICH, S. I., SCHNELLE, J. F., GANT, D. S., & McNEES, M. P. An evaluation of daily report cards with minimal teacher and parent contacts as an efficient method of classroom intervention. *Behavior Modification*, 1977, *1*, 381–394.

LINDSLEY, O. R. An experiment with parents handling behavior at home. *Johnstone Bulletin*, 1966, *9*, 27–36.

LOSEN, S. M., & DIAMENT, B. *Parent conferences in the schools: Procedures for developing effective partnership.* Boston: Allyn & Bacon, 1978.

McDOWELL, R. L. Parent counseling: The state of the art. *Journal of Learning Disabilities*, 1976, *9*, 614–619.

McDOWELL, R. L. *Managing behavior: A parent involvement program.* Torrance, Calif.: Winch Associates, 1978.

McKENZIE, H. S., CLARK, M., WOLF, M. M., KOTHERA, R., & BENSON, C. Behavior modification of children with learning disabilities using grades as tokens and allowances as back up reinforcers. *Exceptional Children*, 1968, *34*, 745–752.

McLOUGHLIN, J. A., EDGE, D., & STRENECKY, B. Perspective on parental involvement in the diagnosis and treatment of learning disabled children. *Journal of Learning Disabilities*, 1978, *11*, 291–296.

McWhirter, J. J. A parent education group in learning disabilities. *Journal of Learning Disabilities*, 1976, *9*, 16–20.

Mira, M. Results of a behavior modification training program for parents and teachers. *Behaviour Research and Therapy*, 1970, *8*, 309–311.

O'Dell, S. L., Mahoney, N. D., Horton, W. G., & Turner, P. E. Media-assisted parent training: Alternative models. *Behavior Therapy*, 1979, *10*, 103–110.

Patterson, B. R., McNeal, S., Hawkins, N., & Phelps, R. Reprogramming the social environment. *Journal of Child Psychology and Psychiatry*, 1967, *8*, 181–195.

Patterson, G. R. A learning theory approach to the treatment of the school phobic child. In L. P. Ullmann & L. Krasner (Eds.), *Case studies in behavior modification*. New York: Holt, Rinehart & Winston, 1965.

Patterson, G. R., & Gullion, M. E. *Living with children: New methods for parents and teachers*. Champaign, Ill.: Research Press, 1968.

Rutherford, R. B., Jr., & Edgar, E. *Teachers and parents: A guide to interaction and cooperation*. Boston: Allyn & Bacon, 1979.

Ryback, D., & Staats, A. W. Parents as behavior therapy-technicians in treating reading deficits (dyslexia). *Journal of Behavior Therapy and Experimental Psychiatry*, 1970, *1*, 109–119.

Schumaker, J. B., Hovell, M. F., & Sherman, J. A. An analysis of daily report cards and parent-managed privileges in the improvement of adolescents' classroom performance. *Journal of Applied Behavior Analysis*, 1977, *10*, 449–464.

Wiederholt, J. L., Hammill, D. D., & Brown, V. *The resource teacher: A guide to effective practices*. Boston: Allyn & Bacon, 1978.

Williams, C. D. The elimination of tantrum behavior by extinction procedures. *Journal of Abnormal and Social Psychology*, 1959, *59*, 269.

Zeilberger, J., Sampen, S. E., & Sloane, H. N., Jr. Modification of a child's problem behaviors in the home with the mother as therapist. *Journal of Applied Behavior Analysis*, 1968, *1*, 47–53.

INDEX

AUTHOR INDEX

SUBJECT INDEX